THE SERBIAN PE
ITS ADVERSARIES

By the same author

Legitimacy and the Military: the Yugoslav Crisis (1992)
Iraq, the Gulf Conflict and the World Community (1993)
(co-edited with Richard Paterson and Alison Preston) *Bosnia by Television* (1996)
Triumph of the Lack of Will: International Diplomacy and the Yugoslav War (1997)
(with Cathie Carmichael) *Slovenia and the Slovenes: a Small State in the New Europe* (2000)

JAMES GOW

The Serbian Project
and its Adversaries
A Strategy of War Crimes

HURST & COMPANY, LONDON

First published in the United Kingdom by
C. Hurst & Co. (Publishers) Ltd,
38 King Street, London WC2E 8JZ
© James Gow, 2003
All rights reserved.
Printed in India

A Cataloguing-in-Publication data record for this book is obtainable
from the British Library.

ISBNs
1-85065-646-0 *casebound*
1-85065-499-9 *paperback*

Cover photo
Villagers watch as the body of Ali Belaj is exhumed for reburial,
Studenica, Kosovo. Photo by George Georgiou 1999.

INSTITUTIONAL ACKNOWLEDGEMENTS

The work for this book was assisted by institutional and financial support from a variety of sources. The office of the Prosecutor at the International Criminal Tribunal for the former Yugoslavia, particularly in its early stages, as well as other parts of the Tribunal provided opportunities (albeit sometimes painful) to develop my understanding of issues in essential ways and to provide the context for this work. The Harry Frank Guggenheim Foundation provided support for a joint research project with my colleague Christopher Dandeker, which made possible some research on the early international military engagement. The Department of War Studies at King's College London granted me sabbatical leave and gave financial support which enabled the book to be drafted. Large parts of it were researched, written or edited thanks to the hospitality, encouragement and support of three venerable North American institutions: the Institute of War and Peace Research at Columbia University in the city of New York, one of the best contexts possible for engaging with issues of strategy; the Liechtenstein Institute on Self-Determination and the Center of International Studies at Princeton University, home of friendships and he finest scholarship; and the academic paradise that is the Woodrow Wilson International Center for Scholars in Washington, DC.

IN PLACE OF PERSONAL ACKNOWLEDGEMENTS

This project, like any other, has benefited from other people. The number of people and the number of ways involved have led me to conclude that naming any of those people and ways, or not naming them, would end up being invidious to some or all. So there are no specific acknowledgements, just a general appreciation to all who have contributed something along the way to the appearance of this volume. And of course I take responsibility for the text as it leaves me.

London, November 2002   James Gow

CONTENTS

Contents

GLOSSARY OF ACRONYMS

ABiH	*Armija Bosne i Hercegovine* (Army of Bosnia and Hercegovina)
AVNOJ	*Antifašističko Veće Narodnog Oslododjenja Jugoslavije*
CIA	Central Intelligence Agency
CSCE	Conference on Security and Cooperation in Europe
EC	European Community
EU	European Union
FCO	Foreign and Commonwealth Office (UK)
FPRY	Federal People's Republic of Yugoslavia
FRY	Federal Republic of Yugoslavia
FSS	Federal Security Service
FYROM	Former Yugoslav Republic of Macedonia
GPD	General People's Defence
HDZ	*Hravatska Demokratska Zajednica* (Croatian Democratic Union Community)
HINA	Croatian news agency
HOS	*Hrvatski Odbranbeni Savez* (Croatian Defence League)
HV	*Hrvatska Vojska* (Croatian Army)
HVO	*Hrvatsko Vijeće Odbrane* (Croatian Defence Council)
IFOR	NATO-led Implementation Force in Bosnia and Hercegovina
JNA	*Jugoslovenska Narodna Armija* (Yugoslav People's Army)
JSO	*Jedinica za Specijalne Operacije* (SDB Special Operations units)
JUL	*Jugoslovenska Ujedinjena Levica* later *Jugoslovenska Levica* (Yugoslav Left, the party of Mira Marković)
KDOM	Kosovo Diplomatic Observer Mission
KFOR	NATO-led peace force in Kosovo
KOS	*Kontraobaveštajne Služba* (Yugoslav Military Counterintelligence)
KVM	Kosovo Verification Mission
LDK	Democratic League of Kosovo

MBO	Muslim Bosniak Party
MUP	*Ministarstvo Unutrašnjih Poslova* (Ministry of Internal Affairs)
NAC	North Atlantic Council
NATO	North Atlantic Treaty Organisation
NDH	*Nezavisna Država Hrvatska* (Independent State of Croatia)
OSCE	Organisation for Security and Co-operation in Europe
PJP	*Posebne Jedinice Policije* (Police Special Units)
RAF	Royal Air Force
RS	*Republika Srpska*
RSK	*Republika Srpska Krajina*
RRF	Rapid Reaction Force (Franco-British-Dutch, Bosnia and Hercegovina)
RTS	*Radio Televizija Srbije* (Serbian Radio and Television)
SAJ	*Specijalna Antiteroristička Jedinica* (Serbian MUP Special Anti-Terrorist units)
SAO	*Srpske Autonomne Oblasti* (Serbian Autonomous Regions – SAR)
SČP	*Srpski Četnički Pokret* (Serbian Chetnik Movement)
SDA	*Stranka Demokratske Akcije* (Party of Democratic Action)
SDB	*Služba Državine Bezbednosti* (Serbian Security Service)
SDG	*Srpska Dobrovoljačka Garda* (Serbian Volunteer Guard)
SDS	*Srpska Demokratska Stranka* (Serbian Democratic Party)
SFOR	NATO-led Stabilisation Force in Bosnia Hercegovina
SFRY	Socialist Federative Republic of Yugoslavia
SG	*Srpska Garda* (Serbian Guard)
SHAPE	Supreme Headquarters Allied Powers Europe
SKJ	*Savez Komunista Jugoslavije* (League of Communists of Yugoslavia – LCY)
SK-PJ	*Savez Kommunist-Pokret za Jugoslaviju* (League of Communists-Movement for Yugoslavia)

SNO	*Srpska Narodna Obnova* (Serbian People's Renewal)
SNR	*Srpska Nacionalistička Stranka* (Serbian Nationalist Party)
SPO	*Srpski Pokret Obnove* (Serbian Renewal Movement)
SPS	*Socijalistička Partija Srbije* (Serbian Socialist Party)
SRS	*Srpska Radikalna Stranka* (Serbian Radical Party)
SVK	*Srpska Vojska Krajine* (Serbian Army of the Krajina)
TO	*Teritorijalna Odbrana* (Territorial Defense Force)
UBVJ	*Uprava Bezbednosti Vojske Jugoslavije* (Security Administration of the Military of Yugoslavia)
UÇK	*Ushtria Çilirimtare e Kosovës* (Kosova Liberation Army – KLA)
UN	United Nations
UNCRO	United Nations Mission in Croatia
UNCHR	United Nations High Commissioner for Refugees
UNPREDEP	United Nations Preventive Deployment
UNPROFOR	United Nations Protection Force
UNSC	United Nations Security Council
UNTAES	United Nations Transitional Administration in Eastern Slavonia
VJ	*Vojska Jugoslavije* (Army of Yugoslavia)
VRS	*Vojska Republike Srpske* (Bosnian Serb Military)
WEU	Western European Union
ZNG	*Zbor Narodva Garda* (Croatian National Guard)

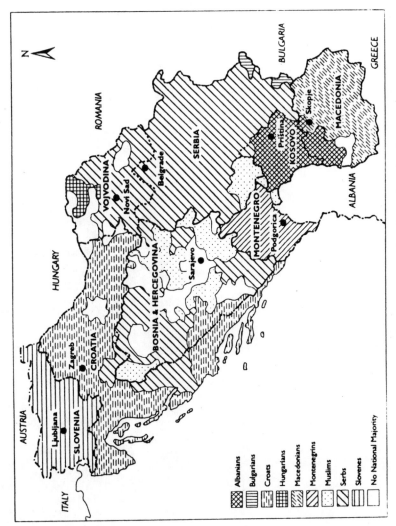

Republics of the SFRY with ethnic distributions.

xiii

1

INTRODUCTION
STRATEGY AND CRIME

For Serbia and the Yugoslavs history is often made on 28 June.[1] It was perhaps no surprise, therefore, when on that date in 2001 Slobodan Milošević was transferred to the Scheveningen detention center of the United Nations International Criminal Tribunal for the former Yugoslavia in The Hague. This was ten years and one day after the Yugoslav war began, and twelve years to the day since Milošević had warned a gathering of 600,000 people at Gazimestan in Kosovo that Serbia might use 'other means' to solve the problems it had with its neighbors. The man who had led Serbia into a decade of fruitless war, and the Yugoslav lands into an abyss of mass murder and human misery, and who was widely deemed to bear overwhelming responsibility for that cheerless history, was in jail. Whatever the outcome of the trial, this was an historic moment.

Many had been skeptical that the transfer of the man who had been at different times head of state of Serbia and of the Federal Republic of Yugoslavia would ever occur. Even after he had been arrested on 1 April 2001, only six months after his ouster, on different charges by the authorities in Serbia, most people seemed to doubt that he would ever face international judicial process in the Netherlands. Once apparently untouchable, the so-called 'Butcher of the Balkans' now had to arrange a defense against charges of committing crimes against humanity and breaching the laws and customs of war. This would test not only the skills and capacities of the Office of the Prosecutor at the Tribunal and the historical record

[1] Beginning with the much-vaunted Battle of Kosovo Polje in 1389, where King Lazar led Serbs and others against the Ottoman Empire but was defeated, notable events have occurred on this date – albeit, sometimes, with a clear sense of decisions having been made to act on that date – Vidovdan (St Vitus' Day) – for symbolic purposes. Other major events include the passing of the deeply contentious first Yugoslav constitution in 1921 and the Soviet expulsion of communist Yugoslavia from the international communist movement in 1948.

of the previous ten years of war; it would also become a philosophical as well as legal exploration of the boundaries of political leadership and responsibility in war, and of the limits of what may be deemed acceptable in war.

As will be seen in the course of this book, the committing of war crimes was the essence of Serbian strategy in the war. Milošević's deadly mission was to lead Serbia into war in order to create a new equation of territory and inhabitants. As the Yugoslav federation dissolved, a Serbian project was implemented to establish the new borders of a set of territories linked to Serbia that would be 'for' the Serbs – and which would mostly be ethnically pure. The only way to achieve Belgrade's ultimate aim in the war was to remove not only armed resistance, which stood in the way of this ambition, but also whole population groups.

This book investigates the link between strategy and war crimes in the context of the Yugoslav war. The link between war and war crimes runs throughout the book. This includes the distinction that war crimes give to war. The link is essential in understanding the attempt to use armed force to achieve the Serbian new state project amid the ruins of the Yugoslav federation, carved from the territory of neighboring states and rendered by the hollowing out of Serbia's existing demographic structure. It is also important in understanding the approaches taken by the local adversaries of that project (and protagonists of alternative state projects), which were not free from the stain of war crimes. And it is vital in understanding the very distinction between, on the one hand, the legitimate use of armed forces within the bounds of the norms, laws and customs of both armed conflict and humanity, which characterized the international military engagement in the Yugoslav war, and, on the other hand, martial operations marked at best by gross negligence and want of care in the use of force, and at worst by the conscious and deliberate violation of international humanitarian law and any sense of humane restraint in the conduct of war. Finally – and most strikingly – the link between war crimes and war is manifest in the way the war ended. This is true in two senses. First, it determined the end of armed hostilities, where it was the International Tribunal's indictment of Slobodan Milošević for crimes against humanity and war crimes that decisively (and to the surprise of the outside world) pushed him to end armed hostilities over Kosovo in 1999. And secondly it was the detention of

Milošević and his transfer to The Hague to face trial on those charges that finally brought the war he had started and the project he had set in train to an end. His appearance in the trial chamber effectively marked the end of the war and the Serbian state project. And despite a continuing stream of repercussive problems throughout the region, it was the real starting point for a new and better future for its people.

I begin this exploration of war and war crimes in the Yugoslav conflict by offering a rudimentary introduction to the terms 'strategy' and 'war crimes'. I also explain the significance of the material presented in this volume for the furthering of international law, and international peace and security through the work of the Tribunal in dealing with crimes against humanity and war crimes; this will be my purpose at the end of the present chapter. Before that, it is necessary to focus, first, on the Serbian state project; secondly, to the responsibility of particular individuals such as Milošević, in their socio-political context, for that project and its defining horror; and, thirdly, on the decision to address the war aims and approaches of the project's adversaries – that is, those directly subject to it and those who became obliged to engage against it. To do any of this it is necessary first to understand the demographic distortion caused by a strategy of murder and forced expulsion, which tested the limits of both European security and the fundamental qualities of humanity, and which were the first traces in the forensic trail of war crimes.

Something to explain: demographic change

The Yugoslav war produced enormous changes in the level and distribution of people across the land that in 1991, when the war began, was the Socialist Federative Republic of Yugoslavia (SFRY). Along the way over a quarter of a million people would be killed in Bosnia and Hercegovina in the early 1990s, 7–8,000 of them in one small place whose name, Srebrenica, has become etched indelibly on the European consciousness. This dwarfs the 11,000 or so killed in the Kosovo phase of the conflict at the end of the 1990s. Yet the horror there was in many ways greater, being more sharply focused and yet better concealed while fully in the gaze of international attention. In both cases, and also in that of Croatia, the common features are impossible to ignore – above all, that the

overwhelming majority of those killed were not military or paramilitary personnel, nor were they killed in combat or as a contingency of combat. Most of them were murdered or unlawfully killed
in other ways. They were deliberately killed as part of the Serbian
project to establish new state borders from which unwanted communities would be removed – ethnically cleansed. They were variously Croats, Slav Muslims and Albanians (although each group,
given the opportunity, arguably might happily have seen Serbs
cleansed from the region). Their removal had two principal elements – physical elimination and mass expulsion, or inducement
to flee. Many young people from all the numerous Yugoslav communities fled to avoid the war and seek a better life elsewhere.
However, for most there was little or no room for maneuver as the
SFRY collapsed and Belgrade sought to create an essentially Serb
phoenix from the ashes of the multi-ethnic, multi-confessional,
multi-lingual conglomerate that was Yugoslavia – a new variant on
the weary eagle adorning nationalist Serbian flags and symbols.

The SFRY comprised six republics: Bosnia and Hercegovina
(two regions joined as a common political and territorial unit since
at least 1878, hereinafter 'Bosnia'), Croatia, Macedonia, Montenegro,
Serbia and Slovenia; and two autonomous provinces within Serbia,
Kosovo and Vojvodina. This federal structure embraced a complex
mix of population groups, as the table shows.

ETHNIC BREAKDOWN OF 1981 AND
1991 CENSUSES (%)

	1981	1991
Serbs	36	34.8
Croats	20	18.9
Muslims (Bosnians)	9	10.1
Slovenes	8	7.5
Macedonians	6	6.6
Albanians	8	9.3
Hungarians	2	1.7
	89	88.9

In addition to these larger and politically more significant groups
there were numerous others: Gypsies (Roma), Czechs, Slovaks,
Bulgarians, Ruthenians, Ukrainians, Wallachians (Vlasi), Romani-
ans, Italians, Greeks and Germans and between 5% and 7% of the

population, many from Bosnia, who identified themselves as Yugo-slavs. Together they comprised about 11% of the population.

The ethnic composition and homogeneity of the republics differed markedly. According to the 1981 census, the majority ethnic groups in the six republics were as follows:

Slovenia	90.5	Slovenians
Croatia	75.1	Croats
Montenegro	68.5	Montenegrins
Macedonia	67.0	Macedonians
Serbia	66.4	Serbs (85.4% without Kosovo or Vojvodina)
Bosnia and Hercegovina	39.5	Muslims

No ethnic group was wholly contained within any republic. For example, one-third of the total number of Serbs lived outside Serbia, mostly in Bosnia; one third of the Yugoslav Albanians lived outside Kosovo, mostly in Montenegro and Macedonia. According to the 1991 census, about 44% of the 4.4 million inhabitants of Bosnia identified themselves as Muslims, 31.5% as Serbs, 17% as Croats, 5% as Yugoslavs and the rest as belonging to other nationalities.

A variety of languages was used in the federation. Most of the people of Croatia, Bosnia, Montenegro and Serbia speak Serbo-Croatian, with minor regional variations. Slovenian and Macedonian are related but distinct Slavonic languages. Albanians and Hungarians speak separate non-Slavonic languages. Serbo-Croatian was the dominant language in Yugoslavia, spoken as a first language by about 80% of the population. Serbo-Croatian has one, single orthography, but different alphabets predominantly the Latin script is used in Croatia, and Cyrillic in Serbia and Montenegro. In Bosnia, Serbs used both alphabets.

Religious diversity and mixing was also a characteristic of the Yugoslav construct. The main religions in the area were and remain: Roman Catholicism, among Slovenes, Croats and the Albanians living in Montenegro; Eastern Orthodoxy, among Serbs, Montenegrins and Macedonians; Islam, among the Slav Muslims in Bosnia, the Albanians of Kosovo and Macedonia, and in the Sandžak region lying across the border of Serbia and Montenegro. There are two major Muslim groups, Albanian and Slav, each with about 2 million people. The Albanian Muslims have a distinct language and culture, whereas the Slav Muslims distinguish themselves from their Christian neighbors only by their faith and culture.

In the years after 1991 there was massive disturbance of the population throughout former Yugoslavia, especially in Bosnia and Hercegovina and in Croatia (affecting both Croats and, in the latter stages of the war in the Western parts of these lands, Serbs). The United Nations High Commissioner for Refugees (UNHCR) estimated in 1994 that about 750,000 non-Serbs had been displaced from Northern and Eastern Bosnia alone. The accompanying UNHCR chart illustrates some of the population changes.

Region	Ethnicity	Pre-war	July 1994	
Western Bosnia	Serb	304,017	450,000	
	Croat	40,638	10,000	mixed
	Muslim	261,003		
Western Hercegovina	Serbs	43,595	5,000	
	Croats	245,586	300,000	
	Muslim	111,128	40,000	
Sarajevo	Serb	157,526		
	Croat	35,865	455,000	mixed
	Muslim	259,085		
Enclaves (Srebrenica,[2]	Serb	20,000	115,000	mixed
Goražde and Žepa)	Muslim	80,000		
Zenica	Serb	79,355	20,000	
	Croat	169,657	122,000	
	Muslim	328,644	428,000	
Tuzla	Serb	82,235	23,000	
	Croat	38,789	36,000	
	Muslim	315,000	600,000	
Northern Bosnia	Serb	624,849	719,000	
	Croat	180,593	30,000	
	Muslim	355,000	40,000	
Bihać region	Serb	29,398	1,609	
	Croat	6,470	7,000	
	Muslim	302,310	300,000	

[2] The figures for the enclaves were, of course, altered dramatically, around a year later, in summer 1995, when Serbian armed forces overran two of them, Srebrenica and Žepa, cutting 40-45,000 people off this list through mass murder and forced eviction.

These enormous changes were not accidents of war – regrettable necessities contingent on armed conflict. They were the result of a deliberate aim, in a war characterized as a matter of course by grossly inhuman acts. Crimes against humanity and war crimes explained these population changes, their commission being integral to the Serbian new state project.

'Slobo', the Serbian project and the adversaries

The initial war crimes case against Slobodan Milošević consisted of two discrete allegations. The first was that, as the political leader during the relevant period in Kosovo, he bore ultimate superior responsibility under Article 7.3 of the Statute of the Tribunal for the crimes committed as part of the Serbian campaign. The second was more direct, namely that he took the leading part in defining a strategy characterized by the commission of war crimes and crimes against humanity. This included planning, instigating, and ordering those crimes, aiding and abetting their preparation and execution, and over time giving the direct instruction to attempt a strategic cover-up of those crimes.[3]

An apparently strategic cover-up, at the practical level, if perhaps not legally 'beyond reasonable doubt', confirmed the other elements of criminal action. It was ordered by Milošević, on 30 March, just under a week after Belgrade had been confronted by NATO air power and put its own ground operations into ethnic-cleansing overdrive. The cover-up concerned digging up bodies, which had been placed in mass graves in Kosovo, and removing them for re-burial where it was thought that the evidence would never be found. These locations were inside Serbia proper and nearly all on land under the control of MUP, SAJ and Security Service JSO units[4] – in other words, they were among the most secret and well-protected of sites. There were a few exceptions to this pattern – for example, at least two container trucks containing ethnic Albanian corpses were simply dumped into the River Danube outside Belgrade.

Milošević and his cronies believed that this evidence would never be found and that they would therefore be able to mock any

---

[3] Individual responsibility for these actions is defined under Article 7.1 of the Tribunal Statute.

[4] See Chapter 3 for discussion of these forces.

international calls to investigate suspected mass grave locations by allowing them access, only to find nothing. A situation of this kind would have served Serbian propaganda perfectly – playing to both domestic and international audiences that had been skeptical of NATO action over Kosovo: everything would be seen to have been a fabrication and could have been dismissed as NATO lies, as Belgrade and its apologists had claimed all along. The Serbian leaders no doubt felt fairly sure about this scenario. There was a belief in some US and British circles that Belgrade had been made aware of aerial intelligence-gathering by that Alliance, which had confirmed at least seven mass graves. By hiding the evidence Milošević was preparing to inflict a post-conflict embarrassment on NATO.

In reality, after he had been deposed in October 2000 and then detained on corruption charges in April 2001, Serbia's new authorities began to probe further, including investigating the possible commission of war crimes and crimes against humanity, and it was these investigations that began to reveal the buried bodies. During the month preceding Milošević's transfer to The Hague, the Serbian media carried reports on new mass gravesites being discovered and opened. This no doubt facilitated public acceptance of the transfer of the former head of state to the Netherlands.

It is important to focus both on the decisive role of Milošević and others in the Serb élite in orchestrating a strategy founded on criminal action, and to acknowledge the degree to which there was an authentic 'Serb question' and popular support for those claiming to pursue it. Since the early nineteenth century there had been a legitimate national question about the inclusion of all Serbs in one state – this is discussed in the following chapter. The creation of Yugoslavia had been one way of doing this, and the dissolution of the Yugoslav federation clearly raised the prospect of Serb communities becoming separated from each other, given that they were primarily spread across three of the six Yugoslav states. There was undoubtedly a legitimate Serb political question, both historically and in the context of the Yugoslav break-up – just as there were legitimate national and political questions for the other Yugoslav communities. Yet despite the undoubted existence of a legitimate Serb question, much of it came to be obscured by the decisions and actions by which Milošević, his allies and his agents sought to exploit that question through war.

Even though the positions of Serbia and others in the Yugoslav framework were probably irreconcilable, both mutually and absolutely, and made war highly likely and in the circumstances, even inevitable, it was Milošević's Belgrade that saw in Yugoslavia's disarray a perfect opportunity to redraw the map; that planned and instigated war (primarily through the use of the Serbian Security Service and a wide range of armed forces), and that defined, above all, the strategy that made widespread, systematic abuse of human rights central the military-political campaign. It was this approach that defined the Serbian campaign and hence the war as a whole. This is why it is the Serbian project that provides the focus for this study rather than any attempt to seek more rounded understanding of the interaction in war of the various parties to the conflict.

The peculiar features of the Serbian project were what gave it prominence and provoked international attention. Attempting to revise borders by force breached the one fundamental rule of the international system and would have been unacceptable without the accompanying abuses – even allowing for particular transitional circumstances, such as those of the Yugoslav dissolution. It would also probably have led to a focus on the Serbian campaign in academic military history. However, it is the strategy itself, a combination of means and ends that ensured elimination of whole populations as a matter of policy, which compels attention to the Serbian project.

Insisting upon the Serbian project as the primary and defining element in the war is important for understanding the conflict itself, as well as the approach taken here to analysing it. Treating the Serbian project specifically rather than 'the Yugoslav War' as a whole is essential both to exploring the true character of the war and to recognizing the central responsibility for what happened. However, in taking this approach, one should clarify the way in which the term is used.

The use of this term has three key features: the use of 'Serbian'; the addition of 'project'; and the distinction between 'project' and other terms such as 'plan'. First, using the label 'Serbian' runs the risk that either all Serbs will be understood as being covered by this term, or that they will feel that they are covered by it. But while I recognize this risk, there is absolutely no intention of branding all Serbs with responsibility for the actions of some in the Serbian cause. Indeed, the use of 'Serbian' rather than 'Serb' is intended, even if vainly, to make a distinction between the state, whose agents are responsible for formulating and implementing the policy which is the focus of this study, and the Serbs as a people – who, like any other, are diverse and varied. It is a misfortune of the shorthand forms of communication involved in discussing these issues that the use of the terms Serb and Serbian is relatively indiscriminate. As a further qualification, I should also stress that identifying the variety possible under those two umbrella terms is not to suggest a spurious taxonomy of 'good' and 'bad' Serbs and things Serbian. To say this is not to offer easy exoneration to the very large numbers of Serbs who were involved in, or supported, the campaign begotten by Milošević.

Relations between leaders and followers can be complex. In the context of Serbia and the Serbs outside Serbia, including the crowd which gathered to hear Milošević speak at Gazimestan, large numbers of them supported the broad aims of the Serbian nationalist project and were receptive to the idea of Serbian victimhood. The Milošević campaign was predicated on the notion of redressing this mood of victimization and restoring the sense of Serbian pride and, most important of all, power. There was always a receptive audience for this dominant message, even though there can be no doubt that it was Milošević and his agents who controlled it.[5] However, that audience was never complete and the success of the Serbian authorities over the years rested not so much on the strength of the message in Serbia itself and direct, strong support for it but on ensuring the absence of real alternatives.[6] However, the overriding concern in the present context is to ensure an understanding in which the political and strategic singularity of the Serbian project with Milošević at its head is separated both from historical

[5] See Mark Thompson, *Forging War* (London: Article 19, 1994).

[6] See Eric D. Gordy, *The Culture of Power in Serbia: Nationalism and the Destruction of Alternatives* (University Park, PA: Pennsylvania State University Press, 1999), perhaps the most important book to emerge on Serbia, which explores the way in which the authorities under Milošević ensured that not even a normal daily life could be a serious alternative, let alone a coherent political or social movement. In the end, the key to Milošević's overthrow was the sense both outside the country and, more important, inside it of the need to limit social and political atomization. The emergence of Vojislav Koštunica as the figurehead for an opposition coalition during 2000 owed much to the realization that the authorities' success had been sustained by their ability to keep Serbian society, culture and politics fragmented. The mood and the messages outside Serbia among the Serb communities in Croatia and in Bosnia and Hercegovina were different and generally more straightforward.

understanding of the Serbian question and from any general assertion of Serb culpability for criminal actions for which particular individuals are responsibile.

But in separating the responsibility of particular individuals from any broad-brush condemnation of the Serbs, there is no desire to minimize the degree and scope of culpability. The naming of Milošević and the focus on his sponsorship and leadership of the distinctively criminal strategy intrinsic to his Serbian project should not be taken as an indication that only the corrupt and manipulative 'dictator' was really to blame.[7] Numerous prominent individuals also bore responsibility. Among these the names of the leading Bosnian Serb agents of the project ring loudly: the political leader Radovan Karadžić and military commander General Ratko Mladić. At the highest levels and at the heart of the project many others were involved and implicated, many of them publicly indicted by the International Tribunal, while others were presumably indicted under seal. And there were many others in the organizational tiers of the Serbian project who might be brought to account.[8]

The second aspect of the designation 'Serbian state project' (or 'state project') is the inclusion of the label 'project.' This is used to help distinguish between, on the one hand, Serb political perspectives and the legitimate questions of political community that arose as Yugoslavia fell apart and, on the other, the corruption of that cause. The 'project' was an ambitious strike for power, an attempt not only to garner and mobilize Serbian support and take control of territory, with ethnic Serb solidarity as its core idea, but also with more extensive aspirations. The issue is the 'project' – the particular aims of Milošević's war and the means used, through war, to achieve them. It is not the broader Serb question.

The third aspect of the designation is the distinction between the term 'project' and others, such as 'plan'. While the Serbian

---

[7] The term 'dictator' was often applied to the Serbian leader, although it did not fit well, given that Milošević tended to lead through manipulation, intimidation, confusion and ambiguity, rather than the direct application of power and threat that the term might connote. While he might have no compunction about sanctioning any act of brutality, including the murder of former cronies, his manner of rule generally had greater subtlety – and arguably, therefore, greater strength.

[8] Again, one should note that this does not necessarily mean that all those involved share equal responsibility.

campaign surely entailed planning, the whole enterprise could only in the very broadest terms merit the label 'plan'. 'Project' is intended to capture the nature of the Milošević approach, couched in ambiguity, seeking to achieve the overall strategic objective: linked territories for the Serbs, carved from parts of Croatia and Bosnia and Hercegovina, free from alien populations; and constant awareness of thresholds that might be better not crossed, of the possibility of opportunities emerging that could be exploited, and the advantages of deception and multi-layering in a situation marked by transition and uncertainty. In short, there was a project, inherently adaptable and flexible. But there was not a single, full plan setting out the full details of how to achieve the political ends of snatching territories, making them all contiguous with Serbia, congregating the Serbs within them, and ensuring the absence of other communities from the territory that had been contested (including contested land within Serbia, namely, Kosovo). The plans came and went, depending on need and opportunity, but the project continued.

Attention to the Serbian war project leaves Macedonia outside the scope of this volume. While it would need to be treated in a full history of the Yugoslav War it is not relevant to the present study. Although the ethnic Albanian insurgents who instigated the armed conflict there early in 1991 must be seen as a spillover, or by-product, of the Kosovo conflict towards the end of the Serbian project, it is at best no more than contingently linked to it. In the end Macedonia, despite some initial fears about it, was not directly affected by the Serbian project.

Macedonia is ignored here because it was not an adversary of the Serbian project. Those who were its adversaries are considered. It would have been possible only to examine the Serbian project in its different aspects, and in some ways this would have been easier, given that treating the adversaries as well as the Serbian core of the war meant difficult decisions at times over where to place parts of the analysis. However reasonable a focus purely on the Serbian project and its criminal core might have been, there are good reasons too for some space to be given to the adversaries, even if it is on a far smaller scale than the equal treatment they would deserve in a fuller history of the war.

Because of the character of the Serbian project, the Yugoslav war was subject to deep controversy in public and international discourse, with many accusations of bias being aimed. Against this background, a focus on the Serbian project alone might have evoked problems of this type – one of the more dismaying features of such an attitude was the fact that honest attempts at accurate analysis of one element of the conflict could be taken to signify prejudice.

Dealing with the Serbian project's adversaries provides a wider context for understanding that central element in the war. Those adversaries are considered in two categories: the local, who on the whole could not escape being enmeshed in the war, and the international, who were drawn into it. The conduct of some of the local adversaries fell short of that displayed by Serbian forces only in scale – the difference being explained by the greater means available to the Serbians and the dominant position this offered. However, even in comparison with the local adversaries (and without guessing what they might have done had circumstances been different) the Serbian project consisted of not only the initiative for war but also the conceptualization of means and ends that took the deadly form of ethnic cleansing. Most of all, the character of the Serbian campaign was thrown into relief by the armed response of its international adversaries. In the circumstances there was, perhaps inevitably, a test of standards, with emphasis being placed at the opposite extreme from the Serbian campaign that international action sought to alleviate. Among other things, the question of standards was a factor in making the international response a test of ingenuity for those engaged in framing that strategy. Just as Serbian abuses were crucial to comprehending the philosophical essence of strategy, so too was the integrity of the Serbian project's international adversaries, as will be discussed below.

Strategy

Strategy in its original and most literal sense (Greek, *strategos*, a general) is the business of generals. Each of the many contemporary uses of the term exploits an aspect of the original usage, namely the relationship between means and ends. Military strategy is about relating the means and ends of war to each other, and is thus the central element in warfare – although there are numerous other elements, all feed into the strategic equation. In its most simple and authentic version, strategy is about the creation and application of force to achieve political ends (that is, in the famous definition of Karl von Clausewitz, the aim of war).[9]

It is the means of war – armed forces – that distinguish it from other aspects of politics. Politics concerns the processes by which it is possible to settle disputes (real or imagined) over the authoritative allocation of resources and values – who gets what, when, where, how and why.[10] War occurs when the disputes (whether imagined or genuine) are mutually exclusive and non-belligerent processes are judged to offer no hope of success. To move a little beyond the Clausewitzian definition, war is a social phenomenon involving the use of organized human groups for the management of restrained coercive violence for political purposes.

The use of organized human groups – armed forces – is one of war's necessary components. One of the major concerns of strategy is the development of armed forces – the creation of force – in the first place. The other key concern is the use of those armed forces, at a later stage, for political purposes. From this elementary starting-point – the creation and application of force – a vast, often subtle and possibly infinite array of conceptual issues proceeds (these lie beyond the scope of this introduction). However, despite its obvious practical connotations, strategy is in its essence a conceptual and philosophical enterprise.[11] It is about embracing the

[9] Much attention has been paid to the hyper-version of strategy, grand strategy, in which the whole economic, social and political wherewithal of a state (or other form of political community) is considered as part of the strategic equation both under conditions of war and those of peace – peacetime, as much as time of war, is one in which political aims and the resources available to the political community and (therefore), if needs be, to its military are to be developed, nurtured, harnessed and protected. For one of the more prominent examples of this fashion, see Paul Kennedy (ed), *Grand Strategies in War and Peace*, New Haven: Yale University Press, 1991.

[10] This is the augmented compound definition that I have used elsewhere, combining and refining other key definitions. See James Gow, *Legitimacy and the Military: the Yugoslav Crisis*, London: Pinter/New York: St Martin's Press, 1992, where reference to original definitions is given.

[11] In many ways, the evolution of nuclear strategy is the epitome of this high conceptual and philosophical understanding of strategy, where the most rational interpretations of the means and ends involve embracing apparent paradoxes. See Lawrence Freedman, *The Evolution of Nuclear Strategy*, 2nd edn, Basingstoke: Macmillan for the International Institute of Strategic Studies, 1989.

totality of a situation and reducing it to an ideational structure in which the available means, the desired ends and the various limitations on each – including considerations of prudence and ethics, destructive capacity, maneuver and other factors – are all balanced. This is by no means simple; indeed, as may be understood from the pages that follow, especially concerning international engagement (discussed in Chapter 8), the attempt to reconcile all the factors in one serviceable approach can sometimes be excruciatingly difficult. That difficulty can be amplified in environments of open discussion such as exist in liberal democracies, where critics abound who have no more than an incomplete grasp of a situation.[12]

The focus has to be on the political objectives to be achieved, but there has to be realization that many roads may lead to Rome, some of which could be more economical than others but not easily recognizable. While it is relatively straightforward in the abstract to conceive of war as a pure and total phenomenon, reality suggests otherwise. There is a theoretical version of war in which all means are devoted to its pursuit and the war itself is everything – although even to discuss 'total' war is problematic, since 'total' can mean different things in different contexts.[13] However, even more problematic is the issue of 'limited war', because it can have no fixed definition short of 'not total'. While some have argued that no war can be limited, others have tackled the need to reconcile means and ends where either the ends or the means are limited – or there are limits to both aspects. (It is unlikely, after all, that total means would be devoted to achieving a limited aim – an uneconomical use of the resources available.) In the many varieties of limited warfare the emphasis on getting the conceptual equation

---

[12] This is an awkward point for an academic to make, given that it is our very purpose and profession to discuss these matters – and I have certainly made my own public comments, both seeking to understand and to expand the scope of strategic discussion on the Yugoslav war. I also note that there are times when such public discussion might lead to better and more elegant conceptualization, as well as to improvements in practice. However, my research and experience also leave me acutely aware of the immense frustration those actively seeking to solve very difficult equations might feel when the chorus of commentators becomes part of the strategic equation or applies friction so as either to distort it, or to make it harder to implement.

[13] There is no doubt, for example, that Ludendorff meant something very different from Clausewitz when discussing total war, and that neither of those conceptualizations could have dealt easily with the prospect of nuclear war.

finely tuned is even more important than it is for total war – in the latter, after all, in theory, there are no limits to the resources that might be committed. In many senses the Yugoslav war – despite the horror of premeditated acts of murder, mutilation, rape and mass expulsion – was a laboratory of different approaches to limited war. Although these are treated in this volume, the very different approaches taken by Serbia, Slovenia, Croatia, Bosnia and Hercegovina and the various extra-Yugoslav actors (the last-named, especially, innovating in their strategic approach) will to some extent be implicit in the relevant sections of the book. However, for each actor there were – crucially – political objectives, questions of resources and limitations of various kinds, all of which made the approach taken seem rational to the protagonist in question.

This sense of the rational can also embrace the use of mass murder and forcible mass expulsion; with the desired political end and the means available, this can be seen on one level as strategically rational. However, strategic equations do not operate only on one level. One of the limitations of this approach – a very strong one, as it turned out – was that it breached the boundaries of the acceptable. While massacre and population removal as a policy had been less problematic at other times and in other places (for example, the Highland Clearances carried out by the forces of the English Crown in Scotland in the late 1740s), in the late twentieth century they had come to be wholly unacceptable in a world that found itself in a position to notice and – however hesitantly, reluctantly and ineptly – to act against an approach in which such acts were central to their perpetrators' military-political purpose.

In addition to the political purpose in war, therefore, it is essential to note the importance of restraint and management in the use of armed force. War is not a matter of bloodlust and random savagery. It is about the disciplined and calculated use of armed force and its destructive capability for specific political purposes. That calculation is the core of strategy: understanding the elements available through the creation of force and the ways in which they might be most effectively applied. The calculation involved is rarely, if ever, simple and straightforward. There will always be awkward balances to be struck between different concerns and different means (as discussed in Chapter 8, there were certainly no straightforward options for those NATO countries seeking to counter the Serbian project, either in Bosnia and Hercegovina or in Kosovo).

A crucial part of gauging strategy is an understanding of the required restraint. This is important in three ways. First, one practical aspect of good strategy is the conservation of force – the wise general will never use more of it than necessary, simply to ensure that capacity will be retained for future use. Assessing just how much force is required in a particular case is no easy matter. A commander will want to err on the side of being sure, which sometimes means applying greater force than is actually needed. The crux of this is that it is rarely possible to know for certain in advance how much force will be required. And warfare is a blunt tool. To begin too weakly, intending that fine-tuning of quality and quantity will be made along the way, would be to leave one's own force potentially at risk if in the opening moves one has not seized the initiative. However, it is clear that there can be no reason to waste force or to use it in ways, at times, or in places that are not justified by the strategic calculation. A good calculation will conserve force as far as possible.

Secondly, restraint is advisable as a matter of self-protection. No leader of soldiers can afford to take a chance that might unnecessarily risk lives and security – hence the difficult dilemmas over the treatment of prisoners: for example, taking prisoners alive in dangerous circumstances might create too great a liability later, and thus a no-prisoners approach may be adopted. But, equally, no officer would wish to exceed the bounds of necessity, simply because doing so could only encourage opponents to behave the same way. In the ugly business of war there is an important element of 'Do unto others as you would have them do unto you'. This does not mean that restraint is equal on different sides in a conflict, that the 'Do unto others' outlook is always reciprocated, and that excesses would ever be found on one side only. Indeed, the present volume demonstrates how this is clearly not the case. But, because it is not always necessarily the case, restraint is no less desirable as a matter of self-interest; in general it protects one's own, as much as it avoids the unwarranted devastation inflicted on others. 'Unwarranted' is the key word here: there may well be occasions where the calculation of restraint, in context, still requires a level of destruction that leaves little room for mercy towards the opponent. Among the problems of war is the process of making external, *a posteriori* judgments regarding its conduct.

Both making external judgments and the composite issues of proportion, purpose and self-interest are relevant to the third dimension of restraint, sticking to the rules, which is vital to the definition of war. It is the rules and conventions of war that, along with political purpose, distinguish it from violent mob clashes and similar phenomena, and their existence makes the status and conduct of soldiers quintessentially different from those of a hooligan rabble. Although these rules and conventions have changed through time and by context, they seem to be ever-present.[14] Hence the devising and application of rules and conventions in warfare are not primarily twentieth-century features of Western international liberalism, as might be thought, but products of the self-interest of those responsible for warfare. It is the codification of some rules and conventions and the un-codified elaboration of others during the second half of the twentieth century that gives particular focus to the emergence of war crimes as a major issue.

Crime and war

The opposition between right and wrong in war has always existed, and has been characterized and debated since time immemorial in terms of the decision to wage war in the first place and the way in which it is waged – the ancient concepts of *jus ad bellum* and *jus in bello*. Indeed, these concepts have been essential to the ethical conduct of war. The interpretations given at any particular moment might have changed, but without affecting the underlying sense that there were boundaries to what was acceptable in war. These took the form of rules, which might be set out as the rules of God or decreed as part of a human code of chivalry, or eventually written as rules of law. Whatever the form, and certainly whatever the detail, there were rules, mostly ones that relied on a blend of conscience, fear and self-restraint on the part of the protagonist. They were not enforced, and indeed it can be argued that they were mostly unenforceable.

The principles underlying notions of *jus ad bellum* and *jus in bello* began to be codified as aspects of international humanitarian law

[14] See Michael Howard *et al.* (eds), *The Laws of War: Constraints on Warfare in the Western World*, New Haven: Yale University Press, 1994.

from the late nineteenth century onwards.[15] The difficult boundaries of 'right' and 'wrong' in the ethical sphere gained definitive legal character. However over time there has been far greater emphasis on standards in the conduct of war than on the reasons for going to war: whatever has been restricted and outlawed, it has not been the fact of going to war itself (although the idea of waging 'aggressive war' has come under increasing condemnation). In the course of the twentieth century the foundations laid in 1899 in The Hague Conventions were developed extensively. The terms of the Geneva Convention of 1929 and their considerably more robust descendants in the 1949 Geneva Conventions, amplified by the protocols of 1977, are central to the laws of war. The Geneva Conventions are treaty law, signed between states and, in the manner of traditional state relations, deeply protective of the state and its interests. They do not apply where there is an internal conflict (an issue discussed below), the one exception to this, under the terms of the 1977 Protocol II, being that 'Common Article 3' is accepted by those who signed and ratified the Protocol as applying to internal conflict. In other words, Article 3 of each of the four Geneva Conventions has the same wording and this common thread applies equally to all forms of armed conflict.

The adoption of Protocol II by a large number of states has contributed to an understanding in which the terms of Common Article 3 are argued to have entered the canon of customary international law, as distinct from treaty law signed between states, which only applies to the signatories. Thus there is a separate category of law, which evolves over time. It can be derived from factors such as major international agreements – when treaty agreements are so widely accepted that their terms are said to extend more generally, even to non-signatories; or it can consist of normative expressions, for which there is considerable support among states; or it can operate simply through state practice and international precedent. The customary approach also embraces aspects of natural law – law considered so essential, basic and immutable that it endures through time and space and – according to the notion of *jus cogens*, cannot

---

[15] This is not to say that there was not a truly legal dimension to war crimes in earlier ages – there was. However, it was only at the end of the nineteenth century that the laws of war really began to be codified in international treaty agreements. See Adam Roberts and Richard Guelff (eds), *Documents on the Laws of War*, 2nd edn, Oxford: Clarendon Press, 1989.

be overridden by another legal agreement. Thus while the Geneva Conventions constitute a clear, treaty-based set of rules for the conduct of war, they also contribute to a wider body of laws on armed conflict, existing outside treaties.

Within the scope of customary law, the notion of crimes against humanity emerged after the Second World War. Although there was no clear basis for what, in the Statute of the International Military Tribunal at Nuremberg, was essentially an invention, there was a strong and understandable argument that the behavior of the Nazis had been such as to require an exceptional measure – the *ex post facto* invention and application of law – appropriate to the offense committed. While the category of crimes against humanity became embedded in international humanitarian law, one of the key aspects it had been invented to cover – the attempt to destroy, wholly, or in part, a national, ethnical, racial, or religious group as such – was distilled into the Genocide Convention of 1948.

It is this register of laws and potential crimes that, in the Yugoslav war, focussed international outrage at the conduct of Serbian forces and later of other parties to the conflict. It also provided the keystones for the Statute of the International Criminal Tribunal for the former Yugoslavia, devised by the UN and representatives of the Security Council states and adopted by the UN Security Council in Resolution 827 of 25 May 1993. This extraordinary use of Security Council power and authority to establish international judicial intervention was seen by many as a fairly empty political gesture. It did indeed focus attention on the atrocities being committed and demonstrate international concern, but beyond this there were problems.

Many of the problems were practical – beginning with finding personnel and premises. Others, understandably, were more conceptual. Unlike the Nuremberg and Tokyo Tribunals, this *ad hoc* body would be an international civil court, not a military one – with vastly different authority and operational and ethical considerations; it would be conducted by a mixture of third parties – outsiders – on behalf of the UN, rather than by the victors in the conflict; and it was created partly as a deterrent while the war continued, rather than as a purely post-conflict instrument of justice. Most strikingly and as a consequence of all the preceding factors, whereas the victorious Allies in the Second World War had twenty-two major figures in custody to try even though some far bigger players escaped justice through death or flight, the Tribunal in The Hague had no suspects in custody and no obvious means of remedying that position. Nonetheless, it began over the years to work effectively and to expand.

In line with the developments in international humanitarian law outlined above, there were four crimes with which defendants could be charged at the Tribunal. These were encapsulated in Articles 2–5 of the Tribunal State. However, there were potential problems associated with the application of each aspect, purely in terms of establishing jurisdiction. Just because much of the world was horrified and indignant at these wrongdoings did not necessarily make them crimes in the eyes of the law. Not only would the Prosecutor have to produce evidence to persuade the Trial Chamber beyond reasonable doubt of a suspect's guilt, but, before that evidence could be considered by the judges, they would have to establish jurisdiction for the crime in question to be considered. The terms for each Article of the Statute were different.

Article 2 of the Statute provided for action over Grave Breaches of the Geneva Conventions. However, to apply it the Prosecutor needed to establish that the alleged offenses were committed in the context of an armed conflict and that this conflict was international and not internal before the alleged victims could be regarded as protected persons under the law. Given the context of the war – the dissolution of the Yugoslav federation, later significantly amplified by inter-communal strife – this was not necessarily straightforward. For a victim in Bosnia and Hercegovina to be deemed a protected person in terms of the Grave Breaches provisions of the Geneva Conventions, the directing role and ultimate responsibility of military and political leaders in Belgrade (or Zagreb) would have to be established.

In terms of the Laws and Customs of War, it was necessary under Article 3 of the Statute to prove that there was an armed conflict, as with the Grave Breaches provisions. What was not at first clear was whether this also required international character. Although the Tribunal's Appeals Chamber significantly clarified this along the way by placing Common Article 3 of the Geneva Conventions clearly in the domain of custom, this was not obvious at the outset. Even so, there was still the question of establishing that the alleged crime was committed as part of an armed conflict. Although there might be a presumption that this should be a straightforward matter, again things can be otherwise in terms of the law. An armed conflict requires two or more parties to be engaged in armed hostilities and each of those parties to have its own 'uniforms' (even if loosely interpreted as common symbols of mutual recognition) and to be actively fighting. For example, there were arguments in some cases that there had been no crime in terms of the Trial Chamber's right to deal with the case because the particular location was clearly under control and no fighting was taking place there. Although there might be a commonsense approach of regarding the whole territory as part of the war, even if there were no direct hostilities on portions of it, this was a question that had to be settled before there could be jurisdiction to consider the detail of the charges.

Genocide (Article 4) and Crimes Against Humanity (Article 5) had a rather different set of requirements. In terms of the Tribunal Statute, the latter required a link with armed conflict, in contrast to the conventional understanding of such crimes as having international character and therefore being subject to universal jurisdiction, requiring no connection to an armed conflict; the later Statute of the International Criminal Tribunal for Rwanda and the Draft Statute of the International Criminal Court both reverted to the being interpretation in international humanitarian law and dropped the link with armed conflict.[16] However, Article 5 did entail the Prosecutor's establishing that the alleged crimes were part of a widespread or systematic pattern.[17] It was therefore not enough simply to record that, say, a murder had occurred. Rather, it had to be established as being *committed* in a context of widespread or systematic commission of relevant crimes. While the former might be established by presenting evidence of similar actions (of an undetermined frequency) in a suitably defined geographical area or set of areas by the same or similar actors, the latter required evidence of planning, organization and intent.

Intent, along with planning and organization (the 'systematic' criterion), was vital in establishing jurisdiction to present charges

[16] It may be presumed that the nexus with armed conflict was inserted because of the inevitably conservative and state protective role that the framers of the Statute were taking, given the extent to which this measure was an innovation and one to which there were grave sensitivities among states to ensure that there were limits on this peculiar body, which radically transcended the traditional sovereign state system, albeit in the particular and limited circumstance of the war surrounding Yugoslavia's break-up.

[17] It should be noted that the requirement is widespread, or systematic, not widespread and systematic – jurisdiction did not require both conditions.

of genocide. Indeed, jurisdiction and the elements of the crime may well have been intrinsically bound up. The only distinction might be where jurisdiction to hear genocide charges existed on the basis of evidence showing systematic features, including planning and intent, but where it was not established at trial that the motivation of the individual in question conformed to the already-mentioned definition of intent to destroy, wholly or in part, a national, ethnical, racial or religious group. Whatever the merits of the individual case, evidence of a more general 'plan' or, otherwise, a systematic approach might clear the way to establishing jurisdiction.

In practice, there were major issues over jurisdiction. Until a surprisingly late stage the issue of armed conflict troubled the Office of the Prosecutor regarding Kosovo – his team had problems determining whether or not, during 1997 and 1998, the Kosovo ethnic Albanian military–political movement constituted an armed force. There were major questions to be settled covering the 'widespread or systematic' category. Many had jumped to the conclusion that the war was simply a chaotic maelstrom of uncivilized 'Balkan' peoples exorcizing their ghosts in orgies of primordial bloodletting (including some in official positions who should have known better), and there was thus a considerable challenge to reveal how the appearance of confusion and uncertainty was, among other things, part of a strategy deliberately steeped in ambiguity, so as to limit the chances of the Serbian project being seen for what it was and crossing the threshold that might warrant international action.[18] It was

[18] The need for pretence of this kind was less pronounced regarding the local adversaries, given that their aims were generally more consistent with the interests of the outside world. Nonetheless, there were clear patterns of manipulation and deception as part of their strategic approach, much to the deep irritation of those in the international community who might have been generally more supportive, had the local adversaries been straighter in this respect. There can be no doubt that there were substantial elements of shadow dancing and ambiguity in the international approach – just as the Serbian campaigns in Croatia and in Bosnia and Hercegovina had initially been dubbed 'peacekeeping' operations, but in fact were instruments of territorial control serving the Serbian project, so in many ways the international peacekeeping force in Bosnia and Hercegovina was an attempt implicitly (and explicitly in most of its conduct at the tactical level) to counter the Serbian project (and at times those of its adversaries) without either being pushed into alliance with the local opponents of the Belgrade program, or openly entering into direct, major armed confrontation with Serbian forces. Serbian forces pretended not to be waging a war of ethnic cleansing and border changing, and the international community pretended not to be

necessary for jurisdiction to show the planning, organization and strategic purpose fundamental to the project. These elements also had some correspondence with the need to demonstrate international armed conflict.

The issue of internationality was particularly difficult. At what point were the states to be regarded as having independent international personality? Was the 'Yugoslav' army really the Serbian army? When it formally ceased to exist and was transformed into three separate forces, were the Serbian forces left in Croatia and in Bosnia and Hercegovina – specifically managed primarily by Croatian and Bosnian Serbs – actors in an internal conflict, or were they agents of Serbia in an international one? In the original Trial Chamber verdict on the first trial, there was a split decision on this issue, with two of the three judges indicating that, although there was an international armed conflict, the victims were not protected persons because the defendant belonged to Bosnian Serb forces and was not among the 'international' actors – i.e., the forces from neighboring Serbia (at one stage the rump of the old Yugoslavia, and at another, of the new Yugoslavia that had been declared). The dissenting opinion of one judge, Judge MacDonald, clearly laid out some of the arguments that the Prosecution had not advanced, based on the evidence offered[19] – a failure that might have gone some way towards irritating Judges Stephens and Vlora, and no doubt made them take a tough line on the interpretation of internationality and the degree to which this factor was recognized as being present.

There were some who rushed precipitately to interpret this mistakenly as determining that there was only an internal conflict and no question of there being an international one.[20] In the end, when

---

opposing that project – because the Serbian project was unstated, opposition to it could not be clearly stated.

[19] The material in this volume, in large part, relates to the evidence in question, which was introduced to assist the Prosecutor in establishing jurisdiction.

[20] The majority opinion was mostly misunderstood as characterizing the conflict as 'internal' rather than 'external.' The judges clearly noted the internationality of the conflict, but deemed that this was not pertinent to the alleged crimes, as they were not committed as part of what those judges regarded as the international armed conflict. This is an important but subtle distinction – one that was overlooked by Robert Hayden, who served as an expert witness for the defense in the case and sought to introduce evidence to demonstrate that Bosnia and Hercegovina did not exist, but that, in so far as it might be said to exist, the conflict there was an internal contest between its three communities – Serbs,

the matter went to appeal and the Prosecutor improved on the arguments offered to the original Trial Chamber, the Appeals Chamber ruled clearly in line with Judge MacDonald. It thus recognized the key elements that made the whole conflict international in character, i.e. the initial purpose of Milošević's Belgrade and the clear evidence of deliberate attempts to disguise its decisive role. This was clear in the continuing support offered through direct involvement of Belgrade troops in some cases (which the original Trial Chamber majority had acknowledged as constituting 'international armed conflict'), and in the certainty that the purportedly Bosnian Serb forces and political actors were proxies of Belgrade's Serbian state project – albeit, very willing ones of Bosnian (or in other cases, Croatian) Serb origin.

Most of the present volume draws on material relevant to this process of establishing jurisdiction. Understanding of the ICTY Statute and the requirements for determining jurisdiction makes up the conceptual and legal context for this study. This is complemented by a military-political context, with strategy as a central component of war, involving the creation of force and its application for a political purpose – the matching of means to ends. This is characterized by restraint, rules and conventions, which contribute to the laws of war. They create the distinction between acts of war that are legitimate and legal and those that are not – namely war crimes and crimes against humanity. Strategy and war crimes were intrinsically linked in the Yugoslav war of the 1990s and remain so in its investigation.

The defining feature of the war was the strategic application of ethnic cleansing. In the Yugoslav context, allegations of war crimes and crimes against humanity led to the creation of the International Tribunal, yet for the Tribunal to raise indictments and make

---

Croats and Muslims. In 'Bosnia's Internal War and the International Criminal Tribunal', *Fletcher Forum of World Affairs*, vol. 22, no. 1, 1998, Hayden curiously claims a personal victory, describing the achievements of the 'expert for the defense'. The piece seems to have failed to understand that the role of the expert witness is to provide factual material on behalf of one side in the case that can be tested by the other side and then incorporated by counsel in their arguments. It is not the expert witness who makes the case to the court. Equally surprising is the failure to read the verdict carefully so as to note that the issue for the judges was not internationality *per se* – as noted, they found that there was an international armed conflict, the opposite of Hayden's claim – but that the crime was not part of that international armed conflict and so the victims were not protected persons, in the terms of the Geneva Conventions.

successful prosecutions the Prosecutor had to establish jurisdiction for relevant charges – war crimes, crimes against humanity and genocide. This meant establishing the presence of an international armed conflict as a context for the commission of crimes, depending on the charge. In the often unclear and complicated circumstances of the Yugoslav morass, where many issues were disputed and blurred (and some remain so), a strong and lucid strategic understanding was necessary to the prosecution. That same understanding is essential outside the Trial Chamber.

Establishing jurisdiction

This book springs from a footnote to a set of histories that includes international criminal law; international relations; the integrative subset of international politics and international law that is international peace and security and the evolution of the United Nations; the evolution of the laws of war; the outcome of the Yugoslav war; the assertion of human rights; and the calibration of the use of power. The footnote is in fact twofold. I have the curious minor distinction of being the first person ever to give evidence before an international criminal court and before an international criminal court in a trial – each of which will be touched on below.

These and other cases where I gave evidence were part of an often frustrating, sometimes painful experience over four years of involvement providing expert advice to the Office of the Prosecutor (OTP) at the United Nations International Criminal Tribunal for the former Yugoslavia (ICTY) in The Hague. Despite the exasperation caused by working with the OTP, it was also worthwhile and the right thing to do. In some sense it seemed to be a matter of destiny. In the early-1980s I had begun studying the Yugoslav military, and that virtual accident seemed like prescience when, a decade later, the SFRY dissolved in war. Of the very few people with knowledge of military-political affairs in the region and able to read Yugoslav material, I appeared to be the only one not of Yugoslav extraction.[21]

---

[21] There were two analysts of Croatian extraction active in this period, both working in US military education. Milan Vego taught at the US Naval College, and Norman Cigar at the US Marine Corps College. Others who had written occasionally on military or defense-related issues as aspects of general attention to Yugoslav affairs – including the inestimable Dennison Rusinow, Ross Johnson

By the time the Tribunal was seeking at last to move forward, it was under considerable pressure both from public and media criticism of apparent inaction (reflecting no understanding of, or even will to understand, the practicalities involved) and from those in the international community (the key members of the UN Security Council) who had been responsible for its creation. In the early years the latter did not offer comprehensive commitment to their remarkable innovation and indeed it was probably the half-hearted character of that support that led the Prosecutor to seek out someone like me. By contrast, in later years, when the Tribunal had survived and proved itself far more useful than would have seemed credible when the original gesture was made, the commitment of Western governments to it was wholehearted. They also found ways to make key evidence available that allowed it to be adduced as such, including working out arrangements for key officials to provide it in sensitive cases. Had these better-placed and better-informed individuals been allowed near the Trial Chamber at the beginning, there might well have been no need for my services. As it was, I was familiar with the military-political and international aspects of the conflict and had analysed coherent patterns of behavior, and was aware of the rare cases in which there was publicly available evidence to support the analysis drawn from other sources. Thus I had become the one-eyed man in the kingdom of the blind.

My involvement began in August 1994, a little more than a year after the UN Security Council had authorized the ICTY's creation,[22] when the practical aspects of a working Tribunal were beginning to be put in place. First of all, the UN General Assembly had been required to appoint judges in a selection process, where politics clearly counted for more than experience and competence; then it had been necessary to found a registry and Judges' chambers; and lastly a Prosecutor's office, incorporating investigators, legal analysts and trial attorneys, needed to be established. Alongside these offices and underneath them (literally, as it turned

and Slobodan Stanković, all stalwarts of the Cold War Yugo-watching community – were no longer doing so.

[22] UN Security Council Resolution 827/25 May 1993. UN Doc. S/Res/827. For fuller discussion on the establishment of the Tribunal, see Rachel Kerr, 'International Judicial Intervention: The International Criminal Tribunal for the former Yugoslavia', *International Relations*, vol. XV, no.2, August 2000.

out) there was a UN bureaucratic-administrative office (unlike each of the others, it was arguably quite unnecessary in operational terms – only the 'UN way' required this cumbersome addition and diversion of resources). Finding premises in The Hague and moving into them, as well as the recruitment of sufficient personnel (by the UN and at this stage by governments for secondment) so as to have a rudimentary operation in place, took over a year. The search for a Chief Prosecutor was also long drawn-out, mainly because of UN politics.[23] In spite of these realities, the Tribunal was already coming under pressure to have demonstrable results.

This was the context in which Terree Bowers left me a voicemail message at the beginning of August, giving no more than his name and a number. Neither knowing him nor having anything else on which to go, I intended to reply within a day, but never did so. After several days' absence from my office, I received a second message. This time Bowers identified himself as working for the OTP, and thus prompted I returned the call. He explained that someone at the US State Department had advised them to contact me, believing that I might be able to help the OTP. When he had established that I had some familiarity with relevant issues, and could shortly meet him or someone else in London, a date was set. The person who came was Minna Schrag, with whom I was to spend many hours in the OTP over the next year. At first I challenged her to persuade me that the Tribunal was for real and would not simply be part of a futile UN charade or political gesture. She convinced me that, at least as far she and her colleagues were concerned, they were in earnest. Minna came from a background in both criminal prosecution and private practice in New York City, and was mercifully direct. When she left her position as Senior Trial Attorney at the Tribunal for personal reasons in the fall of 1995, it was a major loss. She persuaded me to visit The Hague to 'perform' for a small audience of people from the OTP and answer questions, some of which began to make clear their precise requirements – and the grave difficulties in some cases of finding suitable evidence to introduce as criminal evidence. This session seemed to suggest that I could help in a number of ways, each of which could assist the Prosecutor in establishing jurisdiction: military-political and strategic, international and diplomatic, intra-

[23] Richard Goldstone, *For Humanity*, Yale University Press, 2000.

Yugoslav and extra-Yugoslav. The key was to provide not background but the substantive material that could be used by the Prosecutor to argue for jurisdiction – as discussed above. With some difficulties on the way, this is eventually what happened.

There may be an additional, separate footnote to add: the contribution made by the Tribunal's success and its impact on international law, international politics and, eventually, strategy. In the summer and fall of 1994 the future of the Tribunal was not assured. There was considerable pressure to get at least a first indictment publicly issued – to show that ICTY was going somewhere and had purpose. Otherwise, there was concern – not least from the part of the Chief Prosecutor, Justice Richard Goldstone – that funding from the UN General Assembly might not be forthcoming. Once there was an indictment, there was pressure to have additions to the catalogues and, even more, to see trials begin. (Ironically, as later became clear, the principal way in which ICTY could get suspects into custody was with assistance from Western governments.)

Without the factual material introduced by the evidence presented in court (and presented in a new way in this book), it is highly improbable that the Prosecutor would have been able to argue the case for jurisdiction to prosecute the charges successfully, even in the less demanding context of obtaining a public indictment, and certainly not faced with the need to establish a case beyond reasonable doubt at trial. (Indeed, at first, the Prosecutor failed to make the case regarding some aspects of jurisdiction; even with this evidence, the matter had to be settled on appeal, when the evidence was used more effectively and the appropriate case was argued as explained below.) The wherewithal to offer this evidence was unique, at that time – for the most part, not even aspects of it could have been covered otherwise. Later, as the Tribunal was increasingly supported by key governments both publicly and covertly, this picture changed. Government officials, far better placed than any academic could be, might appear in court under specially arranged terms, but in those early days, this was not realistic prospect.

Because the Prosecutor could establish jurisdiction, material evidence pertaining to individual criminal acts could be introduced and the judicial process satisfied. Without jurisdiction there would have been no trials, and without trials there would have been no

Tribunal. Without the Tribunal, the outcome of the war in Bosnia would probably have been different and that over Kosovo would most certainly have been different (as is argued in Chapter 8). And whatever the specific impact on the empirical case of the Yugoslav war, there is also no doubt that the Tribunal's failure would have changed the history of international relations, of the UN, of international peace and security (both in practice and as a field of study), of international humanitarian law and, in so far as this emergent sub-discipline exists, international criminal law. Among the various levels on which this proposition holds, perhaps the most significant is the rapid work towards establishing the International Criminal Court.[24] It is arguable, therefore, that the evidence provided contributed significantly to a change for the better.

The first trial evidence presented at the Tribunal was in the Prosecutor vs. Dušan Tadić, which opened in May 1996, following initial appearances and wrangling over pre-trial issues that lasted a year. Earlier, in the same case of Prosecutor vs. Dragan Nikolić where, under Rule 61 of the Yugoslavia Tribunal's Rules and Procedures, there was a public hearing of some of the evidence in the indictment against the accused, in November 1994. This evidence was heard by a Trial Chamber consisting of three judges who proceeded on the basis of reasonable grounds to confirm the original indictment approved by a single judge and on this basis to issue an international arrest warrant for Nikolić. In neither of these instances, or in others where I appeared, did the evidence concern the actual misdeeds alleged by the Prosecutor against the accused. Nor, as often seems to be assumed, was that evidence merely a tedious historical summary to provide background to the cases – although parts of it did in some sense offer context. The point was to establish factual evidence relating to matters of jurisdiction, primarily by explanation of the Serbian strategy at the heart of the war and the strategic context in which it was applied. This determined the framework for the commission of war crimes and crimes against humanity, not merely as contingencies of war but as its very essence. A strategy of war crimes defined the war.

---

[24] On the remarkable development of the International Criminal Court, especially the swiftness with which it emerged and came to the brink of existence, see Vesselin Popovski, 'The International Criminal Court', *International Relations*, XV, 3 (November 2000).

2

POLITICAL AND HISTORICAL BACKGROUND

The Yugoslav war was a clash of statehood projects. At its most basic, it was a contest between, on one side, a Serbian project to create new state borders and a new correlation between state borders and population groups, and, on the other, the interest of the other states involved in preserving their territorial integrity (although at times Croatia's policy echoed Serbia's as well as opposing it). The core problem was the Serbian state project and the decision to pursue the realisation of that project through organized armed violence.

The Yugoslav federation created by the communists after the Second World War, and which collapsed at the end of the Cold War, was an attempt to reconcile competing national projects. The break-up of that federation was impelled by competition of those national projects and by dissatisfaction with the attempt that had been made to reconcile them. The war itself was a way to resolve the conflict between mutually exclusive political positions over statehood by Clausewitz's 'other means'.[1] While the rest of this book is concerned with those other means, the purpose of the present chapter is to outline the immediate political developments that created a trajectory towards war and to identify key aspects of the historical background to it, including the constitutional definition of statehood and sovereignty that provided the framework for independence, and the context in which the conflict acquired an international dimension.

Historical and political context

Yugoslavia was created on 1 December 1918 as the Kingdom of Serbs, Croats and Slovenes. It was renamed the Kingdom of Yugoslavia in 1929, and recreated, following its destruction by the Axis

[1] Karl von Clausewitz, defined war as 'the continuation of politics by other means.' Clausewitz, *On War*, Peter Paret *et al.* (eds), Princeton University Press, 1976.

powers, as a communist republic at the end of the Second World War, when it was known as the Federal People's Republic of Yugoslavia (FNRJ). It was renamed the Socialist Federative Republic of Yugoslavia in 1974 and dissolved in a process that began in the late 1980s as a result of a compound of political, constitutional, social, legal, military and international events. On 27 April 1992 the last of the successor states proclaimed its new statehood.

The name 'Yugoslav' means 'South Slav' and most of the people who lived in that country, in its various manifestations, were southern Slavs, defined primarily by their use of particular languages of the Slavonic family. Yugoslavia represented an ambitious attempt to embrace within the territorial boundaries of one relatively small state a complex mixture of diverse peoples, cultures and historical and religious traditions.

The political, sociological, cultural, religious and economic differences within the frontiers of Yugoslavia were partly reflections of the area's remarkable diversity of terrain. Distinct natural regions include the northeastern plains, where half the population lives, the lowlands of Serbia and the steppes in Vojvodina. Most of the land is covered and divided by mountains, some all but impenetrable, and along the coast there is a small strip with thousands of offshore islands. Along with geophysical diversity is climatic variation. For example, Podgorica (formerly Titograd) has an average monthly temperature 6°C. higher than Cetinje, only 25 miles to the east; annual rainfall in Podgorica is half that in Cetinje.

Geography determines an historical and cultural cleavage that divides the Yugoslavs along an East–West line that reflects the experience of living for centuries under different imperial regimes. The ancient schism between the Western and Eastern Christian churches, based respectively in Rome and in Constantinople, underlies subsequent divisions. The schism led to rule by Rome in the west and Byzantium in the east, followed later by the Habsburg (Austro-Hungarian) and Ottoman (Turkish) empires. The schism in the Christian Church has relevance today: in the East are still found the Orthodox Church and the use of Cyrillic script; in the West the Roman Catholic Church and the Latin alphabet.

For a period of between four and six centuries most Yugoslavs lived under the imperial rule of either Austria-Hungary or the Ottomans, and often considered themselves exploited and oppressed. It should be noted that the East–West line through the southern

Slav lands is often said to run through Bosnia and Hercegovina, which as a whole only came to lie on the Western side of the line in 1878, following annexation by Austria in accordance with the provisions of the Congress of Berlin. This area experienced different patterns of unrest as the power of the Ottomans waned.

The diversity found in Yugoslavia as a whole was especially notable in Bosnia, where Roman Catholic, Orthodox and Muslim populations coexisted until the country was enveloped by political tension and, eventually, armed hostilities in the early 1990s. To the north and west of Bosnia are the Catholics of Croatia-Slavonia, coastal Dalmatia and Slovenia; to the south and east are the Orthodox Christians of Serbia, Kosovo, Montenegro and Macedonia. In Bosnia itself, as well as in parts of Serbia (including the Province of Kosovo) and Montenegro, there are large populations of Slav Muslims, as well as of non-Slav Muslims.

The Muslims of today are descended from ancestors who converted when the area was brought under Turkish rule in the fifteenth century. For a long time, the Slav Muslims of Bosnia were often thought to be linked to a particular heretical Christian sect, the 'Bogomils' ('lovers of God'), which had been persecuted by both the Eastern and Western Churches. However, recent scholarship has indicated that the Slav Muslim conversion came predominantly from the Eastern Orthodox and Roman Catholic populations of the region. Their voluntary conversion saved these ancestors from much of the oppression experienced by other Slavs under Turkish rule, and they flourished as a sort of aristocracy in the Ottoman Empire, unique to Bosnia.

During the nineteenth century two national ideals of a state in which all the Yugoslavs would live together were developed. These were not mutually exclusive. One was developed by the Serbs on the Ottoman side of the historical dividing line: this was the idea of a 'Greater Serbia'. The other, the 'Yugoslav idea', was developed on the Habsburg side of that line by South Slav intellectuals. Both ideas involved the creation of a common state, embracing more or less the same peoples and more or less the same area.

The basis for the idea of 'Greater Serbia' lay in Serbian emancipation from Turkish rule. In the early nineteenth century, the Serbs, amidst great bloodshed, revolted against Turkish rule. Backed alternately by Austria and Russia, 'narrow Serbia' (that is, Serbia without the territory of the modern Provinces of Kosovo and

Vojvodina) gained its independence as a quasi-independent king-dom. Serbia gained its full independence from the Ottomans in 1878.

Serbian national ideology developed in relation to this growing independence of the nineteenth-century Serbian state within its established borders. Large populations of Serbian Orthodox were left outside those borders, as were southern Slavs of other confessions who were sometimes thought of as 'non-Orthodox' Serbs. The notion underpinning Great Serbian ideology was that all the Serbs should live in one state. The Serbian government before the First World War promoted this version of a common state when it gave assistance to nationalist terrorists operating in Bosnia and Hercegovina (in the Austro-Hungarian Empire), as well as during the First World War.

The corresponding national ideology developed in the Habsburg lands, predominantly by Croat intellectuals, was the 'Yugoslav idea'. Based on the notion of 'self-determination', this was a vision of a common state for all the Southern Slavs, a state not limited to the Serbs or to those who spoke Serbo-Croatian, and one that would be a framework for the self-determination of the various Southern Slavs.

This national ideology was promoted particularly by émigrés forming the Yugoslav Committee in London during the First World War. There was a competing variant on this idea, promoted, at the same time by the National Council in Zagreb, within the Habsburg Monarchy. This was the 'Trialist' solution, which held that the best framework for the self-determination of the Habsburg South Slavs would be a rearranged Monarchy in which the South Slavs would be added to the Austrians and Germans as pillars of the Empire.

The course of the First World War and the dissolution of Austria-Hungary meant that the Habsburg South Slavs found themselves in a weak position compared to the Serbs. As Austria-Hungary broke up, the National Council in Zagreb proclaimed the 'State of Slovenes, Croats and Serbs' (comprising the Habsburg South Slav communities in contemporary Slovenia, Croatia and Bosnia and Hercegovina) on 18 October 1918. However, faced with the prospect of Italian occupation, the National Council agreed to the formation of a common state, largely on Serbian terms, before the end of the year.

The settlement after the First World War created the first Yugo-slav state as a constitutional monarchy which had parliamentary

form and a King from the Serbian Karadjordjević dynasty. Throughout the first decade of that state there was a succession of constitutional, financial and agricultural crises. The largest Croatian political party (the Croatian Peasants' Party – *Hrvatska Seljačka Stranka*)
boycotted the passing of the Serbian Government's 'Vidovdan'
Constitution on 28 June 1921 and was prominent in the nationalist
politics of the 1920s. Its leader Stjepan Radić was murdered in
Parliament in 1928, an event that led King Alexander to declare
a Royal Dictatorship in January 1929. Royal Government became
increasingly unpopular and in 1934 Alexander was assassinated.

On the eve of the Second World War, Yugoslavia was politically,
socially and economically weak. Faced with threats of invasion
unless he acceded to the Axis, the Regent, Prince Paul, agreed to
sign the Tri-Partite Pact with Hitler's Axis powers on 25 March
1941. A group of predominantly Serb Yugoslav Air Force officers,
outraged that their country should surrender, carried out a *coup
d'état* on 27 March. Although the military leaders quickly saw the
impossibility of their country's situation and sought an accommodation with the Axis, Hitler's army invaded on 6 April and overran
the country, routing the Yugoslav army within ten days.

Between 1941 and 1945 around 1 million Yugoslavs died, according to calculations broadly accepted by non-partisan experts.
Most of them were killed by fellow-Yugoslavs in a complex war
in which the struggle for liberation against Germany and Italy was
combined with intra-Yugoslav war and communist revolution. The
major parties to this conflict were the Axis occupiers, Germany
and Italy; the Ustasha, a Croat nationalist and fascist terrorist movement which had been cultivated by the Fascist regime in Italy during
the 1930s and which had been installed as a Nazi puppet regime, ruling an 'Independent State of Croatia' (*Nezavisna Država
Hrvatska* – NDH) covering contemporary Croatia, plus contemporary Bosnia and Hercegovina, and which fought with the Axis
powers – the leader of this regime was Ante Pavelić; the Chetniks,
Serbian nationalist military formations (intended for guerrilla
warfare) loyal to the Serbian monarchy – the leader of this movement was Colonel (later General) Draža Mihailović, an officer in
the Royal Army at the outbreak of war; and the Partisans, a communist-led movement which conducted vigorous guerrilla warfare
before transforming itself into a regular army as the war developed – this movement was led by Josip Broz, known as Tito, who
was to become leader of Yugoslavia after the war. All parties to

the conflict at some stage envisaged co-operation with the others, although, in broad terms, the Partisans seem to have been the least inclined towards this practice.

The Partisans were the prime beneficiaries of the anti-Serbian campaign of terror in which tens of thousands of Serbs in certain parts of Croatia and Bosnia were brutally killed, mutilated, or driven away. The impact of the Ustasha terror caused the majority of Serbs in these areas to join the Partisans, which they did because the Partisans were successfully offering active resistance, whereas the nationalist Serbian Chetniks were largely passive, waiting to capitalize on Allied action in the Yugoslav theater. The Serbs from Croatia and Bosnia became the core of the Partisan movement, and of the post-war communist regime. Parallel to the Ustasha terror, the Chetniks massacred thousands of Muslims in eastern Bosnia.

The Partisans prevailed, since Tito and his followers were able to create a broad base of support. They were attractive because they had actually fought the fascists, because their aims were socially progressive and, above all, because they did not pursue vengeance for any one particular nationality or religious group. Instead, they represented a concerted liberation struggle for a more just future in a post-war state that would be federal in form and communist-ruled. The Partisans offered those dissatisfied with the first Yugoslavia the prospect of a second version of the country in which their aspirations would be accommodated by a federation – this was particularly important in gaining support in Croatia and Macedonia.

Memories of the Second World War remained important in the post-war era and perhaps contributed to the poisoning of relationships in Yugoslavia and the final deterioration in the 1990s. Many of the most senior serving generals in the Yugoslav state in the early 1990s were Serbs from the areas in which Ustasha terror had been most severe and who had joined the Partisans as teenagers.

From 1943 onwards Tito's Partisans established a system of government on liberated territory based on regional councils. This followed the two meetings of the Anti-Fascist Council of National Liberation of Yugoslavia (*Antifašistčko Veće Narodno of Oslobodjenja Jugoslavije* – AVNOJ), at Bihać in 1942 and Jajce in 1943. At the second AVNOJ meeting, the new Yugoslav state was declared, and the regional councils were recognized as the governing bodies on liberated territory. These were the basis for the formal federal state structure of post-war Yugoslavia. This comprised republics and autonomous regions. (There was one exception to this: Sandžak, the Slav Muslim-dominated area straddling the contemporary border between Serbia and Montenegro, which was represented as an equal element at AVNOJ, but did not achieve political status in the post-war federal structure.)

After the war the communists took power throughout the country. The new state was given a federal constitution, with six sovereign republics and two autonomous regions (both within Serbia); these were derived from the structure of AVNOJ and were formally understood as providing the framework for the self-determination of the Yugoslav peoples. These units, in particular the sovereign republics, were deemed voluntarily to have formed a new state in common – which, while federal in form, was in practice highly centralized, with power concentrated in Belgrade, the capital of both Serbia and the Federation. This was a hallmark of communist power.

Communist Yugoslavia's political and economic ties were at first very close to the Soviet Union, but after Tito and Stalin split in 1948, the latter expelled Yugoslavia from the global communist organization, the Cominform, because of its failure to adhere to Soviet leadership. This forced the country to become increasingly independent and to search for an alternative model, whereby it would retain communist rule but not hold to the Soviet model. The Yugoslavs developed their own ideology – 'socialist self-management.' Inherent in this notion was the idea that, while centralized communist rule would be retained, some decision-making would be decentralized. The tension between centralized and decentralized authority was the seed of Yugoslavia's eventual dissolution.

Throughout the post-war period, Yugoslav political and economic policy debates followed a pattern established long before Tito's accession to power. Political leaders in the wealthier areas, historically and culturally associated with Central Europe, generally argued for greater decentralization of power, along with economic and political liberalization. Those in the poorer eastern and southern parts of the country tended to favor more authoritarian centralism and more conservative economic and political controls. Slovenes, in particular, and Croats argued for realization of market measures; the Serbs and Montenegrins supported the remnants of the command economy (although the most progressive elements in Yugoslavia in 1971 – when an unprecedented era of political openness was quashed – were to be found in Belgrade). The economically less-developed south wanted the redistribution of wealth; the northern republics sought to secure reinvestment in their own economic infrastructure. The latter demanded greater autonomy from Belgrade; the former urged a tightening of central control.

Despite Tito's efforts to strengthen the federal system, the mosaic of geographic, political, economic, historical, cultural, linguistic, religious and ideological factors that formed Yugoslavia contained strong decentralizing tendencies. It was a measure of his personal and political abilities that he was able to balance the divergent factions and hold the country together.

Throughout post-1945 Yugoslavia, power shifted gradually to the constituent republics, sometimes fuelled by nationalist movements. The dissipation of power and the claims against the center became so extensive in the late 1960s that by 1971, when Croatia began to discuss its separate membership of the UN, Yugoslavia appeared ready to divide. Encouraged by the army, Tito asserted his personal authority and prevented collapse. Constitutional amendments made at the time, and later confirmed by a new constitution in 1974, made clear that there would be tighter control, but that this would be decentralized and exercised at the republican level.

The 1974 Constitution confirmed the evolution of Tito's Yugoslavia into a highly decentralized quasi-confederation. Aside from Tito's personal authority, power lay with the republics, and the status of the autonomous provinces in Serbia was raised to give a measure of self-rule to communities with significant non-Serb populations, while allowing Serbia to retain ultimate sovereignty. The preamble to the new Constitution affirmed that each constituent nation of the Socialist Federative Republic of Yugoslavia had the right of self-determination, including the right of secession. This counterbalanced the provision in Article 5 that changes in the territory, or borders, of the SFRY, the republics or the provinces could only be accomplished on the basis of the assent of all the republics and, where appropriate, the provinces.

Under the 1974 Constitution, the 'nations and their Socialist Republics' were freely associated in a federation (Article 1) based on the sovereignty of the republics, each formally conceived of as a state (Article 3). While the republics were sovereign states, the autonomous provinces were not (Article 4). 'Nationalities' (that is, national minorities such as the Hungarians) were not entitled to republican status because they had kin-states outside the Yugoslav framework. For the 'nations' of Yugoslavia (Serbs, Croats, Slovenes, Montenegrins. Macedonians and, since the 1960s, Muslims) there was no other state. The 'nations' were considered to be 'founding peoples' in the structure of nation-states within the SFRY.

The political connotations of these constitutional provisions became important as the republics asserted their sovereignty. Serbia acted first to press its authority with regard to the autonomous provinces, at the same time reacting against other republics' reaffirmation of sovereignty. It argued that while the Republic of Serbia was a sovereign state in which the Serbs were the titular nation, the sovereignty of the other republics, where significant numbers of Serbs also lived, was limited. This purported limitation was created by the notion that the Serbs as a whole were a founding people wherever they lived in the SFRY (it was certainly argued that this was the case according to the Constitution of the Socialist Republic of Bosnia and Hercegovina). In response, the political leaderships in the other republics increased their commitment to their own republics' sovereignty and territorial integrity.

The distinction in the 1974 Constitution between nations (the peoples entitled to be state founders in the republics) and nationalities (the minorities with kin status *vis-à-vis* a state outside the SFRY) was crucial. This was so, not only for the basis it gave the republics to assert their sovereignty in the 1980s and early 1990s, but also because of a linguistic sleight of hand: in the context of the distinction between 'state forming' and 'non-state forming' peoples, the exact status of Serbs and Croats living outside Serbia and Croatia was not clearly defined

The 1974 Constitution established a collective Federal Presidency. This consisted of one representative from each of the republics and both autonomous provinces, the Minister of Defense (who did not have voting rights), and Tito, who was designated 'President for Life'. A constitutional provision addressed the problem of Tito's succession by creating a system in which the title of President would pass annually in a pre-set sequence from one member of the collective body to the next.

The mechanisms of the 1974 Constitution appeared to work while Tito was alive, mostly because his personal authority enabled him to intervene in and settle disputes. After his death in 1980, there was no longer any real political authority at the center, and, moreover, economic conditions worsened and sharpened internal tensions. The disintegration was in part due to a lack of faith in the federation. Throughout the late 1980s the lack of commitment to a united Yugoslavia was evident in the inability of the various leaderships to co-operate to resolve the country's economic crisis. Regional divisions were, in a circular way, both the cause and effect of the economic problems, as each regional leadership protected its own interests at the expense of all-Yugoslav economic requirements.

The road to breakdown

In 1986 the Serbian Academy of Arts and Sciences drafted a 'Memorandum' which questioned the constitutional arrangements of the SFRY, suggesting that Serbia and the Serbs were the victims of existing political arrangements and that the question of the Serbs living outside Serbia itself would have to be addressed. The Memorandum asserted that Serbia had suffered discrimination within the Yugoslav federation, especially in relation to the more prosperous republics of Croatia and Slovenia. It called for the Serbian people to regain their pride and for Serbia to assert its role in leading Yugoslavia. This document reflected the support of some of Serbia's leading intellectuals for militant ethnic nationalism and became the ideological underpinning of the Serbian nationalist program. The federal government criticized the Memorandum and tried to prevent its dissemination, but although it was not officially published at the time, it began to create unease among non-Serbs and in republics other than Serbia.

Reflecting that nationalist program, in March 1989, Serbia amended its own constitution to assume control over important responsibilities in both of its autonomous provinces, transferring control of the police, Territorial and Defence judicial systems to the Serbian authorities in Belgrade. The campaign for 'anti-bureaucratic' revolution, as it was known, met little resistance in Vojvodina, resulting in firm Serbian control, but in Kosovo most of the Albanian population reacted to the amendments with great hostility. Indeed, it was general (though perhaps not absolute) inter-communal animosity between Serbs and Albanians in the province, and even more between Serbs outside the province and the ethnic-Albanian majority in the province, that had catalyzed Serbian discussion of its constitutional position. The seemingly implacable ill-feeling between Serbs and Albanians had historical tributaries.

The Kosovo problem had two mainsprings which created the conditions for conflict over the long term. One was Serbian-Albanian rivalry over several centuries; the other was the post-1945 socio-economic development of the province. The territory itself was historically and symbolically important for both Albanians and Serbs. For Serbs it was held to be the bosom of their Orthodox Christian church, which had its seat at Peć in Kosovo in the Middle Ages. Kosovo Polje, west of the capital Priština, marked the plain on which Serbian legend reports the Serbs fighting the Ottoman hordes alone, thereby standing for Christendom against Islam. According to Serbian mythology it was their battle on St. Vitus' Day (Vidovdan) in 1389 that saved Europe; the Turkish attack at the time was so much reduced, it is said, that it lacked the momentum to take Vienna. Although the Serbs were defeated at Kosovo Polje, the nobility found in having stood up against overwhelming Ottoman forces remained an important part of Serbia's self-image. Kosovo was said to be the cradle of the Serbian people, however, it also held the cradle of modern Albanian nationalism. The first Albanian political movement was formed at Prizren in 1878, and it was a later group, from Priština, which secured autonomy from Ottoman rule in 1912. Thus the province is important politically and culturally for both Serbs and Albanians.

Kosovo was incorporated in Serbia after the Balkan wars of 1911–13 and for several decades thereafter was part of it – after 1918 within Yugoslavia. During the Second World War, as Yugoslavia was dismembered, this position changed for a period throughout which there were tensions between Serbs and Albanians, with the Serbian authorities often using violent and repressive means to exercise control over Albanians in the province. These long-simmering antagonisms emerged as a major political question in Serbia and in Yugoslavia in the 1970s and particularly after 1981. This was the result of the post-1945 socio-economic and political development of the province, of which there were four key elements.

The first was repression and the absence of political freedoms for the ethnic Albanians, despite official pronouncements. This situation lasted till after 1966, and created underground, nationalistically-oriented opposition groups. Secondly, after the situation of the ethnic Albanians began to improve after 1966, there was an expansion of Albanian-language education, following the creation of a university in that medium at Priština in 1970. However, this had resulted in a large number of educated, but unemployed and disaffected young Albanians, by the beginning of the 1980s, when there were protests which sparked a Serbian and Yugoslav clampdown, including deployment of the Yugoslav People's Army. Thirdly, the growth in the size of the ethnic Albanian population, especially with its educated youth and the many people working abroad in Switzerland and Germany who sent money back to their families, resulted in a parallel growth of social pressures in Kosovo. Albanians were buying up the property of Serbs, who were increasingly leaving the province, feeling threatened by the demographic change and, in some cases, clearly put under pressure and intimidated by some Albanians. Inter-communal tensions were stoked as Serbs felt pressured to leave, on the one hand, and, on the other, by the discontent of the Albanian majority, who saw Serbs disproportionately employed, especially in the best jobs. Finally, all of these factors were compounded by the province's generally low level of economic development. Despite massive assistance, economic conditions in the 1970s only worsened.

Albanian protests in 1981 resulted in Serbian repression. This started the cycle of political and social action, including violence, which would eventually lead to armed conflict. In the late 1980s, following the election of Slobodan Milošević as Serbian leader, Kosovo's autonomous status was gradually revoked. The main ethnic Albanian political figure to emerge in response to this was Ibrahim Rugova, leader of the Democratic League of Kosova (LDK). However, all opposition in Kosovo was forcibly suppressed.

Against the background of Serbian unease with the position of Serbia and the Serbs in the SFRY, there was a reaction in the other parts of the federation. Other states and peoples on the territory of the SFRY sought to secure their own destinies. Largely this was a defensive reaction to growing Serb nationalism and militancy, and it was also partly an opportunity for some in all the other states to pursue their own agendas. There was a blend of democratization and nationalism, with the former allowing scope for the latter. In each case there was undoubtedly some sense of self-protection – as, of course, there was among the Serb people since all the South Slavs faced uncertain and changing circumstances.

In 1988 the Slovenian communist political leadership began to allow the formation of what were called 'informal' social and political movements. At first this was within the framework of a party-dominated structure, but later wholly autonomous social and political bodies were permitted. This meant the creation of pluralist politics within Slovenia. The process of democratization and homogenization of political perspectives in Slovenia was driven by reaction to the perceived growth of Serbian national militancy and its apparent manifestation in the behavior of the JNA. The critical moment was the trial in the summer of 1988 of three Slovenian journalists and a non-commissioned officer by a military court. This spurred Slovenes towards swifter democratic change and solidarity, as a result of which competitive multi-party elections were set for April 1990.

The establishment of pluralist politics in Slovenia created both the context and the momentum for pluralist politics to evolve in other Yugoslav states, including Croatia. In December 1989 Ivica Račan became leader of the League of Communists of Croatia, and quickly announced that there would be multi-party elections there, to be held around the same time as the elections in Slovenia. With the shift to democratization the door was opened for a return of nationalism in Croatia, of at least as militant a character as that which had emerged among the Serbs.

The strongest movement to emerge in opposition to the ruling communists in Croatia was the HDZ (*Hrvatska Demokratska Zajednica* – Croatian Democratic Community, also translated as Croatian Democratic Union) formed during 1989: a group held a secret meeting to plan a political program on 28 February that year, before holding the founding HDZ Congress in Zagreb on 17 June. At that Congress the party was formally given its name and Franjo Tudjman was elected as its leader.[2] Tudjman had served with the Partisans, the wartime resistance movement led by the communists under Tito, and been a general in the Yugoslav People's Army; he had also made a name as a revisionist Croatian historian. He had also been an intellectual figure associated with a Croatian nationalist political movement in the late 1960s and early 1970s, and imprisoned for that activity.

[2] Stipe Mesić, *Kako Smo Srušili Jugoslaviju: Politički Memoari*, Zagreb: Globus, 1992, p. vi.

The first congress of the HDZ was held on 24-25 February 1990. A nationalist program was espoused, emphasizing ethnic Croatian demographics and the history of the Croats. The congress was attended not only by Croats from Croatia itself, but also by ethnic Croats from neighboring Bosnia and Hercegovina, Serbia and Montenegro, as well as emigrés from around the world.[3]

In the spring of 1990, a Serbian nationalist party, the SDS (Serbian Democratic Party – *Srpska Demokratska Stranka*) was formed in Croatia, under the leadership of Jovan Rašković. The Serbs comprised 11.6 per cent of Croatia's 4.7 million population. About half of these lived in rural areas, in particular forming a historic community in the areas known commonly as 'Krajina' bordering Bosnia to the east, and the formation of the SDS partly reflected the growing fears among the Serbs who lived in that region. These Serbs numbered 150-200,000 out of a total Serb population in Croatia of 600,000. The Krajina Serbs saw the adoption of the red and white checkerboard coat of arms by the HDZ and later by the whole of Croatia as a symbol of the past.[4] It had been used by the Ustasha, the pro-Nazi puppet regime that had attempted during the Second World War to implement a policy of killing one-third of the Serbs, expelling another third and converting the final third from Serbian Orthodoxy to Roman Catholicism.[5]

In 1990 the transposition of legitimacy and power from federation to the republics was formalized by the holding, at the republican level, of the first multi-party elections in Yugoslavia since before the Second World War. In Slovenia a former communist was elected president, with a coalition of former opposition parties holding a parliamentary majority. In April and May 1990 competitive democratic elections were held in Croatia, and the nationalist HDZ led by Tudjman gained an overwhelming victory. The HDZ gained 206 seats in the parliament of 356 members.[6] At that stage parliament elected the country's President, and Tudjman was easily chosen.

---

[3] Mesić, *Kako Smo Srušili*, p. vii.

[4] Croats will point out two things regarding the flag. The first is that its provenance is older than the Ustasha period and dates back to medieval times. The second is that current usage begins with a white square, whereas the Ustasha-period flag began with a red square. Neither of these nuances could be expected to make much difference to agitated Serb opinion.

[5] This policy was given expression by the Croatian Deputy Leader and Education Minister Mile Budak in June 1941; cited in Andrew Bell-Fialkoff, 'A Short History of Ethnic Cleansing', *Foreign Affairs*, 72, 3 (1992).

[6] *The 1990 Elections in the Republics of Yugoslavia: Reports of the Election Observer*

He proceeded to nominate a prominent figure in the HDZ, Stipe Mesić, to become the Croatian representative to the federal presidency.

In Bosnia the major political parties were constituted along nationalist rather than ideological lines. The distribution of seats was broadly proportional to the ethnic composition of the Bosnian population, with the predominantly Muslim Party for Democratic Action (*Stranka Demokratska Akcija* — SDA) gaining about one-third of the Parliament, followed by about 30% for the SDS and about 20% for the Croatian Democratic Union (HDZ). Non-nationalist candidates took another 13.5%. The seven-member presidency elected by the Parliament included representatives of the three major parties. Alija Izetbegović, the SDA leader, became President of the Presidency. In Serbia, Slobodan Milošević won an easy victory to become President of the Republic of Serbia. In Montenegro there was a victory for the communist authorities, who had emerged from a Serbian-inspired 'anti-bureaucratic' revolution in 1989.

The results of these elections were both an expression of dislocation at the political, constitutional, social and ethnic levels and, perhaps even more, a contributing factor to the break-up of Yugoslavia. Votes for nationalist parties were expressions of identity and acts of self-protection in face of the evolving political-constitutional climate. Disintegration at both the political and social-ethnic levels was mutually reinforcing, psychologically and substantively.

Signals of further disintegration surfaced in the autumn of 1990. In the second half of 1990 and the first half of 1991, as a result of the election outcome, inter-communal tension increased in Croatia, and violent Serb-Croat incidents and clashes began to occur in mixed areas, while Serbian majority areas reacted strongly to the program of the HDZ.

In particular, the adoption of a new constitution was a major issue. Discussion of the draft version in the parliament in June greatly increased Serbian alienation by altering the status of the Serbs in Croatia from being co-equals as state-forming peoples to being, in effect, a minority. The new phrasing ran: 'The Republic of Croatia is hereby established as the national state of the Croatian nation and a state of members of other nations and minorities who are

Delegations, Washington, DC: National Republican Institute for International Affairs, 1991.

its citizens: Serbs, Muslims, Slovenes, Czechs, Slovaks, Italians, Hungarians, Jews and others. . . .'[7] The previous formulation had placed the Serbs as a 'nation' (or 'people') after the Croats at the beginning of the definition. This was a small change, but one of immense symbolic importance to Serbs and Croats.

Serb concerns were reinforced by the efforts of the new authorities to make certain institutions 'more Croat'. For example, Tudjman had complained that, of the seven heads of television and radio stations at that time, six were Serbs and the other half-Serb. The new administration sought to exclude communists and Serbs from positions such as these and to put Croats in their place.[8]

Another area in which the presence and influence of Serbs and communists was judged by the new administration to be disproportionately high was in the interior ministry and in the police force. The HDZ government sought to redress this matter swiftly through a restructuring of both institutions, the purpose of which was to purge Serb and communist officers, at once both an anti-communist and a nationalist, anti-Serb program. These steps were absolutely rejected in the predominantly rural areas of Croatia, which had Serb majority populations, principally in Krajina. The name Krajina derives from a period when the Austro-Hungarian Habsburg Empire's borderlands with the Ottoman Empire were known as Vojna Krajina – Military Frontier. Occupied by a mixture of Slovenes, Croats and Serbs, it provided a *cordon sanitaire* between Austria-Hungary and the Ottomans. Military units were raised from the Serb population in these areas in particular, but by no means exclusively, for the defense of the Habsburg frontiers. The label Krajina came to be commonly used before 1995 to refer to rural Serb-inhabited Croatia.[9] But this 'Krajina' was just one part of that territory in Croatia, while parts of the original territory lie in what is now Slovenia, Bosnia, the province of Vojvodina in Serbia and the area of Transylvania in Romania. The largely Serb-populated area of Bosanska Krajina across the border in Bosnia and Hercegovina

[7] Preamble, 'Constitution of the Republic of Croatia Promulgated on 22 December 1990' Snežana Trifunovska, *Yugoslavia Through Documents: from its Creation to its Dissolution*, Dordrecht: Martinus Nijhoff, 1992.

[8] Interview with Franjo Tudjman, *Borba*, 18 April 1990.

[9] At that point, almost the entire population of 150,000 was displaced in connection with major military operations by the Croatian army – a matter covered in Chapters 6 and 9.

also became a cause for concern in the spring of 1991 – as will be seen in Chapter 7.

The ethnic composition of Krajina was an important factor. In 1991 some parts were almost exclusively Serb, others were over 50 per cent Serb and still others had large Serb minorities. However, the same patterns could be found for Croats. Relations between them and the Serbs were increasingly tense. The Croatian Interior Minister Josip Boljkovac was almost lynched during a visit to the town of Knin on 4 July 1990 to discuss changes with the ousted local police chief Milan Martić. The Krajina Serbs reacted by holding an unofficial referendum on autonomy. Martić, having been dismissed by the new HDZ government, distributed arms from the police station weapons store to Serb groups, which then barricaded roads and kept the Croatian security forces from entering. At this early stage the Serbian political leadership and the JNA supported the Krajina Serb rebellion. The JNA gave weapons to the Krajina Serbs, ostensibly for self-defense.

The deteriorating military-political situation in Croatia was set against a background of inter-state and constitutional discussion at the governmental level within the Yugoslav federation. In 1990 several ideas emerged concerning the future of Yugoslavia. One, proposed by the then President of the Federal Presidency, Borisav Jović, a Milošević ally, had support from Serbia and the JNA. Jović's proposal contained many features of the existing federation and would have strengthened the role of central federal institutions and, therefore, of Belgrade.

The Slovenes and the Croats rejected the Jović proposal. To the former, who were not prepared to remain part of a Yugoslavia built on the 1974 Constitution, a proposal for even greater central control was unacceptable. Instead, they and the Croats said that they would only remain as part of a more loosely federated, or confederated, Yugoslavia; they sought an arrangement that would confirm the *de facto* confederation established by the 1974 Constitution, so that Belgrade (whether Serbia or the federation) could not challenge their sovereignty. If that could not be achieved, they would insist on being independent.

In other parts of Yugoslavia, responses to the Jović proposal were divided. The Montenegrin leadership favored the proposal. Bosnia tended towards retaining the federation, but would have also accepted a confederation of existing republics. In declaring itself for either option, provided all constituents remained part of Yugoslavia, the Bosnian leadership, conscious that the broader Yugoslav framework offered protection from competing nationalist pressures, avoided offending either side, while advancing its own interest in preserving some sort of Yugoslavia. Macedonia initially supported the federal option, but later leaned towards confederation. The Albanians in Kosovo were sympathetic to the confederalists but also wanted their own republic, because a confederal arrangement with Kosovo as a province would have left them even more subject to Serbian control and formal sovereignty. Confederalists identified federation with the old system of Serb-dominated centralism; federalists saw it as the only way Yugoslavia could continue to exist. For the federalists, confederation was a code for dissolving Yugoslavia, while the confederalists saw it as a way of keeping some from of Yugoslavia intact. Meanwhile, Serbia declared that if Yugoslavia became a confederation, it would support political autonomy for the Krajina Serbs and that it would 'unify' Serbia if the Croats attempted to become independent.

While the republics and provinces debated the merits of confederation and federation, the economic program of the then Federal Prime Minister Ante Marković was widely supported. At the end of 1989 Marković had revealed a radical reform plan to tackle inflation, which was running at 2,600 per cent per annum. The central feature of the reform was monetary control. Marković froze wages for six months and removed price restrictions from 85 per cent of commodities, leaving only certain raw materials and essential utilities under control.

The Marković program was impressive in its first six months. The month-on-month inflation rate fell, hard currency reserves rose, and the country's debt declined. In the first months of 1990, Marković's federal government appeared to become the most important element in the Yugoslav political system but he was less successful later in the year. Republics blocked further reforms and constitutional amendments, refused to agree to essential measures, withheld required financial contributions to the federal government and made their own laws. In effect, they moved towards independence. The crisis deepened.

Discussions about future relations and constitutional arrangements between the Yugoslav states produced a series of summit meetings between the leaders of Yugoslavia's states, but by May

1991 these were deadlocked. The federation was gradually ceasing to operate as, from different angles, it ceased to have the support of a number of its component states. On 9 May 1991, with the Yugoslav Defense Secretary-General Veljko Kadijević having threatened that if there were no settlement the army would impose one (on this evolving role, see Chapter 3), the Federal Presidency agreed six points for resolving the crisis, but this was merely a means of creating breathing-space. Statements by leading Croatian and Serbian politicians, including the presidents, were warlike. At an event labeled a peace rally in Serbia, the leader of the main opposition party, Vuk Drašković, called on Serbia and Serbians to prepare for war. President Slobodan Milošević of Serbia announced that, wherever there was a Serb, there was Serbia. Tudjman made it clear that Croatia would be prepared to defend itself. Tudjman and Milošević were hostages to their national constituencies and political ambitions, and the Croatian leader and his government were hostages to circumstances.[10] The final countdown had begun.

On 23 December 1990 Slovenia held a referendum which voted overwhelmingly in favour of declaring its independence from the federation if, within six months, the constitutional crisis had not been resolved. Slovenia accelerated the passage through its parliament of laws to prepare for eventual independence. Violence and unrest grew in Croatia through the spring (see Chapter 6). On 15 May 1991 Serbia blocked what should have been an automatic procedure, and prevented Croatia's Stipe Mesić from becoming President of the Collective Presidency of the SFRY. At this point Yugoslavia was left without a technical head of state. The federal system in Yugoslavia no longer worked.

On 19 May 1991 Croatia held a referendum on independence. A substantial majority voted to declare it at the end of June if the constitutional crisis persisted. In the mean time, on 12 May, the 'Serbian Autonomous Region of Krajina' had held a plebiscite (albeit one not sanctioned in Croatian law) to ratify a declaration of union with Serbia. The vote gave the declaration the support of 90 per cent of those who voted (95 per cent of those eligible to vote did so).[11] The Krajina referendum was held in anticipation of Croatia's 19 May referendum. Finally, on 25 June 1991, Slovenia and Croatia

[10] *Politika, Vjesnik, Delo*, 10 May 1991.
[11] *The Times*, 14 May 1991.

issued declarations of independence, initiating the final phases of the dissolution of the SFRY. International involvement and armed conflict of a mixed internal and international character, in which the role of the Yugoslav army and Serbian paramilitary forces was central, followed immediately.

3

THE MEANS: ARMED FORCES –
THE LIFE, DEATH AND LIFE
AFTER DEATH OF THE JNA

The first requirement of war is to have an armed force. Therefore, as the SFRY disintegrated and war loomed, it was necessary for Serbian President Slobodan Milošević to gain a military capability. The SFRY was replete with weaponry and a militarized population, given the official doctrine in which all citizens would be engaged in the defense effort should an invasion occur. However, the preponderance of military might lay with the regular army, the one part of the Yugoslav patchwork that owed its existence and its loyalty to Tito's Yugoslavia. If Milošević were to have the means to prosecute a war and create new borders and political realities, he would need the strength of that army and its arsenal. However, with its Titoist history that army was not necessarily an instrument that the Serbian President could control easily or completely. Thus it was necessary not only to gain control over the regular military, but also to ensure that there were alternative armed forces available for practical, political and personal purposes. Together, these alternative armed forces and the various elements of the old federal army and its inheritors constituted the means for Milošević's war. The present chapter focuses on the creation of force for the war, and considers how the means to conduct the Serbian war project were generated and developed to the point where, during the Kosovo campaign in spring 1999, Milošević finally had formal command of all armed forces.

The role and character of the JNA in the SFRY

The armed forces of the SFRY comprised two elements. The first tier, the JNA, was a regular armed force, including ground, air and naval services. The second tier, a Territorial Defense Force (*Teritorijalna Odbrana* – TO), was an irregular force, derived from the

51

Partisan tradition in guerrilla warfare. The Federal Secretariat for People's Defense (*Savezni Sekretarijat za Narodnu Odbranu* –SSNO) was responsible for the JNA, while Repub-lican Secretariats for People's Defence were responsible for the various TOs.

Both tiers were intended to be components of a unified defense capability within the doctrine of General People's Defence. In this doctrine the role of the JNA was to be the first mobilized. The TO, together with elements of the JNA, would then carry out defense in depth by conducting warfare, especially from the heavily wooded mountain heartland of Bosnia, to harass and exhaust the invader. The command structure for both the JNA and the TO was highly decentralized, given the nature of the war envisaged which could not rely on the maintenance of a command and control network across the territory of the SFRY if there were an invasion. The primary aim of this defence doctrine was to deter attack by persuading a potential invader that the costs of invasion would be militarily and politically too great.

The origins of the JNA lie in the Second World War Partisan movement that brought Tito's regime to power. The Partisan army had been originally a guerrilla force, but as the war progressed, it took the shape of a regular armed force, and in 1945 became the army of the new Yugoslavia. It was known first as the Yugoslav Army (*Jugoslovenska Armija* – JA), but was renamed the Yugoslav People's Army (*Jugoslovenska Narodna Armija* – JNA) after the Soviet-Yugoslav split in 1948. Supplemented by the territorial defence forces, the army was preoccupied with the external threat. Yugoslavia initially perceived this as originating in the West and therefore turned to the USSR for assistance.

After the 1948 split with Moscow, Yugoslavia believed it was in danger of external invasion from the East. It further built up the domestic arms industry which had proved important to the Partisans during the Second World War. By 1952 the JNA had 500,000 men under arms and 25 per cent of the national income was spent on defense. Eventually, Yugoslavia produced 90% of its military needs. Many of the key defense manufacturing facilities were consciously located in Bosnia, where access was difficult, to protect them from outside invasion, and where they would be close to strongholds of resistance foreseen in the General People's Defence doctrine.

In the 1950s the Yugoslav military was primarily concerned with developing the defense capability of the country and had no political role. Because of its emphasis on hierarchy, discipline and responsiveness to command, the JNA was regarded as being relatively successful at overcoming ethnic and political differences, and it therefore saw itself as a champion of 'Yugoslavism'. In the late 1960s, as the republics were asserting more autonomy, efforts were made to 'republicanize' the JNA. Under pressure from the Republics, it attempted to achieve fully proportional representation from each in the officer corps. It also adopted the principle that 25 per cent of the troop contingent from each republic should be based on home territory. At the same time, the territorial component of the defense system was strengthened. The TOs became co-equal with the JNA, with joint command structures.

Through constitutional amendments made in 1971 and the new Constitution of 1974, the JNA gained a leading role within the governing party, the League of Communists of Yugoslavia (SKJ – *Savez Komunista Jugosjavije*), receiving equal status with the two autonomous provinces in the SKJ's new 166-member Central Committee. As Yugoslavia seemed to be falling apart in 1971, the JNA leadership became essential in maintaining the stability, cohesion and authority of civilian political institutions.

The JNA's political role increased in part because it was a pan-Yugoslav institution. Its loyalty was not to any one republic, but to the Yugoslav Federation. Its own legitimacy and survival depended on Yugoslavia continuing to exist. As a result, the JNA leadership was cautious about intervening in politics, physically or otherwise, beyond its allotted constitutional role. The Constitution was central to the military's role in the political system. In 1971 General Ivan Mišković said that 'only in cases where the constitutional order was threatened would the army become an instrument for solving internal difficulties.' As long as some central civil authority remained, the army would constitutionally be the coercively instrumental partner in an alliance with that authority and would not itself usurp the political process.

This formalized, legitimate political role for the JNA was based on the notion that it would ensure a 'pan-Yugoslav' voice in politics, inheriting Tito's mantle when he died. Tito emphasized this: 'Brotherhood and Unity are inseparably linked with our army . . . I believe that our army is still playing such a role today. . . [it] must not merely watch vigilantly over our borders, but also be present inside the country. . . There are those who write that one day Yugoslavia will disintegrate. Nothing like that will happen because our army ensures that we will continue to move in the direction we have chosen for the socialist construction of our country.' This role was given substance by the appointment of generals to key government and party leadership posts in the 1970s and '80s.

In 1988, as nationalist sentiments grew stronger throughout Yugoslavia, civil military-relations in Slovenia deteriorated. In May the JNA arrrested and tried three journalists and a soldier on suspicion of betraying a military secret. There followed a trial that incited the Slovenes because it was conducted *in camera* and in the Serbo-Croat language rather than in Slovene; even though the 1974 Constitution assured the equality of all Yugoslav languages in the JNA (Article 243) – the reality was that increasingly Serbo-Croat had become the *de facto* command language, used in almost all circumstances. The use of Serbo-Croat at the trial reinforced the notion among many Slovenes that an ever more vigorous Serb nationalism was emerging. It also catalyzed Slovene national sentiment.

At the end of 1988, quietly and without public discussion, the JNA reorganized, replacing the old Army Districts, often identical with borders of the republics' borders and always associated with the republics' TOs, with new Military Districts, the boundaries of which were different from those of the republics. The importance of republican authorities in defense matters diminished, as the new Military District headquarters and their commanders exercised broader discretion in the field.

The increased autonomy of the Military Districts from superior JNA command and republican political authorities had important consequences as the SFRY entered its final phase of dissolution and armed conflict. In the case of the Knin Corps, based in the principal town in Croatia's Krajina region, the 1988 rearrangement meant that as early as the summer of 1990 the Corps' command could give the local Serb population access to JNA arms and equipment – one of several ways in which elements of the JNA increasingly acted in collusion with Serb political forces.

While the autonomy of a Military District allowed an individual commander to support local Serb interests, the JNA leadership was equally interested in protecting Serbs outside Serbia. Many Serbian military officers, such as General Kadijević and his Chief of Staff General Blagoje Adžić, came from the regions of Croatia and Bosnia where Ustasha terror in the Second World War had driven them, or their parents, to become the core of the Partisan movement. The decreasing numbers and influence of non-Serbs in the JNA also contributed to the army's tendency to align itself with Serb interests.

The structural and political consequences of a growing Serb dominance in the JNA had already become evident in the spring of 1991 – when, seeking reliable and usable forces, the JNA formed ethnically homogeneous Serbian units for special deployment in Slovenia. The growing Serbian orientation of the JNA was also evident in April and May 1991. While General Kadijević was in hospital, General Adžić authorized the JNA to deploy in parts of Bosnia and Hercegovina and in about one-third of Croatia, the deployments in Croatia, especially in the Krajina region, being to protect armed Serb civilian insurgents who had created areas which the Croatian police could not enter. This action was one manifestation of the JNA's increasingly important role in the SFRY crisis. Previously General Kadijević, who was regarded as a cons-titutionalist, had argued that martial law could be imposed only if the Presidency ordered it, but General Adžić favored acting re-gardless of whatever the Presidency might do.

General Kadijević's concern for constitutional requirements was illustrated by an incident in March 1991. The JNA Supreme Com-mand schemed with Serbian political leaders in Belgrade to get the Federal Presidency to declare a state of emergency and allow the army to impose martial law. At two specially convened meetings, held not in the normal Presidency building but in the cold base-ment of an army building, pressure was put on the eight members of the Presidency by General Kadijević and other military leaders.[1] They were also pushed into declaring a state of emergency by the chair of the meeting, Borisav Jović who was formally President of the Yugoslav Presidency at that time and one of Serbian President Slobodan Milošević's closest confidants. After two tense meetings, in which the Croatian representative pointed out that this was ef-fectively a move towards war and General Kadijević retorted that,

---

[1] The Slovene representative to this collective body, Janez Drnovšek, did not attend the first of the meetings.

if the Presidency would not act, the JNA would be forced to take matters into its own hands, there was a split decision. The representative from Bosnia, Bogić Bogicević, though a Serb, surprised Jović and his allies by voting against the proposal.[2] This meant that a state of emergency was not declared.

Milošević and Jović had a fallback plan. This was to create the conditions in which the Federal Presidency would not function, so that the Federal Secretary for Defense, General Kadijević, would become *de facto* commander-in-chief of the armed forces. He would then be able to impose a state of emergency and martial law himself. The President of the Presidency, the Serbian representative Jović, resigned in order to set the stage for the realisation of this plan, but this did not happen. Part of the explanation lies with activity in the Presidency without Jović. The Vice-President of the Presidency, the Croatian representative Stipe Mesić, surprised the JNA and prepared to take over the Presidency in Jović's absence. This left the Presidency potentially functioning. The other factor was General Kadijević himself, who could not bring himself to proceed with this momentous step if it meant acting in an unconstitutional manner, and therefore did not pursue the plan.[3] Once it was clear that the JNA was not going to act as arranged with the Serbian political leadership, Jović quickly returned to his post after the Serbian parliament, controlled by Milošević, rejected his resignation.

A final possibility for JNA intervention in the fading political life of the Yugoslav federation occurred in May 1991, but the JNA's proposals were again rejected as the storm clouds gathered over the lands of the South Slavs. In these situations the JNA Chief of Staff, General Blagoje Adžić, appears to have argued for acting without an order from the Presidency, but Kadijević opposed this. However, despite Kadijević's sense of constitutional propriety, as well

[2] Whereas the Serbian camp – Serbia, its two autonomous provinces – Vojvodina and Kosovo, and Montenegro – supported the action, the four other republican representatives from Slovenia, Croatia, Macedonia and Bosnia rejected it.

[3] While Kadijević seems to have had little sense that plotting with one part of the Presidency against others, among other things, might have been unconstitutional action, it seems clear that he was not prepared to intervene and declare martial law without some kind of an order from the Presidency formally to authorize this. This assessment is confirmed by his predecessor as Defense Secretary and adviser, Admiral Branko Mamula in *Death of Yugoslavia*, Part 2, Brian Lapping Associates for the BBC, 1995.

as his aversion to Serbian President Milošević, he and his army had become ever more aligned with the political leaders in Belgrade. This perhaps occurred predominantly by force of circumstance and the institutional prejudice and culture that remembered Croatian nationalist independence leading to mass murder of Serbs. This political drift was to be confirmed by the approach and effects of war. These would see a change in the demographic character of the army, the JNA formally ceasing to exist, and Milošević bringing about increasing Serbian control over the army – in part, through preference for other armed forces, as will be seen below.

Serbianization: Milošević and the military

When Belgrade retired generals after a meeting of the Supreme Defense Council on 25–26 August 1993, Serbian President Slobodan Milošević's effective control of the Yugoslav military was confirmed and all but the very last traces of the JNA were removed. Its principal successor – Belgrade's new military, the Army of Yugoslavia (*Vojska Jugoslavije* – VJ) – continued a process of Serbianization that had already begun in the JNA during Yugoslavia's descent into war and dissolution. That process meant transformation from a multi-ethnic armed force to an almost purely Serbian organization, and the accrual of command and control of the military by the Serbian President. Yet not until the Kosovo campaign of 1999 would he have generals in charge on whom he could absolutely rely, and even then the prospect of adverse civil-military relations remained, as will be seen below.

In the course of the armed conflict surrounding the dissolution of the SFRY, the character of the JNA changed substantially in ethnic and ethno-political terms. Before 1990–1, the JNA was a mixed force of regulars, almost entirely commissioned and non-commissioned officers, with a conscript cadre. In the highest ranks an 'ethnic key' principle operated to ensure proportional representation of all the major communities in the SFRY, although the most senior posts were almost invariably held by Serbs. The middle and junior ranks were dominated by Serbs.

In the officer corps as a whole, 60 per cent were Serb, 6.2 per cent were Montenegrin, and 5.4 per cent described themselves as 'Yugoslav'; probably the majority of these were Serbs and Montenegrins. Most shared a perspective on Yugoslavia that coincided generally with that of the Belgrade political leadership. The remainder comprised Croats, 12.6 per cent; Macedonians, 6.3 per cent; Muslims, 2.4 per cent; Slovenes, 2.8 per cent; Albanians, 0.6 per cent; Hungarians 0.7 per cent; others 1.6 per cent. Until 1990–1, the JNA was unquestionably a multi-ethnic conscript-based force of 80,000. Serbs made up 36 per cent of the conscripts and 42 per cent of the total. On the eve of the declarations of independence in the summer of 1991 and of the subsequent wars, figures from the Federal Defense Secretariat reported a slightly lower proportion of Serbs, but a more or less consistent picture.

The dissolution of the state and armed conflict had a marked impact on both the ethnic composition and the ethno-political character of the JNA. Purely in terms of its ethnic composition it was reported in March 1992 that no more than 11,000 non-Serbs (including some 6,500 Montenegrins) were still on the army payroll. This was less than 10 per cent of the official total for the armed forces, although perhaps slightly over 10 per cent of the ground forces. With over 3,000 Montenegrin officers and around 3,500 Montenegrin conscripts among the non-Serb component, who were mostly (though not always accurately) seen as allied to the Serbian cause, the picture was starker. This meant that those who were clearly non-Serb constituted less than 5 per cent of the official total, implying that overall the Serb component of the army had risen from about 40 to 90 per cent.

Through defections to Slovenia, Croatia and then other republics, resignations from disillusioned officers who could not defect, and an apparent program of retiring non-Serbs, the army progressively became Serbian dominated. The combined effect of circumstance and active Serbianization was that when the JNA ceased formally to exist on 19 May 1992 (see below), out of 150 generals serving exactly one year before, only twenty-four remained. Aside from defections, this was a result of the resignation of General Kadijević in January followed by pensioning off 20 mostly non-Serb or Yugoslav-oriented generals in March 1992 and a further 38 in May. In terms of the army's ethno-political character, the effect of this was augmented by the impact of the circumstances in which the army found itself. The JNA was forced to adjust to the idea that the SFRY was no more and that there was a priority to establish the borders of a new *de facto* Serbian state (see Chapters 5–7). There was also an active campaign to re-orient the JNA towards a Serbian political character.

In May 1992 the JNA, by then over 90 per cent Serbian in com-position, was formally disestablished and divided into two (although some parts of it, especially command and control, had already been inherited by the armed forces of the Krajina Serbs in Croatia, thus maintaining Belgrade control). This followed international recog-nition of the independence of Bosnia at the beginning of April and the proclamation of a new Yugoslav federation, comprising Serbia and Montenegro, at the end of that month. The proclama-tion of the new state and the division of the armed forces were made in response to the imposition of comprehensive, mandatory UN sanctions on Serbia and Montenegro, with the aim of getting the JNA to withdraw from Bosnia. Belgrade tried to sidestep the issue by dissolving the JNA and dividing its assets between the self-styled Serbian Republic (of Bosnia and Hercegovina) (*Srpska Republika Bosne i Hercegovine*)[4] and the new 'Federal Republic of Yugoslavia' (*Savezna Republika Jugoslavija* – FRY), comprising Serbia and Montenegro.

This was a move carefully conceived and planned several months beforehand. Following an assessment that Belgrade's campaign against Bosnia would meet with a hostile international response and accusations of aggression, Milošević and Jović prepared to deal with this possibility by deception. On 5 December they instructed JNA chief General Kadijević to re-deploy all Serbs from Bosnia to JNA units in the country, while removing Serbs not from Bosnia from those units, as far as possible. Only ten days later the General, who had been reluctant to do this even though Jović (who had consulted no one else) claimed to speak on behalf of the Federal Presidency which was formally the Commander-in-Chief of the JNA, reported that this redeployment was complete. Thus when the time came, Belgrade would claim not to be involved in the Bosnian war, asserting that those who were fighting were Bosnian Serbs. Despite this allegation, Belgrade's original conception of the war ensured that it would retain ultimate control.

As a result of the May division, the VRS and the VJ each gained around 80,000 personnel.[5] In both cases the units involved mostly kept the equipment at their disposal, although the VRS did not inherit some of the old JNA's most modern capabilities – notably

---

[4] This entity was later to be renamed 'Republika Srpska.'

[5] Milan Vego, 'Federal Army Deployments in Bosnia-Hercegovina', *Jane's Intel-ligence Review*, October 1992, p. 445.

aircraft.[6] While remaining formally divided, the chain of command within the old federal army did not change. The VRS continued to be under Belgrade's command,[7] albeit with broad operational authority given to the commander in Bosnia, General Ratko Mladić, who could be relied on to prosecute the campaign largely without reference to Belgrade, thereby enhancing the superficial fiction.

The division of the JNA represented an apparent success for those such as the youngest of the generals at that time, Colonel-General Vuk Obradović. These were 'young Turks' who, looking to the future, had been arguing that realities would have to be accepted. These included recognition that the army's responsibility was to get on with securing its own future on the basis of the new state – with Serbian identity at its core, a new doctrine and greater professionalization. Obradović appeared to be the leader of a faction which, by its open position, was seeking to change the political leadership as well as the army's own. However, he resigned when his promise to the parents of soldiers serving in Bosnia that their sons would all be returned to them by 19 May could not be fulfilled. This enhanced his popular reputation, although it left open to question the full explanation for the resignation of a clearly ambitious young general. Whatever this was, it made Obradović a significant figure. By the end of the 1990s, having apparently retained good links with some of his former military colleagues, he had emerged as political leader of one of Serbia's numerous political parties, Social Democracy (*Socijalna Demokracija*). Meanwhile he continued the campaign to change the political leadership.

Much of what was most visceral about the JNA had become the VRS, with the notorious General Mladić as its commanding officer. Some estimates put the proportion of Bosnian Serbs among the total number of Serbs in the JNA as high as 80 per cent. While this was probably an exaggeration, it was conceivable that a majority of Serbian officers were Serbs from outside Serbia. Certainly around 80 per cent of the JNA force in Bosnia remained there when the new FRY authorities formally recalled its citizens in the army from Bosnia in view of splitting the JNA into two.

---

[6] The VRS inherited, in fact, forty three aircraft, of which the most important were Yugoslav produced Galeb G-4 ground attack aircraft.

[7] See Vego, 'Federal Army Deployments.'

Mladić and the military in Bosnia served Belgrade's purposes and clearly acted in line with Serbian nationalist political objectives. However, problems of reliability remained regarding the VJ, in which great changes occurred after the division of the JNA. There was extensive replacement of top personnel regarded by the Serbian leadership as unreliable, and there was an intra-military takeover during 1992 of senior positions by airforce hardliners, whose role in the purges was critical. This was especially true of Colonel-General Božidar Stevanović, who became airforce chief in January 1992 following the shooting-down of an EC helicopter which led to the removal of his predecessor, Colonel-General Zvonko Jurjević (one of the remaining Croats at that time) and his intelligence chief, Colonel-General Slobodan Rakočević.

Stevanović's appointment had an interesting background. In June 1991, at the time of the first armed clashes in Slovenia, he had requested normal retirement but, extraordinarily, he was allowed to have his application withdrawn after being so advised by the Serbian leadership.[8] Following this, in August, he made public a letter from pilots in the 5th Corps (Zagreb) demanding the replacement of the then military leadership of Kadijević, Jurjević and Admiral Stane Brovet; this was part of an internal campaign in support of Serbianization and the Serbian political leader's ambition, conducted by a 'thread' of those with links to the Serbian Security Service and 'in the know' – including General Mladić. Serb officers were recruited by members of Milošević's Security Service into a 'clandestine network';[9] they were not likely to cling to the 'Yugoslav' and 'Titoist' orientation of those, such as Kadijević, in the JNA command. To some extent this web of Serbian officers, known as the Vojna Linija (the military line), may have rejected Tito's multi-ethnic Yugoslavia and the JNA because the emphasis on the ethnic key at the highest levels, despite the preponderance of ethnic Serbs in the JNA, denied them promotion. This could certainly be inferred from charges made by General Mladić, as well as his assertions regarding Tito's crimes against the Serbs, – which, he alleged, included making Serbs second-class citizens.[10]

[8] *Vreme*, 19 April, 1993.

[9] Tim Judah, *The Serbs: History, Myth and the destruction of Yugoslavia*, New Haven and London: Yale University Press, 1997, p. 170.

[10] Ljiljana Bulatović, *General Mladić*, Belgrade: Biblioteka Svedočanstva, 1996, p. 188.

Through Squadron 252 of the air force, based at Batajnica, General Stevanović, seemingly without the knowledge of the General Staff, initiated aerial attacks against Croatia. Batajnica appears to have been a focal point for the Serbian camp within the JNA, and among it functions was furnishing the extremist paramilitary leader Vojislav Šešelj (whose units also received arms from Stevanović) with military helicopters. This squadron became known as the 'First Serbian' because of its close links with other paramilitary leaders, including Mirko Jović, leader of the White Eagles (Beli Orli), Captain 'Dragan', an Australian Serb who led the Serbian fight in parts of Croatia, and Željko Ražnjatović 'Arkan', leader of the Tigers force (see below).

Stevanović organized an Airforce Intelligence (*Ratno Vazduho-plovstvo-Obaveštcajna Služba* – RVOS) operation, which was responsible for engineering greater Serbian political control of the armed forces. In May, following the removal of twenty generals in February, a further thirty-eight were purged as 'traitors' and 'unreliable' elements. Stevanović and his team were responsible for preparing the list of those to be purged and in some cases arranging smear campaigns. The impact of this campaign on the 150-strong cadre of generals in the army has already been noted. This process sought to eradicate any residual 'Yugoslav' character in the armed forces.

During 1992 Stevanović effectively arranged an Air Force takeover of military intelligence. He appointed a new head of the RVOS, whose job was to identify and remove 'spies' and 'traitors' from the military as a whole. The appointment was curious, as Colonel Nedeljko Bošković was brought out of retirement by Stevanović to take up this appointment and was promoted to major-general, in spite of insufficient qualifications. The Stevanović-Bošković campaign culminated in December 1992 when the hardliners successfully gained a complete grip on military intelligence. They achieved this when they replaced the last army personnel in significant positions in the Security Administration of the Military of Yugoslavia (*Uprava Bezbednosti Vojske Jugoslavije* – UBVJ).

Towards the end of 1992 there were several indications of the harder line resulting from increasing RVOS dominance of intramilitary politics. In October, Serbian Interior Ministry troops occupied the Federal Interior Ministry. They kept the Federal Minister

Pavle Bulatović, an appointee of the then Prime Minister Milan Panić,[11] who was trying to steer Belgrade away from war, out of the building, and at the same time allowed Mihajl Kertes, the former Deputy Interior Minister and Head of the Federal Security Services, back to his desk. Kertes had been sacked by Prime Minister Panić for his involvement in attempts to bug the August 1992 London Conference. These had been detected by the British Security Service MI5. He was also fired over his role in the organization of ethnic cleansing and what Panić described as resisting his policy of opposing ethnic cleansing.[12] The VJ Chief of Staff, Colonel General Života Panić (no relation to the Prime Minister), declared that the military would keep out of politics. This meant that they would not come to the aid of Panić and his government by restoring his position in the Interior Ministry and *vis-à-vis* the Serbian republican forces, which had carried out the occupation.

Another indication of the dominance of hardliners was the sudden appearance of the war in Bosnia and Hercegovina on the pages of the army weekly *Vojska*. This had been an otherwise strange omission from the publication's launch in May 1992 as successor to the old *Narodna Armija* until the appearance of such references in December. The publication of reports from the Bosnian battlefields in *Vojska* indicated that behind-the-scenes divisions had been settled in favor of the hardliners. The division here was between those who favored Panić's option, or at least thought it wiser not to oppose it publicly, and those clearly against it. Those opposing the search for peace and harmonization with the other former Yugoslav states and the international community had clearly won.

The clearest manifestation of the VJ's position came from a mysterious and anonymous group called the 'Collegium of the Ministry of Defense', which issued a statement at the beginning of

[11] Milan Panić was a Yugoslav-born US citizen and a businessman with a large California-based pharmaceuticals firm but also major investments in Serbia. (The Serbian part of his business empire was nationalized by the authorities in 1998 in the course of a financial and political struggle.) Panić had become Prime Minister as elements in Serbia and the diaspora sought to change the country's image, if not Serbia itself. As regards image, it was in Milošević's interest in 1992 to present a more agreeable face to the West. However, Panić was unable to bring about any genuine change before he was removed.

[12] 'Intervention of Milan Panić', London Conference, 26 August 1992.

December that Prime Minster Panić, who also held the federal defence portfolio, was not competent for the latter role and should
resign from it. Although there was another statement later the same
day from the General Staff denying that any of its members were
part of this 'informal group' (none of its members was known), the
denial could not remove doubts about civil-military relationships
in Belgrade. It was hard to imagine that members of the General
Staff did not share the opinions of their neighbors in the Defense
Ministry.

This represented a change in military attitudes to Prime Minister Panić. The General Staff had at first appeared to be wholly behind the federal team of Panić and President Ćosić. Early issues of
the new publication *Vojska* even seemed to be beginning to treat
Panić as a potential savior, giving him the kind of attention the
JNA had given to Tito in the old days. However, there was a rupture
in September when Panić said that the VJ would withdraw from
the Prevlaka Peninsula in southern Croatia, which it had continued to occupy since fighting stopped in Croatia at the beginning
of the year. This was part of the Panić program of normalizing
rela-tions with Croatia and moving towards mutual recognition.

The peninsula was a vital strategic question for the VJ, as for the
JNA before it. It dominated the northern coast of the Bay of Kotor,
the location of the one naval facility the VJ had inherited from the
old state. If that coast were to be in Croatian hands, the operation
of the naval base – and naval operations as a whole – would always
be vulnerable. This left aside the legal issue of international mari-
time boundaries. The VJ was extremely unhappy at this suggestion. Yet, in spite of some emollient words from President Ćosić,
which indicated that his sympathies were with the military, the VJ
withdrew under an agreement made with the UN-EC envoys,
Cyrus Vance and David Owen.

The loss of Prevlaka stung the VJ – the operations in southern
Croatia had been the only ones in the war in Croatia carried out
by the JNA on its own, not in conjunction with Serbian locals or
irregulars, and had been done for specific strategic reasons connected with the creation of a new state. This was demonstrated
by a sixteen-page special color insert in the 1 October edition of
Vojska – which even included a summary in English, presumably
for distribution in a propaganda campaign. The reluctant withdrawal weakened the links between Prime Minster Panić and the

VJ and strengthened the hardliners, who through the machinations of General Stevanović were gaining the upper hand.

In this context, the statements by the Chief-of-Staff, General Panić, that the military would not be involved in politics and that it was against a use of force to change the government, were not necessarily what they appeared to be on the surface. What looked like statements favorable to the government – that the military would not remove it – were in reality just as much statements that the military would not protect the government. Hence, when Serbian troops took over the Federal Interior Ministry, the VJ sided with Serbia *de facto* by not making itself available to assert governmental authority.

Finally, while Stevanović was constructing an army free from Yugoslav impurities, which would be wholly subordinate to Milošević from within, Milošević himself was strengthening the army's subordination to him from without. Command and control of the VJ was established on a different basis from that of the JNA in the old state. Significantly, a body called the Supreme Defense Council, rather than the federal presidency, became the ultimate authority over the armed forces. This council comprised the Presidents of the Federation and of Serbia and Montenegro. The Federal President acted formally as its spokesman, but orders were determined by the Council.

This indicated that, whatever the policies and positions of federal politicians in Belgrade, command of the military had moved significantly into the hands of the republics. In particular, Serbian President Milošević had in fact some degree of official, direct and formal control over the VJ – which he did not have over the JNA. Indeed, he only needed the backing of one of the other members of the presidential troika for the VJ to be following his orders, officially. Given that the appointment of the Federal President was made by the Federal Parliament (which was, in turn, controlled by Milošević's Serbian Socialist Party), the Federal President was, *de facto*, a Milošević appointment. This was confirmed when, facing the prospect that he could not constitutionally stand again as President of Serbia, he had himself chosen by the parliament as President of the FRY. His long-time political ally, Milan Milutinović, was appointed in his place as President of Serbia. More than ever before, therefore, Milošević was the key figure in Yugoslav military-political affairs.

General Perišić and the persistence of ambiguities within the army

Although so many generals had been removed, relatively few new appointments were made. When Ratko Mladić was promoted general in October 1991, along with four others, he was among the last to achieve this status in the JNA. During the first half of 1992, the forty-two generals removed from their positions by Stevanović's Serbianization campaign gave way to only one new appointment. This was the naming of Colonel General Momćilo Perišić, formerly commander of the 3rd Army, as Chief of Staff to replace Colonel-General Života Panić. The promotion of Perišić was important in the context of civil-military trends in Belgrade following the declarations of independence by Slovenia and Croatia and the onset of war in June 1991.

One of the notable question-marks hanging over the VJ was the position of the Chief of Staff, General Panić. His predecessor General Adžić was retired by Belgrade as part of the trend towards Serbianization, although he had been considerably more hardline and apparently pro-Serbian that General Kadijević (whom he replaced as Federal Defense Secretary on an acting basis when the latter resigned), who was too 'Yugoslav' for the new circumstances. There was a need to find a serving general to replace him who fulfilled two criteria. The first was to be reliable, or pliant, enough for the Serbian regime. The second was to have been born in Serbia itself. Because the heights of the army command were traditionally held by Serbs from outside Serbia, such as Generals Adžić Kadijević and Admiral Mamula, this was not as simple as it might have been. Panić came from the General Staff, but had previously been commander of the 1st Military District, with headquarters in Belgrade. This was the highest point in the command of the fading JNA to be taken by a Serb from Serbia. It was Panić's forces which were responsible for the destruction of Vukovar in Croatia in the autumn of 1991. In addition to rank and origin, one other factor was important in the appointment of Panić – he was more a career soldier and less a politician than his predecessors.

General Panić does not appear to have been an outright supporter of Milošević. During 1992 he became publicly associated with Milan Panić and Dobrica Ćosić, respectively Prime Minister and President of the new Yugoslav federation. Although neither would have been appointed without tactical advantage to Milošević, it was clear that first Prime Minister Panić and later President Ćosić were seeking to undermine and unseat the Serbian President from within. Once Milošević had engineered a vote of no-confidence in Panić in December 1992, at the same time as General Stevanović had seized control of the military through the intelligence services, it was only a matter of time before the Chief of Staff would also be changed. After Ćosić was replaced as president of the federation in the spring, it seemed that the move would be imminent. As a result, with effective control of the Supreme Defense Council, Milošević was able to shake out the top of the military.

The sign that Milošević was ready to get rid of Panić came when Vojislav Šešelj, leader of the ultra-nationalist Serbian Radical Party, began to demand the Chief of Staff's removal. Šešelj alleged that Panić's son had been engaged in smuggling and war profiteering in Eastern Slavonia and Vojvodina, which had fallen within the 1st Military District of the JNA which General Panić had commanded before taking his post as Chief of Staff. Panić himself was linked to this. Hence, Šešelj pushed for changes in the army leadership. Only a few weeks before his discharge, the General was still able to hope that matters 'with regard to the affair linked with my name' would be 'clarified by the Supreme Defense Council in the shortest time, on the basis of information from the state commission'.[13] Whatever clarification came regarding the alleged corruption, it did not save General Panić's job.

Instead, the Serbian Radical leader's campaign intensified, with his party leading opposition to the federal budget, on the grounds that it would not sanction funding of the armed forces while incompetent and corrupt generals remained in charge. Some saw this as Šešelj flexing his muscles against the Serbian leadership, but it was hard not to see a recurring pattern of Šešelj demanding something that Milošević was seeking to do and Milošević's apparently doing it, according to the rules of this game, under pressure from nationalist extremists.[14] Thus the Radical leader's posturing was part of the Serbian leader's move to clean out the army command.

When the shake-out came, there were some surprises, including one for the Serbian President's opposition sidekick. What was unexpected also was the extent of the changes and that they

[13] Interview carried in *Vojska*, 15 July 1993.

[14] Miloš Vasić, 'Konkurs za zvedice i lišće', *Vreme*, 30 August 1993, described the double act as 'their cultivated joint maneuver', with one playing the government and the other playing the opposition, or 'good cop, bad cop'

affected Šešelj: General Stevanović was surprisingly included in the purge. It had been expected that when Panić was ousted, he would not go alone.[15] In July the Belgrade weekly *Vreme* reported that General Panić would only remain in post for as long as it took to find others to accompany him. In all, another forty-one generals were retired or sacked on 26 August 1993.[16] As a result, only nine officers already holding the rank of general remained, of whom the new Chief of Staff was the only one with field experience.[17] This was a major blow against the military by Milošević.

The most surprising elements of the purge were the retiring of General Stevanović and the appointment of General Perišić as Chief of Staff. As the man who had been rescued from the brink of retirement by Milošević in 1991, and who had been the scourge of anything pro-Yugoslav in the military, Stevanović seemed to be set to complete his renaissance by becoming Chief of Staff. Indeed, Belgrade circles were reported to have been buzzing with news of his appointment the day before it was announced that Perišić was to have the job.[18]

There were two possible explanations for the by-passing of Stevanović. The first was that, through his knowledge of events, his increasingly outspoken public statements and his links with leaders of paramilitary groups, particularly Šešelj, he might develop an independent power-base that could threaten Milošević. It certainly made sense for Milošević not to allow someone like him to become an autonomous locus of power. The second explanation was more rooted in pragmatic factors. Rather than acting politically in getting rid of Stevanović, Milošević was simply recognizing the

[15] 19 July 1993.

[16] *Politika*, 27 August 1993, published the full list of names.

[17] The nine generals were General Perišić; Major-General Radomir Damjanović, deputy commander, of the 2nd Army, based in Podgorica; Major-General Milovan Bojović, commander of the Priština Corps; Major-General Dragoljub Ojdanić, Commander of the Užice Corps (later to replace Perišić as Chief of Staff in 1998); Colonel General Mile Mrkšić, commander of Special Forces (later to be appointed as commander of Krajina Serb forces to manage their withdrawal in 1995); Major-General Tomislav Radovanović, chief of the legal administration in the Ministry of Defense; Colonel-General Momčilo Lazović, Rector of the Military Academy; Major-General Dr Jovan Bijelić, deputy commander of the Military Medical Academy; and Major-General Prof. Dr Milan Ćusić of the Military Medical Academy.

[18] Vasić, 'Konkurs'.

reality that he was superannuated and politicized. The army needed a good professional rather than a political conspirator. In particular, the need to rejuvenate the army command was offered as the reason for overlooking Stevanović and another contender, former assistant Chief of Staff Colonel-General Dragoljub Simonović.[19]

In this context, Perišić, at forty-nine and with a proven record in the field, represented a new generation of militarily competent officers ready to shape a professional army. He was born on 22 May 1944 in Koštunići and his secondary school education was in Čačak, after which he went to the Military Academy for Ground Forces, where he trained as an artillery officer. He was later to graduate in psychology from the Higher Military-Political School of the then JNA. During his active service, he held fifteen posts before being promoted to the top position in the VJ. During the break-up of Yugoslavia, he saw action at Zadar in Croatia, where he began the war with the rank of colonel as commandant of the artillery school there. He was uncompromising in his bombardment of the town, while under a Croatian blockade – although he later explained this action by saying that he was 'defending a still existing country against rebels'.[20] After successfully breaking the blockade, he was transferred from Zadar to Bileća in eastern Hercegovina, where he became corps commander. From there he was active in the Dubrovnik campaign. Later, in Bosnia, he was to be involved in engagements at Foča, as well as at Mostar, where he gained the nickname 'the Knight of Mostar', following his part in the destruction of the centuries-old town.[21] Both temperamental and intelligent, he was a man with verve whose mind was not closed; he was reported to have shown some remorse at the destruction of Mostar, but nonetheless retained a strong reputation as a tough soldier who inspired those who served with him. Before being nominated Chief of Staff, he was commander of the 3rd Army, with its headquarters at Niš.

While consideration of soldierly qualities partly explained the appointment of Perišić, this had to be measured against the overall position in which this round of changes left the VJ. By leaving it

[19] *Pobjeda*, 29 August 1993.
[20] Quoted in *RFE/RL Newsline*, 13 August 1999.
[21] It should be pointed out that the most significant part of the destruction of this beautiful medieval town was the responsibility of Croatian forces, which, in a venal act of vandalism, deliberately destroyed the 700-year-old bridge that had survived all other wars through its history.

temporarily with only nine generals, three of whom were not field officers, Milošević does not appear to have been concerned for the welfare of the VJ. Instead he could be more sure that it could not turn against him. He would also, no doubt, have promotions available as inducements and rewards for service in his cause.

The naming of Perišić appeared to catch Šešelj off balance. Šešelj and Stevanović were thought to have a good relationship. However, Perišić was certainly an appointment beyond reproach, as far as nationalist opinion in Serbia was concerned. Thus, although Šešelj was not fulsome in praise for the choice of Perišić, he was not disrespectful either. For Šešelj the new Chief of Staff was an 'honorable man and a competent commander'. Moreover, officers were not to be regarded as divided into his supporters and opponents, only 'into those who are honorable and competent and those who are not'.[22]

It was not entirely co-incidental that the changes were made on the same day as the latest adjustments to the federal budget were finally approved in the federal parliament. According to the Federal Secretary of Defense, Pavle Bulatović, there was no connection between the two and 'this was a regular change.'[23] However, the proximity of the decisions and the fact that the changes were announced after a hastily convened meeting of the Supreme Defense Council suggested a connection. In addition to this, the Perišić appointment was the only replacement made – no other posts were filled and no new generals appointed in the following month. Moreover, there was a direct, albeit probably secondary, link. The withholding of required funding was an incentive to weaken resistance in the military to the changes. Officers were already comparatively poorly paid in relation to Serbian Interior Ministry troops (*Ministarstvo Unutrašnjih Poslova* – MUP), and thus there was a choice between the sacrifice of generals and the sacrifice of salary. The material position of the army had become extremely difficult, as Prime Minister Radoje Kontić noted.[24]

With inflation running at 1,000 per cent per month, stable financing of federal institutions was increasingly difficult. Only in the previous July a new budget was agreed which was expected

[22] Quoted in *Borba*, 27 August 1993.
[23] Ibid.
[24] *Vojska*, 22 July 1993.

to cover the period until the autumn. At that time the military took 946,362 from a total federal budget of 1,277,756 billion dinars. Even that, according to Federal Secretary of Defense Bulatović, only represented 43 per cent of the VJ's real needs.[25] The new budget was 122 times greater than that made the previous month. The total was 155.9 million billion dinars (approximately DM 770 million), of which 117.6 million billion was set aside for the VJ.[26] This represented around 8 per cent of the planned share of social production in the country for the year (somewhat higher than the figure of 4.94 per cent of social product envisaged and 3.58 actually spent in 1988, when the high-spending military was under pressure to cut costs).[27]

Against the background of accusations against Panić, criticisms of other senior officers as incompetent, and problems with the budget, the selection of Perišić seems to represent a political compromise, which focused on military reliability. The decision to pension off not only the 'moderates' but also the 'hardliners' indicated that there was no agreement on the appointment of a more political figure, such as Stevanović. The relative 'moderates' included General Panić, his assistant Simonović, and Colonel-General Dimitrije Baucal, who had been reporting progress on the transformation of the armed forces, with which he was closely involved.[28] Many hardliners, including members of Milošević's Serbian network in the army, also fell. As well as General Stevanović, their ranks included Generals Radovan Radinović, Andrija Biorčević and Tomislav Šipčić.

Perišić had a hard but essentially non-political profile. Like General Mladić, his reputation was that of a 'soldier's soldier', highly regarded by his fellow officers and men. This was borne out by the testimony of those who served under him in and out of combat:[29] his troops were said to be extremely loyal, and he was an inspiration to those who served with him.[30] It was said that his

---

[25] *Borba*, 27 August 1993.

[26] Ibid.

[27] *Narodna Armija*, 22 December 1988.

[28] Maj.-Gen. Dimitrije Baucal, 'Osnovni pravci transformacije i neki rezultati', *Novi Glasnik*, God. I, no.1, March–April 1993.

[29] See, for example, Ivan Marković's profile of artillery Major Radomir Ilić: 'Ja na Krf da idem neću', *Vojska*, 3 June 1993.

[30] *Borba*, 28–29 August 1993.

appointment also suited General Mladić and that they had similar outlooks as soldiers.[31] Both gained experience during the war and both demonstrated the tendency to be ruthless on the battlefield.

There was one further reason for General Perišić to be given the job of Chief of Staff. With the situation both in Croatia and in Bosnia and Hercegovina continuing to be uncertain and volatile – and with the prospect of American-led air strikes not quite completely out of the picture, circumstances might emerge in which Milošević would need an army. Soon after his selection as the new Chief of Staff, General Perišić gave an interview to the Belgrade daily *Politika* in which he emphasized the prospect of war spreading to Sandžak and Kosovo, in particular the latter where 'secessionist people' had failed 'from the war so far to draw any lessons.'[32] The thinly disguised threat inherent in this was reinforced by the fact that all the field generals who kept their places were those who would be in charge of operations in Sandžak and Kosovo. Although Milošević had developed the MUP as a Praetorian Guard, there remained several instances in which he would need a Chief of Staff with the best military credentials, given the heavy blows already inflicted on the top levels of the military.

As the VJ continued its transformation from the multi-ethnic, communist-led JNA to an essentially Serbian and professional army, it was important to have a strong and respected figure in charge. This soldier could also be useful if the need emerged to use this army in combat. Thus, Milošević had weakened the army politically, especially with the countervailing build-up of Interior Ministry troops, as well as functionally. But he did not leave it completely unusable, should the need arise – as it did in Kosovo (see Chapter 6).

It was the issue of Kosovo that, combined with the even more distressing case of Montenegro, led to the ouster of General Perišić at the end of 1998. On 24 November 1998 he was sacked as Chief of Staff. This was part of a purge that had begun the previous month, during which Milošević, a leader who always dealt with problems cautiously and separately, had purged fifteen members of the Security Service who were regarded as potentially disloyal. Most significantly, he sacked two of the most important figures from the

---

[31] Vasić, 'Konkurs.'
[32] 29 August 1993.

military-political campaigns of the 1990s: General Perišić and the head of the Security Service, Jovica Stanišić.

General Perišić's sacking capped an uneasy relationship over the years with President Milošević who always distrusted and disliked him and marked the General's differences with most of his colleagues. Before he was sacked, Perišić had made public his dissatisfaction over Milošević's policy towards Kosovo, telling the Serbian newspaper *Blic* that Yugoslavia was without friends and allies and in the impossible position of being 'at war against the world', adding that 'no country can afford to be in that position.'[33] He then lay the responsibility for this isolation on the political leadership of Milošević and his wife, Mira Marković, who led the Yugoslav United Left (JUL), one of the parties in the Serbian government coalition. This was supplemented by rumors that the general had been in contact with reformist and Western-backed Montenegrin President Milo Djukanović. Some of these rumors suggested that this contact concerned shared doubts about Milošević's policy towards Kosovo. Others suggested that the general might be helping to engineer a coup d'état in Belgrade to install Djukanović in Milošević's place.

Reports in Belgrade had long suggested that Perišić was opposed to the campaign in Kosovo, just as he had been publicly reluctant in late 1996 to allow the army to be used against opposition demonstrators. This was confirmed by his being bypassed in the Kosovo campaign during 1998. The commander of the 3rd Army at Niš, General Dušan Samardžić, was given formal command over the VJ operation, while effective command lay with the 52nd Corps in Priština, in association with MUP commanders who took orders directly from the political leadership in Belgrade. Perišić may have feared a further diminution of the VJ's position *vis-à-vis* the MUP, which was more actively involved in Kosovo, but this same motivation caused some others in the army to draw the opposite conclusion. Perišić judged the Kosovo campaign to be against the army's better interest, and saw it as further evidence of the President's cultivation of the MUP and a diminishing of the VJ's position given its effective subordination to the MUP. Some of his colleagues concluded that the army had to be more involved so as not to fall further behind the MUP in institutional standing. The

[33] *Blic*, 20 October 1998.

latter were therefore keen to commit the VJ to the fray, while General Perišić attempted to limit its involvement. This was further evidence confirming Milošević's distrust of Perišić and the generals.

An even more decisive reason for distrust and for the general's sacking concerned Montenegro. Plausible rumors regarding Perišić's links with the Montenegrin leadership linked his removal to the sacking three weeks previously of the Security Service chief, Jovica Stanišić. Although no one but Milošević's wife knew more about the workings of power in the regime, or its involvement in war, there had been persistent rumors over several months of strong differences of opinion between Stanišić and Serbia's Macbeth and his Lady. These involved the Security Service chief's refusal to become involved in plans to remove the Montenegrin leadership and tied in with Perišić's contact with Djukanović and signals that he would be reluctant to use the VJ against Montenegro. Although it appears unlikely that the two would have been conspiring against Milošević, either of them might have been exploring such possibilities.

Both Perišić and Stanišić issued statements suggesting that they might continue publicly to oppose Milošević, although Stanišić retired from view and tried to mend fences with Milošević. Perišić, in contrast, charged that his removal had been 'inappropriate and illegal' and that his alleged new post as adviser to Bulatović was fictitious. At the same time he confirmed the political thrust of the sackings by adding that the country's leaders were seeking to exclude those who thought for themselves and were of 'high integrity'.[34] Both sackings confirmed that Milošević and his wife felt deeply threatened as they sought to eliminate any potentially unreliable elements from their close circle. However, they were to feel more comfortable with Perišić's successor, General Dragoljub Ojdanic. A supporter of Mira Marković's JUL, and said to be close to her – Milošević's wife, his appointment put Milošević in a stronger position regarding the army than ever before. He finally had a Chief of Staff in Belgrade who was his and could be relied on to do that which the Serbian leader wanted – even if it meant leading the country and its armed forces like lemmings into an unwinnable conflict with NATO over Kosovo. In the meantime, Milošević's

---

[34] *RFE/RL Balkan Report*, vol. 2, no. 47, 2 Dec. 1998.

campaign to acquire the means to prosecute a war had led to the appearance, in name at least, of other armed forces.

The Serbian ghosts of the JNA: the VJ and the Krajina and Bosnian Serb forces

Implementing the decision to divide the JNA greatly reduced Belgrade's open participation in the war in Bosnia. This was part of an attempt to persuade the outside world that the new Federal Republic of Yugoslavia was not involved in events there or responsible for them. The reality was very different. In May 1992 the federal Yugoslav army divided itself into the Serbian Army in Bosnia (later the Army of the Serbian Republic – VRS) and the Army of Yugoslavia (VJ). While the VRS remained to carry on the Serbian war against Bosnia and Hercegovina, the VJ became the armed force of the Federal Republic of Yugoslavia, which consisted of Serbia and Montenegro. In fact these two were part of a troika. An element of division had already occurred at the beginning of 1992 when the Armed Forces of the Republic of Serbian Krajina (Oružanie Snage Republika Srpska Krajina – OS RSK) were the manifestation of Serbian military might in Croatia after the 2 January 1992 ceasefire there.

The key part of the troika remained the one formally attached to Belgrade's political leadership – the VJ, which comprised all three services: land, air and sea. The ground forces were organized into three armies, with headquarters at Belgrade, Podgorica and Niš, and within each there was a corps structure. For a time command positions in the VJ were unclear, until on 7 September the Supreme Defense Council nominated the following to become commanding officers of the three armies, the airforce and the navy: Colonel-General Jevrem Djokić, 1st Army; Major-General Božidar Babić, 2nd Army; Major-General Dušan Samadžić, 3rd Army; Major-General Miloje Pavlović, Air Force and Air Defence; Contra-Admiral Dojčilo Isaković, Navy. However, as noted above, none of these was even to remain in post for a year.[35] While change continued in Belgrade, the specter of the JNA loomed in Croatia and Bosnia.

This ostensible division and distance from Belgrade were belied by events. The VJ offered great assistance to the military forces that

[35] *Vojska*, 16 September 1992.

remained in Bosnia and continued support to those in Croatia. The Krajina Serbs in Croatia had inherited from the JNA a military capability and command and control structures, as did the Bosnian Serb military after its division. This was unlike its conduct when it withdrew from its installations in the remainder of Croatia and in Slovenia, Macedonia and other parts of the former Yugoslavia. In the latter cases it removed all its equipment and destroyed everything else, down to the light fixtures and electric outlets. However, the JNA left its installations intact in Bosnia and gave significant military equipment, including tanks and ammunition, to the VRS.

The OS RSK was the successor to forces led by Milan Martić, the Serb who had been dismissed as police chief in Knin, the central town in Krajina, in July 1990, as was seen in Chapter 2 (on the forces themselves, see below). Although Martić remained a prominent figure, this was in the political sphere, as RSK leader. The armed forces themselves retained vital linkages with Belgrade, including membership of what was effectively a common officer corps. Although officially the officers were part of the OS RSK, they remained on the Belgrade military payroll – numerous current Belgrade pay- and passbooks were found after Croatian operations in western Slavonia in 1995 – and in some cases were rotated with positions in the VJ. The most notable example of this involved General Mile Mrkšić. He had been involved in the JNA 1st Military District siege of Vukovar, before holding positions in the VJ, including Deputy Chief of Staff immediately before he was transferred to take command of the OS RSK in May 1995. Although many perceived this as a move to strengthen the OS RSK, which had just suffered defeats in Western Slavonia, in reality the appointment of General Mrkšić was to manage military withdrawal from Croatia.

In terms of armaments, much of the heavy weaponry of the JNA and the local Serbian forces in Croatia had been technically placed under joint control with UNPROFOR, the UN peacekeeping force deployed after the cease-fire. Some of it, though, remained in the hands of what was called a police force, but was effectively a paramilitary force for the Krajina area. It remained extremely well-armed, especially in lighter weapons. The OS RSK was around 25,000-strong, with some 40 tanks and 150–200 artillery pieces. Although most of these were in the joint UN-Serbian stores after the deployment of UNPROFOR, weapons remained outside these stores and the OS RSK was not averse to taking munitions from them. In addition, the OS RSK had eight Mi-8 and Gazelle helicopters and a number of MiG-21 aircraft.

The VRS was the name given to Serbian forces in Bosnia. This was essentially the former JNA 2nd Military District Command, covering Bosnia, now turned into a formally separate army, with the old command structures in Sarajevo withdrawn to the wartime command location of Han Pijesak and transformed into a General Staff. It also incorporated those elements of the old territorial defense system, which had been mobilized in Serb-dominated areas by the JNA throughout the second half of 1991 and especially in January 1992, shortly before General Mladić took over the Sarajevo command. The VRS inherited a 60–80,000 strong force, although some estimates were higher and in practice, operational strength may have been closer to 50,000. The VRS fought under the command of General Mladić, who had been the last Commanding Officer of the 2nd Military District of the JNA. The VRS also inherited from the JNA over 300 tanks, mostly of types T-54/55, but with perhaps 50 of the more modern T-72/M-84A; 2–300 armored cars; 5–600 artillery pieces, including 76mm, 105mm, 155mm guns and howitzers giving it an enormous advantage over its adversaries in Bosnia. In addition, the VRS inherited an air capability of 5,000 personnel and 35 aircraft (14 fixed wing: Galeb G-4, Jastreb-2, Orao; 21 helicopters: 12 Mi-8; 7 Gazelle), though the imposition of an 'air exclusion zone' by the UNSC restricted use of this air capability.

The VRS also benefited from continued support from the VJ, the troops coming across the River Drina from Serbia. The level of these reinforcements varied, but was estimated to run up to 20,000 personnel and over 100 pieces of armor. As reported by observers along the Drina River between Serbia and Bosnia, the JNA continued to supply the Bosnian Serb army with troop reinforcements and equipment long after the 19 May formal division of forces.

General Mladić was reported to maintain daily contact with the federal Yugoslav Defense Ministry in Belgrade (the Bosnian Serb Defense Ministry offices and the Yugoslav Defense Ministry were near neighbors). Bosnian Serb officers in the field were reported to claim that they could not hold their fire until they received orders from Belgrade, while some Bosnian prisoners were transported in JNA helicopters to military jails inside Serbia, where they were imprisoned for several weeks in 1992. The shadow of the JNA that linked the troika of Serbian forces gained a more substantive, though little noted, manifestation in the official 'agreement' in February 1994 to have 'joint' military intelligence activities.[36]

One example illustrates well how the VJ remained closely involved in the war in Bosnia after the 19 May division. In January 1993, Bosnian government troops near Bratunac succeeded in pushing Bosnian Serb forces across the Drina River into Serbia. As the Bosnians fired on the retreating Bosnian Serbs, VJ troops openly became involved in the conflict, firing on the Bosnian troops. A more constant and crucial instance of Belgrade's involvement with the VRS involved payment and rotation, as in Croatia. One prominent case concerned Colonel-General Djordje Djukić, Chief of Logistics in Mladić's army. In 1996, after the 1995 Bosnian peace agreement, Djukić was arrested by Bosnian forces,[37] and was found to be carrying a VJ passbook.[38] Although he was formally Chief of Logistics in the VRS, a putatively separate force, he was in practice co-ordinator of VJ supplies into Bosnia through the VRS Staff Headquarters at Han Pijesak.

These examples confirm what General Stevanović had made clear at the time of the transformation of the JNA. It was a move to 'secure the conditions for strengthening the hold on Serbian land in Bosnia and Hercegovina', which, it was hoped, would 'be the future Yugoslavia.'[39] This, backed by his message to his troops on his appointment in February ('I offer you only work and war'), showed the Belgrade military's commitment to their comrades in Croatia and Bosnia. While they might all have been forced into apparently different armies for the sake of Milošević's games of international deception, they retained common cause and common *esprit de corps*. As was seen in the discussion of General Perišić,

---

[36] *Danas*, 22 February 1994.

[37] This operation was tantamount to entrapment, or a kidnapping, and provoked strong protests and tension which obliged the Bosnian authorities to give an undertaking not to repeat such actions.

[38] See Ed Vulliamy, 'Serbian lies world chose to believe', *The Guardian* 29 February 1996.

[39] *Monitor*, 20 November 1992.

above, this did not mean that the army was reliable from Milošević's point of view. Not until the Kosovo campaign of 1999 would the senior levels of the regular armed forces be truly loyal to him, and even then this appeared to be loyalty from a small group at the top who owed their positions to him. Underlying military disaffection remained a potent risk for Milošević, even after he had secured full control of the Supreme Command. Because the army was a potential problem from the outset *vis-à-vis* reliability, Milošević had continually to bolster his efforts to marshal the regular military. He did so through the creation and strengthening of alternative sources of armed force that both complemented and competed with the regular army.

Paramilitary forces and a Praetorian Guard: politics and purpose

There were three main reasons why President Milošević nurtured militarized alternatives to the JNA and its successors. The first of these was practical. The organization of 'volunteer' paramilitary units served the purposes of strategic deception and ambiguity, whereby supposedly independent forces could be blamed for atrocities, the appearance of chaos could be maintained in the field and the army's professional reputation could, in contrast, be bolstered. In operational terms, paramilitary forces provided a cadre of infantry 'shock troops' that could carry out tasks the regular army could not be counted on to perform. These included close combat and street-to-street fighting. Crucially, their role also included commission of the catalogue of acts that added up to ethnic cleansing: murder, mutilation, torture, rape and terrorization.

The second reason why alternatives were used was more political. Irregular paramilitary groups could carry out action, that required support from the JNA or its successors, thus putting pressure on the regular army to follow the Serbian line. Similarly, paramilitary groups organized by the Milošević security service apparatus also competed with Serbian formations that might have been created independently. Thus, Milošević's paramilitaries could be used not only to drag the regular army into the Serbian corner, but also to crush any other groups who claimed the Serbian mantle. In either case, the Serbian leader's control was consolidated.

The third reason to build alternative sources of armed force concerned loyalty. In this context, the development of the Interior

Ministry Troops in Serbia proved crucial. Better trained, equipped, fed and paid than Belgrade's regular army, the MUP and its special units became Milošević's Praetorian Guard. The MUP was a vital competitor to the VJ in terms of old-style communist bureaucratic politics, and one of its roles was to keep the VJ in its place. Another, more chilling, role was to be the vanguard of ethnic cleansing in the Kosovo campaign. Unlike their paramilitary counterparts, however, the MUP was a highly organized, large force, capable of action on a far greater scale than that of the various paramilitary forces that had peppered the war in Croatia and in Bosnia. First and foremost, the MUP remained Milošević's key instrument of power and terror. Although no formal Serbian army was to emerge from the ashes of the JNA, one effectively appeared with the MUP. This was the core of the campaign to have armed forces wholly subordinated and loyal to Milošević.

At least six irregular groups participated on the Serbian side during the conflict in Croatia. Five of these were the paramilitary branches of political parties; the other was somewhere between a party-army and an element of the old territorial defense forces. In effect, this last group behaved like a party-army, with loyalty to specific politicians in Krajina, although there was no party to which it was formally connected. It also incorporated aspects of the old Yugoslav territorial defense system (formally designated for the Republic of Croatia, but used against it).

The emergence of these groups occurred after the first signs of unrest following around Knin in the Krajina in August 1990 after Milan Martić's removal from his post by the Croatian interior ministry. This was the beginning of what was essentially a form of party-army in Krajina. The force was assisted and organized by the Serbian Security Service (SDB), with Service Chief Jovica Stanišić overseeing the campaign, along with another senior figure, General Radmilo Bogdanović, and head of operations, Frenki Simatović, implementing it. It was originally led by Martić and popularly known as the 'Martićevci.' This force was reported to number up to 50,000, although its real strength was probably less. It later also became known alternatively as the 'Knindže' after Martić became *de facto* 'Minister of Defense' in Prime Minister Milan Babić's government of the self-proclaimed 'Serbian Autonomous Region of Krajina', which later declared itself to be a 'republic.'

With the backing of elements of the local Knin Corps of the

JNA, which allowed access to weapons and munitions during the year leading up to the Slovenian and Croatian declarations of independence, the Martićevci created an effective no-go area. This was an exclusion zone into which the Croat authorities could not gain entry without risking bloodshed. A product of the perceived threat to the Serb community from the Croatian government, this group pushed north in the early stages of the conflict in Croatia, led by the near egendary Captain Dragan (Dragan Vasiljković, an Australian Serb who became extremely popular among Serbs in general). He built a reputation as the man who transformed Krajina's volunteer units into a formidable armed force, despite a very limited military background among the ordinary ranks in the Australian Defense Force and rumors of a criminal history.[40] However, having made moderate territorial gains, the Krajina leadership and its forces, in conjunction with the JNA, seemed intent on consolidating control of their region in order to wait for eventual recognition of a *fait accompli* – although this territory was less than that initially envisaged (see Chapter 6).

Four political parties organized five irregular groups involved in the war on the Serbian side. These were the Serbian Guard (*Srpska Garda* – SG), the Serbian Volunteer Guard (*Srpska Dobrovoljačka Garda* – SDG), the Serbian Chetnik Movement (*Srpski Četnički Pokret* – SČP), and, lastly, Dušan Silni and the Beli Orli – both military units of the same party (see below). Each of these had its own political identity and each tended to fight in certain areas. All were commonly called 'Chetniks' by the Croats and by much of the western press, although only one of them formally bore this title, while they were referred to as 'territorials' or 'volunteers' in the Serbian media. Although each was attached to a particular political organization, and these forces set the pace for the JNA in Croatia and collaborated with it in both Croatia and Bosnia, all but one owed their prominence to support from the SDB. These units appeared to be separate actors in the chaos of conflict, yet they were eventually officially subordinated to JNA command, whether they accepted it or not.

The SG was formed by a consortium of opposition nationalist parties at the beginning of June 1991, but almost immediately Vuk Drašković's Serbian Renewal Party (*Srpski Pokret Obnove* – SPO),

---

[40] See, for example, the articles in *Intervju*, 16 August 1991 and *Duga*, 30 August 1991.

which had initiated the guard, became its only patron. Although the initiative came from Drašković, two other SPO members Djordje Božović-Giška and Branislav Matić-Beli (both alleged criminals) established the force. Both, however, were killed. The former, who was paymaster for the guard, was machine-gunned in the street, gangster-style, by the occupants of two cars; the latter was killed on the battlefield near Gospić in Croatia (initial reports that he had died heroically were later undermined).[41] After Božović-Giška's death, command passed to Branislav Lainović-Duga, owner of a Novi Sad night club that was bombed at the end of October 1991. Lainović alleged that the bombing was connected to a dispute between Lainović and his 'staff', on one side, and the SPO's Initiative Committee for the Guard's formation, led by Zoran Djordjević and Zvonko Osmajlić, on the other.

Although one of the principal reasons for forming the guard was to provide opposition leaders, especially Drašković, with personal protection, it soon became involved in the war, especially in the Gospić region. The movement was said to number 80,000 members, in large part from Vojvodina, although some 1,500 at most were involved in the paramilitary force. Those who did see action came increasingly under JNA command, thus precipitating the civil-military clash over control of the SG between the Initiative Committee and the Guard's 'Staff'. The latter argued for practical co-operation with the army, while the Committee ardently opposed collaboration with the communist-dominated JNA. This was essentially a dispute about the SG's identity as an anti-communist party-army. Lainović-Duga argued that the SG did not belong to the SPO, which he alleged had not supported it – although over eighty per cent of those at the front were SPO members – and that the JNA was 'changing its profile' to become 'pro-Serb'.[42] The line taken by Lainović-Duga suggests that he was in league with Stanišić's SDB, a key political aim of which was to prevent independent action by opposition elements in Serbia. This provided one of the reasons for organizing and supporting other paramilitary groups: to draw support from the SG.

With involvement from the SDB, two other opposition parties formed their own military wings: the Serbian Radical Party (*Srpska Radikalna Stranka* – SRS) created the SČP – the 'Chetniks' and

---

[41] Stojan Cerović, 'Obilići garavoga lica', *Vreme*, 23 September 1992.

[42] Gradiša Katić, 'Čije je carstvo gardijsko?', *Borba*, 4 February 1992.

the Serbian People's Renewal (*Srpska Narodna Obnova* – SNO) formed two units, 'Dušan Silni' and 'Beli Orli', both of which were active in the spring of 1991. The SNO sent Dušan Silni as an 'unarmed mobile unit' into Slavonia in April,[43] and the SČP was the first Serbian unit into action when it claimed responsibility for the deaths of twelve Croatian government 'Specials' at Borovo Selo over a month before fighting broke out in earnest in late June.

The Chetniks were organized by Vojislav Šešelj, leader of the SRS, who in previous incarnations had been a Titoist party member, reserve officer and critic of the regime who was expelled from the Bosnian party in the early 1980s. By the mid-1980s he, like his parallel on the Croatian side, Paraga, had been imprisoned for 'nationalist' and 'anti-Muslim' crimes by the regime and was regarded, ironically, as a dissident in the West. Šešelj advocated the most extreme form of 'Great Serbia', one which would incorporate all the territories of the old Yugoslavia except those northwest of the Karlobag-Karlovac-Virovitica line. Despite Šešelj's ambition, the SČP remained a small, albeit vicious, outfit of around 185 members.[44] It was involved, *inter alia*, in the central Croatian region of Banija, where some of the ugliest fighting and most confirmed atrocities occurred, as well as in up to thirty-four places in Bosnia where alleged crimes against humanity were committed.

Dušan Silni and Beli Orli, under the command of Dragoslav Bokan, were created by the SNO, run by Mirko Jović. The SNO was labeled a 'pure Nazi organization' by Miloš Vasić, one of the best-informed independent journalists in Serbia, and its leader was 'in the pocket' of the Vojvodina interior ministry forces.[45] Dušan Silni was probably also involved in May 1991 at Borovo Selo in Croatia, but during the course of the war in Croatia and in Bosnia both it and Beli Orli, the more important of the two units, operated in a variety of zones. Šešelj and Jović were friends and appear to have shared a friendship with another significant figure, retired General Dušan Pekić, who was also important as the organizer of the SDG, effectively the paramilitary wing of the 'General's party', the League of Communists-Movement for Yugoslavia (Savez *Komunist-Pokret za Jugoslaviju* – SK-PJ, led by Milošević's wife,

[43] *Delo*, 8 April 1991.

[44] Svetlana Vasović, 'Vse Srbske Vojske', *Mladina*, 27 August 1991.

[45] Cited by Vladimir Jovanović, 'Play it Again Slobo', *Monitor*, 29 November 1991.

Mirjana 'Mira' Marković). The SDG had emerged from the pro-Serbian group within the party.[46] Indeed the SDG as good as absorbed large parts of the other parties, paramilitary groups, particularly the Chetniks, thanks to the proximity of Šešelj and General Pekić. Šešelj's close links with senior figures such as General Pekić probably owed something to correspondence between the borders he wished to establish in his scheme and those in the JNA's plans.

The SDG was formed by pro-Serb SK-PJ figures as a rival to other Serbian irregular groups, the SG in particular. The SDG, better known as the 'Tigers', was the leading force in eastern Slavonia in Croatia and was active in at least 28 points in Bosnia. Its leader was Željko Ražnjatović, popularly known as 'Arkan', who among other things, was an Interpol suspect in the murder of émigré Croatians on behalf of the Yugoslav secret services, a convicted and escaped armed robber in several West European countries, as well as an agent of the Serbian interior ministry's Security Service. Estimated in some reports to have up to 40,000 members, far fewer than this – 1,500–5,000 – were in fact active. This group was formed essentially as competition for the SG politically, as well as to be a murderously effective instrument for close combat and ethnic cleansing, and special units of the Tigers led the assault on Vukovar in Croatia in November 1991.[47] Its headquarters were established at Erdut, once the Croatian MUP had been evicted. Operating in the 'Serbian Autonomous Region of Slavonija, Baranja and Western Srem', it effectively became the armed force of any putative political authority attached to that entity. This meant that, in principle, these forces should be accountable to Goran Hadžić, the region's putative prime minister and another recruit of Jovica Stanišić's SDB.[48] The Tigers criticized the federal army for its conduct of the war in Croatia, but operated jointly with it, co-coordinating operations in eastern Slavonia and throughout Bosnia.

Arkan had some 100 instructors who were reported to be inducting about 1,000 volunteers per month in October 1991. In many cases, those involved had criminal backgrounds, either formerly, or current convicts recruited directly from prison on the promise of pillage, rape and liberty in exchange for risk and cold-blooded killing. Those responsible for the SDG training center

[46] Branislav Matić, 'Strogo Pov Patriote: Rado Ide Srbin u Gardiste (Sve Srpske Vojske)', *Duga*, 30 August–13 September 1991.

[47] *Borba*, 18 October 1991.

[48] Judah, *The Serbs*, p. 171.

hoped that the Serbian government would found similar centers throughout Serbia. They also asserted that all Tigers' activity would have to be legalized within one framework and placed under one flag – that of Serbia. Given the origins of the SDG among hard-line elements of the JNA, the SK-PJ and the SDB, this was disingenuous to say the best. In fact, it coincided with the avowed position of Drašković and the SG. Thus the real purpose of these statements and one of the roles of Arkan's Tigers was to draw support away from paramilitary groups outside the Serbian authorities' control.[49]

There was much discussion of forming a Serbian army during 1991. General Tomislav Simović was appointed to begin training a Serbian army, *Politika* – widely viewed as the Belgrade mouthpiece for Milošević – having declared that a Serbian army would be formed 'within three months'.[50] No Serbian army was formed. Instead, as noted above, the JNA became more overtly Serbia's army. A few weeks later, Simović was replaced by General Marko Negovanović, who had been head of the military counter-intelligence service, KOS, during the clashes in Slovenia in June, before becoming an Assistant Minister of Defense and, effectively, the JNA's press officer. Reportedly close to both General Adžić and, more importantly perhaps, President Milošević, his appointment as defense minister put an end to the idea of a Serbian army. Ultimately, all the paramilitaries had at a minimum consulted with the JNA and the federal defense ministry and most, by November 1991, had co-coordinated operations with the army and accepted its command.[51]

The actions of the paramilitary forces in Croatia amplified the 'Serbianizing' of the JNA and paramilitary leaders approved the continuation of a 'Yugoslav' army: Lainović assented in February 1992; Šešelj had done so earlier. The latter had even gone so far as to consent to the JNA's continuing use of the communist

[49] In October, Arkan insisted that what he called the 'SG' was not a 'party-army', and nor was it connected to Šešelj or Drašković. Rather, the 'SG' was the 'foundation of a true Serbian army.' Three days after he had presented his group as 'the Serbian Guard' in *Borba*, Božović-Giška's mother, Milena, protested that the two guards were radically different, that the real SG did not want to be under the control of the SK-PJ and that this SG had only three units in the field, none of which was in eastern Slavonia with Arkan. As she opined, the SDG was 'stealing our ideas and our fighters.' *Borba*, 21 October 1991.

[50] *Politika*, 7 November 1991.

[51] Milan Bežejić, 'Šajkače, nalevo ravnas', *Borba*, 13 November 1991.

five-pointed red star. Šešelj regarded it as a Serbian symbol, as well, because, in eastern Slavonia, unlike fifty years before, Chetniks and 'Partisans' (that is, the army) fought together. However, this unity, while Serbianizing the JNA and leading it towards its mutation into three effectively Serbian armies, still did not give Slobodan Milošević an indubitably loyal force. This had to be created in Serbia.

To compensate for the latent unreliability of the otherwise necessary Yugoslav military, Milošević ensured that he would have complete control over one force, the MUP in Serbia. The ultimate purpose of developing the MUP into the best-trained armed force in the FRY was to protect Milošević's regime. It also offered the political benefit of keeping the regular army in check and, as with the paramilitaries on the western front, the reality of a force that would be in the forefront of repression and, ultimately, ethnic cleansing on the southern front. The MUP, directly linked to the Security Service through the Interior Ministry, constituted Milošević's Praetorian Guard and his 'shock troops.'

Throughout the 1990s, Milošević built up the MUP as a two-pronged alternative instrument of coercive power to the regular army. The first prong involved what was effectively a light infantry force embraced by the police as special units. These were supplemented with small specialist 'anti-terrorist' units attached to the force. The second, far smaller, prong was in many ways the more important. It ran through the SDB, also under the interior ministry, and was linked to the organization of the paramilitary web described above.

The largest part of the MUP comprised Police Special Units (*Posebne Jedinice Policije* – PJP). Although the MUP was thought to number tens of thousands, its real strength lay in its reserve forces. The standing force strength was around 5,000 personnel. These troops were organized into six detachments, based at Belgrade, Novi Sad, Kragujevac, Užice, Niš and Priština, each normally with a battalion level strength of around 700. Each of these special units co-coordinated with yet larger local MUP forces, organized through public security centers. The combat units were highly trained with specifically recruited personnel and equipped with armored personnel carriers, mortars and heavy machine guns. Each of these detachments had a Specialist Anti-terrorist Unit (*Specijalna Anti-teroristička Jedinica* – SAJ). This was a separate part of the MUP structure comprising around 400 personnel. The SAJ was attached to each of the MUP detachments at around the strength of three or four platoons – that is, 60 to 80 personnel. These were very specially selected forces, generally between19 and 24 years old, recruited for their absolute loyalty, their fitness and their psychological profiles. While on one level this force could be equated with counter-terrorist units elsewhere in the world, in the Serbian context, they could also play a role in agitation. This was the case in 1997 when opposition rallies were disrupted by plainclothes members 'of the anti-terrorist squad. The SAJ could also be likened to a special forces unit attached to light infantry battalions for specialist tasks such as intelligence gathering and liaison, as well as operations requiring specific skills and small numbers.

These roles were also undertaken by the Security Service special operations unit (*Jedinica za Specijalne Operacije*), in addition to which the JSO was also involved in other activities including *murder*, both of individuals and groups. Like the SAJ, JSO recruitment was targeted to find individuals who had the exceptional physical and mental capabilities for the job. As with the SAJ, these recruits were subject to thorough psychometric testing in order to ensure they could do whatever it might take – including close quarter killing. Unlike the SAJ, however, JSO members came almost exclusively from army special forces backgrounds, where they had already demonstrated their aptitude for these tasks.

The JSO had a total strength of 500 individuals. Organized under the operational arm of the SDB, these units were in some sense siblings of the paramilitary forces used in the field in Croatia and in Bosnia. Like the latter, the JSO was organized by the Head of Operations in the SDB, Frenki Simatović. Highly secretive, this specialist force wore distinctive red berets. They were organized into squads of around twenty and used modern armored vehicles. If the MUP as a whole provided Milošević with a Praetorian Guard, the JSO was probably the Praetorian Guard's ultimate expression. Trained to the highest standards, highly motivated and capable of acting as instant execution squads, they were, according to one British officer, 'very dangerous'.[52] When the time came, it would

---

[52] Maj. Julian Moir, Ministry of Defence briefing, 1 April 1999. Moir's briefing was included in 'Briefing by The Foreign Secretary, Mr Robin Cook, and the Deputy Chief of the Defence Staff, Air Marshal Sir John Day' at http://www.mod.uk/news/kosovo/brief 010499.htm at 5 April 1999.

be the MUP that provided the assault troops for the Kosovo campaign and ethnic cleansing, but it was the JSO that supplied the lead 'shock troops' and murder squads. It was these same troops that could be the ultimate ring of protection for Milošević.

While the MUP as a whole, let alone the specialist units, could not outnumber or outgun the regular army, they were always ready to use their cohesion and troop quality as a force multiplier in any conflict with it. The army would inevitably be less well prepared and likely to be divided, and this, together with the allocation of resources and preferences to the MUP over the VJ in the 1990s, ensured that the army would be the institutional loser and thus kept at bay. However, with the Kosovo campaign in 1999, Milošević, by this time President of the FRY, finally gained formal control of all the armed forces, as he formally became commander in chief of all forces when the MUP was subordinated to the VJ on 24 March 1999. This was the point at which the force which Milošević had developed as his own in Serbia, the MUP, was placed under the authority of the VJ, of which he had always been distrustful. By now, the man who had always hated the generals could not but love them. He had a Chief of Staff, General Ojdanić, who was his to control, as well as others in the most senior positions whom he could afford to trust – including, it was reported (but also denied) one of his wife's relatives, General Nebojša Pavković, as commander of the 3rd Army fighting in Kosovo. Milošević had ensured that both the MUP and the VJ would do his bidding in battle. However, even with his own men in command of the VJ for the first time, the MUP continued to provide Milošević with the only force that would be wholly and truly his. But this was still not enough of a guarantee if circumstances turned against him – along with the people and the bulk of the army. Most significantly, Milošević had for the first time put himself in a position of indisputable formal and legal responsibility for the commission of crimes against humanity.

It took Slobodan Milošević nine years finally to have all the armed forces properly and officially under his control. The war's impact on the ethnic composition of the Yugoslav military had effectively put most of the JNA's capability at his disposal. To achieve this degree of control, he had to resort, for political and practical reasons, to other fighting groups of a more purely Serbian orientation, as well as of a more vicious character. These were complements to and competitors for the regular army. Alongside this, it had been necessary to enlist a cadre of those within the old JNA who could secure the means to Milošević's ends. When international circumstances required the JNA to be divided into three, the ghost of the old army remained, not only through personal and informal connections, but also through continuing links of personnel, command and control. Notwithstanding significant Serbianization, Milošević could not trust the regular army implicitly to do his bidding, as was seen with the sacking of General Perišić, as late as the end of 1998. Even then, with true loyalists running the army for the first time, it was still the MUP that offered Milošević undiluted loyalty and the means both of action and of protection, even if the latter could not be guaranteed in all circumstances.

4

THE MEANS: CAPABILITY AND CALCULATION – THE SUPERIORITY SYNDROME AND THE GULF CONFLICT

The creation of force requires more than the subordination of troops to political purpose. It also requires those soldiers to be armed and to be able to use their armaments. This involves not only acquisition of weapons, but also assessment of the balance of power between an armed force and its likely adversaries. Calculations have to be made regarding the conditions under which armed force will be employed. It is these conditions and calculations that form the subject of the present chapter. Within the Yugoslav context, as Serbian political leaders developed a manpower capability to prosecute war, they also acquired overwhelming superiority over their enemies in terms of armaments. Even where there were relative problems with manpower, this superabundance of weaponry would allow Belgrade's armed forces to dominate the battlefield. The only way in which Serbian firepower could be countered was if substantial superior force were to be introduced from outside the Yugoslav lands.

With this consideration in mind, military leaders in Belgrade paid close attention to the demonstration of overwhelming Western destructive capability against Iraq in the Gulf War of 1990–1, as will be seen below. Two crucial conclusions emerged from this analysis for the conduct of the Yugoslav war. The first was that European capabilities were not sufficient to mount an intervention without the United States and that this made such an intervention unlikely in the Yugoslav context, given prevailing conditions. A corollary of this was that so long as certain thresholds were not crossed, it was unlikely that a major Western use of armed force would emerge. The second conclusion was that Iraq's biggest error had been to confront sophisticated and massive Western force more or less on its own terms. Iraqi defense had been static. The key to survival lay in dispersal of forces, decoys and mobility if a Western attack were to occur. The starting point for a review of Belgrade's military calculation at the outset of the war in 1991 is an understanding of the conditions for its strategic dominance in armaments and associated issues.

Arms and Yugoslavia: mountains of weapons

The imbalance of armaments between Serbian forces and their enemies was one of the most striking aspects of the Yugoslav war. It was also one of the most emotive in international intellectual and political discourse. Arguments over this issue were focused on the UN arms embargo which was imposed early in the conflict, the effect of which was to consolidate Serbian superiority. Serbian forces began the war with the vast arsenal of Tito's Yugoslavia at its disposal, including weapons and munitions stored under the SFRY's many mountains.

As war broke out while the SFRY disintegrated, the overwhelming bulk of that arsenal fell into Serbian hands. The JNA began the war with 1,850 tanks, of which 300 were M-84 Yugoslav updates of the Soviet T-72; a further 850 were T-55s and T-54s. In the first six months of fighting there was some attrition of this capability. It was known to have lost 65 T-55s in good working order at Varaž-din, while another 100 (for the most part M-84s) fell into Slovene hands and, by the army's own admission, a further 170 tanks were captured in Croatia. Battlefield losses were not admitted, but these could not have exceeded another 100. In all, by the time the JNA had split into the VJ, VRS and OS RSK, it had lost much of its equipment and had divided it between three armies. In addition, the air force while relatively inactive lost 40 combat planes and 30 helicopters.

Nevertheless Serbian forces retained overwhelming superiority in quantity and quality of weapons. Even when, by 1993, the Army of Bosnia and Hercegovina (*Armija Bosne i Hercegovine* – ABiH) had built up its level of equipment, this remained the case. The ABiH had around 40 T-34 and T-54/55 tanks and Armored Personnel Carriers, at this point, as well as larger numbers of artillery pieces of 76mm, 105mm and perhaps even 155mm caliber (these were mostly the fruit of one successful operation north of Tuzla in which a single 100 vehicle column was captured, which also provided light armament and ammunition for up to 15,000 troops). The Bosnian Army did not lack light weaponry, although ammunition supplies presented problems. There was some weaponry manufactured in government-controlled territory, notably in Novi Travnik where limited production continued of artillery, multiple rocket launchers and munitions. The Bosnian Army also had 60mm, 82mm and 120mm mortars, as well as good supplies of shoulder launched anti-armor rocket systems. There were also 50 Bosnian air force personnel and one Jastreb-2 aircraft (not in use) and 4 Mi-8 helicopters. Despite all of this, there was an enormous imbalance in heavy weapons. When it came to the weapons that secured battlefield dominance – tanks, guns and howitzers – the JNA and its successor, the VRS, usually had a ten-to-one, or greater, advantage.

By the 1995 Dayton Peace Accords for Bosnia, the position remained such that a ratio of 5–2–2 was established between the VJ and its formal counterparts in Croatia and Bosnia. Thus it was assumed the VJ would be one quarter larger than the forces of the other two countries combined. However, there was more to this than the apparent picture this arms control agreement suggests. In fact, one third of the Bosnian total was allocated to the VRS, thereby increasing the formal Serbian entitlement, given the realities on the ground. Moreover, while the arms control ceilings represented a relative parity across the region, the figures proposed as default levels at Dayton envisaged a level to which both the FRY and the Bosnian Serbs would have to disarm in order to meet, but levels often well in excess of existing arsenals in Croatia and the rest of Bosnia.

At the end of the war in Bosnia, Serb forces remained the most substantially armed and equipped of the former Yugoslav countries. In the absence of international forces, this left them militarily dominant. Thus, the degree to which Serbian political leaders were able to acquire and increase control over the enormous arsenal of the JNA was a key strategic factor in prosecuting their campaign. This advantage was compounded by the difficulties their opponents faced in obtaining weaponry, particularly in the more important heavier categories. The basic imbalance established at the outset of the war was effectively cemented by well-meaning but often questionable international efforts to prevent the import of weapons into the region.

One week after Slovenia and Croatia declared their independence from the Socialist Federative Republic of Yugoslavia (SFRY) at the end of June 1991, the United Kingdom announced an embargo on the sale of arms to any part of the SFRY. This was soon followed by a similar ban imposed by the European Community, in the framework of European Political Co-operation and the soon-to-be Common Foreign and Security Policy, which was being drafted at that time. In September the United Nations Security Council passed Resolution 713 banning all transfers of arms to the SFRY or any of its territories. The embargo is a particular mechanism designed to control arms transfers. While trade may be one aspect of the study of arms transfers, it is not the principal focus of an embargo, the aim of which is to cut the flow of weapons into certain hands. For this reason, trade is not considered in the following analysis, which is limited simply to questions of transfers – that is, the supply of military capability by one party, or parties, to another.

As the conflict in Yugoslavia deepened and intensified, questions arose about the role of an embargo in a war of this kind. Some of these were entirely technical, concerning how the proscription of arms transfers was circumvented. Others were of a more philosophical and even moral nature. In order to understand these issues one has to delve into the former Yugoslav federation as it approached break-up, in particular the peculiarities of its defense system.

The doctrine of General People's Defense (GPD) in Yugoslavia developed a two-tier system of armed forces. One part was the Yugoslav People's Army (JNA), a highly trained standing army based on conscription and run by the federal defense ministry. The other was a territorial defense force, which would mobilize up to 85 per cent of the population into a resistance force, responsibility for which lay with the republics. Thus Yugoslavia had one technically advanced federal armed force and a series of less well-equipped republican-based armed forces. These became the basis for the formation of republican proto-armies as Slovenia and Croatia sought full statehood.

The JNA, aware of the role the territorial forces might play, impounded virtually all of the weaponry designated for the Croatian force and about 40 per cent of that for use by Slovenia following the first democratic elections there in spring 1990. It later carried out a similar program in Bosnia in 1991, following elections there at the end of the previous year. The weaponry involved included artillery, anti-air and anti-tank rocket systems (and rockets). Croatia, for example, had 200 of each type of rocket system and 9–10,000 rockets for each.[1] Both countries immediately sought to replenish their denuded stocks by making purchases outside Yugoslavia.

The only transaction officially reported was the sale by Hungary of 10–20,000 Kalashnikov automatic rifles to Croatia – and this deal only came into the open after a series of reports forced the Hungarian government to admit the sales.[2] Otherwise, equipment was obtained in or from at least ten countries, including Austria, Italy, Czechoslovakia, Poland, Switzerland, Singapore, the two Koreas and Germany;[3] this also included some items of Yugoslav provenance re-channeled from Lebanese militias that no longer required them. Secret arms markets were held in Austrian forests about 50 km. from the Slovene border and became prime points of purchase.[4]

Secrecy was necessary in light of the difficulties all involved faced in making deals which could not include Yugoslavia's federal authorities. Arms trade of any kind should have been subject to two federal laws – one on import-export transactions and the other on the production and transfer of arms and military equipment. However, the constitutional status of the republican secretariats for defense and internal affairs gave the transactions attributes of legality.[5] Arms sales were not made, therefore, to rebel insurgents; they

[1] Slaven Letica and Mario Nobilo, *Rat Protiv Hrvatske*, Globus, Zagreb, 1991, p. 72.

[2] Judith Pataki, 'Relations with Yugoslavia Troubled by Weapons Sale', Radio Free Europe, *Report on Eastern Europe*, 22 February 1991.

[3] *Borba* (A pan-Yugoslav daily, published in Belgrade and Zagreb by the Federal government, using both Serbian and Croatian variants of Serbo-Croat), 15 January 1991, gave a detailed account of a delivery by a Czechoslovak company of 5,000 pistols to Zagreb.

[4] *Mladina* (a Slovene weekly published in Ljubljana, instrumental in undermining the communist system and critical of the Slovene government; it was also a regular source of information on armed forces issues), 4 December 1991.

[5] Stanoje Jovanović, 'Jasno definisan postupak opremanja oružanih snaga', *Odbrana i Zaštita* (A monthly publication published by the Federal Secretariat for

were made to appropriate constitutional entities. Although many of the purchases ought to have been dealt with through the federal defense ministry, some republican defense acquisitions, such as 4,000 horses (for pack work in mountains) from Poland, would not necessarily be subject to Defense Ministry vetting. Other items were disguised or imported in pieces, avoiding the gaze of the defense ministry and not seeming to be objects of concern to those responsible for import-export trade. All this, including acts of direct smuggling, was activity conducted in a haze of semi-legality: institutions entitled to buy arms did so from organizations entitled to sell them. The Slovenes either disguised them from Yugoslav federal agencies, such as the army, which, having already removed weapons designated for the territorial forces, could not be thought likely to sanction such arrangements; or they by-passed the federation. Secrecy was also a product of the awkward dislocation between the Yugoslav reality of states within a state and international principles proscribing arms transfers that would affect territorial order. For international purposes, Yugoslavia remained one state; internally, it had really become several. To deal with de facto governments, those trading arms had to by-pass *de jure* authorities.

States followed a deliberate strategy of buying only that which would be most cost effective and useful, particularly Soviet, American and German anti-tank and anti-air weapons, including SAR-80s, SAM-7s and German Armbrust anti-tank rockets. In both republics, liberal laws on hunting weaponry at both federal and republican levels also played a role. Licenses were plentiful for those wanting to take advantage of Austria's liberal gun laws, where individuals could walk into a shop with a license from one of the Yugoslav republics and buy a wide variety of armaments. The biggest snag proved to be for those who were clumsy enough to try and bring fifty items at once without an export license, whereupon the Austrian authorities seized the weapons at customs. Otherwise, larger items were smuggled in bit by bit.[6]

These imports added to the enormous number of weapons already in Yugoslavia. In addition to the weaponry under official federal

---

National Defense in Belgrade, using the Serbian variant of Serbo-Croat, but Latin script), vol. XXVII, no. 1, January 1991, p. 40.

[6] *Mladina*, 22 January 1991.

or republican control, there was an astonishing number of personal firearms. In 1990, there were more licensed personal and private firearms in Yugoslavia per household than either motor vehicles or washing machines.[7]

The arms embargo: philosophical and technical aspects

Once open hostilities had broken out in Slovenia and Croatia, for the respective authorities in those republics, acquiring arms became a priority. Both were able to use the armaments already at their disposal to capture weaponry from their enemies, but all discussion of Slovenia and Croatia in this context pales at the side of Bosnia and Hercegovina. Whereas the former republics had some military capability, access to the Adriatic Sea and borders with sympathetic countries, Bosnia's position was different. Although some arms remained in the non-Serbian communities in Bosnia, these were limited mostly to personal firearms (there were some armed Croat groups in western Hercegovina). The Muslim community, especially, was relatively unarmed – in large part the result of a campaign, backed by the authorities in the republic and implemented jointly by the Yugoslav army and the republican interior ministry forces, to disarm and disband groups wherever the potential to create paramilitary formations existed.

In Bosnia, there was not only a stark imbalance in access to the armaments produced by the defense industry of the old state, but also a vital need for protection as the Serbian forces began campaigns of 'ethnic cleansing' throughout northern and eastern Bosnia. The aim of this policy was to create swathes of territory which were ethnically homogeneous and, therefore, free from elements potentially hostile to the Serb population. Ethnic cleansing involved massacre, rape, mutilation and torture, and some have argued that it constitutes an act of genocide. In these circumstances, the ban on arms transfers became critical: for the Muslims in Bosnia, just as it would be for any other ethnic community fighting to preserve the integrity of the state, access to arms was to be a matter of life and death.

In Bosnia there existed a block on arms transfers to a war zone in which there was an overwhelming weapons imbalance, and those with the preponderance of materiel were accused of attempting genocide. This left those without weapons unable to defend

[7] *Mladina*, 4 December 1991.

themselves. The question this raised was a moral one. Whether or not the Muslim population in Bosnia and Hercegovina had the humanitarian right, either to be protected by those with the wherewithal to do so, or to try to defend themselves. While various European countries, under the auspices of the UN had tried to limit the extent of the horror in Bosnia through humanitarian relief operations, the Bosnian Presidency and government persistently called for the arms embargo to be lifted in its favor, arguing that the state and its threatened people should have the right to defend themselves.

In formal terms, the Bosnian arguments and those of their supporters were wrong. The arms embargo, brought about by a UN Security Council Resolution to deal with a threat to international peace and security, was mandatory on all states. Enforcement measures authorized by the UN Security Council under powers given in Chapter VII of the UN Charter supersede any other provision and become binding international law. So, in this case, the right to self-defense claimed by the Bosnian government under Article 51 of the UN Charter was subject to the condition 'until' the UN Security Council had taken measures necessary for the restoration of the peace. However, the certainty of this arrangement under international law did not prevent the Bosnian authorities and their international sympathizers from claiming that the embargo was illegal. These charges also raised the philosophical and practical dimensions of the case: was it right effectively to maintain the obvious imbalance of armaments between the parties, and was it practical to do so?

All of this raises questions about whether attempts to control arms supplies should take into account local specifics *before* they are made reality. In the Yugoslav case, the effect of the embargo was minimal on the one side which had a preponderance of weapons and quite extensive on those without. As a matter of principle, it seems questionable to impose heavy restrictions, no matter how well intentioned, on all parties in a situation where the sides are grossly unequal. There is little point in placing a blanket proscription on those who already have arms in abundance, and it is hard to defend decisions, effectively, to subject those without the means of self-defense to a similar regime, even though the imposition of an embargo may limit the intensity of the conflict.

There is a further sense in which the imposition of complete controls is questionable. This is the reality that in Bosnia, especially in carrying out acts of ethnic cleansing, sophisticated weapons systems were not required. The war in Bosnia, although significantly shaped by the possession of certain categories of equipment on one side, was in no way dependent on modern weapons. Technological advantage may be important in some senses – such as the Serbian maintenance of sieges with heavy artillery – but it was generally irrelevant as ethnic cleansing resulted often from the use of personal weapons, often not even firearms.

Finally, the usefulness of attempts to prevent the supply of arms is open to question. It was evident that, in spite of controls in source countries and of considerable efforts by UN forces tasked with preventing the provision of arms to those subject to sanctions, arms still got through. There are two points worthy of note here. The first concerns the relative ease with which the parties in Bosnia and those in neighboring countries acquired arms. The second involves the types of equipment transferred – a critical factor in Bosnia. The types of armament that would tip the strategic balance in Bosnia (heavy artillery and armor) were just the sort that it was hardest to smuggle and transfer illegally. It was these weapons which the Serbian side possessed in abundance from the outset and which the Bosnian Army, the Kosovan armed forces and, to a lesser extent the others, lacked. The Bosnian government forces were, on the other hand, able to acquire all kinds of portable weaponry, including 5,000 MILAN shoulder launched anti-armor systems, with munitions, which had a telling impact on the fortunes of the Bosnian Army in the spring of 1993, along with other deliveries of portable systems.

The weapons that would have most affected the course of the war were those which were subject to the UN embargo. (Various practical difficulties would have, however, remained had there been no embargo, for example, delivery through hostile neighboring countries.) Allied to this, those weapons with which the embargo could be breached played the greatest part in violence against civilians and in actions to frustrate UNPROFOR and other international actors. These included hand grenades, mortars, various mines, automatic pistols, automatic rifles and even crossbows.[8] The size and nature of heavy categories of arms, especially in the case of an

[8] On the devastating effects of British-made crossbows in Croatia, Bosnia and Kosovo, see *Sunday Times*, 8 August 1999.

enforced embargo, make the imposition of sanctions on this type of weapon effective, but not on portable weapons, which proved relatively easy to transfer despite the prohibition.

Analysis of the technical aspects of attempts to control the illicit transfer of weaponry belongs in the sphere of classified information. Without access to such information, one can only sketch in some of the technical aspects of illicit arms transfers on the basis of the few cases which were openly reported. All parties in the Yugoslav war received arms through transfers in defiance of sanctions, which only serves to highlight the embargo's shortcomings. As early as September 1991, three British businessmen were arrested in connection with an aircraft hangar full of arms destined for Croatia although the case was not reported further. There can be little doubt that businessmen in Bedford, Windsor and many other places in Britain and Europe were engaged in similar activities. Serbian intelligence and Mafia networks were believed to have a series of arms caches throughout Europe, especially in the Federal Republic of Germany. However, those willing to export arms to the former Yugoslavia were to be found in all corners of the globe.

Weapons identified in Bosnia and in Croatia of external provenance are probably too numerous to mention. In addition to the MILAN anti-armor systems already mentioned, US Stinger anti-air rocket systems could be found, as could Soviet (mainly SA-2) systems. Mortars, mines and automatic weapons were identified which originated in the Russian Federation, Ukraine, Moldova, the former East Germany, Poland, the Czech and Slovak Republics, Romania, Malaysia, China and Singapore, among others. British and (West) German assault rifles were identified, although these appear, in a sense, not to have originated in their 'parent' country (although there may be nuances to add to this – see below).

Austria had a key place in secret arms transfers. From time to time, advertisements with a Vienna telephone number might appear in publications such as *Jane's Defence Weekly*, offering, for example, large quantities of former Warsaw Pact kit. With the Soviet retreat from Eastern Europe, there was a surplus of former Warsaw pact weaponry swilling around Europe. Operators in Austria, but also, of course, in other places, acted as middlemen, linking potential buyers and sellers. Having established financial arrangements and completed agreements, the remaining issue was delivery. There were two elements to this. One was provision of legal cover for the transfer. The other was physically to arrange delivery to the user. The provision of legal cover meant forgery, or government complicity. Of these, the latter was the more effective. One example serves to demonstrate this. An Austrian citizen, Rudolf Breiner, living and working out of Marbella in Spain, arranged for the transfer to Bosnia of 5,000 automatic pistols with ammunition, 25,000 Scorpion 7.62 combat rifles with ammunition, including armor piercing bullets, and 200,000 Uzi sub-machine guns, reconditioned in Austria, plus ammunition. It was officials in the Czech Republic, dealing with the application to export the pistols and ammunition from two factories near Prague who disrupted Breiner's scheme. He twice applied for permission to get the arms exported. The first time, he was turned down outright, as the Bolivian General whose signature was on the end user certificate produced was, the Czechs found on enquiry, retired. A second attempt was made using Panamanian end-user certificates for the whole consignment, that is, including the Scorpions and Uzis. Parts of the shipment were taken by waterway to Rotterdam, while others were said to have been delivered to an airstrip in a 'small European country'. The attempt to transfer was again stymied by the Czechs who, noticing the same names involved with the same consignment, but for a new destination, asked the US to confirm with the Panamanians that the certificate was genuine – something for which there was reasonable doubt, given that at the time, Panama was a country without an army, or a real police force and had just been invaded by the American military. The certificate was bogus and had been illegally provided by the deputy head of the office dealing with arms transfers in Bolivia. The matter was subject to international criminal investigation and Breiner and two others were convicted in Spain.

In many cases end-user certificates were not so closely interrogated and it was commonplace for the whole, or some part, of a consignment of arms never to reach the designated end-user point. In these cases, it was still necessary to arrange delivery to the point of use. To this end Slovenia obtained assistance from the Pope in one case. Slovenian security forces proudly flew camouflaged Bell helicopters, purchased after the arms embargo was put in place, which were originally sold to the Vatican for transport purposes. Shortly afterwards, they were re-exported to Slovenia and others purchased from the manufacturers on the grounds that the Pope had been an impeccable civilian user, one to overcome any doubts in that crucial gray zone of 'dual use' technology.

Other attempts were more blatant. Shipments believed to be from Iran were intercepted. On one occasion in September 1992 an aircraft ostensibly carrying humanitarian aid was discovered at Zagreb carrying Kalashnikov automatic rifles. At other times, weapons were discovered in humanitarian convoys travelling in Bosnia. The most obvious initial route to the former Yugoslavia was by water, either along the River Danube into Serbia, or to the port of Bar in Montenegro, or to one of the ports on the Croatian coast. On several occasions, ships were intercepted carrying weapons to some part of the Yugoslav region. One vessel, sailing out of a Greek port, was stopped carrying arms being re-exported by Serbia to Somalia. Behind all this activity, for it to be successful there had to be assistance from elements in some governments, as in the Panamanian case, or from the governments themselves and their secret services. A clear example of this was the identification of an arms consignment at Maribor airport in Slovenia in July 1993. The consignment, intended for the Bosnian Muslims, engulfed the Slovenian Ministry of Defense in scandal. The accompanying documents reported in the press indicated that not only had senior figures in the Slovene MoD and Slovene intelligence been involved in this operation, but so apparently had an intelligence officer from a Western European country, who had been flying helicopters with arms into Bosnia. The presence of such an operative raised a new set of questions about arms transfers and the war in Yugoslavia.

The questions surrounding arms transfers to the former Yugoslavia were in some ways straightforward – tracing routes, identifying those involved in a network and assessing the qualities of dual technology. However, the issue of arms transfers raised other sets of problems, ethical and philosophical, linked to the question of self-defense. The key element in all of this was that Serb superiority of weapons allowed territorial domination against all of their opponents in the former Yugoslavia (even if Slovenia was an irrelevance in this context). The international arms embargo ensured that the dominant position Serb forces enjoyed before and as the conflict began would be maintained. In doing so, it also confirmed that the only factor that could disrupt Serbian ambition was external intervention. Having established strategic domination of its neighbors through weapons superiority, military–political leaders in Belgrade weighed up very carefully the prospect of international intervention, the one thing that might block their plans. Analysis of the US-led and UN-authorized operations against Iraq in 1990–91 played a vital part in their calculations.

The superiority syndrome

In between the Iraqi invasion of Kuwait on 2 August 1990 and the deployment of units of the JNA in the Republic of Slovenia at the end of June 1991, the Yugoslav military-political elite became extremely confident about their military superiority, in the light of the performance of first the Iraqi armed forces against Kuwait and, later, the effectiveness of the US-led international coalition against Saddam Hussein. They strongly believed that armed forces with superior organizational and technical capabilities would easily overrun those who were significantly weaker in either or both qualities.

The Gulf War ran concurrently with the penultimate phase of the Yugoslav break-up, and the Iraqi invasion of Kuwait affected thinking in the Yugoslav military. As tension mounted and preparations were being made for the ever-more likely contingency that one or more republics would secede from the Federation, these and other assumptions bred a careless confidence in the Yugoslav military. In the run-up to the Slovenian referendum (2 December 1990), a prominent Belgrade military analyst promised that if Slovenia were to declare its independence there would be a scenario akin to 'Kuwait in the Alps.' This promise was issued, not on the basis of the as yet unleashed Operation *Desert Storm*, but from a confidence that the 'battle management' skills deemed responsible for Iraq's six-hour invasion of Kuwait would give the JNA an even greater advantage in Slovenia.[9]

Subsequent events in the Gulf seem only to have confirmed the view that forces both larger and better equipped would easily overcome weaker opponents. According to Slovenian Defense Minister Janez Janša, the generals in Belgrade expressed the belief that there would be a two-day, mini-*Desert Storm*. He even cites Slovenian intelligence sources as reporting that one of the top generals assured US Secretary of State James Baker that the JNA would perform

---

[9] 'Miroslav Lazanski, `Kuvajt na Alpima', *Intervju*, 23 November 1990.

its own *Desert Storm*, should Slovenia proceed with its declaration of independence.[10]

Slobodna Dalmacija, in September 1992, carried a serialized account of the final days of the SFRY according to the country's last Prime Minister, Ante Marković.[11] This serialization was based on official documents of government sessions and other meetings retained by Marković. This account also indicates that the JNA leadership was confident that operations in Slovenia would be straightforward and that *Desert Storm* would be the model.[12]

However, any assessment of this confidence must be addressed with caution in one respect. This involves consideration of not only the beliefs of the Belgrade military *vis-à-vis* the Slovenian military, but also the political dimensions of the situation. KOS, the Yugoslav military counterintelligence service, performed badly. Its assessments seem to have incorporated two crucial miscalculations about the situation in Slovenia. The first was that Slovenia's Territorial Defense Force would be neither able, nor willing to respond to a show of force. This was a serious intelligence failure which has to be explained in part by assumptions about Slovenia – first, that those responsible for defense and interior ministry forces were inexperienced, having come from the ranks of the anti-military opposition; secondly, that the Slovenes were not fighters; and thirdly, that the 'secessionist' leaders in Slovenia did not have the support of the people.[13]

For whatever reason, the military-political elite in Belgrade appears to have believed that simply a symbolic show of force would be enough. In spite of the projections of a mini-*Desert Storm*, which

---

[10] Janez Janša, *Primiki*, Cankarjeva Založba, Ljubljana, 1992, p. 98.

[11] *Slobodna Dalmacija* is a daily newspaper published in the Croatian port of Split. It became widely regarded as the 'best' and most objective newspaper in Croatia. As a result of its open policy, including publication of the series referred to here, and criticism of the Zagreb authorities, it was 'nationalized' by the Zagreb authorities and a new, pliant editorial board imposed.

[12] *Slobodna Dalmacija*, September 1992.

[13] One of the most prominent JNA officers in Slovenia (at the time, a colonel) later recounted how he simply did not believe that what he regarded as his fellow countrymen would fire on the JNA. Rather, he and his colleagues assumed that their concern was with difficult political leaders who were out of touch with their own population. General Milan Aksentijević in *Death of Yugoslavia*, Program 3, Brian Lapping Associates for the BBC, 1995.

the JNA launched a policing operation similar to that it briefly effected in March 1991 when it put tanks on the streets of Belgrade (and also similar to the operations by elements of Soviet Armed Forces during the Moscow *coup*-attempt). The JNA did not, it may be concluded, think that it was going into battle.

There were, however, obvious divisions within the JNA command. Some, most notably the Chief of the General Staff, Col. Gen. Blagoje Adžic, seem to have favored something more than a policing mission. Adžic told a meeting of one hundred and fifty officers in Belgrade that the army should have used greater force.[14] He argued that should sufficient force be employed to supplant the Ljubljana leadership and eliminate large elements of the Slovenian Territorial Defense, this would be accepted then by the international community. He avered that, although there would have been protests from Western countries, these would die down after three months and everything would return to the *status quo ante*. In effect, the General was identifying a pattern in Western behavior and expecting it to be repeated: as had happened in other cases, China and the Tiannamen Square protests being the most notable, the West would declare its disapproval, but then normalize relations after a short period. Belgrade's calculations may also have been disrupted by the degree to which the international community particularly the European Community became involved in attempts to end the conflict – and the speed with which they acted.

Assessing international engagement: linking the Gulf War to the Yugoslav crisis

As the international community, in particular the EU, became increasingly engaged in efforts to end the fighting in Yugoslavia, the Belgrade military-political elite woke up to the possibility of external intervention. They began a series of studies both of the Yugoslav crisis in the context of the 'New World Order' and of the international community's intervention in the Gulf: would Belgrade find itself in the same position as Baghdad?

The editor of the leading military-theoretical journal, Colonel Jovan Čanak, published a selection of these studies in *Vojno Delo*. Although there were small differences of interpretation in the

---

[14] 5 July 1991.

contributions (for example, whether or not the US-led campaign was an example of the application of classical air-land battle theory, or an adaptation of it), they all contributed to the general conclusion that the Gulf War was unique – and would not, therefore, be repeated in the Balkans. In considering the overall consensus, it is important to bear in mind that *Vojno Delo* was the major theoretical organ of an armed force organized and controlled within a communist system. Although elements of the control formerly exercised were receding, there was still a high degree of official control. And although Čanak was editor of the volume, the journal was heavily supervised by an editorial committee, itself overseen by a council. The control exerted ensured that what appeared in print represented an 'official' view.

Čanak explained in his introduction that, while the Yugoslav crisis in its international context was obviously of interest, the events in the Gulf could and should be linked to the situation in Yugoslavia. The war in the Gulf was 'a true paradigm for the use of modern technology and a credible model for the use of force in a hypothetical war in similar military-political circumstances, something which (with reference to our crisis and its possible internationalization) cannot leave us indifferent.' The Gulf War 'could be a model for the instrumentalization of the UN, as a system of global collective security, serving to realize the global strategic interests of the greatest world powers.'[15]

This last statement reflected a curious interpretation of the intervention in the Gulf, one set in a Marxist mode of thought. According to Čanak, the idea that the Gulf War was a model for wars against Third World countries (as the JNA seems to think it was supposed to be) only 'disguised the real strategic intentions of those who were really directing these wars.' This reflects the tone of the article which won the JNA's '22 December' Prize in 1991 and, even more, of congratulatory articles and statements. The crux of these was that the Yugoslav crisis could not be understood without reference to the geopolitical 'games' played by Western political-economic interests.[16]

[15] Col. Jovan Čanak, 'Uvod', *Vojno Delo*, vol. XVIII, nos 4–5, July–October, 1991, p. 12.

[16] 22 December was 'Army Day' in Tito's Yugoslavia and the prize was awarded for the best article on a military theme published during the preceding year. The prize winner was: Dr Živojin Rakočević, 'Koreni i geopolitička dimenzija

For the JNA leadership, the findings were extremely important. The overall conclusion was that specific conditions applied to the Gulf; that those conditions did not apply to their own situation; and that both the Gulf and Yugoslavia were cases *sui generis*. An implicit assumption followed from this, namely that although there was reason to be concerned about international interference in Yugoslavia, there was little reason to expect armed international intervention. This notion was reinforced by the fact that the United States was not significantly involved and that EU countries, through the WEU, could not undertake meaningful military operations without minimal US backing.

There were other reasons to conclude that there would be no external military intervention.[17] An ad hoc intervention under the auspices of the CSCE would require Yugoslav agreement – and so could be ruled out. An intervention in what would be the internal affairs of a state could not be authorized by the UN Security Council unless the situation were defined as posing a threat to international peace and security. This was judged unlikely because it would require the agreement of all five permanent members of the Security Council whose views on the Yugoslav question were quite different. Moreover, it was recognized that, if they acted, although Western forces would eventually suppress armed conflict, this would not solve the problems – a finding reinforced by the assessment that most Yugoslavs would oppose intervention.

Consideration of organisational and technical matters confirmed the small likelihood of a Western European intervention. Although the events in Yugoslavia had spurred discussions about the formation of purely European military institutions, these could not, in any event, be ready until after 1992. NATO's Rapid Reaction Corps was seen as one arm of a European military response, but this too would not be ready in time; the alternatives, of creating new institutions or building a Western European military through the WEU, were even more remote. Moreover, establishing a unified political position as a basis for unified military action was seemingly far off

jugoslovenske krize', *Vojno Delo*, vol. XLIII, nos 4–5, 1991, pp. 21–86; elaboration was given in Battleship Captain Professor Radivoje Jovadžić, 'Jugoslavija u igri geopolitike', *Vojno Delo*, vol. XLIV, nos 1–2, 1992, pp. 254–64.

[17] Milan Radaković, 'Evropska zajednica – mogučnosti vojne integracije', *Vojno Delo*, vol. XVIII, nos 4–5, July–October, 1991, pp. 188–203.

and sensibilities about the United States' military presence in Europe meant that any talk of a European military would be within the framework of a 'European pillar' in NATO. In this context the US role was seen to be paramount: on the one hand, the Americans would oppose any European moves towards a wholly autonomous capability, on the other, the Europeans did not have a capability to engage without US backing.

Analysis of the Gulf War affected other matters too including international and regional relations, military operations and the role of information media. The most important features of those studies are presented below with a view to offering a relatively coherent understanding of international strategic questions, including the assessment of the uniqueness of Operation *Desert Storm*.

The Gulf War altered the regional balance of power, making not only the United States but also Iran, Israel and Syria victors. The fact that, as a result of the war, borders remained as they had been before 2 August 1990 was taken as significant, although not dwelt upon. The principal innovation was seen to be the use of US, UK and French troops to protect the Kurds in northern Iraq at the end of the Gulf War. This was interpreted as being the possible foundation of a Kurdish statelet, formed at the expense of a defeated Iraq: 'Whether the Western military, financial and humanitarian involvement has already begun the *de facto* founding of a Kurdish state remains to be seen.'[18] Thus, although no border changes resulted directly from the Gulf War, the possibility that there could be a change in the future was anticipated, if not assumed.

The JNA's analysis concluded that there was no existing basis for this action in the UN Charter; instead the Kurds were protected on the basis of Security Council Resolution 688, linked to the Convention on Genocide. It was noted that each Security Council resolution became a precedent for action in similar situations and that these could involve human and ethnic rights, as well as internal conflicts, which were deemed to threaten international peace and security. There was no extrapolation to the Yugoslav case, although the implications for that conflict were clear. There was, however, the suggestion that the events in the Gulf, particularly the emphasis on the extension of humanitarian considerations, could constitute a type of 'neo-imperialism.'

[18] Oliver Potežica, 'Zaliv posle rata', ibid., p. 221.

Thus the Gulf War seems to have been judged to be so much of a special case that any implications for the Yugoslav situation were deemed insignificant. The singularity of the Gulf War was found in many respects. In particular this applied to the specific international circumstances in which it occurred. The end of the Cold War and the definition of Iraq as the aggressor by both superpowers (albeit each with their own particular interests in the zone) enabled the US to concentrate fully on preparations for the war – including the removal of half its forces from the Central Front in Europe – and the building of the international coalition.

The ending of superpower competition created a situation in which virtually every country in the world condemned Iraq, freeing the Security Council to authorize, ultimately, the use of force. The way in which Iraq was left on its own without allies was noted as a lesson about alliances for all countries, 'including our own'.[19] Although not stated, it seems fair to assume that two consequences were understood from this. First, that allies or supporters could not be relied upon if their interests required opposition to Belgrade – presumably a matter for concern for those in Belgrade who sought to rely on 'traditional' good relations between Serbia and, for example, France. Secondly, there was the converse of this: utter isolation and the formation of an alliance against a particular party, that is, Belgrade, could be avoided if potential members of that alliance could be persuaded that it was not in their interest to back such a coalition. As will be indicated below, the Serbian camp made strong efforts to persuade potential military interveners that such a course would not be in their interest.

Other general characteristics were noted. One of these was the co-ordination of elements from twenty-eight countries' armed forces, particularly the use of ten in the campaign to evict the Iraqi army from Kuwait, in particular the role of the AWACS. Another was the long period in which the coalition's forces were assembled, also giving time for many practice operations. This meant that the war was almost 'won' in the preparatory period, a development aided by the passivity and positional nature of Iraq's defensive preparations.

Vital too was the use of sophisticated technology – particularly,

[19] Gen. Maj. Ilija Nikežić (retd), 'Vojnostrategijski aspekt rata u Zalivu', ibid., p. 283.

of electronic and electronic counter-measures systems, of Precision Guided Munitions and of the *Patriot* anti-rocket defense system. The post technological level of the Iraqi forces, especially their 1960s generation air-defense system, was also a key factor in the conflict.[20] There was at least one voice of caution, expressing the view that, as with all other wars, the decisive feature was not so much the technology itself as those using it.[21] (The 'human factor' was a strong conceptual element in the doctrine of General People's Defense operated by the combined regular and territorial forces of the Socialist Federative Republic of Yugoslavia.)

The 9:1 proportion of time taken up by the initial air campaign *vis à vis* the ground assault in Operation *Desert Storm* was yet another outstanding feature.[22] The protracted initial air assault was judged to have been a major contribution to the brevity of the ground campaign, but was not decisive.[23] Nonetheless, the technical and technological levels of the aircraft meant that more guided munitions were used to greater destructive effect than ever before. Noteworthy, too, was that, in spite of the accuracy and destructiveness of the Allied assault, the Iraqi tactics of camouflaging, dispersal to outlying bases and engineering and camouflage of aerodromes resulted in a significant degree of protection from being destroyed on the ground. This finding was to prove significant when NATO air power went into action over Kosovo in 1999.

Yet, even with the immense destructive capacity of these forces, a leading air power specialist noted that many of the most modern aircraft were only effective so long as their support systems were functioning. Earlier experiences (the Bekaa Valley was cited as an example) were confirmed in the Gulf War: up-to-date combat aircraft are of low effectiveness if their command and guidance

[20] Col. Gen. Zlatko Rendulić, 'Uloga i značaj veoma preciznih oružja u ratu u Zalivu', *Glasnik RV i PVO*, vol. XLVII, no. 6, November–December 1991, pp. 12–18; Col. Dr Todor Mirković, 'Neka obeležja rata u Zalivu', *Vojno Delo*, vol. XLIII, nos 4–5, July–October, 1992, pp. 306–7.

[21] Maj. Gen. Angel Ončevski, 'Vazduhoplovna komponenta rata u Zalivu', *Vojno Delo*, vol. XVIII, nos 4–5, July–October, 1991, p. 326.

[22] The air campaign was studied within the context of the general *Vojno Delo* study – see ibid. At the same time as the aforementioned study, the air force and air-defense journal carried a series of analyses of Gulf air operations; see, *Glasnik RV i PVO*, vol. XLVII, no. 6, November–December, 1991.

[23] Ibid., p. 326.

systems are neutralized. This was said to be particularly true of fighters, which do not possess autonomous means of identifying targets in low and high 'hemispheres.' The Gulf War was considered to offer little instruction concerning tactics and the use of these aircraft in combat. The key reason for this was the virtual absence of air-to-air encounters.[24]

A fifth peculiar feature of the conflict was terrain (a matter of significance with regard to assessments of the Yugoslav situation). Although, it was noted, there were difficulties adapting to desert conditions, requiring arduous training, these were overcome. Moreover, the geographic and topographic features – flat desert terrain in Kuwait and southern and central Iraq – facilitated the use of the advanced technology which gave the coalition such an enormous advantage, particularly when it came to the uninhibited, direct identification of targets lying on the desert plains. This factor, in particular, as well as the others, meant that the War in the Gulf was unlike any war in the past and any war to come. Extrapolation from the Gulf War to other situations would therefore be incomplete and could quite readily lead to mistakes being made, it was concluded.[25]

The unreliable nature of any extrapolation from the Gulf War, it was argued in an analysis of American military doctrine in relation to the war, was compounded by Iraqi behavior.[26] In this analysis, the Gulf War was seen as a test for the American doctrines of rapid reaction and low-intensity conflict, both of which were seen as designed for war against 'Third World' countries. In the end, neither was really tested in operations. Rather, an ad hoc, *sui generis* and more or less new doctrine was worked out which, nonetheless, included some components of established air-land war theory.

This 'new' doctrine could not, however, be used in other cases, particularly against the United States' key strategic rivals. The principal reason for this was the behavior of the Iraqi army. Its passive defense meant that any lessons learned from the combat were devalued. Indeed, the general assessment that the effectiveness of

---

[24] Angel Ončevski, *Lovački Avioni: Juče, Danas, Sutra*, VIZ, Belgrade, 1992, p. 115.

[25] Col. Dr Todor Mirković (retd), 'Neka obeležja rata u Zalivu', p. 307.

[26] Battleship Captain Prof. Anton Žabkar, 'Ameriška vojna doktrina i pomorska komponenta rata u Zalivu', pp. 351–3.

coalition air power caused the rapid disintegration of Iraq's armed forces had to be qualified: in spite of an almost constant thirty-eight-day offensive, using 80,000 tonnes of munitions, 50 per cent of Iraqi combat aircraft and 40 per cent of heavy weaponry remained intact.

The lessons from the Gulf War for the Americans, it was judged, were even more modest than this suggested because Iraq offered no defense. Apart from the *eighty-one* Scud missiles launched against Israel and Saudi Arabia, the night attack on Khafji and a few attacks on naval vessels, plus ecological measures such as releasing oil into the sea or setting oil fields ablaze, Iraq did nothing to counter the coalition attack. Against such inactive defense few valuable lessons could be learned and little of significance applied to other situations.

However, Iraq's passive and positional defense did have limited lessons to offer. In particular, the Iraqi use of camouflage was felt to have offered beneficial lessons which 'for our armed forces are particularly significant'[27] – again, as was to be relevant during the Kosovo campaign in 1999. Of importance here was not only the camouflaging of units and firing positions, as well as airfields (see above), but also the creation of false targets using decorative and 'scenographic' methods. The latter was judged to have given the impression from the air that a target attacked was completely destroyed – leading the opponent to reach false conclusions. Among specific features considered here was the use of model Scud launchers. In the end, 'Saddam's line' – that is, the fixed defensive positions in Kuwait – was at some points a 'superficial arrangement.'[28] Deception of this kind, in the view of the Chief of Staff-to-be, was a key element of operational art.

In spite of the positive assessment of this element of Iraq's defense, the general conclusion was that use of positional defense was a failure. Such a defense could only limit the effects of an air attack, but could not bring success in battle. The clear implication here was that the enemy should not be confronted with such passivity, nor given such a clear run in its preparations. A significant lesson

---

[27] Col. Gen. Života Panić, 'Karakteristike inžinjerskog obezbedjenja u ratu u Zalivu i savladjivanje prepreka oklopno-mehanizovanim sastavima', ibid., p. 369.Col. Gen. Panić became Chief of Staff in April 1992.

[28] Ibid., pp. 361–2.

learned was that the conservation of forces for a 'decisive battle' was disastrous.[29] Waiting to defend entrenched positions was a successful counter-infantry strategy in the war fought against Iran during the 1980s, but was inappropriate when faced with an alliance disposing of immense concentrations of high-technology weapons systems.[30]

Positional defense was the central, doctrinal mistake made by the Iraqis. This was compounded by tactical mistakes, such as concentrating ground forces close to the coastline where they would become trapped, or displacing the most advanced elements of the air force to Iran, making them unavailable thereafter. In addition to this was the very low morale and motivation of the Iraqi army. This was evident at 'all levels of command in the course of the war.'[31] Although this criticism of the Iraqi armed forces was noticed, the lesson did not appear to have been learned by the JNA which underwent a deep crisis of morale during the war in Croatia in the second half of 1991 – a crisis which was, as with the Iraqi case, founded on poor leadership.[32]

Overall, the JNA leadership and, presumably, their political allies seem to have drawn comfort from their analyses of both international involvement in the Yugoslav conflict and the Gulf War. The features which appeared to make the Gulf War a unique case, both diplomatically and militarily, reassured Belgrade's military-political elite that it was not a model that could or would be readily transferred to other regions. They consciously recognized that their own case had parallels with that of Saddam Hussein, but these were limited. Certainly, the Gulf War would not be repeated in their region.

Above all, that international involvement in the Yugoslav conflict had been led by the European Community was deemed significant. Even through the WEU, involving nine of the Community Twelve, Western Europe had no ready-made means of intervention. Any ad hoc development would be possible only with US backing, effectively involving NATO. The key role played by the Americans in the Gulf War, including the use of the UN Security Council, defined the international isolation of Iraq. Belgrade, on

[29] Maj. Gen. Ilija Jikezić, 'Vojnostrategijski aspekt rata u Zalivu', ibid., p. 286.
[30] Žabkar, 'Ameriška', p. 352.
[31] Ibid., p. 353.
[32] See Chapter 3.

the other hand, was faced with a situation in which the US was taking a back seat and in which the EC, acting through and on behalf of the CSCE, took the lead. Those making calculations about the possibility of an armed intervention could be sure that the supporting role taken by the US, as well as the different course being taken by the international community, meant that, whatever else was taken into account, there would not be one. This confidence seems to have been in doubt, however, in the spring and summer of 1992 after the United States became prominently engaged in dealing with the Yugoslav crisis as widespread violence unfolded in Bosnia.

'Balkan Storm' apprehension

In the spring of 1992, the US became more prominently involved in the international handling of the Yugoslav crisis. Alongside this, the UN Security Council became far more actively engaged, discussing the situation in Bosnia and issuing a series of resolutions. The crux of this was the growing and clear identification of the Serbian camp as bearing responsibility for the aggression and the concomitant increasing isolation of the Belgrade authorities by the international community.

As a result of the growing pressure, the assessments of Fall 1991 that there would be no repetition of the Gulf War appear to have been reconsidered. The US lead in obtaining a series of UN Security Council resolutions against Belgrade offered similarities with the pattern of events which preceded the Gulf War. Although there remained a general confidence that armed intervention would not materialize, there was also widespread concern that Belgrade would suffer the same fate as Baghdad.

In this phase, Belgrade made the strength of the air-defense system, particularly that around Belgrade, a matter of public confidence. While there was probably no sense that Belgrade was impregnable, it was believed that the losses inflicted on an aggressor would be so punitive as to deter an attack.[33] Announcements that Belgrade's air-defense system was on full-alert and that the military

---

[33] Air Force and Air Defense Chief Col.-Gen. Božidar Stevanović assured Belgrade's citizens that 'the air-defense system is prepared and all the rocket systems withdrawn from the territory of the independent republics have been positioned around Belgrade.' Interview with *Večernje Novosti*, 30 March 1992. In discussions

were ready 'to defend ourselves with everything we have got'[34] were balanced with realism: 'we could counter-attack, if our early-warning system functions properly and if we survive the first strike', an air force officer soberly told Western journalists.[35]

At the same time as reassuring the population, the prominence given to the air-defense in the official news media may also, of course, have served the Belgrade regime in another way: talk of a possible attack helped consolidate popular support around the leadership of Slobodan Milošević. At once, people were alarmed enough to seek solidarity against a potential external aggressor, yet sufficiently reassured enough so as not to be so anxious as to be crippled with fear.

However, there is evidence that the threat of an air attack was not simply a matter of manipulating the population. Attention was paid to the air-defense system and to the question of stealth technology in military journals,[36] reflecting the thinking of the military leadership. In addition, there are other indications, including reorganization of the air-defense system, that there was concern, at least temporarily, that there could be an aerial attack.

The reason for supposing that there might be an attack of this kind is a matter of speculation. One possible explanation is that the growing international isolation of Belgrade and condemnation of the Serbian camp outside Serbia's borders appeared to be a repeat of what happened to Saddam Hussein's Iraq. If the pattern of the Gulf War were to be followed, then it would seem obvious that absolute condemnation and isolation by the international community and the imposition of sanctions would be followed by the use of military force if (or when) these other measures did not achieve compliance with UN Security Council resolutions.

---

in Belgrade during the summer of 1992, I was assured that if anybody decided to bomb Belgrade they would lose at least half of their aircraft.

[34] Airforce and Air Defense Chief, Božidar Stevanović. quoted in *The Daily Telegraph*, 1 June 1992.

[35] Major Živojin Petrović, quoted in *The Sunday Times*, 9 August 1992.

[36] Col. Gen. Božidar Stevanović, Commander of the Air Force and Air Defense, 'Stanje i perspektiva razvoja RV i PVO u novim uslovima', pp. 1–4, and Maj. Gen. Angel Ončevski, 'Pedeset godina stvaranja i razvoja našeg Ratnog vazduhoplovstva i protivvazdušne odbrane' in *Glasnik RV i PVO*, vol. XLVIII, nos 1–2, January–June 1992, pp. 5–13; *Idem*. 'Mogučnosti za otkrivanje i uništenje letelica stelt-tehnologije', *Vojno Delo*, vol. XLIV, no. 3, May–June 1992, pp. 183–200.

Analysis of the Gulf War had offered little in the domain of air-defense.[37] The US-led coalition clearly used overwhelming means to suppress air-defense radar systems, but even this did not produce absolute success.[38] It was noted that most of the 8–9,000 artillery components of the air-defense system survived the initial attack and, although incomparable in terms of effectiveness with rocket systems, nonetheless disposed of considerable potential (these systems were responsible for 83 per cent of American aircraft brought down during the Vietnam War). The implication of this was that at least the artillery element of an air-defense system, if properly used, would enable some resistance to be offered.

The key factor in successful air-defense was considered to be the positioning of fixed systems, the mobility of others and camouflage. In this regard, it may be of note that the highly advanced air-defense system, which had been withdrawn with the JNA from Slovenia, where it guarded Ljubljana, the Slovenian capital, in April was re-positioned as part of Belgrade's air-defense system.[39]

At this stage, following the harmonized recognition of Bosnia as an independent entity by the United States and the European Community, Belgrade may have believed that events were moving in the direction of an attack. But as the main Belgrade daily assured its readers in a commentary, a 'Balkan Storm', or US intervention, was unlikely because the Balkans was not one of its major spheres of interest.[40] Thus, although doubts may have been raised, the official view seems to have been that an American-led intervention was still out of the question, though intervention by other Western forces remained a possibility (see below).

Given the official control of *Vojno Delo*, the appearance of an article describing stealth technology aircraft and discussing the possibilities of revealing and destroying these planes was of note. It included the suggestion that although it might not be impossible to detect and destroy stealth aircraft using the most advanced fighters, let alone specialized technology, this would be far from an easy task. Conventional aircraft would need to operate on a massive scale

[37] Col. Momčilo Sakan, 'Dejstva vazduhoplovnih snaga i protivvazdušne odbrane u ratu u Zalivu', *Vojno Delo*, vol. XLIII, nos 4–5, July–October 1991, pp. 383–408.

[38] Maj. Gen. Angel Ončevski, 'Vazduhoplovna komponenta rata u Zalivu', pp. 316–17.

[39] TV Beograd 'Večernje Vesti', 18 April 1992; *Politika*, 19 April 1992.

[40] Ibid.

in a limited area using specialized tactics and procedures to stand any chance of combating stealth technology. Discussion of this topic, in conjunction with the attention paid to air-defense capability, suggests that serious thought was being given to the prospect of a major aerial attack, one that remained a remote possibility, and would implicitly have required American participation. Hence so long as US involvement was absent, external constraints on Belgrade's actions would be of limited effect.

At the beginning of July, *Nedjeljna Dalmacija*, one of the few publications in Croatia free from political control or interference, published what was claimed to be a document produced secretly by the military leadership in Belgrade for the president of the Federal Republic of Yugoslavia, Dobrica Ćosić.[42] In this alleged 'Report on the condition of the Yugoslav Armed Forces', air-defense and other preparations for a possible attack by NATO forces were emphasized. Although elements of the text read credibly, doubts regarding its authenticity were strong, for one superficial reason: the document constantly refers to the 'Yugoslav Defense Forces' (*Jugoslovenska Odbrambena Snaga* – JOS), whereas the new name used by the Belgrade military was 'Military (or Army) of Yugoslavia' (*Vojska Jugoslavije* – VJ). Judging this issue correctly involves answering some deconstructivist questions. Is it possible that the Belgrade military might use a different term for themselves than that used publicly? Would anyone wishing to fake such a document, on the other hand, make such an obvious error? These questions are important: if the document were authentic, then it is of great interest, given the perspectives and perceptions it offered of the West.

Whatever the credibility of the 'report', there was clearly concern that a 'Balkan Storm' was not out of the question. This was true at the popular and at the elite level. Although the Belgrade military-political elite continued to believe that there would be no such an attack, the relative confidence established by the *Vojno Delo* studies the previous autumn was undermined.

International intervention was the major obstacle that Belgrade's war for new borders would face. Having subordinated most of the old Yugoslav federation's military while running paramilitary squads to create ambiguity and perform the tasks regular soldiers, especially conscripts, could not be relied upon to perform, the military-political elite in Belgrade had a dominant position among the protagonists involved in the Yugoslav war. International concern was expressed initially through the imposition of a legally binding arms embargo, the inadvertent effect of which was to cement an imbalance of arms capabilities in the region. Because only international intervention could alter this strategic balance even in the medium term, assessments in Belgrade before and during the war were vital to its conduct. Although there were later concerns that the initial conclusions might be brought into question by US engagement, and in spite of initial misjudgment over Slovenia, the strategic calculation remained the same throughout. So long as operations remained below the threshold that would precipitate Western military intervention, the Serbian project would be successful. It was on this basis that the campaign for new borders was carried out in Croatia and Bosnia.

5

MEANS AND ENDS: THE STRATEGY
OF ETHNIC CLEANSING

Once Slobodan Milošević and his collaborators had established a
military capability and made calculations over the balance of armed
forces, there was a question over how to translate these means into
achieving ends. The use of armed force required political purpose.
The Serbian new state project meant war. It meant war of a particular kind. This could not be a war of established force against established force. It was a war against civilians. In this sense it might
terminologically go beyond a conventional understanding of war
as a social phenomenon involving the use of organized means of
restrained coercive violence according to conventions and rules to
settle a political conflict. While armed forces were involved, the
essence of the Serbian strategy was control of territory through removal of the population. This practice became known as 'ethnic
cleansing.' Generally the inhabitants of whole regions were not
displaced as a contingency of war, seeking safety from the fighting.
Although there were certainly some who fled fighting, the overwhelming majority was subject to forced migration, directly, or
indirectly. Where this was indirect, it was as a function of the direct
impact of ethnic cleansing elsewhere. The political aim was complete control of territory. The strategy to accomplish this was use
of largely unrestrained coercive violence to eliminate any potentially hostile population.

Ethnic cleansing is the strategic use of excessive violence against
civilian population centers, demonstrative atrocity and mass murder in order to remove that population. While it involves killing
in some cases, in others, the intention is not to murder all members of an ethnic group, but to induce all members to leave the
territory in question, through the use of demonstrative violence.
It is accompanied by the complete destruction of property so as
to ensure that return is not possible. The intent of this strategy,

which is also conditioned by ethno-national ideology, was to secure the territory in question by removing the prospect for opposition, whether purely political, or violent.

The latter was the more important. Terrorism and, especially, guerrilla warfare, rely on armed groups operating within a supportive community. In the famous doctrine of Mao Tsedong, the guerrilla among the people is like a fish in water. The point of ethnic cleansing was to drain the water, making it impossible for the fish to swim. This blunt application of armed force to the ends of territorial control crossed the boundary between that which is acceptable in the awful, bloody course of war and that which is not. And it was this strategy that Serb forces implemented in the areas they controlled in Croatia, in Bosnia and in Kosovo.

The scale, range and consistency of the methods used to terrorize the non-Serb populations of many different areas in Croatia, Bosnia and Kosovo did not and could not have resulted from a spontaneous eruption of local resentment. The political and military organization that is required before a campaign is considerable – as was seen in a different context when international forces inevitably took far longer than critics believed possible to deploy troops and materiel to the theatre, once it had been decided to do so.[1] Setting up, supplying and staffing the many camps and detention centers that disfigured the Bosnian landscape required significant co-ordination and planning. The purpose of this terror was solely in furtherance of the goal described above: to ensure that the population remaining in the secured areas would be 'reliable'.

The term 'ethnic cleansing' (Serbo-Croat *etničko čišćenje*) became widely used to describe the practice of creating ethnically pure territories, primarily through the use of terror, including the killing of individuals and groups to strike fear into the hearts of others. The heritage of this concept is linked to the practices of the Turks and their agents during the Ottoman occupation. The term ethnic cleansing first appeared in documents penned by Serbian

---

[1] There seems to be a sense among Western publics, especially among journalists and activists, that in an age of instant communication and instant gratification, it should be possible instantly to deploy tens of thousands of troops, as though it involved no more than the double-click of a computer mouse. In the Gulf Conflict of 1990–1, for example, it took over six months in relatively straightforward and conducive circumstances to deploy the international coalition that eventually effected the eviction of Iraq from occupied Kuwait.

generals in the Royal Yugoslav Army in 1931, *vis à vis* Muslims. It also appeared in documents of the Ustasha regime in the Second World War Independent State of Croatia, *vis-à-vis* Serbs. Its usage in the Yugoslav War was said to have been coined by Vojislav Šešelj, leader of the Serbian Radical Party and leader of the Chetnik paramilitaries – although he was later disingenuously to suggest that he had only meant peaceful population exchanges. While most criminal activity covered by the term 'ethnic cleansing' was committed as a key part of the Serbian cause, the practice was not limited to Serbian forces. As the war progressed, following the Serbian lead, ethnic cleansing was practised by the Croats in western Hercegovina and central Bosnia during 1993, and in the Krajina region in 1995. On a lesser scale, and often overlooked, Muslims in Bosnia were involved in similar practices. After the 'liberation' of Kosovo by NATO-led troops in 1999, the international force struggled for two to three months to control low level acts of violent intimidation that saw over three quarters of Serbs 'cleansed' from the province.

The application of the strategy at the tactical level began with a trial run in April 1991 at the village of Kijevo in the Krajina region of Croatia. A striking event to those who noticed it at the time, this remained unnoticed by most analysts and observers well after its namesake village in Kosovo had passed under the shadow of both Kosovan and Serbian ethnic cleansing in 1998 and 1999. Under the command of the then Colonel Ratko Mladić, JNA troops surrounded the predominantly Croat village set in a preponderantly Serb region. The siege of Kijevo lasted two weeks, during which time, almost no one was allowed into Kijevo and no one was allowed out and back in again. All supplies were cut. While the water, fuel and food supplies were eventually allowed back in, it would only be a matter of months before Kijevo would again be encircled, after which the other elements of ethnic cleansing were applied (see Chapter 5).

The practice appears to have been begun in earnest in eastern Slavonia and other parts of Croatia in the autumn of 1991, where it continued in a low-key way long after armed hostilities ceased there, according to international observers. In reality, in Bosnia it was the trial run for implementation where it was that ethnic cleansing gained notoriety. This was the result of a strategic aim combined with a virulent Serbian ethno-national ideology. The aim, as stated, was to create the boundaries of a new state in which there would not be a hostile, or potentially hostile, population to mount opposition, or even guerrilla resistance, leaving only Serbs and those who accepted second-class status to inhabit the lands in question. The same understanding was applied to Kosovo, with the exception that the need was to consolidate the formal borders of the state and through ethnic cleansing to remove a problem that had come to involve armed insurgency, once and for all. In all cases the equation was simple: remove those resisting violently and secure the territory for Serbian control.

In every case, the stories told by so many deportees, refugees and survivors were eyewitness testimony to what happened. While eyewitnesses can always be capable of some degree of unreliably, the consistency found among so many reports from so many individuals in so many different places, often gathered with great speed and timeliness, permits a clear and indisputable picture to be drawn, from which the pattern of ethnic cleansing emerges. The conduct of Serbian attacks, including the manner in which the JNA, MUP and paramilitary groups deployed and treated the non-Serb population, was similar throughout the war zones. The speed and high level of co-ordination that these attacks required make clear that they were centrally coordinated and planned. The places attacked in the Bosnian offensive, graphically illustrate the systematic nature of the attacks and the strategic importance of their locations. The main characteristics of the strategy of ethnic cleansing are described in this chapter, the four principal elements being preparation and provocation, takeover and the use of force, concentration camps and, lastly, elimination through expulsion and execution.

Preparation and provocation

The Bosnian Serbs were well prepared for their takeover – from the very outset they had official letterheaded paper, documents and stamps ready to administer the bureaucracy of ethnic cleansing. For those whose ethnic community was being systematically destroyed – primarily the Slav Muslims of Bosnia and Hercegovina – there was a stark choice between on the one hand, summary murder, or death after deprivation and torture in camps, and, on the other, paying to sign away their possessions, their property and their right to remain in their homeland on specially prepared documents that would receive the specially prepared rubber stamps of the new Serbian administration.

The Bosnian Serbs were prepared in other ways. Plans for the takeover of each municipality (or *opština*) had been made according to one centralized program. Radovan Karadžić's Bosnian Serb leadership laid out this scheme, almost certainly under the tutelage of the Serbian Security Service. A document, marked 'strictly confidential', was a set of instructions titled, 'For the organization and activity of organs of the Serbian people in Bosnia-Herzegovina in extraordinary circumstances'. [2] It is a paper prepared by the leadership of the SDS, which indicates the processes that were implemented by the Serbian élite in order to facilitate its plan. From late 1991 onwards, in addition to the steps already mentioned, preparations were made for the creation of what were effectively shadow governments to be ready for the time when the plan would be put into operation. This involved the creation of 'Crisis Headquarters',[3] which made preparations primarily for the political, but also some of the military aspects of the takeover.

The 'crisis headquarters', derived from a concept designed for wartime conditions under the defense doctrine, were a vital part of political preparations for taking control further to the declarations of Serb autonomous regions. (See below.) In Bosnia, at least from the end of 1991 onwards, the SDS in conjunction with security service centers was preparing to take control in certain areas and making the provision for shadow secret governments using the crisis headquarters which would take up their role in office at a designated point. The SDS document, dated 19 December 1991, was circulated to relevant individuals in the party and concerned the organization and activity of the 'organs of the Serb people' in Bosnia and 'emergency' circumstances. It indicated preparations for the creation of para-governmental structures through the establishment of the crisis headquarters.

The document provided two versions of the plan, one for areas of Bosnia in which there was an absolute Serbian majority, and the other in which there was not. In either case, the aim was to

[2] This document was produced as prosecution Exhibit 70 in the case of 'Prosecutor vs. Dusan Tadic' IT-94-7 and prosecution Exhibit 206 in the case of 'Prosecutor vs. Delalic *et al.* (Celebici)' IT-96-7 at the ICTY in The Hague.

[3] 'Crisis Headquarters' is a translation of the Serbian '*Krizni Štab*', where headquarters is used in preference to 'committee', which is sometimes used (including on early occasions by the author) and 'staff', which is a more obvious literal translation (also used sometimes), yet has too strong a military connotation in English. The term staff reflects the defense heritage of the concept, associated with the political dimensions of a liberation struggle under the old defense system.

prepare loyal Serbs for the takeover and to prepare for coordination, for example, with the JNA. The designation of a Serbian-majority area was arbitrary, rather than being made on a straight demographic basis. It was not a simple calculation that said where Serbs constituted 50 per cent plus one of the total population, that constituted a majority. Instead, calculations were also made on the prominence of loyal, ethnic Serbs in official positions and on official bodies. For example, although Konjic was not a majority Serb area, it was designated to become Serbian territory because of the number of representatives from the Serbian community in local political bodies. On this basis, the Serbian political leadership played a particular role in arming the population. The SDS 'Headquarters' in Konjic, for example, distributed around 400 weapons to local Serbs.

The steps elaborated in the document divided those planning the creation of these governmental forms into two categories. One approach described as option (A) was to operate in areas in which the Serbs formed the majority; the other was for areas in which Serbs were in a minority – option (B). The remainder of the document dealt with the two options and envisaged each passing through different stages. The key elements of the preparation, apart from identifying appropriate candidates for particular tasks, also involved ensuring preparations for taking over control and also contacts with public security service centers in certain areas. The principal security services center was in Banja Luka, although there was one in each of the principal towns of the Serb Autonomous Regions.

In early 1992, throughout Bosnia, there were signs of a high state of readiness in JNA military preparation for the coming war. The JNA positioned troops and equipment in strategic areas. For example, just before the Bosnian referendum on independence, their tanks, artillery and anti-aircraft units were deployed on the Serbian side of the Drina River, across from Zvornik, to assist the forces inside Bosnia. In Foča, the JNA placed artillery in the surrounding hills in positions to shell the city, while in Brčko and Bosanski Šamac it activated, staffed and stationed reserve units, in Serbian neighborhoods and at strategic points.

The JNA supplied the paramilitary groups and Bosnian Serb volunteers with weapons and ammunition directly from its own inventories and redistributed the weapons it took from the non-Serb TOs. In places such as Zvornik, local Serb 'authorities', in coordination with the JNA, confronted non-Serbs who had given licenses and demanded that they relinquish their weapons. In Brčko, Bosanski Šamac and Zvornik, the JNA conducted training exercises for local Serb volunteers and paramilitary personnel. In Vlasenica, high-ranking JNA officers visited the irregular Serb military units that had organized themselves in neighboring Serb villages. In Sarajevo, the JNA's efforts to disarm non-Serbs were supported by a Bosnian government attempt to disarm the entire civilian population.

Paramilitary units were also in planning. In Zvornik, Arkan himself negotiated with the main Muslim political party and, under threat of violence, compelled the Muslims to divide the city and give the industrial section to the Serbs. In Brčko, several paramilitary groups, including The Tigers, Black Panthers and Šešelj's forces were organized in advance so that they were prepared to fight when hostilities erupted. In Foča, a unit of the White Eagles mobilized. Witnesses from several different places observed that just before the military attacks began, armed strangers appeared in their communities, some speaking dialects that were said to be unique to Serbia.

Part of the military preparation included elimination of organizations that could resist the Serb take-over. The JNA and local authorities dismantled the TOs that had a significant non-Serb membership. In Bosanski Šamac and Brčko, the TO commanders themselves assisted in dismantling their units. Where the TOs had predominantly Serb membership, they excluded non-Serbs and began the preparations. In Zvornik, local Serbs established a new TO under the command of the local JNA garrison. Serbs in the Vlasenica area formed their own ethnically 'pure' TO units as early as August 1991.

The JNA and Bosnian Serb leaders also made every effort to undermine the local police. In Brčko, the local JNA commander pressured the police chief to permit JNA soldiers to join police patrols. In Vlasenica, the Serbs exclusively staffed the police reserves and disobeyed an order from the national police authorities. Belgrade television explained the presence of numerous JNA units in Zvornik, for example, as necessary because of an impending attack by Muslim extremists.

In the face of increasingly strident demands and threats from Serb leaders, many non-Serb authorities continued to negotiate, hoping to avoid violence. They did little to prepare for the possibility of war. For example, in Brčko, after a few Muslim volunteers seized some JNA weapons, the Muslim political leadership ordered that they be returned. The Serb leaders took advantage of the non-Serbs' eagerness to negotiate and continued to talk, even though they knew that they soon would be using force to obtain their objectives.

In late 1991 Serbs in Prijedor and elsewhere in Bosnia were directed by the central SDS leadership to assemble a shadow government. Local Serb leaders were instructed to ensure their ability to control all levels of municipal life, including police, finance and communications and to ensure co-operation with the JNA. Apparently consistent with this instruction, a Serb 'Crisis Headquarters' was in place to govern Prijedor after 30 April 1992.

Another part of the preparation was ensuring the readiness of active and reserve members of the police forces, the TO and Civil Defense units so that they would have adequate numbers in place at whatever time would be appropriate. Finally, in this connection, the document indicated the need and intention to co-operate throughout with units of the JNA: instructions went out to equip wartime units with personnel, military resources and livestock reserves according to JNA designations.

During the war in Croatia, Banja Luka had been the command center for the JNA campaign across the border in western Slavonia. As JNA forces withdrew from the conflict in Croatia in early 1992, many remained in Banja Luka and in the Prijedor region. Local residents noted the increasing presence of soldiers, many speaking dialects from Serbia. Artillery and troops were deployed on Mount Kozara, where they looked down on the population below.

This area provides a clear example of the political background to the Serb takeover. The *opština* of Prijedor is in northwestern Bosnia,[4] bordered by the *opštinas* of Banja Luka (to the east), Bosanska Dubica (to the north), Bosanski Novi (to the west) and Sanski Most (to the south). Its largest town is also named Prijedor, and several small, and two large, villages, Ljubija and Kozarac, are contained in the *opština*. The *opština* is dominated by heavily forested areas and by the Kozara Mountains, which lie to the north of Kozarac. The Sana River runs through the *opština*.

Prijedor is located within a strategically placed corridor that connects Serb-dominated areas in the Croatian Krajina to the west with the FRY (Serbia and Montenegro) to the east. People of Serb

---

[4] An *opština* is a local municipality within a republic or province.

descent had lived in Krajina, the traditional name for the land on either side of the border between Croatia and Bosnia, for generations. During the Second World War, the heart of Ustasha terror against Serbs and others was in the area around Prijedor. The 1991 Serb-Croat conflict in Croatia focused on Serb claims to Krajina as an independent Serb republic with direct ties to the 'new Yugoslavia.' The corridor in which Prijedor is located took on enhanced military significance in the light of that conflict.

Before the war, the population of Prijedor was almost evenly divided between Muslims and Serbs. According to the 1991 census, the opština had a total population of 112,470 people of whom 44% were Muslims, 42.5% were Serbs, 5.6% Croats and 5.7% Yugoslavs with 2.2% others (Ukrainians, Russians and Italians). According to the report of the Commission of Experts established pursuant to Security Council Resolution 780 (1992), by June 1993, over 43,000 of nearly 50,000 Muslims in the *opština* had left Bosnia or been killed. By the end of that year, no more than 1,000 Muslims remained there.

When the multi-party system of government was established in 1990 in Prijedor, the two largest parties were the Serb SDS and the Muslim SDA. In the 1990 elections, the SDA won a plurality of seats in the *opština* assembly. Nevertheless, during the succeeding months, Serb officials, who had previously dominated key positions in the opština, resisted a reallocation of key positions consistent with the electoral results. On 11 and 12 April 1991, Serb politicians in Banja Luka, the regional center about 45 km from Prijedor and in neighboring *opštinas* proclaimed an association, or community, of Krajina Serbian Opštinas. Later on 16 September 1991, the local SDS declared the SAO Krajina.

Another example of the political and practical preparation was found in Vlasencia in eastern Bosnia. This *opština* is 50 km. from the border between Bosnia and Serbia, on the main road and rail line from Belgrade to Sarajevo and Pale. It is the regional center for bauxite mining and aluminium production. Again, the main town shares the same name as the *opština*. According to the 1991 census, the *opština* of Vlasenica had a population of 33,187 people of whom approximately 55.3% were Muslims, 42.5 were Serbs and 2.2% were 'others'. The town's population was 7,500, of which 4,800 were Muslim. There are forests to the west of the town in the direction of Kladanj, a nearby, predominately Muslim, town.

The woods became an escape route for Muslims fleeing Vlasenica after the Serb take-over in April 1992.

In the town of Milići, near Vlasenica, there is a bauxite mine, of considerable strategic importance, which employed about 2,500 people, with much of its output processed at the Vlasenica Alpro factory, where 650 people worked. Before the war, Muslims held many of Vlasenica town's leading positions, including chief of police.

Here too the two main parties were the Serb SDS and the Muslim SDA. Although Serbs in the *opština* were 42 % of the population and Muslims 55 %, the opština assembly was almost evenly divided, with the SDS winning 27 seats and the SDA 26. Nationalistic parties such as the Serbian Nationalist Party (SNR) were also present, and nationalistic leaders such as Šešelj were popular. In April 1990, the Belgrade media reported that the authorities in Vlasenica had attempted to ban a political meeting in Milići that Šešelj was scheduled to address. In January 1992, Serb leaders in several *opštinas*, including Vlasenica, declared themselves as the 'Serbian Autonomous Region of Birać.' Included were Zekovici and Vlasenica and parts of the opštinas of Bratunac, Zvornik, Srebrenica, Kalesija, Kladanj, and Živinice. Milenko Stanić, president of the assembly of the commune of Vlasenica, was appointed prime minister designate.

Before April 1992 residents of the *opština* had been able to receive Bosnian as well as Serbian television. In April Bosnian television was cut off. Belgrade television was reported to have repeatedly broadcast distorted reports designed to inflame Serbs by suggesting that Muslim extremists were intent on establishing an Islamic state in Bosnia. On 13 April, Vlasenica SDS representatives pressured the SDA leaders to agree to divide the town.

On a broad level these preparations were part of a process of action and reaction in Bosnia. Certainly, members of the Serb communities in Croatia and Bosnia, seen in some of their documents and declarations, regarded the Bosnian declaration of sovereignty and the declaration of independence as being a provocative act. However, on another level, with regard to operational questions and activities in specific areas, it is clear that there was a pattern to the churn of events in several places such as Bijeljina and Zvornik. In these cases, there was a clear act of direct provocation within the town, which provided the justification for action by the JNA. The latter in all cases had already placed artillery usually outside the town. It was also a pretext for paramilitary forces to enter the town. In both Croatia and Bosnia, there was a repeated pattern of the JNA's providing the heavier weaponry, but not having the manpower and resources to go into built-up areas and hence relying on the volunteer paramilitary forces.

Provocation was a common element in the transition from preparation to implementation of the Serb takeovers. Across Bosnia during the weeks preceding the war, local Serb politicians increased the pressure on their municipal governments. Serb leaders in Zvornik and Brčko demanded that the towns be divided into Serb and non-Serb areas. In Bosanski Šamac, the Serb party announced the creation of a local Serb 'commune' and later met with representatives of other parties to insist that they agree to establish an expansive Serb area of control. This would require Croat villagers to evacuate the area and secure a broad path from Bosanski Šamac to Brčko, within the strategic Posavina Corridor linking Serbia with Serb strongholds in western Bosnia and Krajina.

In some cities there were orchestrated incidents designed to portray the police as incapable of maintaining order, thereby preparing the way for the JNA intervention. In Bosanski Šamac, a series of explosions, including ones that destroyed long-distance cables, created a pretext for the JNA and local Serb leaders to criticize the effectiveness of the police. In Brčko, detonation of explosives on two bridges over the Sava River not only signaled the start of hostilities, but also served as a supposed justification for the JNA to usurp police functions. In Bijeljina, grenades thrown through shop windows were the pretext for action. On 29 April 1992 Radio Sarajevo reported that the Bosnian Serbs were circulating a telecopied document that purported to be the orders for the non-Serb Bosnian TO to attack the JNA. The Bosnian government immediately denied such orders and described the document as a hoax to provoke hostile action.

Television signals to Prijedor were mostly transmitted from a tower on Mount Kozara, which was protected by a fence guarded by a JNA unit. In the winter of 1992, Prijedor residents were no longer able to receive television program broadcast from Sarajevo or Zagreb, but only from Belgrade and Banja Luka. It was announced that a paramilitary group had taken over the tower and that the matter was under investigation by the authorities. Belgrade television broadcast anti-Muslim and anti-Croat propaganda, which escalated in intensity, repeatedly warning that non-Serb extremists were planning to destroy Serbs. Before the Serb take-over of Vlasenica, Serb media and local Serb leaders complained of actions by Muslim extremists. According to a soldier from the JNA Novi Sad Corps, the SDS in Vlasenica sent a telegram to the JNA asking for troops, alleging as the pretext that Muslims had killed some Serbs.

Takeover and the use of force

The first Serb attacks in Bosnia followed similar patterns. Usually, artillery was used during the initial stages. At Brčko, Bosanski Šamac, Foča, Kozarac and Zvornik, artillery units, either JNA-staffed, or trained, shelled non-Serb neighborhoods into rubble. The shelling discouraged resistance, expelled non-Serbs from targeted areas and, where resistance occurred, crushed it with a greater-than-necessary show of force. Often, as in Brčko, Bijeljina and Zvornik, the shelling was co-coordinated with street-fighting conducted by paramilitary squads.

From Prijedor to Foča, Serb paramilitary groups from outside the particular area under siege joined with local Serb irregulars to conduct street fighting, round up non-Serb civilians and secure the area. Local Serb irregulars sometimes requested the intercession of paramilitary groups, particularly those of Arkan and Šešelj. Reports indicated that Arkan's forces operated in 28 different municipalities throughout the former Yugoslavia, Šešelj's in as many as 34.

Arkan sometimes incited local Serbs through speeches and radio addresses, as at Zvornik. Arkan and Šešelj usually provided ground forces in the area, which ordinarily co-ordinated activities with JNA commanders, as at Brčko and Bijeljina. Often, JNA troops and yet other paramilitary squads worked together with Arkan and Šešelj to clear a city or town, as at Brčko, Zvornik, Bosanski Šamac and Foča. By itself, the unfettered movement of the paramilitary forces, co-ordinated with the closely timed series of attacks and provision of materiel in so many different locations, confirms that they were not acting independently.

In each location, police, broadcast and civil administration were taken over by local Crisis Headquarters, composed entirely of Serbs, which had been organized pursuant to instructions issued in December 1991 by the SDS. Acting consistent with a central instruction that required close co-operation with and support for JNA units and adopting the mantle of governmental authority, local officials worked with paramilitary units to identify and interrogate non-Serb residents and evict them from their homes.

Throughout Bosnia, as soon as Serb forces secured a location, local Serbs immediately established a Crisis Headquarters to serve as a provisional government. These worked closely with the military and usually had military representatives as members. In Brčko, the former commander of the TO became the military representative in the crisis headquarters. The Crisis Headquarters established curfews, restricted travel of local residents, dismissed non-Serbs from their jobs and positions of authority (in many cases), or allowed them to continue (in a few cases) under license, and helped identify individuals for detention. Although on a few occasions members of the paramilitary squads participated in these provisional governments, ordinarily, the paramilitary forces departed for other areas of fighting.

Once paramilitary units entered a city, they systematically identified, collected and segregated the non-Serb population. Soldiers, irregulars and Serb policemen worked together to comb the non-Serb neighborhoods. In towns like Zvornik and Brčko, the occupying troops took special care to neutralize, by arresting, killing or expelling, non-Serb political, academic and military leaders. The JNA sometimes assisted in the round-ups by broadcasting over the local radio station that non-Serbs concerned for their safety should go to the JNA garrison. Those who accepted the invitation were detained and segregated just like the rest of the non-Serb population.

Serb forces segregated the military-age men from the women, children and elderly, although sometimes all males were included with the military-age men. The segregation gave the occupying forces better control over the non-Serb population and later left the women more vulnerable to organized rape. Terror tactics, such as killings, rape and torture were used, and apparently condoned, by JNA and paramilitary commanders during the sweeps through the non-Serb neighborhoods. The terror served to intimidate and discourage resistance and also compelled non-Serbs to flee the area. After the first weeks of the war, the mention of the expected arrival of certain paramilitary squads, by itself, induced flight. Serb forces also looted non-Serb neighborhoods in an organized manner. Much of the booty reportedly found its way to the Belgrade black market.

In the occupied areas Serb forces destroyed the cultural and religious symbols of the non-Serb community. Serbs bombed and burned mosques and Roman Catholic churches and sometimes bulldozed the sites, removing all traces that a sacred building had once been there. Serb forces also destroyed houses and businesses owned by non-Serbs.

Throughout the territories they controlled, the Serbs expelled the non-Serb population. Most of those released from prison were deported immediately. The few non-Serbs who were not imprisoned and remained in their homes were harassed and came under increasing pressure to leave. Non-Serbs often had to pay significant sums for 'permission' to leave. Serb authorities required non-Serbs to sign statements that they were 'voluntarily' giving up all rights to their homes and property. In many places, including Bijeljina, Brčko and Prijedor, the Serb officials then resettled Serbs from outside the area in the homes of expellees.

The administrative structure for processing the expulsions and resettlement was operational almost immediately after the first attacks. As mentioned above, in early April, the Bosnian Serbs were already using 'official' letterheads, documentation and rubber stamps. The quick implementation of the procedures, combined with the organized and widespread nature of the expulsion program, strongly suggests central planning and co-ordination.

Prijedor, again, provides a detailed example. On the night of 30 April 1992, Serb forces seized Prijedor town, there having been no meaningful resistance, non-Serb police surrendering their arms to their Serb colleagues. The following morning, Serb flags flew from all official buildings and Radio Prijedor broadcast that the Serbs had taken over the *opština*, which henceforth would be called Serbian *Opština* of Prijedor (*Srpska Opština Prijedor*). Control of all government and business institutions was in the hands of Serb authorities. Non-Serb officials, police and government employees were suspended from their jobs, although a few retained their positions by swearing oaths of loyalty to the new Serb government.

Over the next three weeks Radio Prijedor repeatedly broadcast demands that non-Serbs surrender all remaining arms, even licensed hunting weapons. Muslim officials met with Serb authorities to negotiate a way the communities could co-exist peacefully. During this time, travel for non-Serbs was increasingly curtailed and communication lines from predominantly Muslim villages to the outside were cut. Meanwhile, JNA helicopters, military trucks and officers were observed making 'night time' visits to predominantly Serb villages. Soon afterwards, rumors spread that the Serb residents of those villages had new weapons. At the checkpoints, both Serb and Muslim, that sprang up throughout the area, the Serb guards displayed modern automatic weapons, while the Muslim guards had hunting rifles or antiquated weapons dating from the Second World War.

On 22 May 1992, during a confrontation at a Muslim checkpoint in Hambarine, a predominantly Muslim village, two Serbs were killed. The next day Serb forces launched an artillery and tank assault on the village. Most of Hambarine was destroyed and its population fled. By this time, Serb forces had blockaded Kozarac and the predominantly Muslim villages nearby. Major Radmilo Zeljaja, the local military commander, demanded that local Muslim leaders pledge loyalty to Serb authority or face imminent attack. While the Muslim leaders were attempting to negotiate a peaceful resolution, the attack on Kozarac was launched on 24 May.

Intensive shelling of Kozarac, most of which was destroyed, continued for two days, while the residents fled to the mountains and nearby woods. After two days, Muslim leaders negotiated a ceasefire based upon the surrender of the population and any weapons that remained in their hands. Behind white flags, thousands of non-Serbs emerged from hiding. Serbian soldiers and local armed citizens ordered them to form columns, remain silent and keep their heads bowed. The non-Serbs marched to Kozarac, to the taunts and curses of Serb onlookers. Some were pulled from the line and beaten or killed. Muslim police officers were particularly vulnerable. Their corpses were left beside the road as the columns marched by. Men of military age were segregated from women, children and the elderly men. Some were taken to the Prijedor police station or to the JNA barracks, where they were beaten and questioned by police and soldiers. Most of the men were sent to the camps at Omarska and Keraterm, others to the Trnopolje camp (see below).

On 30 May a small group of local Muslims and Croats launched an unsuccessful attempt to retake Prijedor town. The resistance was quickly crushed. Non-Serb residents were instructed by radio broadcast to display white flags from their homes as a sign of loyalty. JNA tanks and infantry then swept through areas identified by the flags destroying homes and gathering non-Serb residents for transport to the camps at Omarska, Keraterm and Trnoploje. In the following weeks, local armed Serbs and paramilitary bands terrorized non-Serb neighborhoods, plundering homes and collecting most of the remaining residents for imprisonment in Omarska and Keraterm. Many people were simply killed on the spot.

Neighboring villages on the left bank of the Sana River, lying within the Prijedor *opština*, were also embraced by the Serb takeover in the months after the seizure of Prijedor town. On 20 July the last pocket of non-Serb residents in the area was attacked, as Serb military forces swept through the predominantly Muslim hamlets on the left bank of the Sana River and across northern Bosnia, including the villages of Ljubija, Bišćani, Tukovići, Sredice, Hegić, Durtović and Čarakovo. Before hostilities began, there were about 20,000 Muslims in these villages. By September 1992, they were desolate.

From 20 to 26 April Serbian and JNA forces, including elements of the Novi Sad Corps, which operated from the province of Vojvodina in Serbia, took over the town of Vlasenica. Some soldiers had masks over their faces and wore camouflage. The occupation forces had armored vehicles and heavy machine guns and placed barricades and checkpoints throughout the town. Radio announcers and local officials driving through town with megaphones proclaimed that Vlasenica was now Serbian, and that all Muslims should turn in their weapons immediately. Those local Serbs who had not already been mobilized were mobilized immediately. Serbs who had JNA uniforms wore them, while others wore white armbands. Regular soldiers from the JNA were seen in Vlasenica for about the first two weeks. Reserve soldiers were present until the end of May. When the JNA withdrew, it left behind its equipment for the Serb forces that remained

Immediately after the attack, Serbs took over positions in the municipal government that had formerly been held by Muslims. All non-Serbs were dismissed from the police force. Muslims were required to have special permits from the municipal assembly or their employer to pass through the checkpoints. Searches were conducted on vehicles and personal belongings. Paramilitary forces also patrolled the town, working together with former JNA troops and locals, and searched the woods for non-Serbs. Many non-Serbs were killed in the initial takeover of the town and in the subsequent sweeps of the woods. For example, public reports indicate that in the village of Zaklopaća, uniformed Serbs killed 83 Muslims. After the Serb forces secured Vlasenica, they used it as a staging ground for attacks on nearby towns. On 1 May, for example, it was reported that artillery from Vlasenica shelled nearby Srebrenica. Just before and after the takeover, many Muslims fled Vlasenica. After the take-over, Serb municipal employees prepared lists of the Muslims who remained and went from house to house, registering the occupants.

From early May, efforts accelerated to rid Vlasenica of those Muslims who remained. Non-Serbs were dismissed from their jobs. Limits on the amount of money that could be withdrawn from banks were enforced only against Muslims. The local police called Muslim men into the police station for interrogation and beat them. Serb officials, often armed and in uniform, and civilian municipal officials or employees appeared at Muslim homes and ordered Muslims to appear at the bus station at scheduled times, or escorted the Muslims to barricades or the bus station for pickup. At the bus station, Muslims had to turn over the keys to their homes and vehicles. Then they were bussed out of Vlasenica. Municipal employees then removed the property from the Muslim homes and businesses, ostensibly so that it could be inventoried and safeguarded.

The Serbs arrested most of the remaining Muslims. Sometimes, the Serbs rounded up the entire Muslim population of a street or small area at the same time. Some people were sent directly to the camp at Sušica, to the Vlasenica jail or to a school that was being used as a makeshift prison, before being transferred to Sušica.

Concentration camps

The Serbs established a network of camps throughout Bosnia (and some prisons inside Serbia too) to serve as detention facilities for the huge numbers of non-Serbs they had collected. In these locations, non-Serb men of 'military age' and many non-Serb women were imprisoned. Some of the camps were set up in school gymnasiums and were apparently run by civil authorities, while others used regular army facilities and were run by military and police units. Women and children were often held in the camps until the Serbs transported or expelled them to non-occupied areas. In most camps where women were detained, the camp commanders organized, or at least condoned, repeated and systematic rape. According to witness reports, non-Serbs were systematically killed, beaten, raped and mutilated in all of these camps. Many camps, like Batković, featured daily beatings; others, like Omarska and Luka, appear to have operated in part as 'killing' camps, where camp commanders either participated in, or permitted the beating and killing of prisoners. The brutal conditions in all of these camps were part of a campaign of terror designed to persuade the non-Serbs to abandon their homes and leave the area. By September 1992 this design had been largely accomplished. Most of the survivors in Bosnia were eventually deported to areas beyond Serb control.

The camps came to light in July 1992, when the Bosnian government alleged that Serbian forces had established over ninety 'concentration camps.' These allegations were investigated by western and other journalists, beginning with Roy Gutman of New York's *Newsday*, who first reported their existence on the basis of interviews, but most notably by Ed Vulliamy of *The Guardian* and Penny Marshall and Ian Williams from ITN television news, both from Britain. It was Vulliamy and others who discovered a number of camps, including those in north-western Bosnia, at Omarska, Trnopolje, Manjača and Prijedor and revealed them to the world. There was argument over the term concentration camp, with the Serbs claiming that these should be called detention, or transit, camps. However the term 'concentration' was an accurate description of camps in which Muslims, as well as some Croats and some Serbs who had refused to join the Serbian campaign, were gathered together. Quite literally, these parts of the population were 'concentrated' in the camps. From the onset of the war in Bosnia there were consistent reports of camps and rape factories,' but were these 'concentration camps' along the lines of the 'death camps', that were central to the Nazi extermination policies of the Second World War? As evidence mounted that what was called 'eliteocide' – the killing in the camps of Muslims with higher education – had taken place, the argument was immaterial. By the time it came to Kosovo, these were peripheral arguments of degree.

In response to these reports, the UN Security Council appointed the former Polish Prime Minister Tadeusz Mazowiecki to head a commission of investigation into the camps and into ethnic cleansing. Later, the Security Council also created the International Criminal Tribunal for the Former Yugoslavia to carry out legal processes against those involved in ethnic cleansing and other atrocities in the former Yugoslavia.

From the beginning, the camps played a vital role in the Serbian war effort by providing a source of forced labor, as Serb troops on the front line used prisoners to dig trenches and perform other dangerous work. The Serbs also used the camp populations to increase the numbers they had available for prisoner exchanges.

The best-known, and most infernal, camps were in north-western Bosnia. Beginning in late May, thousands of non-Serbs from the Prijedor opština were rounded up and sent to camps at Omarska (a former mining complex), Keraterm (a former ceramics factory) and Trnopolje (a former school). Conditions at all of these camps were brutal, especially so at Omarska and Keraterm. The camps were organized to serve different but complementary functions. Trnopolje was the primary detention site for women, children, elderly men and those somehow considered appropriate for relatively lenient confinement before expulsion from the area. Omarska held those who were prominent in intellectual, political or business circles, including a very few women. Prisoners at Omarska were systematically murdered, beaten and otherwise degraded. Other males were sent to Keraterm, where the brutality was only slightly less intense. There was evident co-ordination between the camps, as prisoners were transferred from one to another.

The subjugation of prisoners at Omarska and Keraterm was achieved in similar ways. New prisoners were ordinarily greeted by beatings administered by the prison guards, while camp commanders looked on. Prisoners frequently were not fed for several days after arrival, and then they received meager rations once a day. At the height of summer, water was often withheld and when provided was visibly contaminated. Toilet and hygiene facilities were inadequate. Prisoners were forced to sing, and listen to, Serbian nationalist songs; at Omarska, the song '*Ko Kaže, Ko Laže, Da Je Srbija Mala?*' ('Who Says Who Lies, That Serbia is Small?') was played repeatedly. Beatings were routine, especially at mealtime and at night. Almost every night, some prisoners were killed. Corpses were stacked up most mornings, waiting to be removed by truck. At each camp there was at least one mass killing.

Most of the camp guards were from Serb villages near the camps. The interrogations there were principally conducted by police officials and teachers from Prijedor and Banja Luka. From time to time, members of special military forces and some local civilians came to the camps and administered particularly brutal beatings and other tortures. Serb officials from Prijedor, such as the newly installed police chief Simo Drljača, frequently came to the camps and there were occasional visits by SDS leaders from Banja Luka. In early August, the international press and International Red Cross were granted permission to visit the camps. Immediately before the visits, most prisoners were transferred from Omarska and Keraterm to Trnopolje or to another less severe camp at Manjača, which was already monitored by the International Red Cross. Eventually, the surviving prisoners secured their release from the camps, but only after they agreed to relinquish their property and leave the territory. A few returned to their homes. They found the Muslim intellectual and political leadership wiped out. Most also found their homes destroyed or occupied by Serbs, their mosques razed to the ground, no prospect of work and a hostile and unprotected environment. When they at last prepared to leave Prijedor, as the humiliating final experience of ethnic cleansing, they encountered countless bureaucratic obstacles and demands for fees.

The camps were not confined to north-western Bosnia. In eastern Bosnia, for example, at Vlasenica, there was the Sušica camp. This was a former TO storage facility, located on the outskirts of Vlasenica town, and run by the VRS. Starting in at least mid-June, Dragan Nikolić was commander of the camp. Estimates of the number of Sušica inmates vary, but it appears that at anyone time at least 500 people were kept there. As many as 8,000 people may have passed through it.

The camp had two large buildings, one hangar, approximately 50m x 30m, used to house all the prisoners, and another for uniforms and equipment. There was also a small house with two rooms, one used for interrogations and another where the guards ate their meals. The camp was enclosed with barbed wire and concrete posts and there were two towers with floodlights. Just outside the camp, across a creek, there were two small houses used for sick prisoners. Food was scarce and there were no showers. Usually, the prisoners were permitted outside only to eat or use the toilet. Some prisoners were brought outside to perform work. Certain prisoners guarded the others and kept order during the night. Sušica came under the spotlight by July 1992, after which many prisoners were transferred to Batković, run by the army, located in northern Bosnia. By the end of September 1993, Sušica was no longer used as a camp.

Although the focus in the Kosovo campaign came to be principally on rapid expulsion and killing, detention facilities also operated there. These included the Djeneral Janković cement factory, where around 5,000 men were reported to have been held, as well as the ferro-nickel factory at Glogovac, which had already been reported as an execution site during 1998. In addition, when NATO troops entered Kosovo in June 1999 they found some 60,000 ethnic Albanians in concentration camps created out of burnt-out villages. The five villages in question were near the town of Podujevo and most of those incarcerated in them had been rounded up in brutal campaigns to take them from mountain camps and hideouts during the previous April. These were the places to which they had fled to avoid capture or death. The villages were surrounded by troops and tanks. Anyone trying to escape was shot. Inside the camps, the inmates, including children, were given identity cards with their name, number and the name of their 'prison village.' Serb snipers in the hills overlooking these concentration camps were reported to have shot people at random.[5] Other reports of major detention centers included 20,000 Kosovans being held in a munitions factory at Srbica and reports concerning the Trepča mines.

Elimination

There were two methods by which the non-Serb population could be eliminated in pursuit of the strategic end of purely Serb territories. One was expulsion. This was often induced by demonstrative examples of the other – killing. As seen above, the brutal administrative processes for expulsion of those who had not already fled in fear ensured the expulsion of millions of Muslims from Serb-controlled parts of Bosnia. However, the most acute case of expulsion was that of the ethnic Albanians from Kosovo in 1999. As with Croatia and Bosnia, this mass expulsion was backed by cold-blooded killing.

Following a year long program of low-level ethnic cleansing – a village a day kept NATO away – in the spring 1999 Serb forces

[5] *The Daily Telegraph*, 20 June 1999.

in Kosovo initiated an overwhelming campaign of expulsion. With 300–400,000 Kosovan Albanians already refugees or deportees from Serbian campaigns during 1998, in a matter of days, Serb forces were able to turbo-charge their ethnic cleansing. This scale of cleansing was always the ultimate goal of the Serb operations in Kosovo. However it was only when a commitment to force had been made by the Atlantic Alliance that the exercise of self-restraint in order to prevent NATO action was abandoned.

In the last week of March and the first weeks of April 1999, about one million Kosovans were forced from their homes and land. This included 750,000 refugees and deportees who were given shelter primarily in the neighboring lands of Macedonia, Albania and Montenegro. Estimates suggested that up to 700,000 Kosovans were also internally displaced in Kosovo itself, unable or afraid to remain in their homes but lacking the means of escape.

The process of expulsion was rapid and simultaneously random and systematic. The random element in the systematic expulsion was the application of violence, whether beatings and rape, or murder, as well as the fact that at certain points the process would simply be stopped. The systematic quality was evident in the process by which expulsion occurred in Kosovo. MUP, JSO or paramilitary units would knock on the door of a Kosovan home. Those inside would be told immediately to leave. If they did not move fast enough they would be shot immediately. The men would generally be separated from the women and children. The former would often be shot nearby, or taken away for questioning. The latter would either be scared into fleeing, or would be taken at gunpoint to pre-arranged buses or trains to be carried to the border. In most cases, as well as extortion of money for safe passage, the Kosovan Albanians were stripped of all documentation to establish their identity. Presumably, this was so as to leave them without proof of legal right to property and citizenship – thereby enabling the Belgrade authorities to allege that those in question were not from Kosovo because they did not have the document-ation to prove it. At the border they would then be ordered from the trains at gunpoint and marched into no-man's land to cross the border.[6]

In the birthplace of the Serbian Orthodox Church, Peć, on the morning of 25 March 1999, the cleansing operation began.

[6] *Daily Telegraph*, 17 April 1999.

Although it was an important place in Serbian history, it was predominantly inhabited by ethnic Albanians. A week later the 80,000 Albanians were gone. On the first morning of the cleansing operation, VJ, MUP and paramilitary units wandered through the streets. They looted and burned shops owned by ethnic Albanians. Already some of the Albanians had begun to leave their homes to seek refuge, or to hide. The following day, the cleansing operation began in earnest. Beginning in the western parts of the town, MUP and paramilitary squads worked their way across the town, street by street, knocking on doors, instructing the inhabitants to pack whatever they could carry and to leave within half an hour. Within an hour one suburb, Kapašnica, was empty and its residents moved to the town center, before being forced to leave altogether. The same occurred throughout the town over the next few days, with many residents leaving in fear before the knock on the door arrived. There was reason to flee in fear – in one street alone fifteen people were shot.[7]

One of the most dangerous moments in the process of expulsion from Kosovo was the decision to stop it on two occasions. The first of these was on 7 April 1999. Abruptly, Serbian forces closed the borders across which they had been forcing hundreds of thousands of people for two weeks. The same refugees that had been driven to the border at gunpoint were then turned back at gunpoint. There were two reasons for this. The first was the potential to use the Kosovan Albanians as human shields against NATO attacks, the second was to limit the impact that the images of deported and distraught Kosovans had made on public opinion around the world, strengthening the resolve and commitment of NATO countries seeking to stop the ethnic cleansing of Kosovo. An implication of this second reason was ominous. It was precisely at the point when the Nazis ceased to feel able to expel Jews and other undesirables in 1942, and the war began to go against them, that they conceived of the idea of a Holocaust and began to implement mass extermination by industrial murder in the gas chambers of the Third Reich's six death camps.

The reports of killing in Kosovo were numerous. While all could not always be verified at the time, or in the immediate wake of the conflict, there was sufficient evidence from the first months of

[7] *Daily Telegraph*, 17 April 1999.

KFOR, the NATO-led military peace force, to provide sample confirmation of what had happened. With existing reports of mass graves to be investigated, new ones also came to light. It was judged necessary for international investigation, carried out by representatives from the International Tribunal in The Hague and, even before that, by representatives from governments, notably from the UK, to concentrate on fifty sites. The first waves of evidence led to the conclusion that around 11,000 Kosovans had been deliberately killed during the Serb campaign. Among the reported killings, not all of which were investigated in the first phase and so remained unconfirmed, were those of hundreds, perhaps thousands of bodies being incinerated at the Trepča smelting plant (see Chapter 8). Other incidents included the killing of sixty men in a water tank at Kutlin,[8] in southern Kosovo, as well as the discovery of Kosovan children, each shot with a bullet through the back of the head, in the village of Bela Crkva west of Prizren in the Orahovac opština.[9] This was in addition to sixty-five adults known to have been killed there.[10] There was evidence to support reports of the killing of around 100 people held at the Istok prison in Rakoš,[11] as well as video evidence backing reports of the killing of 150–160 Kosovans in Velika Kruša.[12] In the case of one group killed there, a survivor told of his own fate and that of fourteen others. They were separated from around 200 other men and taken to a barn where they were shot and then doused in petrol and set alight. This last action seems to have been intended to destroy the evidence. However, Selami Eshami was only grazed on the shoulder by the gunfire and then, having sustained heavy burns, crawled

---

[8] *Daily Telegraph*, 29 March 1999.

[9] 'Child Massacre Uncovered in Kosovo', *BBC Online Network* World: Europe at http://news2.thls.bbc.co.uk/hi/english/world/europe/newsid%5F385000/385372.stm 4 July 1999.

[10] 'The Prosecutor vs. Slobodan Milosevic *et al*.: Indictment' International Criminal Tribunal for the former Yugoslavia Doc. IT37/99

[11] Serb authorities showed 45 bodies on 24 May following a NATO attack on the prison. It was not clear at the time, however, how the deaths had occurred. Investigators exhumed bodies from a site 10km to the west of Istok. At the same time, 120 bodies were recovered at Donja Stubla. 'Bodies Recovered From Mass Grave' *BBC Online Network* World: Europe at http://news.bbc.co.uk/hi/english/world/europe/newsid_420000/420801.stm 14 August 1999.

[12] 'Erasing History: Ethnic Cleansing in Kosovo', US State Department, May 1999 p. 23.

from under the corpses that had offered him some protection once there was hope that the Serb forces had gone and the flames were unbearable. In Eshami's words, 'God saved me to come out and tell.'[13]

The Serbian campaign in Kosovo provided the material with which the International Tribunal raised an indictment against Slobodan Milošević and his cronies. This documented the killing of hundreds of Kosovans, including some of the cases mentioned above and that of 130 Kosovans from Izbica in the Srbica opština, killed in two groups, as well as others. The Prosecutor appended a list of the known names of those killed. This indictment also included action before March 1999, in particular the one incident which brought added urgency to Western policy over Kosovo, even if it did not inform policy makers to the extent that it should have done, regarding the scale and brazenness of Serbian intentions and potential regarding the ethnic cleansing program. This was the killing of forty-five men, executed with bullets through the back of the neck, at Račak in January 1999. The impudence of Serbia's approach was such that they countered the judgment of the head of the OSCE's Kosovo Verification Mission (KVM), Ambassador William Walker, by saying that the men in question had been killed in the course of fighting, whereas every indication was of execution.[14]

This shameless disregard for international opinion regarding mass murder could also be found in earlier years. In one of the very first attacks at the beginning of the Bosnian war, at Bijeljina, the approach was starkly clear. At the end of a three-day operation to capture the town, Serbian troops rounded up Muslim political activists and leading members of the Muslim community and murdered them. The same pattern occurred in countless other places, including Zvornik, as was discussed in previous sections. The most blatant act of ethnic cleansing in the conflict in Bosnia occurred near Srebrenica, under the gaze of Dutch UN troops manning the 'safe area' declared there. In July 1995 the Bosnian Serb army overcame the Srebrenica 'safe area', expelling over 40,000 Muslims – most of them already refugees from other places where they had been ethnically cleansed – and murdering thousands of men

[13] Quoted in *Washington Post*, 18 April 1999.
[14] BBC News, 23 January 1999.

of military age. The Bosnian Serb attack was relatively easily accomplished. Although there was some resistance from the small Dutch UN force, most Bosnian government troops had withdrawn some twenty four hours before the attack. As Serb troops advanced, several thousand Muslims fled. Around 15,000 people, mostly men, left through the woods from Šušnjari towards Tuzla. This column was intercepted near the village of Buljim and attacked by the Bosnian Serbs. Around one third of the group escaped to Tuzla, the remainder being trapped on Serb controlled territory.

A second group of men, women and children sought security in the Dutch UN compound at Potočari, where they remained from 11 until 13 July, and after which they were transported by bus to Bosnian government controlled territory. As the Bosnian Serb army burned and looted Muslim houses, General Ratko Mladić, the Serb military commander, personally assured the Muslims that they would not be harmed, but would be safely transported out of Srebrenica. However, as the Muslims boarded the buses on 13 July, Bosnian Serb military personnel separated the men from the women and children. The latter were escorted out of Bosnian Serb controlled territory, while the men were taken elsewhere. Although some of the Muslim men were told they would be exchanged for Bosnian Serbs being held by government forces in Tuzla, the majority were taken to Bratunac and then Karakaj where they were killed at two sites between noon and midnight on 14 July. By 23 July, one way or another, the Muslim population of the Srebrenica area had been virtually eliminated in circumstances described by Judge Fouad Riad of the International Criminal Tribunal for former Yugoslavia as 'unimaginable savagery.' Srebrenica, according to the Judge, was a scene 'from hell, written on the darkest pages of human history.' The massacre at Karakaj was perhaps the most callous act in a litany of atrocities during the war in Bosnia. In its scale, even after Kosovo, it was the single largest criminal incident.

The war on the territory of the erstwhile Yugoslav federation was fostered by military and political leaders in Belgrade. Serbian nationalism, based on the notion that all Serbs should live in one state, helped to facilitate the war's eruption. The idea of Serbian solidarity was often expressed in official Belgrade pronouncements and in the Belgrade media. This was consistent with the apparent desire of the Belgrade military and political leadership, evident from the conduct of the war, to control strategic assets and communication routes located in Bosnia, and to remove potentially un-co-operative populations from areas of Serb control. Jointly, Serbian political leaders, the Serbian Security Service, Serbian irregular units and the regular army conceived, planned and implemented an armed campaign in Croatia, Bosnia and Kosovo that involved systematic use of terror to establish the borders of a new Yugoslavia that would include significant portions, if not all, of Croatia, Bosnia and Kosovo.

The principal elements of that terror applied for strategic purpose at the tactical level comprised preparation and provocation, takeover and the use of force, mass detention in brutal and sometimes murderous prison camps, and elimination through expulsion and execution. The scale and range and consistency of the methods used to terrorize the non–Serb population in so many different areas, like the methods used to attack and secure the key communications and strategic locations, could not have resulted from a spontaneous eruption of local resentments. The process of setting up, supplying and staffing the many camps and detention centers alone required significant co-ordination and planning. The purpose of this terror was entirely in furtherance of the goal of ensuring that the population remaining in the secured area would be reliable.

6

THE ENDS: THE QUEST FOR NEW BORDERS IN THE WEST – CROATIA

Having acquired armed forces and made appropriate calculations about the balance of force and how to use the means available to achieve the desired political ends, the question of putting them to use arose. Slobodan Milošević's purpose was to alter state boundaries and structures, especially population structures. In Croatia and Bosnia, the two elements of this went hand in hand; in Kosovo, only the latter came into play. Thus, while in Kosovo the aim was to change the province's demography so as to consolidate control of existing boundaries, in Croatia and Bosnia it was to create new borders from old. Recognizing that the old Yugoslavia could not survive, the Serbian leader decided that force would be decisive in settling what came afterwards. Armed force was used in the attempt to carve new borders from Croatia and from Bosnia and to remove the non-Serb population from the land. In Kosovo, it was used simply to remove the population. Through almost a decade, Milošević and his acolytes applied force to achieve these ends. The present chapter, and the two that follow, describe each of those campaigns, illustrating how initial Serbian success, cloaked with layers of strategic ambiguity, was overturned.

The new state project in the West: carving the borders of a mini Yugoslavia for the Serbs

Immediately after the Slovenian and Croatian declarations of independence, the JNA, together with other Serbian forces, responded with armed force. While hostilities in Slovenia and Croatia began simultaneously, the initial focus was on Slovenia, where the JNA had two operational plans. The more extensive of these involved full mobilization to overwhelm Slovene forces, win control of its territory, implement a state of emergency and arrest all Slovene political leaders. This option was held in reserve. Instead, there was a far more limited operation that constituted no more than a show of force. Under guidance from Borisav Jović, the Serb who was federal president, and acting under an instruction from Prime Minister Ante Marković, it consisted of assisting the civilian authorities in the form of the federal police in securing control of Slovenia's 137 international border posts with Italy, Austria and Hungary.

As noted in Chapter 4, the JNA's assumptions over Slovenia were misplaced. The Slovenian TO proved effective against the limited force deployed by the JNA in Slovenia. Nor would the JNA escalate its deployment because Belgrade had no political commitment to tackling Slovenia – as far as the Serbian leadership was concerned, Slovenia was an obstacle best kept out of the way so that they could deal with Croatia on different terms and, it was thought, without being overstretched.[1] The international community, in the form of the European Community, took an active interest and offered to mediate. As a result, the JNA abandoned Slovenia to concentrate on Croatia.

Having been surprised by the European Community's involvement in Slovenia, the JNA re-assessed its strategy and evaluated the likelihood of Western military intervention in Croatia. It also abandoned the notion that the entire SFRY could be preserved, and thus, according to General Kadijević, the JNA decided to fight to establish the borders of a new Yugoslavia composed essentially of Serbs. Kadijević described this project, as follows, in his 1993 book *Moje Vidjenje Raspada* (My View of the Collapse):

Our assessment was not only that not a single army, including the JNA, could successfully conduct and win a war without a clearly defined state for which the army was fighting and the correct way, as contemporary warfare demands, which supports its army, but also we made the assessment that, as a priority, at the political level, we should mount a counter-offensive which would confront the destroyers of the old Yugoslavia with a new Yugoslavia composed of those peoples who wanted to live together in it and who would not allow the disintegration of such a Yugoslavia.[2]

By late 1991, after suffering disappointments in Slovenia and Croatia (Slovenian independence was a *fait accompli* and it was clear that the

[1] This is confirmed in film interviews with Slobodan Milošević and his close ally Borisav Jović (who was liaising with the JNA command) in *The Death of Yugoslavia*, Program 3, Brian Lapping Associates, 1995.
[2] General Veljko Kadijević, *Moje Vidjenje Raspada. Vojska Bez Države* (Belgrade: Politika, 1993), 132.

government in Croatia would not be toppled or persuaded to remain within the Yugoslav federation), the political leaders in Belgrade adopted a new goal consistent with that of the JNA generals: to establish a 'mini-Yugoslavia' composed of the key strategic infra-structure of the old Yugoslavia and inhabited by reliable Serb communities. This new entity was most likely to be formed as a federation of Serbian states. In its original and most extensive ver-sion, the borders would have run just south of the Croatian capital Zagreb, forming a line from Karlobag on the coast to Virovitica on the Hungarian-Croatian border. Such a state would have in-corporated the whole of Bosnia and Hercegovina, where there was some hope that the leaders of its largest, yet weakest, com-munity, the Slav Muslims, would, out of self-interest, accept the Serbian terms for the new state.

The fallback position from this plan was to consolidate borders in Croatia around predominantly Serb areas and territory adjacent to those areas that could be brought under Serbian control. In Bosnia and Hercegovina, the aim was to take control of most of the country, including all of the eastern region bordering on Serbia itself, the whole of the southern and eastern part of the country (including eastern Hercegovina) that bordered on Serbia and Montenegro, and, crucially, a large swathe of land stretching from eastern Bosnia across the northern and central parts of the country, leaving West-ern Hercegovina, by agreement with Croat representatives,[3] to hard-line leaders of the predominantly Croat population there, as well as those parts of Central Bosnia that they could secure. In the middle of this arrangement to smash Bosnia and Hercegovina, the Slav Muslims would, if they accepted the plan, be allowed to keep a nugget of territory in Central Bosnia as a 'homeland', probably within the triangle marked approximately by Bugojno, Travnik and Zenica – if they did not, they would be removed from the map entirely.

Military preparations were accompanied by political planning. Under the guidance of the Serbian Security Service, Serb political leaders in Croatia and in Bosnia and Hercegovina had been setting

[3] The story of the agreement between representatives of the Serbs and Croats at Graz in Austria in March 1992 has become well known, as has the character of a secret meeting between Milošević and his Croatian counterpart, Franjo Tudjman at Karodjordjevo in 1991. See Laura Silber and Alan Little, *The Death of Yugoslavia*, London and New York: Penguin, 1995, p. 34.

up the political framework in which Croatia and Bosnia and Herce-govina would be subjugated, or if this failed, dismembered and rid of hostile communities. There were three principle elements to this scheme: the proclamation of 'associations of municipalities', by law, and unlawful 'autonomous regions' with the designation 'Serbian'; the formal political unification of these declared 'auto-nomous regions' into 'Serbian Autonomous Republics,' with put-ative constitutional documents, setting out the claimed status of the republic, already framed and adopted, waiting only for their proclamation at the appropriate moment; and, lastly, preparation for political takeover within that framework by the secret forma-tion of 'Crisis Headquarters' as shadow local governments ready to assume power at the moment of takeover and to implement a program of action to remove their opponents.

The template for the Serbian strategic program began in late 1990 with the proclamation of the 'Serbian Autonomous Region of Krajina' by the dominant Serb population in Croatia's Dalma-tian hinterland. The Serbs in this area, with assistance from the Serbian Security Service and the JNA, had created what was ef-fectively a no-go area for the official authorities in Croatia. This 'autonomous region' was later complemented by the declaration of another, the 'Serbian Autonomous Region of Eastern Slavonia, Baranja and Western Srem,' after control had been taken of that territory in June 1991. Finally, with agreement on a ceasefire close, in December 1991 the Serbs in the Croatian Krajina declared an independent and sovereign entity, the 'Republic of Serbian Krajina' (*Republika Srpska Krajina* – RSK), with its capital in Knin, which would be a separate unit within a set of federated structures linked to Belgrade.

By the time of its declaration the RSK comprised less terri tory than the JNA intended in its original projections (which may be deduced from the lines of attack identified by Kadijević in his book, and those pursued in the military campaigns). The JNA adopted what General Kadijević called a 'modified' plan when it recognized that it could not achieve its maximum desired borders because of manpower shortage, loss of morale and the interna-tional political environment. General Kadijević and General Života Panić (at the time Commander of the 1st Military District based in Belgrade and responsible for JNA operations in eastern Slavonia in Croatia) remarked that the JNA was obliged by circumstances to stop short of its ambitions with regard to one part of western Slavonia.

In Bosnia and Hercegovina, the Serbian project followed the same pattern: political preparations began long before the war erupted. While many observers have erroneously attributed the outbreak of war in Bosnia and Hercegovina to immediate political circumstances – the Serbian campaign is seen by such authors as a reaction to international recognition of the country's full independent international personality on 7 April 1992 – the political process had begun a year earlier.

In April 1991 Serb political leaders had begun to form Serbian 'associations of municipalities' in parts of Bosnia and Hercegovina. Although challenged by Muslim and Croat politicians, there was an innocuous legal basis for this action although Serb leaders were soon operating outside the state's legal parameters. The initial move to form associations was made in a context where it was hoped that the more ideological Muslim leadership of Alija Izetbegović, leader of the main Muslim party, the SDA, might be rejected in favor of the more compromising approach to Serb concerns offered by other Muslim leaders, such as Adil Zulfirkarpašič, leader of the smaller Muslim Bosniak Party (MBO) and owner of the newspaper, *Bosanski Pogledi*. Even at that stage, while the formation of these associations went largely unnoticed outside Bosnia and Hercegovina, the implications of this development were understood perfectly by some inside it – notably the cartoonist for *Bosanski Pogledi*, who, in the spirit of Balshazzar's Feast, saw the writing on the wall: his cartoon of 18 April 1991 proclaims the Serbian 'State of Bosnian Krajina' in a graffito, while depicting Muslims in the street wearing crescent and star arm-bands, an image clearly redolent of Jews in Nazi Germany and a foreshadowing of the 'ethnic cleansing' that would come a year later.[4]

By the fall, following several months of armed hostilities in Slovenia and Croatia, the associations of municipalities were upgraded. There were declarations by SDS leaders of the 'Serbian Autonomous Regions' of 'Hercegovina' (12 September), '[Bosnian] Krajina' (16 September), 'Romanija' (17 September) and 'North-Eastern Bosnia' (19 September) and, belatedly, in November, 'Northern Bosnia.' These declarations were accompanied by calls for JNA

---

[4] *Bosanski Pogledi*, 18 April 1991.

protection. After these requests, in conjunction with existing SDB and informal army activity, the JNA formally began extensive collaboration with Bosnian Serb political leaders.

In October 1991, faced with the challenges presented by the Serbian declarations of autonomous regions – which clearly threatened the territorial integrity of Bosnia – the activities of the JNA, rising tension and, finally, emerging international acceptance of the de facto dissolution of the SFRY, the Parliament of Bosnia and Hercegovina reasserted its sovereignty. It was in the heated exchanges in this debate that Radovan Karadžić warned Izetbegović and the Muslim leadership that if they continued to affirm Bosnia's sovereignty, they would be 'annihilated' – a threat that, although seemingly made in the heat of the moment and in direct response to his Muslim opponent, in retrospect, appears to have been no more than confirmation of what was already being planned – and, indeed, implemented in Croatia, although full realization of the systematic character of atrocities had yet to be made public.

In December 1991 Bosnia applied to the European Community for diplomatic recognition and, as had been foreshadowed, the Bosnian Serbs under Karadžić moved their political and constitutional agenda forward. On 9 January 1992, the Bosnian Serbs proclaimed their intention to become independent if Bosnia withdrew from the SFRY and framed a constitution for their prospective Serb republic, which was then adopted on 28 February. This republic was said to comprise the territory in which the Bosnian Serbs claimed control – the five regions of Bosnia where they said Serbs were the dominant ethnic group.

The putative political-legal arrangements for this would-be statelet were published on 16 March in *Službeni Glasnik*, the official gazette of the Serbian people in Bosnia and Hercegovina – one of the many appurtenances of formal statehood that did not previously exist but which remarkably appeared to report, symbolize and make pretensions of legality for the state–to-be. Among the basic provisions of the constitutional document presented in *Službeni Glasnik* was one that defined the 'Serb Republic of Bosnia and Hercegovina, the state of the Serb people and of all citizens living therein', with its capital said to be Sarajevo (although at different times Banja Luka and Pale would serve as de facto capitals and certainly as seats of government). The reference to 'all citizens' was theoretically open to interpretation within a liberal and cosmopolitan tradition and was perhaps an indication that there was the possibility that any non-Serbs who were prepared to remain part of this entity might have a place in it (although in practice, this would mean remaining only on Serb terms). Article 2 indicated that the territory of this Republic was deemed to consist of the Serb autonomous regions, municipalities and so forth, as mentioned in the 9 January declaration. In terms of real Serbian intentions – that is of the new-state project – it was stated that the Republic was a part of the federal state of Yugoslavia. This indicated again that it would be a federal unit linked with Serbia and Montenegro rather than a part of Bosnia and Hercegovina. The constitution was to come into effect upon its proclamation, under article 144. The date of proclamation was to be 7 April 1992, the day of international recognition of Bosnia and Hercegovina's international status.

The evolution of these self-proclaiming states as the political, constitutional and territorial framework for the Serbian project was complemented by preparation of a different kind. This was the secret formation of shadow governments, which would immediately take office at the point the plan was put into action, and which would implement key provisions, such as the identification of key non-Serb political figures (and leading Serbs whose profile defined them as political opponents of the secret project) and arranging for them to be removed from the political scene.

Krajina, central Dalmatia and the Serbian stranglehold

Although the war proper in Croatia did not begin until after the declaration of Croatia's independence on 25 June 1991, the first action occurred almost a year earlier, in August 1990. Serbian military operations in Croatia ended five years later, in August 1995, when there was a virtually complete withdrawal in advance of Croatian attacks and an evacuation-cum-cleansing of the Serb population of the Krajina region. For much of the time in between, there were no major operations. The following sections present a strategic overview of the war in Croatia, considering the significant action at the outset and close of hostilities, as well as the limited operations in the intervening period, primarily from the perspective of the Serbian project – additional consideration of the Croatian perspective is offered in Chapter 9.

The Serbian aim through political and military means was first to remove the parts of Croatia with mainly Serb inhabitants from official Croatian control, then, later, to take control of almost all the Dalmatian coast and large swathes of the central and eastern regions of the country. Ultimately, as major operations were launched in August 1991, there would be three sub-theaters within the Croatian theater of operations. One was in the east, close to the border along the River Danube between Croatia and Serbia. A second was in the far south, along the thin strip of the Dalmatian coast surrounding the elegant town of Dubrovnik and bordering on Montenegro and eastern Hercegovina. Each of these is discussed later in this chapter. The third sub-theater was the largest, incorporating the Serb-heartland of Krajina and regions to the north of it, and is considered in the present section. This was the keystone to the Serbian project, the foundation for territorial extension across the Croatian-Slavonian plain to the east, and westwards and southwards to the Adriatic coast.

The key initial objective, based around the Serb-populated areas, was to break Croatia in two. This would weaken Croatian control in the central part of the Dalmatian coast around Split, a mainly ethnic Croat area open to the Adriatic Sea, but hemmed in by predominantly Serb communities in the mountainous hinterland that dominated the coast. The more that Serbian action could disrupt north-south communications in Croatia, the weaker Croatia's position would be.

Already, from 17 August 1990 or thereabouts, a problematic security situation prevailed in Croatia in an area which began some 80km to the north of Split on the Dalmatian coast and extended further north. This disrupted road and rail communications running north-south in the hinterland of the Dalmatian coast. Rail services were stopped and did not resume until August 1995. In some places, barricades and roadblocks erected by Krajina Serb rebels restricted travel. However, in the initial period – and to some extent, throughout, limited road travel remained feasible in this region. One major route, the Adriatic Highway, running along the coast, was not affected until 18 August 1991, after which stretches of it were no longer passable. Until then, this might have involved taking a longer and possibly more roundabout route, it meant that road communication remained an option. While some travel was possible, communications in Croatia were disrupted and the country was in many senses cut in two – psychologically, if not entirely physically.

When the war proper began in June 1991, the impact of the

Serbian project began to take its toll on Croatia. The security situation in Krajina between August 1990 and June 1991 failed to have anything more than a minor impact on tourism, which continued on the Dalmatian coast, despite the security situation inland, bringing in total revenue worth $2.2 billion in 1990. In 1991, by contrast when there were major armed hostilities, estimates of tourist-derived income fell to no more than $300 million, almost all of which was income for the period to June.[5]

The JNA's presence prevented Croatia's Interior Ministry forces from entering these areas and also prevented movement to or from some Croat communities, which were surrounded and left without basic necessities (such as food, water, electricity and medication). In the case of the Knin Corps, based in the principal town in Croatia's Krajina region, devolution of authority meant that, as early as the summer of 1990, the Corps command gave the local Serb population access to JNA arms and equipment to assist in the creation of Serb 'no-go areas', which the JNA also protected. This was one of a series of instances in which the JNA was deployed outside barracks with the formal task of preventing inter-ethnic conflict, which in terms of the military command, was understood, in Federal Secretary for Defense Kadijević's words, as 'protection and defense of the Serb people outside Serbia.'[6]

In the second half of August 1991, the JNA markedly escalated the war in Croatia, as it began the war for new borders. The principal lines of attack corresponded with those identified by General Kadijević:

The directions of offensives of the main forces of the JNA to be aimed at liberating Serb areas in Croatia and the JNA garrisons, which are in the depth of Croatian territory. Cut Croatia on the routes Gradiška-Virovitica; Bihać-Karlovac-Zagreb; Knin-Zadar; Mostar-Split in that order. The strongest formation of the armored mechanized forces should liberate East Slavonia, and then swiftly continue its attacks moving westwards, connect itself with the forces in Western Slavonia and go on to Zagreb and Varaždin, i.e. toward the border of Slovenia. Simultaneously, the strong forces from the direction of Herceg Novi-Trebinje should blockade Dubrovnik from the ground and reach the River Neretva valley, thus coordinating its activities with the forces moving towards Mostar-Split; after the seizure of certain installations, secure and keep the border of Serb Krajina in

---

[5] EIU *Country Profile*, 1995–6, London: Economist Intelligence Unit, 1996, p. 44.

[6] Kadijević, *Moje Vidjenje Raspada*, pp. 114 and 127.

Croatia, withdraw the remaining troops of the JNA from Slovenia and subsequently withdraw the JNA from Croatia.[7]

By Croatia, Kadijević appears to mean the territory that would remain after the borders of the new entity had been secured. In line with Kadijević's outline, the conflict intensified noticeably in late August, with the siege of Vukovar in Eastern Slavonia by JNA artillery beginning on 19 August 1991 and that of Dubrovnik shortly after, following operations in southern Dalmatia launched simultaneously.

Encirclement and siege were hallmarks of the Serbian campaign. Although the notorious cases in Bosnia and Hercegovina would become better known – Sarajevo, Srebrenica, Bihać, Goražde – and both Vukovar and Dubrovnik were emblematic of the conflict in Croatia, the approach was first applied as part of the broader campaign in the central Dalmatian heartlands of what would be the self-proclaimed Republic of Serbian Krajina, near the village of Kijevo. There were three sub-theaters in the Croatian phase of the war – Eastern Slavonia, southern Dalmatia, and the Krajina-central Dalmatian hinterland. The template of encirclement, siege and ethnic cleansing was laid at Kijevo in the Krajina sub-theater. In April 1991, as an ethnically Croat village, it was completely surrounded by JNA units, under the command of the then Colonel Ratko Mladić, and local Serb forces. For two weeks, all supplies were cut off and no inhabitants allowed in or out. Although discussions with the Croatian authorities brought to an end this apparently bizarre event, Kijevo had gained no more than a stay of execution. Once the war was really under way and the plan outlined by Kadijević was being put into force, it was the first of many places where non-Serb populations were surrounded and removed.

Within a region otherwise dominated by the Serbs, Kijevo was not only an ethnic stain, it was also a key communications point, which if left to its own devices could disrupt Serbian access to areas they controlled. This had given Kijevo importance from the outset – and explains the treatment meted out to it in the spring. With armed conflict under way, the Croats in the village had, not surprisingly, sought to prevent Serbian forces assisting the ethnically Serb villages that lay behind it. Kijevo was again surrounded and its connections to the outside world were cut off. An ultima-

7 Ibid., p. 135.

tum was delivered: the town's Croatian police had to surrender to the local Serbian leader, Milan Martić, the ex-police chief in Knin, otherwise they would be forced to do so. The Croats refused, so Mladić launched a heavy assault on the village, with artillery bombardment by the JNA that destroyed much of it, before moving in to overrun and occupy Kijevo. This was the first time that the JNA had so starkly and openly used its destructive capacity in the Serbian cause (it had previously claimed a 'Yugoslav' and 'peace-keeping' role), and it was the starting point of the Serbian campaign that Kadijević had planned. Meanwhile JNA units were on the move, siege, bombardment and ethnic cleansing being deployed in support of the Serbian project throughout the three sub-theaters in Croatia.

The war in the central sub-theater came to a stalemate relatively early on. While the Serbian-JNA campaign had consolidated predominantly ethnic-Serb areas and expanded these somewhat, it had proved impossible to extend operations successfully to achieve some of Kadijević's key objectives. Although the Serbs had created a salient of controlled land that divided northern Croatia from central-southern regions, they could not press on to capture major objectives on the coast, notably the naval headquarters town of Split, which had a relatively easy war, as the limits of Serbian capability were demonstrated. In the period of civil disturbance and violent unrest prior to 25 June 1991, after which full-scale hostilities broke out in Croatia, communications in the Split region remained largely intact although journeys by road involved longer and more indirect routes. Sea access remained unimpeded but rail links from the Dalmatian region to the northern parts of the country were cut.

After the onset of the war proper in late June 1991, Croatia was effectively cut in two. Split lay some 70–80 km to the south of the salient of Serbian controlled territory, running from the border with Bosnia and Hercegovina to the east, almost to the coast in the west. This area of land included all major communications routes, with the exception of the Adriatic Highway ('Magistrala', Route E27). This was the one north-south route not under Serbian control, but it began to be impeded by fighting after 18 August 1991 and was rendered impassable by the destruction of the Maslenica Bridge on 11 September 1991. The small strip of coast near the Maslenica Bridge, which was not under Serbian control was easily dominated by their artillery.

However, most of the Adriatic Highway remained open and the

area in range of Serbian artillery was avoided by use of a ferry via the island of Pag and back to the Dalmatian coast by bridge. In January 1993, the Croatian Army achieved control of the Maslenica area. This permitted a pontoon bridge to be constructed in place of the destroyed bridge, thus restoring the possibility of north-south road traffic entirely by land. This possibility was constrained by the continuing threat of Serbian artillery and the fact that inter-mittently the bridge was destroyed (for example on 13 May 1993), then rebuilt, and so forth. Road access through the area generally became easier after January 1993, however. This hindered the Serb-ian campaign, but only a detail of what remained a stalemate that seemed to favor the Serbian side. The fine thread of road, some-times interrupted by Serbian power, was a significant improve-ment for Croatia, but it still left the whole central region under Serbian control, or domination.

Occasionally the Split region was directly affected by hostili-ties. Although Split was initially a Serbian objective, lack of resour-ces limited action there to one week, on or around 20 September 1991.[8] There was some naval bombardment and a series of attacks on Split international airport. The area was also directly affected by the naval blockade imposed by the JNA navy of all Croatian ports, beginning on 15 September 1991. The JNA Naval Com-mand at that time was located at Split. During the blockade, shell-ing occurred only on two days. Along with the naval action against Croatia's other ports, the blockade in this area was being scaled down by 23 September 1991; although the JNA would not with-draw from naval bases, such as Zadar till 12 October 1991, and maintained the blockade against Dubrovnik till December 1991, the general blockade after 23 September 1991 was relaxed, ena-bling ports to be used again.

The attempt to subdue the Croat-inhabited territory in Central and southern Dalmatia relied extensively on disrupting economic activity and life in general, given the lack of opportunity and manpower to take the region by force. As well as communications, many power-generating stations, within range of Serbian artillery, were attacked and put out of action and otherwise there were efforts to disrupt the power supply. For example, the main transformer station at Bilice-by-Šibenik, which carried 700 megawatts, had been

---

[8] *Slobodna Dalmacija*, 21 and 22 September 1991.

destroyed by 27 September 1991, as was another installation at Konjsko (an estimated 15km north-east of Split).

The Croatian authorities in an effort to ease the Serbian squeeze constructed gas-fuelled power stations in Dalmatia during the early 1990s, although it is not clear whether this provided significant relief. In addition, it is conceivable that there could have been independent sources of electricity supply in the area. According to Yugoslav military information, there would normally be a separate power supply for major military facilities.[9] Although this clearly could not include all military and military-related facilities, it would probably have meant separate power supplies for Split airport and for the city's naval facilities. During much of the second half of 1991, some of these facilities, notably the Naval Command in Split, were not under Croatian control although Split airport was. After the JNA withdrew from Croatia at the end of 1991, JNA facilities came under Croatian control. The Peruča Dam facility was the principal supply source for the Dalmatian coast and it came under effective Serbian control from 17 August 1990. In February 1992 the Serbians claimed Croatian artillery fire had damaged the transformers and oil barrels. Nonetheless, there was no total interruption of supply while it was under Serbian control and most areas received electricity supply from this facility.

However, the power supply from the Peruča Dam was affected to a sufficient degree for it to be a principal concern of the Croatian authorities, as is evident from the fact that it was one of only three objects of limited operations by the Croatian Army in January 1993, the first such operations for a year.[10] Ironically, electricity supplies depending on the Peruča Dam were interrupted indefinitely after Croatia's operation to capture it in January 1993. Until that point, although it had been run by the Serbs, there had been some supply, simply because they needed the power supply as well. Before conceding the dam, however, Serbian forces mined it. This put it out of action and thereby aggravated the position of the Croat communities along the coast.

It is hard to gauge the exact impact of restricted power supply

[9] *Vojna Enciklopedija*, vol. 2, Belgrade: Izdanje Redakcije Vojne Enciklopedije, 1971, p. 649.

[10] Other operations at this time were focused on the Maslenica Bridge, which was vital for restoring continuous north-south road communication, and access to the Zemunik airport near Zadar – discussed both above and below.

in the period of major armed hostilities after June 1991. Whatever the precise impact at any one stage, overall the impact was significant, but never decisive. Croatia was badly damaged and the coastal communities in the central and southern regions suffered. But, odd exceptions notwithstanding, power was available for half the day or longer across most of the Dalmatian region. This may be deduced from figures for 1993, the worst year for power cuts, which reflected the combined impact of the losses of power caused by the destruction of the Šibenik and Peruča Dam facilities and cutting of supply from Bosnia and Hercegovina during the Croat-Muslim conflict there. In June 1993, consumers of electricity were legally restricted to using 50 per cent of the normal kilowattage, which was further reduced in October 1993.[11] In 1993, the Dalmatian coastal region experienced power cuts of up to 10 hours per day.[12] These cuts primarily affected areas around Zadar and had little effect on the Split region – for which supply from the power stations near Zadvarje appears always, or almost always, to have been available, as well as other sources.[13] Thus the overall impact of the Serbian campaign was some way short of applying a critical blow in central Dalmatia.

Eastern Slavonia and the siege of Vukovar

It was in the Eastern Slavonia sub-theater that the worst of the war in Croatia was most apparent. The siege of Vukovar provided the headlines but this was the focal point of a conflict in which local social-ethnic tensions had led to an upsurge of mutual hostility, a situation exacerbated by the insertion of paramilitary forces, recruited in Serbia by the Security Service and led by figures such as Vojislav Šešelj and 'Arkan' (see Chapter 3). These paramilitary forces were charged with acts of provocation, intimidation and close combat and, not wholly unreasonably in Serbian terms, with defending Serbian communities.[14]

[11] Letter from Croatian Ministry for Energy and Industry to Hrvatska Elektro-priveda, 26 June 1992.

[12] Reported in Ivo Bičanić, 'The Croatian Economy: Achievements and Prospects.' *RFE/RL Research Report*, vol. 2, no. 26, 25 June 1993, p. 34.

[13] It should be noted that the large military presence in Split of the Logistics Headquarters of the UN force in Bosnia and Hercegovina after September 1992 was not affected by power shortages at any stage of its deployment.

[14] See Chapter 9 on some of the Croatian action against Serbs, including personal involvement by senior Croatian figures.

Their first significant act had been in May 1991, on the eve of the declarations of independence by Slovenia and Croatia, and the onset of war. In the prologue to war, Serbian paramilitary units had trapped Croatian MUP units in Borovo Selo, a village near Vukovar. As a provocation, two Croatian policemen were seized in order to set a trap. The special police from the MUP drove into the heart of Borovo Selo, where the Serbian paramilitaries were lying in wait and soon had them trapped. Although the Croats put their buses to good defensive use and fought fiercely for half an hour, they were eventually overwhelmed. Twelve policemen were not only killed but also, as a sign of that which was to be expected later, mutilated (throats were slit, noses cut off, eyes gouged out) – echoes of Ustasha practice in the Second World War. The petrified Croatian leadership tried to maintain calm and did not publish the images of the mutilated policemen in an effort to prevent a further increase in tension.[15]

Eastern Slavonia, which includes the towns of Osijek and Vukovar, has a specific character in terms of history and inter-communal relations. It is the border area between Croatia and the Serbian province of Vojvodina, which was established as the boundary between both Croatia and the Republic of Serbia, but also between Croatia and the 'People's Autonomous Region' of Vojvodina, which was within Serbia. At the end of the Second World War the border was disputed between the Anti-Fascist Council and the communist party of Croatia, on the one side, which had a strong independent character and, on the other, the local district committee of the communist party of Srem in Serbia and the People's Autonomous Province of Vojvodina. It was, overall, a disputed area, one characterized by major population changes in terms of its ethnic mix in the latter stages of the Second World War. The border was defined by a commission, but remained a matter of contention.

One of the first acts of ethnic cleansing in the Yugoslav war of the 1990s also took place in this area, at Ilok, a town with a significant Croat population. In September 1991, the JNA rounded up the local Croat community and ordered it to leave and, with

[15] By chance, I made the trip from Belgrade to Zagreb, passing by Borovo Selo, the day before and had an interview arranged with Darko Bekić, then an advisor to President Tudjman, who showed me pictures of the policemen and explained the position. It was clear that the Croatian authorities feared a heavy blow from the JNA immediately – hence their desperate need to buy time and calm public nerves.

the assistance of international monitors, the population was removed. Serbian forces were also removing ethnic Croats from their homes in other parts of the region. The legacy of the Second World War was clear not only in the actions of the armed forces on either side, but also in the social-ethnic fabric of the region. At a local level, there was violence between extremists on both sides, with intimidation, the firing of weapons, and both arson and bomb attacks on the houses of members of the opposite community. In some cases, rocket grenades were fired at Serb houses – including attacks in 1991 led by the Croatian Defense Minister Gojko Šušak.[16] Conditions were propitious for the violent intimidation of ethnic Serbs and for the forcible expulsion of other ethnic groups by armed Serbian forces.

The Vukovar siege was central to the war in Eastern Slavonia. With ethnically mixed villages, such as nearby Borovo Selo, providing a platform for action, on the Serbian side, and, on the Croatian side, the major towns of Osijek and Vinkovci lying behind and relatively protected by it (though by no means free from attack). Vukovar was pivotal. Vukovar had a population of around 40,000, of which ethnic Croats constituted a small majority, and it found itself under siege and heavy bombardment for 89 days in the fall of 1991. Surrounded by up to 40,000 Serbian troops – around the same size as the town's population before the attack – some 1,500 people defended the town. The defense of Vukovar was iconic for Croatia, both domestically and internationally – although there were differences of perspective between those active in the town's defense and the leadership in Zagreb (see Chapter 9). For the Serbian besiegers, it was an important strategic cornerstone to gaining control of the region. First, it was the launching point for the planned push on Zagreb and Varaždin; and, second, it was seen by the Serbian generals as dear to the Croatian command – the 'battle for Vukovar was a battle with the command of Croatian forces, who wanted to hold Eastern Slavonia and Baranja at all costs.'[17] However this strategic keystone proved difficult to capture, hence demonstrating the limitations of Serbian forces.[18]

[16] *The Death of Yugoslavia*, Program 3, Brian Lapping Associates for the BBC, 1995.

[17] Kadijević, *Moje Vidjenje*, p. 137.

[18] Aside from problems of mobilization, heavy losses were incurred during the Vukovar operations. The Novi Sad Corps' number of deaths was published – 1,300. From this Tus extrapolates total Serbian losses in the Vukovar operation

The final assault on Vukovar was under the overall command of General Života Panić, Commanding Officer of the 1st Military District, headquartered in Belgrade. The boundaries of the Serbian campaign in Eastern Slavonia were those of the 1st Military District, giving the impression that Serbia was seeking the same border. The problem the Serbian-JNA force faced was lack of manpower. Capturing built-up, urban areas is notoriously difficult. The environment favors defenders, so long as they can maintain the willingness to fight and the resources to do so. The greater the destruction caused by an attack, ironically, the better the position of the defenders becomes. Rubble, broken walls and immobilized vehicles create a multitude of defensive positions, in addition to those built by troops. The only way to capture such positions, aside from the surrender of those defending, is through street-to-street, close combat. This form of intensive combat requires high quality troops for close quarters fighting, but most Serbian-JNA forces in the area were conscripts, who could be used for standoff artillery bombardment and for control of the surrounding area – although this still presented problems in terms of morale and skill levels.[19] They could not, however, mount a major assault on the town. For one thing the great socio-political impact of the heavy losses that could be expected in operations of this kind would be untenable; for another there was a lack of quality and competence – as a largely conscript force it had neither high morale, nor was it highly skilled. It was simply unsuited to this form of combat. This problem affected the Serbian campaign throughout the war in Croatia and in Bosnia and Hercegovina. At Vukovar, as in other cases, it was the 'volunteers', the paramilitaries, who provided the wherewithal for such operations. High-caliber forces, these paramilitary groups were the shock troops of the Serbian campaign – not only were they used as an elite infantry-cum-special force for difficult attacks, but they also constituted the most brutal *avant garde* and implementation force of ethnic cleansing (see Chapter 3).

It was the correlation of means and ends that defined the siege of Vukovar and would do so elsewhere. Lacking resources, in terms

---

of 5,000. General Anton Tus, 'Rat u Sloveniji i Hrvatskoj do Sarajevskog Primirija' in Branka Magaš and Ivo Žanić (eds), *Rat u Hrvatskoj i Bosni i Hercegovini, 1991–1995* (Zagreb and Sarajevo: DANI for the Bosnian Institute, 1999) p. 85.

[19] Col. Milan Miletić, 'Iskustva iz Upotrebe Artiljerije u Ratu 1991 Godine', *Vojno Delo*, vol. XLVIII, no. 2, 1996.

of both quantity and quality, the rationale underpinning operations based on encirclement, siege and bombardment becomes more
comprehensible. With force commanders mindful of preserving
the well-being and morale of their troops, as best they could, to
say nothing of their lives, a standoff siege made sense. It guaranteed force conservation, especially as artillery materiel was in plentiful supply, and offered the prospect that, eventually, at the end of
this long, low road to occupation, the objective would be accomplished at far less cost than an attempt to capture it directly, through
street-to-street fighting, which might also fail – the record of urban areas captured in direct combat since the Second World War
is not long.[20] The siege of Vukovar was dreadful and the destruction of the town near complete. There have been allegations that
the bombardment itself constituted a war crime, but the key issue
here was one of judgment – had to be based as much on an assessment of the strategic calculations involved as on the physical evidence of devastation.[21]

Vukovar was utterly destroyed. As the end approached, and after
three months that had included almost constant artillery attack (both
shells and rockets) and, in some periods, aerial bombardment, if
any building remained intact, this was remarkable and went un-
observed. Giant flames engulfed large parts of the town ahead of
the final advance, with the Croatian defenders of the town putting
up house-to-house resistance against a well-trained and brutal
Serbian force, spearheaded by Arkan's Serbian Volunteer Guard –
'The Tigers.' After its capture a veritable crime cemented the fall
of the town that had been dubbed the Croatian 'Stalingrad'[22] –

[20] The only clear-cut case appears to be the Iraqi capture of Khoramshar during the Iran-Iraq war. That most formidable of armies, the Israeli, failed in its
attempt to capture Suez City in 1973. Saigon fell in the Vietnam War, but this
owed more to a case of collapse and surrender.
[21] These are all issues taken up in the final chapter and have particular relevance to the siege of Sarajevo, the capital of Bosnia and Hercegovina, over which
General Stanislav Galić was indicted by the ICTY.
[22] The significance of Stalingrad can be grasped by reference to the titles of
John Erickson's monumental two-volume study of the Nazi-Soviet war: the first
volume is called *The Road to Stalingrad* and the second is dubbed *The Road to
Berlin* (both London: Weidenfeld and Nicolson, 1983). The titles mark the turning
point in the war and its final destination point, the place where it had begun.
The experience and meaning of Stalingrad has been captured in an enormously
popular book by Anthony Beevor – *Stalingrad*, London: Viking, 1998.

and, like Stalingrad, despite the different outcome, came to be regarded as a turning point.[23]

As Arkan's force took over and the ghost town's inhabitants left, moving on foot in columns escorted by paramilitaries, the Tigers handed over control to the JNA as it followed them into Vukovar. This included handing over the hospital, where there were around 400 men, including medical staff and patients, as well as many local political figures and members of the defense force who had taken refuge there. They had done so in the belief that they would be better protected, because the transfer of people from the hospital would occur under international observation. This did not happen. Instead, all 400 were removed from the hospital while negotiations with the staff were in progress. Around 300 of them, mainly men, were taken by bus to a JNA barracks to the south of the town, where 15 of them were released when identified as hospital staff, or their relatives. The remainder were taken to the nearby Ovčara farm, where, after being terrorized and beaten (during which two died and seven were released after interventions from ethnic Serbs), 200 of them (198 men and two women) were murdered by JNA and Serbian paramilitary troops and dumped in a mass grave. At least 50 other people who were taken by the JNA from the hospital on the morning of 20 November 1991 were not seen alive again. The International Tribunal in The Hague indicted three JNA officers who were apparently implicated in this terrible event. The three were Colonel (later General) Mile Mrkšić, Major (later Colonel) Veselin Šljivančanin, and Captain Miroslav Radić. All three belonged to the Guards Brigade, which occupied Vukovar, with Mrkšić in command. Šljivančanin was in charge of security and commanded a special military police battalion, while Radić had command of a special unit involved in the murderous operation.

The Vukovar hospital massacre was one of the starkest and most high profile incidents during the conflict in Croatia but by no means the only one. The clear purpose of ethnic cleansing could be measured across Eastern Slavonia and in the other sub-theaters. At Vočin, in another infamous though less well known case, 48 Croats were not only killed, but shot through the eyes, mutilated and left on display, as a message to others, both in the town and elsewhere,

---

[23] Norman Cigar, 'Srpski Ratni Napor i Okončanje Rata' in Magaš and Žanić (eds), *Rat*, p. 232.

that there was a simple choice – stay this way, or flee. As Paul Garde has suggested in a detailed account of events in Croatia, everywhere 'the scenario was the same' during the summer and fall of 1991:[24] Dalj, Četkovci, Balinac and Čoljug in Eastern Slavonia; Krajlevčani, Dragotnici, Hrvatski Šuntić and Skela (all in the Banija region) are among the examples he cites. The presence of mixed populations in many areas, as well as clear examples of Croatian actions to equal those of the Serbian campaign – including the hands-on, Šušak-led provocations in spring 1991 – often occluded the Serbian goals and the strategy for achieving them. The campaign in southern Croatia was also obscured under the haze of 'ethnic conflict' – a meaningless label that was often applied, but diffused clear appreciation of the war.

Southern Dalmatia and the siege of Dubrovnik

The case of southern Croatia offers much in terms of understanding Serbian military war aims. The operations in the Konavli area in southern Dalmatia, the narrow hinterland to Dubrovnik, begun at the end of September 1991 were the only ones in Croatia carried out by the JNA alone – those in eastern Slavonia also involved irregular units organized in Serbia, those in central Croatia and Krajina involved local Serb populations. The region was largely undefended by Croatia, which had limited capability and seems not to have anticipated an attack on an area in which there had not already been fighting associated with claims focused on local Serb communities. However, it was strategically vital to the JNA. Without control of the southern tip of this region, the Prevlaka Peninsula, use of the naval base at Kotor in Montenegro would be difficult, given that entry to the bay would be controlled on the northern side by Croatia. Boka Kotorska – the Bay of Kotor – would be the only port left to the Yugoslav military if Croatia became independent but access to it would not be secure.[25] Control of the northern side of the Bay was vital.

Having seized control of the region easily, Dubrovnik remained

---

[24] Paul Garde, *Vie et Mort de la Yougoslavie*, Paris: Fayard, 1996, p. 316.
[25] The Yugoslav Navy had bases at Pula, Šibenik, Split, Ploče and Kotor Bay; in addition there were small facilities on some Adriatic islands.

a blot on the landscape. At the end of August the military began to besiege the old Adriatic port from land and sea. Naval vessels progressed up the coast destroying one house after another, as shells also rained on the town itself. In retrospect, that which appeared to be spiteful and senseless had a clear purpose: to drive out an unwanted and potentially hostile population – that is, to cleanse the territory.

Army units secured the territory lying behind Dubrovnik. Had the aim been to capture the town, this could have been achieved in an afternoon by dropping a parachute battalion inside the walls of the old city, where there was next to no defense. By comparison, Vukovar, under siege simultaneously, was a large town with some defensive capability and proved difficult to capture. However, it may be inferred that in both cases the aim was not to capture but to drive out the population to ensure that strategic control of territory afterwards would be unhindered – that is, that there would be no potential opposition that could use political disruption, terrorism or guerrilla tactics to thwart Serbian control.

This strategy was not apparent at the time, but may be inferred in the light of subsequent events. These are the continued expulsion of non-Serb populations from the occupied territories in Croatia under UN protection and the war in Bosnia and Hercegovina where, in combination with a virulent strain of Serbian ethno-nationalism which had begun this practice as early as the spring of 1991, 'ethnic cleansing', the label for this strategy, became a by-word. The conduct of the war in southern Croatia, where the JNA acted without Serb paramilitary or local forces, illuminates the JNA's war aims. For example, the operations in the Konavli area in southern Dalmatia, and the apparently spiteful shelling of Dubrovnik were intended to secure a strategic area and to drive out an unwanted population.

The JNA rapidly took control of the whole region, destroying houses and driving out the inhabitants. Then, although Dubrovnik was virtually undefended and, uniquely among the built-up areas in Croatia, could have been easily captured, the JNA stopped short. Instead, it subjected the city to weeks of bombardment from land and sea. There is no conventional military explanation for this conduct. The only evident goal was to instill terror and to drive people away.

*Ceasefire and Storm: the decay and demise of the
Serbian campaign in Croatia*

The Serbian campaign in Croatia was largely successful: by November 1991, around one quarter of Croatia was under Serbian control. By November, pressure for a ceasefire was growing. In part, this was external pressure from the EC – above all, the prospect that EC member states would soon recognise an independent Croatia carried with it the peril that some, or even all, of them would assist Zagreb under what might be a newly acquired right to individual and collective self-defense. But pressure was also being generated by the conflict itself. Croatia had organized itself defensively and was fighting back to the south of Zagreb, around Karlovac, and in Western Slavonia, in particular, where for the first time Croatian forces were engaging above the tactical level.[26] Meanwhile, crucially, Serbian forces had reached their limits and were starting to be overstretched. Thus, by November growing Croatian capability met diminishing Serbian strength and created a stalemate. From then on, negotiations began, under the auspices of Cyrus Vance, the former US Secretary of State, acting as a UN envoy.

On 2 January 1992, the Croatian government and the JNA command signed the 'Vance Plan', a UN-brokered ceasefire agreement. This was the end of major armed hostilities at this point, but not the end of the war. The Serbian side had been largely successful, but not completely so: having dropped plans to capture Zagreb and the greater part of Croatia, the campaign still had failed to achieve its fallback position, with objectives in Western Slavonia unattained.[27] The Croatian side, if it could find a way to do so, had much pride to restore and the goal of regaining control of one quarter of the country. Over the next three and half years, there would be constant activity, including mostly unnoticed skirmishing and, more significantly, the development of better trained, organized and equipped armed forces by Zagreb. The ceasefire was underpinned by the presence of a large UN peacekeeping force, UNPROFOR, deployed in four sectors – North, South, East and West.[28]

---

[26] Tus 'Rat' in Magaš and Žanić (eds), *Rat*, p. 86.

[27] Kadijević, *Moje Vidjenje Raspada* , p. 142; Col. Gen. Života Panić, 'Iskustva iz rata u Jugoslaviji moraju se analizirati na stranicima Vojnog dela', *Vojno Delo*, nos 1–2, January–April 1992, pp. 222–3.

[28] See James Gow, *Triumph of the Lack of Will: International Diplomacy and the Yugoslav War*, London: Hurst, 1997, Ch.5.

After the January 1992 agreement, there were few notable military operations until those in 1995 that brought the war to a close. The only significant engagements on Croatian territory occurred in May and June 1992 (although the former continued for several months), January and September 1993, October 1994, May 1995 and, finally, August 1995. There were also isolated incidents, sometimes in response to Croatian low-level actions, sometimes seemingly spiteful acts of terror. This latter included use of Serbian long-range artillery (range *c.* 25km) and surface-to-surface rockets (range *c.* 45km). The latter were concentrated in UNPROFOR Sector North, from where they were used against the outskirts of Zagreb in September 1993 and May 1995. These apparently random and terrorist-like actions led to the indictment of the RSK leader, Milan Martić, by the International Tribunal in The Hague.[29]

The engagements on Croatian territory during 1992–3 were quite limited and have been deemed to have had no more than a domestic political purpose – and that, largely, in reaction to events in Bosnia and Hercegovina. The first of these, Operation *Tiger*, was launched on 18 May 1992, its objective being to end the Serbian grip on Dubrovnik and its hinterland. This operation continued until 23 October, mainly at a low intensity. The 159-day operation ended when the order was issued to cease the attack, which while having created some breathing space, had not prevented Serbian artillery from Trebinje, across the border, in eastern Hercegovina, from intimidating and pinning down Croatian forces. Shortly after Operation *Tiger* began, a second operation commenced to occupy the 'Pink Zones' – these were the areas agreed under the ceasefire and peacekeeping deployment plans and were around the edges of the UNPROFOR sectors. While not part of the UNPAs, under the terms agreed, neither Croatian, nor Serbian, forces would enter these demilitarized zones. Unlike the drawn out Dubrovnik operation, this one was completed inside 24 hours.

The two successful operations in 1993 were significant morale boosters and regenerated popular support for the government of Franjo Tudjman – the first of them, with transparent party-political timing, occurred just two weeks before elections in Croatia. This was the operation to seize the Maslenica Bridge, in January. Apart from the positive effect this had on morale in the HV and in Croatia more generally, it was also a learning experience. It was

---

[29] 'Prosecutor vs. Milan Martic' IT-95-11

a clumsy and naïve operation, involving a frontal attack along the whole line of defense, where there had been no reserve force in the operational zone. The HV attacked with all forces, was initially successful as it rushed to occupy the territory taken from Serbian control, but then experienced a counter-attack, in which the HV was driven back again, leaving the town of Zadar vulnerable to Serbian forces. There was no reserve force in the operational zone – one had to be transported from Osijek, in Eastern Slavonia, where forces were also needed. While the bridge was occupied, as discussed earlier, it remained continually vulnerable to Serbian artillery attack and the practical benefit of capture was often limited. Moreover, in the course of the 85-hour campaign, one brigade alone suffered 150 deaths.[30]

The second operation, during 1993, focused on the 'Medak Pocket.' The focal point of the operation was the town of Gospić. Gospić had been subject to attacks in 1991, when forces under the command of General Mirko Norac were reported to have massacred at least 38 Serbs – reports that would lead to the General's being indicted for war crimes in Croatia, amid much public protest, in 2001. Again, during the successful 1993 operation to control the pocket, there were accusations of atrocities committed by HV units – allegations which led to the indictment by the ICTY, made public in July 2001, of one of several ethnic Albanians serving in the army, General Rahim Ademi.

Against the background of these limited, less than accomplished, operations, those in 1994 and 1995 betrayed the signs of an armed force that had begun to acquire some proficiency. While this development was exaggerated by some – for example, Admiral Davor Domazet 'Lošo', who proclaimed that Croatia had become a regional power,[31] it was nonetheless salient in shaping the final stages of the war in the West. The August 1995 operations by the Croatian armed forces led to their recapturing the territory of the Republic of Croatia (as well as success in Bosnia and Hercegovina, as will be seen below) and terminating Serb control.

The first of the two key operations, *Flash* (*Bljesak*), occurred in May. In less than three days, beginning on 1 May, Serbian

[30] Ozren Žunec, 'Operacije Bljesak i Oluja', in Magaš and Žanić (eds), *Rat*, p. 95.
[31] Davor Domazet, 'Lošo' 'Završne Operacije Hrvatske Vojske – uvjerljivost vojne moči i(li) Promjena strategijskog odnosa', *Hrvatski Vojnik*, 22 July 1997.

forces were swept out of Western Slavonia. Using an element of surprise, the Croatian Serb armed forces were in no position to mount sustained resistance, cut off, as they were, from both the Krajina heartland of the RSK, with its border to Bosnian Serb-controlled territory, and Eastern Slavonia, with its border to the province of Vojvodina, in Serbia itself. The strike was quintessentially military. First (in contrast to the Maslenica Bridge operation), there was no single frontal assault. Instead, two principal and two subordinate lines of attack were used, each well protected. This created strength and flexibility. The swift attack split the OS RSK forces and then drove them from key high ground at Lipik and Pakrac, before additional forces completed the rout, with resistance being offered only by one light brigade of the OS RSK. When their resistance ended, the OS RSK 18 Corps collapsed and both it and the Serb population in Western Slavonia fled into Serb-held North-Western Bosnia. Not only had their forces been routed, but, according to the astute Croatian military analyst Ozren Žunec, they had been humiliated.[32]

This was the most complete defeat suffered to date by the Serbian camp, and command changes followed soon afterwards. In one of the clearest examples of the way in which the purportedly discrete Serbian armed forces in Croatia, Bosnia and the Federal Republic of Yugoslavia (Serbia and Montenegro) remained parts of one organic whole, the Deputy Chief of Staff of the VJ in Belgrade, General Mile Mrkšić was appointed to command the OS RSK. Initially seen as a move to strengthen the defensive demeanor of the OS RSK, in fact, his role was quite the reverse. His true mission was to manage the Serbian withdrawal from Croatia. Thus, when Operation *Storm* (*Oluja*) began on 4 August, it was over within 48 hours, largely because Serbian forces, and civilians, were mobilized to flee the land that had been so often proclaimed as 'historically Serbian' by nationalist politicians and outside observers alike. Thus, although the Croatian operations were swift and carried the hallmarks of mobility and penetration, they were not really tested – and the same was true of the early joint operations, which had begun in July, with the Bosnian army. There was no resistance, for the most part – Žunec notes that in some areas, where strong, theoretically high quality forces were deployed, they did 'not lift

---

[32] Žunec, 'Operacije' in Magaš and Žanić (eds), *Rat*, p. 101.

a finger to prevent the HV' advance.[33] Croatia and Croatian forces were jubilant, flushed with pride at their newly acquired and manifest prowess. In truth, their prowess had not been tested.

There continued to be pockets of local Serbian resistance around Lika and Kordun into the fall, with remnants of the OS RSK who had not withdrawn exploiting the mountainous terrain to make life difficult for HV units seeking to gain complete control of the territory. These exceptions went unnoticed, or forgotten, by most Croats as the country revelled in satisfaction at the success of *Storm* and the establishment of control of most sovereign territory.[34] As much as these clashes continued to take the shine off the HV's success, there was another, more serious, blemish on the record, namely the conduct of forces in the newly captured areas around Knin whose behavior left their honor and caliber open to doubt. Some older Serbs, attached to their land, had decided to stay and take their chances. They were found with their throats slit and their homes burned. Thus, the HV's success was stained with the blood of murdered Serbs who had remained – suggesting that the same might have happened to the others, had they stayed.

Serbian strength had evaporated. There were two keys to explaining this turn of events, neither of which was predicated on the quality of the HV. The first was the decision of Slobodan Milošević to seek an end to the war. Some Western military and political figures believed that he had already told his generals, including General Mladić, that the war had to be concluded by late 1995, in the interests of securing Serbian gains from being wasted still further and capitalizing on the economic control and regeneration program that Belgrade's chief banker Dragoslav Avramović had put in place – something indirectly confirmed by his former aide, Borisav Jović.[35] The second was the fact that Belgrade had realized from an early stage that it had insufficient strategic depth to defend Krajina and the other areas in Croatia.[36] The area adjacent to the Serbian province of Vojvodina remained under Serb control for some time after the formal end to hostilities, when

---

[33] Žunec, 'Operacije' in Magaš and Žanić (eds), *Rat*, p. 103.

[34] Confidential Author Interview with a Reserve NCO, September 1995.

[35] Cigar cites an interview in which Jović states this. 'Srpski' in Magaš and Žanic (eds), *Rat*, p. 241.

[35] Radovan Radinović, 'Odmazdom do Pobede', *Duga*, 5 November 1993.

the UN Transitional Authority in Eastern Slavonia (UNTAES) managed a transfer of control, completed in 1998, under an agreement that had staved off an HV attack on the area (one that might not have been so successful as Operation *Storm*, given the strategic depth provided by Serbia's proximity).

The Serbian position over defending Krajina was alternated by a crucial land operation that affected the outcome of the war in the West – and arguably the most important operation of any type. Indeed it went largely unnoticed at the time, even by the most astute and experienced observers.[37] This was the joint HV/HVO-ABiH seizure of Kupres, in November 1994. And perhaps, curiously, this vital operation with regard to the position in Croatia – and the only significant Croatian military engagement of that year – occurred in western Bosnia, where it was also the pivotal moment in the land war there and a watershed in the outcome in that theater. It signaled the Serbian potential for collapse: the Serbian campaign for new borders in the west, taking territory in both Croatia and in Bosnia and Hercegovina, was undone by this one operation, in Bosnia and Hercegovina.

---

[37] One British general, who otherwise applied splendid strategic analysis to the war, was bold and honest in conversation in the spring of 1998, saying he had missed the significance of the operation.

7

THE ENDS: THE QUEST FOR NEW BORDERS IN THE WEST – BOSNIA AND HERCEGOVINA

By the time the Croatians had reestablished control over most of their country, the balance had also tipped against the Serbian campaign in Bosnia and Hercegovina. The two campaigns were complementary. In some ways this mirrored the unity of Serbian ambition in the two countries – seeking to establish ethnically pure territories under their control that would be severed from Croatia and Bosnia and Hercegovina. The joint Bosnian-Croatian ground operation for the Kupres Heights, discussed in Chapter 9, was the key moment in changing the territorial disposition in both theaters. However, as will be seen below, despite the use of siege and ethnic cleansing to conserve forces and hold territory, and notwithstanding the assertions of many critics that the Serbian campaign in Bosnia and Hercegovina was undone by those joint Croatian-Bosnian operations, as argued in the last part of this chapter, in reality initial Serbian success was undone by NATO airpower. NATO's *Deliberate Force* air campaign rendered the Serbian military impotent and, for the first time, unable to control events.

Serbian strategic preparation: the campaign in Bosnia and Hercegovina

As the war in Croatia intensified in 1991, the JNA mobilized Bosnian Serbs into the JNA in Bosnia and Hercegovina, as it co-coordinated with Serb political leaders to incorporate the Territorial Defense Forces (TOs) in Serb-dominated areas. The mobilization was judged by General Kadijević to be of 'vital significance' for the JNA, because 'the Serb people in Bosnia and Hercegovina, by its geographical position and size, [is] one of the keystones for the formation of a common state for all Serb people.'[1]

[1] Kadijević, *Moje Vidjenje Raspada*, p. 144.

172

In the following months, the JNA mobilized Serbs through constant maneuvers in the Bosnian countryside and deployed units at major communications points. This was followed by large troop movements from Serbia and Montenegro into Bosnia and Hercegovina, and from bases in Bosnia. Military preparations were in a high state of readiness by January 1992.

In September 1991, the Bosnian parliament questioned the deployments, the JNA responding that it was 'defending Yugoslavia', and engaged in 'peacekeeping.'[2] The JNA continued to strengthen its position in Bosnia and ordered the potentially unreliable TOs, whose membership reflected the ethnic composition of their respective regions, to surrender their weapons, which were often redistributed to mobilized elements of the Serb population.

On 15 January 1992, the EC Advisory Commission under Robert Badinter advised the European Council that the situation in Bosnia would be clarified if a referendum were to be held on the question of independence. Bosnia held a referendum on independence on 29 February and 1 March 1992 in line with the recommendation of the European Community. 63% of eligible voters participated, of which well over 90% opted for independence. Bosnian Serb political leaders boycotted the referendum and declared its results invalid. The SDS, with the support of armed irregular units, prevented delivery of ballot boxes in some areas, while the air force dropped leaflets urging support for the boycott.

After announcing the referendum results, President Izetbegović declared Bosnia independent and again on 6 March 1992 called for international recognition. On 6 April 1992, the EC decided to recognize Bosnia, and did so the following day, 7 April, as did the United States and Croatia, along with Canada a day later on 8 April, and other members of the international community in due course. On 7 April 1992, in Banja Luka, Bosnian Serb leaders declared the independence of the 'Serbian Republic of Bosnia-Hercegovina', with its putative capital in Sarajevo, and went on to claim by force more than two thirds of Bosnia's territory. Later, in August, they changed the name to 'Republika Srpska'. The pattern established in Croatia was followed – that of declaring autonomous regions and then later proclaiming a republic, which, it was intended, was then to be united with a federated set of Serbian

---

[2] *Delo*, 12, 21 and 24 September 1991.

territories. As with the self-proclaimed Serbian 'republic' in the Krajina region of Croatia, the RSK, the international community did not recognize the new Bosnian Serb entity and a brutal war in Bosnia ensued.

The Bosnian Serbs, working to Belgrade's design, responded politically and militarily to the international independence of the country. Politically, they did so by formalizing their self-proclaimed Serbian Republic in Bosnia and Hercegovina in August, renamed Republika Srpska – the name by which it continued to be known to the end of the war and beyond the Dayton Peace Accords of 1995. The Bosnian Serb entity effectively declared its formal association with Serbia and Montenegro through the constitution, which had been enacted in January 1992, and demonstrated its link militarily by co-operation with the JNA before the latter was divided into the VJ and the VRS, when they jointly began the armed campaign to secure all major communications and access points into Bosnia, so as to create a frame for military and political developments.

The principal objective of the JNA and Serbian armed forces at the beginning of the campaign was to take control of entry or major communication points in Bosnia and Hercegovina. Thus in the first weeks all the major conflicts occurred at places such as Bijeljina or Višegrad, which, once under their control, would enable free access for Serbian movements into Bosnia and Hercegovina or, in some cases, such as Bosanski Brod, would prevent access from outside for those seeking to thwart the Serbian campaign.

JNA army units stationed in Bosnia, paramilitary groups from Serbia and Serb-controlled territory in Croatia, and Bosnian Serb irregular forces launched attacks at key points throughout Bosnia. Between March and May 1992, the JNA, aided by paramilitary groups such as those led by Šešelj and Arkan, engaged in coordinated attacks to secure the main entry points into Bosnia, as well as major communications and logistics lines at, for example, Bosanski Brod (27 March), Bijeljina (2 April), Kupres (4 April), Foča (8 April), Zvornik (8 April), Višegrad (13 April), Bosanski Šamac (17 April), Vlasenica (18 April), Brčko (30 April) and Prijedor (30 April). The offensive left the core of the newly independent Bosnian state surrounded and the periphery under JNA and Serbian military control. There were many (very likely well-founded) rumors of an operational plan, named RAM – the Serbian word for 'frame'. Incontestably, these initial operations to ensure control of access into and out of Bosnia established a frame around the periphery of the country, within which the remainder of the campaign was conducted. As the attacks progressed, Serb forces drove out non-Serbs and 'disloyal' Serbs from occupied areas. This was ethnic cleansing.

One aspect of the processes affecting the JNA, discussed in Chapter 3, had a direct strategic impact on the Serbian campaign in Bosnia and Hercegovina, serving to obscure Belgrade's leadership of, and responsibility for, the war. This was the decision to avoid international responsibility, if at all possible. The JNA formally ceased to exist. The decision to divide the JNA into the VRS and the VJ was announced on 4 May 1992, to take effect from 19 May 1992, from which date it formally became two armed forces. One was designated the VRS, the army of the Bosnia Serbs, the other, the VJ, the army of the newly declared Federal Republic of Yugoslavia, that is Serbia and Montenegro. In practice, the two substantially remained one and the same.

Important steps were taken to facilitate this end. Some months prior to this action in May, the Serbian political leadership and the JNA command redistributed JNA personnel so that, JNA soldiers serving in Bosnia and Hercegovina would be, as far as possible, Bosnian Serbs and that all Serbs who were not from Bosnia and Hercegovina would be transferred to units in Serbia and Montenegro. This was done so that the Serbs in the JNA in Bosnia and Hercegovina could then be said to be an army of Bosnian Serbs, rather than the army of Belgrade. The decision was taken on 5 December 1991 by Slobodan Milošević, at that stage President of the Republic of Serbia, and Borisav Jović, the representative of Serbia to the then defunct or rump Federal Yugoslav State Council (or, more formally, the collective Presidency). The latter was more than merely the Serbian representative, however. He was a close political ally, collaborator, and confederate of Milošević.

Following the decision, General Kadijević, the head of the JNA, was instructed to implement it.[3] In his diary entry, Jović makes the Serbian leadership's thinking explicit: 'Practically, all those who

---

[3] This is confirmed by the diary entry for 5 December 1991 in the selected diaries of Borisav Jović, published as the volume, *Poslednjih Dani SFRJ: Izvodi iz Dnevnika*, Belgrade: Politika, 1995, p. 420. Although Jović published this diary, there are relatively few copies of it available, because the Serbian political leadership, namely Milošević, had it withdrawn from sale as soon as it became clear what it contained.

remain in the JNA are Serbs and Montenegrins, but from all the Serb lands. When Bosnia and Hercegovina is recognized internationally, the JNA will be declared a foreign army and its withdrawal will be demanded, which it is impossible to avoid.' Thus on 5 December 1991, four months before the onset of war, Milošević and Jović had anticipated what would follow from international recognition of the independent personality of Bosnia and Hercegovina. Their decision enabled the overall project to continue, but it was disguised in order to sow confusion over the nature of the armed conflict that they were planning.

The political and military leadership in Belgrade wished to expand the territory under their control amid the dissolution of the Yugoslav federation and the independence of some of the republics which had formed that federation. The intention was to bring together Serbia, Montenegro and the Croatian and Bosnian Serb statelets. Quite clearly, therefore, the formal-but-fictional division of the JNA into successor armies was motivated by the desire to prepare for a situation in which JNA units deployed in Bosnia and Hercegovina were ready to annex parts of Bosnia and Hercegovina for the Serbian new state project. After any international recognition of Bosnia and Hercegovina's independence the JNA would be seen as a foreign occupying force, hence the decision was taken as a means of camouflaging the JNA's role, that is to confuse the issue and to allow observers, as well as their own political leaders, to say that this was, in fact, no longer the same army. By dividing the JNA and by having primarily Bosnian Serbs in the army in Bosnia and Hercegovina, it could be argued that there were two discrete armies, although the new army in Bosnia and Hercegovina had the same structure, and was left with almost all the capabilities of the JNA, as its units had been constituted in Bosnia and Hercegovina before the mytosis.

Belgrade's role was to conceive of and to plan the execution of this project, which would see these territories detached from Bosnia and Hercegovina and re-attached to Serbia or Montenegro. In addition to deception regarding the JNA, it also included the deployment of paramilitary groups organized by the Serbian Security Service in Bosnia and Hercegovina before and during the war, and support provided by VJ-designated units, that is those elements of the old JNA in Serbia and Montenegro, going into Bosnia and Hercegovina. In this regard it is important to characterize the relationship between the Bosnian Serbs and Belgrade correctly as one of unity. In effect, the Bosnian Serbs, without prejudice to the genuine political dilemmas they faced in Bosnia and Hercegovina (and which provided fuel for the Serbian campaign), were acting as agents for, or proxies of, Belgrade in prosecuting an armed conflict. The Bosnian Serbs clearly had their own political concerns and desires, but it was Belgrade that conceived of military operations and saw that they were put into practice, using Croatian and Bosnian Serb manpower in an armed campaign funded, run, and ultimately commanded from Belgrade.

The Bosnian Serbs within the JNA, and within and associated with certain political structures – such as the SDS – were loyal to Belgrade's project. They were effectively (and often in the military, contractually) acting in the interests of, and pursuing a course set by Belgrade, although in doing that, they may well have undermined what would otherwise have been a genuine political grievance for Serbs in Bosnia and Hercegovina regarding their status and constitutional position – an authentic political problem that questioned the legitimacy of existing arrangements for the country's governance. It undermined their political case because it was couched in the framework of an aggressive armed campaign and because they were acting for Belgrade against Bosnia and Hercegovina. Those who were loyal to the Belgrade project did not encompass all Bosnian Serbs. A minority of Serbs sided with the Bosnian government, while others fled Bosnia and Hercegovina and yet others simply became politically disenfranchised because of this course of action.[4]

Serbian operations and strategic limitation in Bosnia and Hercegovina

All parts of Bosnia and Hercegovina were affected by the war, although the swift Serbian takeover meant there was little or no action in large swathes of territory for much of the time. The precise way in which any part of the country was affected depended on whether

---

[4] One consequence of the Bosnian Serbs becoming implicated in Belgrade's resort to organized violence was that the Bosnian government and its predominantly Muslim leadership regarded them as potentially hostile and therefore would either treat them as prisoners of war or suspect them of being agents of Belgrade and therefore, until their status was determined, deemed to be hostile.

it was easily taken over, was engaged in armed hostilities or was on the other side of the line.

In some areas, such as around Konjic, the JNA operated for only a relatively short period. In these cases it did so until May 1992, although once specifically JNA units had been moved out of Konjic bombardments using JNA artillery continued under the VRS standard. In others, the JNA and then the VRS, sometimes with unmistakable support from the VJ, conducted particularly vicious actions – as was witnessed in the long sieges of Sarajevo, Srebrenica and Bihać, or in the harsh ethnic cleansing operations in Bijeljina, Foča and Zvornik, the last-named being a good and unusual example of the Serbian approach. It is a good example because the conduct of Serbian forces was typical. It was highly unusual because the Serbian forces allowed the occupation to be filmed, as well as failing to bar outside observers, such as Jose Maria di Mendiluce, a senior representative of the UNHCR, who testified to the inhumanity in Zvornik that day. The town marked the principal crossing point between Serbia and Bosnia, with Mali Zvornik ('Little Zvornik') on the Serbian side of the River Drina. Zvornik was surrounded by JNA troops, including artillery emplaced on (and later firing from) the Serbian side of the river, and an ultimatum was delivered to the Muslim mayor of the town: disarm the local police and surrender. He was told directly that the town would be Serbian and that he had no alternative but capitulation.

The tanks surrounding the town left little room for maneuver. The JNA provided the heavy support for the operation while Serbian paramilitary forces, organized by the Serbian Security Service, and including Vojislav Šešelj's Chetniks, mounted this operation on direct orders from Belgrade. It was Šešelj who, once the attack was completed within a day, read out the list of names of the Muslims to be killed. The television crew filmed the Serbian military police and paramilitaries identifying Muslims in the town, capturing the palpable fear that the incipient regime of terror induced. With blood on the streets and in homes, soldiers filled four or more trucks with the corpses of civilians – men, women and children. At the end of the operation 2,000 people were missing and all those left alive were expelled, reducing the Muslim population from 49,000 before the war to nothing – and drawing to an abrupt end centuries of Muslim life there.

After 19 May 1992, despite the splitting of the JNA and the formal device of creating a Bosnian Serb army, the VJ continued to play a role in Bosnia and Hercegovina. The VJ, that is, the element of the erstwhile JNA which was in Serbia and Montenegro, contributed actively to the prosecution of the Serbian new-state project in Bosnia and Hercegovina in terms of its personnel and supplies. It did so in a number of cases to support the VRS, that is the JNA units in Bosnia and Hercegovina, where it was called on to provide additional support or forces of a particular kind (often elite special forces). The ghost of the JNA remained, despite its apparently schismatic succession. Some Muslim prisoners were even taken to camps in Serbia – for example, some of those captured at Bosanski Šamac were transported to military jails at Batajnica and Sremska Mitrovica by military helicopter. The ghost effectively continued to act as one body, even though a degree of operational autonomy was given to the commander in Bosnia and Hercegovina, General Ratko Mladić. Nonetheless, for the most part he maintained regular contact with Belgrade.

There were several instances over the years where VJ troops, specifically VJ troops, were clearly identified in the field. These included VJ troops located in Serbia openly becoming involved in the conflict in January 1993, when they brought down artillery fire on Bosnian government troops pursuing Bosnian Serb forces to and across the Drina. Shortly afterwards thousands of VJ personnel, MUP and irregulars crossed the border into Bosnia and Hercegovina with more than 100 tanks and armored vehicles. These troops were sent to accelerate operations in the Drina Valley and reinforce the Posavina Corridor at Brčko – the vital lifeline to Bosnian and Croatian Serbs lying to the west of the corridor. At least 4,000 troops were devoted to securing this *sine qua non* of the Serbian project. At later stages, VJ troops and new equipment were clearly identified in eastern Bosnia and in February NATO aircraft enforcing the 'No-Fly Zone' over Bosnia and Hercegovina responded to one of the purest demonstrations of the continuing unitary character of the three Serbian forces derived from the old JNA. The mission was against Serbian aircraft violating the ban. At this point, a Serbian air operation was launched involving all three forces: pilots serving with the VJ air force were transferred from Podgorica in Montenegro to Udbina in Serb-held Croatia, from where they set out to fly missions for the VRS against targets in Bosnia.

A few months later in May, when the VRS made a push on Goražde (see below), brand new VJ equipment was used in the attacks which could only have been mounted with forces entering from Serbia and, especially, Montenegro (the only road through Čajniče towards Goražde came from Montenegro – meaning, at the very least, that VRS troops had transited through Serbia and Montenegro), and elements of the Niš and Užice Corps participated directly in the battle. There were many other cases where evidence of the Belgrade military's role emerged. Belgrade's commanding position could also be attested by events after hostilities ceased. For example, a report by Ambassador James Pardew, the American special representative for arms control agreements at the Dayton Peace Accords, noted that one of the problems faced in the Republika Srpska was that it was still effectively one army with Belgrade.[5]

There was a special and close relationship between the Bosnian Serb military command and the military political leadership in Belgrade. Belgrade devolved considerable command authority to General Mladić in the theater. He knew well that the objectives were to prosecute the armed campaign and, as far as possible, to do so without bringing Belgrade's role into question. This meant disguising Belgrade's involvement at all costs, wherever possible. Because Mladić was an 'insider', part of the *Vojna Linija* organized by the Serbian security service within the old JNA, he understood fully the strategic requirement to allow the fiction of separation between the Bosnian Serbs and Serbia to be maintained. The government of Bosnia and Hercegovina, unsurprisingly, considered itself to be engaged in an armed conflict with a foreign army, despite the formal division. They were at war with a foreign power – Serbia and Montenegro, the Federal Republic of Yugoslavia. On 22 June 1992, the President of Bosnia and Hercegovina, Alija Izetbegovic made an, official proclaimation to this effect.

Counter-offensives were mounted by the weak Army of Bosnia and Hercegovina and by local Croat forces of the HVO, supplemented by units from the HV. These occurred both in western Hercegovina and in central and northern Bosnia from the outset of the war – although joint Croat-Bosnian efforts were abandoned from around July 1992 until late 1994, while ABiH and Croatian forces were engaged in a fierce struggle in central Bosnia. From April 1993 until the end of the year, Croat and Bosnian Government forces, rather than fighting broadly in alliance, as had been

---

[5] Ambassador James Pardew, *USIA Worldnet*, 14 October 1997.

the case, fought each other. In this period the main fighting between these former allies was in central Bosnia. This conflict ensured that the VRS was less pressured than might otherwise have been the case. With the focus of the war on the HVO-ABiH clash, overstretched Serbian forces were able to hold their positions – though, as discussed below, they found it increasingly difficult to extend them.

At the beginning of the war, in western Hercegovina, Croatian forces, including over 5,000 (and at one stage as many as 20,000) regulars from the HV, were operating jointly with the Bosnian army. In a six-week campaign, the siege of Mostar was broken on 4 July 1992 and the Serbian camp's forces were pushed back several kilometers beyond the town into the Serbian strongholds of eastern Hercegovina. Serb inhabitants in several areas were obliged to flee. However, after this point, Serbian positions were consolidated because the HVO withdrew all support from the Bosnian army, leaving Serbian forces to the east and south of the Neretva relatively untroubled.

In central and northern Bosnia, units of the Bosnian armed forces operating out of Tuzla carried out successful operations in the summer and autumn. Whereas Tuzla had been coming under siege at the end of May, Serbian troops were then forced back 25–30 km to the north and 15 km to the east by September – putting the town at the limit of range of most Serbian artillery to the east and beyond the reach of guns to the north. Indeed, the operations to the north were particularly successful, combining with Croatian units moving from north-west to south-east to harrass the crucial Serbian supply corridor across northern Bosnia.

The critical battles were at Brčko, Orašje and Bosanski Šamac, as well as at Gračanica and Gradačac, the objective being the vital Serbian corridor, which linked Serbia with the Serbs in western Bosnia and in Croatia. These Bosnian army attempts on the Posavina Corridor, the lifeline for Serbian forces in the west of Bosnia and in most of Croatia, could never be completely successful, although at times they compressed the corridor to no more than a 25 km breadth, leaving it vulnerable to artillery fire. The key Serbian objective was always to keep the corridor open and, where possible, to widen it. However they failed to create a wider corridor, incorporating a great swathe of territory running some way to the south of Tuzla, designated a 'Safe Area' by the UN Security

Council, after spring 1993, as well as one of the key cities held by the Bosnian government and moreover held up to the international community as testimony to the multi-cultural character of Bosnia before the war.

The hallmark of the inadequacies of the VRS and the limitations of the Serbian campaign were defined by the failure to create a huge arc of Serbian-controlled territory across north-eastern Bosnia. Following the pattern of Serbian attacks, in which towns or pockets of resistance were gradually encircled and the circumference of the resisting area slowly reduced, like a puddle evaporating, Mladić's intention was to cut a second corridor to the south of Tuzla, along the River Krivaja, between Olovo and Maglaj. If successful, this would have split any connection between the two major towns held by Bosnian Government forces, Tuzla and the capital, Sarajevo, and would have enabled Mladić to close in on Tuzla, until it could eventually come under VRS control. Maglaj was a strategic finger of high ground on the frontline between the VRS and the ABiH in central-northern Bosnia, while Olovo was the most westerly point of VRS control in eastern Bosnia. To have linked the two points via the Krivaja Corridor would have allowed the VRS two logistics lines to forces in Western Bosnia, in addition to facilitating the constriction of Tuzla.

The additional logistical line would have been particularly important not only for the new dimension it would offer generally, but also for three other principal benefits. The first of these was that Olovo lay only 30 km to the west of Han Pijesak, the nerve center of the VRS and, indeed, the whole Serbian military, including the VJ. Designed as the real wartime and operations headquarters of the old JNA, this was the key point in the Serbian military infrastructure, with deep underground command, control and communications and intelligence facilities, linked by deep-laid land lines and a vast network of tunnels. Second, Olovo lay on the main communications axis from the parent command and control center in Belgrade into central Bosnia – meaning that support could be more easily and more quickly channeled to forces in the west, through Zvornik and Olovo, if needed. Third, the corridor would have allowed Mladić considerably greater mobility of his limited forces – as it was, if he wanted to shift forces from eastern and southern Bosnia to reinforce the Posavina Corridor, or through that corridor, to carry out operations against the ABiH 5th Corps in its stronghold around Bihać in northwestern Bosnia, then he had to take the long route, through Serbia itself, with the assistance of the VJ; the Krivaja Corridor would have allowed faster and more direct reinforcement and movement of forces. However, despite Mladić's attempts, little progress was made. The VRS became overstretched and in fall 1994 diverted troops to relieve pressure on the Posavina Corridor directly, rather than indirectly by opening a second thoroughfare.

The lack of Serbian forces was telling. At its own highest (and inflated) estimates, the VRS had 100,000 personnel. Outside military estimates put the highest troop level at 86,000 – a figure that peaked when VJ units were inserted to reinforce the VRS, but was likely to be closer to 60,000 in practice. Even had the force level been 100,000, the arithmetic did not add up easily, with the need to control over two thirds of Bosnia and a frontline more than 1,000 km in length. This posed a serious question for General Mladić, regarded as being among the thirty best active generals in the world (although also regarded as crazy with it), and his colleagues – 'how to fight?'[6]

Sieges, safe areas and Serbian strategy

Unable to conduct more classically elegant operations – involving concentration of forces, surprise, maneuver and speed to capture positions – Mladić had no qualms about taking an uglier, more cumbersome, quasi-medieval approach. As in Croatia, the superabundance of weaponry available to Serbian forces could be used to encircle and besiege towns. The purpose, ultimately, was to win by demoralizing the opponent. The point was to tie down enemy troops and to paralyze ordinary civilian life. The mechanism by which this would be achieved was 'Drive them crazy and fry them,'[7] the key example of this approach being what happened to the capital city, Sarajevo.

The siege of Sarajevo dominated the war in Bosnia and Hercegovina and to a large extent, it obscured conflict in the rest of the country to the outside world. Only in moments of exceptional

---

[6] Filip Švarm, 'Komandant Glavnog Štaba Vojske Republike Srpske', *Vreme*, 9 May 1994, reproduced in Ljiljana Bulatović, *General Mladić*, Belgrade: Svedočanstvo, 1996, p. 171.

[7] Bulatović, *General Mladić*, p. 172.

atrocity did the conflict around places such as Srebrenica distort the focus on the capital. Sarajevo became a celebrity city – known everywhere for its predicament and visited by international celebrities seeking to show solidarity with the beleaguered inhabitants. The siege began as the war in Bosnia began and continued until the very end of the war, when a ceasefire was agreed, following NATO air sorties and the use of artillery by the British-French-Dutch Rapid Reaction Force moderated only for four months at the beginning of 1994.

There was a strategic logic to the use of siege, as explained above. It made sense, given the weaponry available, the relative shortage of manpower and the perfectly understandable military desire for force preservation. The shelling of the city was also not necessarily by definition irrational: Sarajevo was an objective of the VRS, it was the political and military center of gravity for the Bosnian side, and it contained armed forces that were defending the city and firing at the Bosnian Serbs – and who were even unscrupulously co-locating military positions close to hospitals, so as to draw fire onto them and generate international outrage (as if there were not enough already) at Serbian conduct. The city provided legitimate targets. The key question was whether action against those targets was legitimate – a topic that will receive further discussion in the conclusion.

Mladić's approach may have been dictated by the strategic equation of aims and resources, but it was adopted with apparently sadistic relish. He was recorded giving orders that seem clearly to confirm this. 'Vukašinović, Colonel?' he says, checking to whom he is speaking, before he orders the Colonel to direct fire onto the Presidency Building and the Parliament in Sarajevo. The order was for measured torture by artillery bombardment: 'Fire at slow intervals until I order you to stop.'[8] Mladić is also recorded giving instructions to 'target Muslim neighborhoods' and to shell them 'so that they will not be able to sleep' – the aim appears to have been to drive the people out of their minds.

Specific targeting complemented the psychological torture intended in the shelling. Among the buildings destroyed early on were the main post office, the old library and public records center, and other buildings that were centers of either communication or

---

[8] *Death of Yugoslavia*, Program 4, Brian Lapping Associates for the BBC, 1995.

record. This pattern of targeting ensured that the Bosnian Government and the people under siege in Sarajevo would be largely cut off from the world and, crucially, from the remainder of the country. It was not easy for the Bosnian leadership to communicate with its people and troops in the rest of the country. Moreover, the attempt to erase Bosnia's history and specifically to destroy all records, including those of property and people, was an essential complement to the intended seizure of territory and removal of the population.

For over a year, there was one partial gap in the Serbian encirclement of Sarajevo, which was also a gap in the contiguity of Serbian controlled territory between eastern Hercegovina and eastern Bosnia, close to Goražde. To the south-west of Sarajevo, there was a limited and dangerous route over Mount Igman, the one strategic high point that the VRS did not control. Mladić closed the gap in summer 1993 with an operation to seize Mount Bjelašnica, part of the south-western mountain range dominated by Mount Ozren, as well as the peaks of Jahorina and Treskavica. Operation *Lukavac* ('Hunter'), completed on 27 July, was the culminaton of a series of operations – *Mač I* and *Mač II* (Sword I and Sword II), *Podrina* (Drina Valley) and *Cerska* (the name of a town north-east of Sarajevo) which had begun in February. This 'significant' success was a major operation, which gave Mladić great satisfaction because 'the whole of the VRS took part in it.'[9] Mladić flaunted his dominance at this point by flouting the 'No-Fly Zone' ordered by the UN Security Council and landing on the Bjelašnica Ridge in a helicopter, in front of television cameras. The international response to this development, including agreements at various stages to withdraw, or canton, weapons (even if agreements were not honored), meant that Mladić could not drive on to close the circle and to complete the attempt to strangle the capital. But he had tightened his grip on Sarajevo and, perhaps more pertinently from his point of view, had connected Serb-controlled territory in eastern Hercegovina with the larger concentration of territory towards the River Drina and the border with Serbia.

One of the General's most prized targets, Goražde, remained a large blot on the map, following his earlier successes. Lying on the main communications route from Serbia to the Adriatic Sea, it was

[9] Quoted in Jovan Janjić, *Srpski General Ratko Mladić*, Novi Sad: Matica Srpska, 1996.

a key strategic target, impotant for reasons beyond its communications significance. It was home to one of the most important munitions facilities in the integrated defense industry that had underpinned the old JNA. The Pobjeda plant was vital not only for ammunition production, but also because it was the above-ground concealment of a massive underground defense installation, geared for secret wartime production of arms and munitions. As with Han Pijesak (and many other parts of the old JNA infra-structure), Goražde was the hub of a network of tunnels and there-fore a major prize. Indeed, because some of the network was held by the ABiH and some by the VRS, battles were fought under-ground for its control.

Mladić made several attempts to seize Goražde, but never quite succeeded. It was a far larger enclave than the others in eastern Bosnia – Žepa and Srebrenica. Stretching 70–100 km² across moun-tainous terrain, with underground channels, there was always the possibility of defense in relative depth. An additional factor was the decision by the UN Security Council to declare safe havens in six enclaves in Bosnia and Hercegovina surrounded by Serbian forces, one of which was Goražde. It was this status that proved vital in saving the town of Goražde, if not the wider enclave, on two occa-sions. First, in the spring of 1994, the VRS pressed a major attack on the town. Despite the first-ever use of force by NATO, which carried out close air support operations against a VRS command tent and issued an ultimatum backed by the threat of air strikes,[10] General Mladić overran one Bosnian army position after another, although there was fierce fighting over the dominant high ground at Gradina, Point 1046, between Goražde and Čajniče, which chang-ed hands four times. After securing Gradina, the VRS was able to turn along the right bank of the River Drina, eventually capturing 180km² of territory. Only the NATO ultimatum to withdraw 3km from the center of the town made a difference. Even that left Mladić crowing that Goražde was 'militarily settled' and that it only re-mained to 'solve it politically.'[11]

In fact, Goražde was not militarily settled. Part of the success in April 1994 might have been the abandoning of positions by the

[10] Close air support refers to the tactical use of air power in direct support and protection of forces on the ground, with troops on the ground identifying targets and directing strike aircraft towards them. Air Strikes refers to the stra-tegic use of air power against pre-determined targets.

[11] Quoted in Janjić, *Srpski General*, p. 113.

ABiH – presumably in the hope of increasing the chances of NATO air action (a matter that may explain the bitter reaction of the UN force commander, the British General Sir Michael Rose, given that his own troops acting as observers were left exposed and one was killed). In face of stiffer military resistance, the capture of the enclave was not so easy, as Mladić found out a little over a year later, when, at the end of May, he sought to overrun the enclave in the first of a series of operations intended to mop up the three enclaves in eastern Bosnia – after Goražde, Žepa and Srebrenica would be targeted. The first of the trio, however, survived. The VRS used its common stop-start approach, trying to leave both the ABiH and UN forces uncertain as to whether there was a major attack in the making, or simply tactical maneuvering. Although there was some sense that the attack would come, when it did, on 28 May, it was with a sudden spurt that saw both British troops from the Royal Welch Fusiliers in the UN mission and the Bosnian Army battling hard (see Chapter 8). In the end, Mladić could not capture the key strategic ground, Mala Biserna, where the British had held out in one of their observation posts, withdrawing only when the Bosnian Army's defensive positions were stable enough to block the VRS advance. Thwarted, the Bosnian Serb commander changed tack and decided to eradicate the enclaves in reverse order: if Goražde was too difficult, then he would begin with Srebrenica and then move on Žepa – before eventually returning to tackle the stumbling block.

Mladić approached Srebrenica with his classic slow-slow-quick-quick-slow pattern.[12] This worked to convince the Dutch forces deployed as the UN mission in the Srebrenica 'safe area.' Until it was already just about too late, the Dutch battalion believed that Mladić did not intend to take the town.[13] They judged that he was maneuvering for tactical advantage. The VRS (supported by key

---

[12] On Srebrenica, see the impeccable study by Jan Willem Honig and Norbert Both *Srebrenica: Record of a War Crime*, London and New York: Penguin, 1996, which was the first study on this one aspect of the war to appear. Not only does it contain detail that could be found nowhere else when it was written, but it also combines the 'detective' approach with a sound sense of strategy and military operations; see also the strong journalistic account by David Rohde *Endgame: the Betrayal and Fall of Srebrenica, Europe's Worst Massacre since World War II*, New York: Farrar, Straus and Giroux, 1997.

[13] The Netherlands Foreign Ministry quite possibly had information about the Bosnian Serb commanders' intentions, but this certainly does not seem to have found its way to the commander on the ground.

units from the VJ) delivered heavy artillery attacks, moved forward a little, then paused. The pause was to check the prospect of an international military response. In the later stages of the attack on Srebrenica, Mladić's forces waited patiently whenever NATO aircraft were airborne, waiting for a provocative act and a signal to deliver close air support to the UN contingent on the ground. They were able to gauge the prospect of air power's being used because the Belgrade air defense radar system could monitor when NATO aircraft were in the air. As soon as the skies were clear, the VRS Drina Corps' advance, under the command of Major-General Radislav Krstić and Mladić's personal direction, could continue. Set in a valley, covering a small, hard to defend area of only 15km², with only a weak UN force and ABiH units that had curiously been depleted of their senior commanders, recalled to 4th Corps command in Tuzla on the eve of the attack, Srebrenica's only real hope since it was first surrounded, put under siege and then declared a UN 'safe area' in April 1993, had been General Mladić's reluctance to risk provoking a strong international military reaction.

The attack began at 0315 on 6 July, with a rocket artillery barrage. By the time VRS control had been established and the VJ support units had withdrawn after the capture of the town, a little after 1600 on 11 July, Mladić was ready personally to oversee the gravest single atrocity of the war. By 13 July, some 7,000 Muslim men, who were separated from the women and children in the 'safe area' and removed in a well-prepared operation (including the provision of sixty buses, including some from Serbia itself), had been murdered, while several thousand others had been killed as they fled to Tuzla. Despite Mladić's publicly filmed assurances that the prisoners would be looked after, he ordered the shootings. Men were lined up at the edges of mass graves, ten at a time and shot. Those doing the shooting had little choice – those who would not fire were told that they could join the lines of men on the edges of the vast ditches, including the bus drivers, who were forced to take part just for good measure and to ensure that they would be too implicated to risk revealing exactly what had happened (an approach taken from the Nazi textbook). Despite a visit from the Belgrade Security Service chief, Jovica Stanišić, dispatched, it can only be presumed, by Milošević to warn against these executions, the Bosnian Serb commander would not be deflected.

Although there could be a temptation to believe that Stanišić was implicated in the mass murder, based on the conclusion that he must have traveled to Bosnia to give the order to murder the Muslim men and that the order must have come from his political master, this seems unlikely, in the circumstances. It is only reasonable to presume that, although at earlier stages Milošević might have condoned, if not sanctioned and ordered the killings, at this stage he would have been more likely to oppose them. In circumstances where he had already long before told the Bosnian Serb commander that he had to end the war and was seeking an end to armed hostilities that would remove the pressure of sanctions on Serbia, it seems highly improbable that 'the Butcher of the Balkans' would wish to wield his cleaver in a manner that would strongly imperil his one overriding objective. Thus, if the Prosecutor at the International Tribunal were to charge him in connection with the Srebrenica massacre, it may well be that, curiously, this would prove an occasion in which he could demonstrate, contrary to most assumptions, that he had actually made some effort to prevent the action – albeit for the wrong reasons. Indeed, Mladić's bloody determination in this situation almost certainly means that the Bosnian Serb political leader, Karadžić was not involved and knew nothing about it – potentially creating significant problems for the prosecution, if he faced trial for genocide in The Hague, based on the events at Srebrenica.

Three weeks later, the other eastern 'safe area' also fell. Set on top of a peak – almost in the manner of a medieval castle – Žepa was considerably more defensible than Srebrenica. Indeed, some in the local military command, although the town had descended into anarchy, were deeply dissatisfied that their political leaders decided to concede the town. This decision, based on negotiations between the British UN Force commander, Lieutenant-General Rupert Smith, and Mladić, was taken to allow the evacuation of the town's 15,000 civilians, in order to save lives. This was followed by an agreement between the EU's diplomatic envoy, former Swedish Prime Minister Carl Bildt, and Milošević to allow sanctuary in Serbia for the Muslims defending the town – in Serbia, they would be safe from the Mladić meat-cleaver, but the cleaver-wielder could be assured that the ABiH men would not be available to fight his troops on another front. The concern of all involved, even Mladić (he hoped to avoid another outcry that would drive the

West, already committed to using air power against him, after the London Conference of 20–21 July, from doing so),[14] was to avoid another ugly bout of mass killing. Thus, at the beginning of August, the town was conceded, with the last of its inhabitants finally making it to some form of safety on 3 August. Although there was some criticism of both the UN and the Bosnian political leaders for agreeing to the evacuation of the mountain fortress, any reasonable assessment, in the light of Srebrenica and the impossibility of giving timely and meaningful military assistance (if any at all), would see it as a humanitarian triumph.

By this stage in the war, concentrating on the eastern enclaves and overstretched, the VRS was under considerable pressure in western Bosnia. The vital strategic ground of the Kupres Heights had fallen in late 1994 (see Chapter 9), and with its loss the angry Mladić was (rightly) concerned that forces moving north from Kupres might make an ABiH breakout from the Bihać pocket harder to resist because of the pressure applied from the south by advancing Croatian and Bosnian forces. He was determined on regaining the Heights (the loss of which he blamed on politicians, in any case).[15] This was contrary to that which had happened in the previous November. Then, the ABiH had attempted to drive out of the enclave and had been exuberated by their apparent success.

In Operation *Sloboda* – Freedom – the Bosnian 5th Corps had quickly driven the under-strength VRS back. The ultimate aim was to forge a link to ABiH forces concentrated in an extended version of the magic triangle which was to be conceded to the

[14] This prospect was actually quite unlikely given two factors. One was that NATO and UN military commanders had judged that there was no serious option to save Žepa – although it was, in itself, a sound defensive point, it was completely isolated with no reasonable means of logistical communication, it would sooner or later inevitably succumb, therefore, and the UN and NATO forces available were not of an appropriate character to intervene effectively and decisively. The second, and far more important, reason was that those attending the London Conference on 20–21 July seemed to believe that the town had already fallen, so strong was the idea that it had to fall. General Smith was an exception. Even though he no doubt judged the position at Žepa to be a lost cause, he spoke strongly to broaden the horizons of those present from a narrow focus on Goražde, the defensible, remaining 'safe area' in eastern Bosnia, to all the 'safe areas' that were intact. The UN Force Commander was undoubtedly bemused at being party to discussions in which one of his primary continuing concerns was treated as history.

[15] Janjić, *Srpski General*, pp. 174–5.

Muslims, should they accept it: Bugojno, Zenica and Tuzla. If this link could be made, then perhaps 20,000 or more ABiH troops trapped in the north-western enclave could be freed to tip the balance elsewhere in the country. The 5th Corps, with some support from a Croatian brigade, launched an attack on the night of 23–24 October, under the command of General Atif Dudaković.

The 501st, 502nd, 503rd, 504th, 505th and 517th brigades ran along the right bank of the River Drina, along with support from other units, including an engineering brigade and aerial support. The 501st, 502nd Mountain and 517th Light Brigades pushed out from the Bihać pocket towards Petrovac. The 502nd's Reconnaissance and Diversionary unit focused on Gražebo. The 503rd Mountain Brigade headed towards Velika Radica, with additional reconnaissance and diversionary units, as well as support from the 505th Motorized Brigade. Over eight days, the 5th Corps advanced vigorously, taking around 100km² from the VRS. However, this extensive and speedy advance left the Bosnian forces over-extended. It is not clear whether Mladić was surprised by this first significant attempt at an operational move by the ABiH, though he certainly allowed it to continue. He astutely lured the 5th into a position where it could then easily be counter-attacked and mopped up, and this is what happened. Mladić began the counter-offensive on 1 November in the front line, where he sustained a minor throat injury, but soon left the operation to run virtually on automatic pilot, under the command of VRS Chief of Staff Colonel-General Manojlo Milovanović, who saw through the rollback, while Mladić toured the other battlefronts in Bosnia.

The fall of the Kupres Heights just after the Bihać breakout and rollback had major repercussions the following summer. Then, the supreme confidence and skill that had seen Mladić wipe out the ABiH 5th Corps gains prevailed. By the summer of 1995 the 5th Corps was again breaking out, but this time in conjunction with a joint Croatian-Bosnian offensive advancing easily northwards through western Bosnia, threatening to strike at the under-belly of any repeat of the November counter-offensive – and at the same time threatening the Bosnian Serb stronghold of Banja Luka, as well as the psychologically important towns of Prijedor and Sanski Most. This was a situation that tested Mladić. But it was far from being an impossible situation for his forces, even if they were too thin on the ground immediately to thwart their opponents' thrust.

There was one factor that finally rendered him helpless, namely NATO's use of extensive air force, with some support from British and French artillery on the ground around Sarajevo, operating in support of the UN mission, at the end of August.

Deliberate Force and air defenseless

Mladić was to end the month with a military challenge to which he had no answer. This outweighed the difficulties with which he had begun the month. Following the capture of Srebrenica in July and Žepa in early August, he found himself in a civil-military battle. On 5 August 1995, after the retreat of the OS RSK in Croatia, General Mladić held a meeting of his whole command in Banja Luka. Although Srebrenica and Žepa had been captured, it was clear that the pressure being applied by Croatia in alliance with the ABiH would increase. The war in Croatia was just about over and the war in Bosnia and Hercegovina was entering its final phase. The day before, Karadžić had declared that the General Staff had been renamed and that he was personally in charge of the Supreme Command under the emergency war conditions that had been declared a week earlier, while Mladić was named as the special adviser 'for defense of the RS and RSK' – in effect, the General was being removed from command of the VRS and sidelined. Mladić understood this and was far from content, declaring 'I went to war as a soldier and I intend to leave it as a soldier.'[16]

The meeting was attended by Mladić; his Chief of Staff, Milovanović, head of morale, faith and legal affairs (the equivalent of the ideological-political officer under communism); Colonel-General Milan Gvero; chief of logistics, Colonel-General Djordje Djukić; chief of intelligence and security, Major-General Zdravko Tolimir; chief of mobilization and manpower, Major-General Petar Škrbić; Permanent Commander of the air and air defense forces, Jovo Marić; commander of the 1st Krajina Corps, Colonel-General Momir Talić; Chief of Staff in the 1st Krajina Corps, Colonel-General Boško Kelečević; commander of the 9th Operational Group, Major-General Vladimir Arsić; commander of the 30th Infantry Division, Major-General Momir Zec; commander of the 2nd Krajina Corps, Major-General Radivoje Tomanić; commander

---

[16] Quoted in Janjić, *Srpski General*, p. 188.

of the Eastern Bosnia Corps, Major-General Novica Simić; commander of the Drina Corps, Major-General Radislav Krstić; commander of the Hercegovina Corps, Major-General Radovan Grubac, commander of the air and air defense forces, Major-General Živomir Ninković; Chief of Staff of the air and air defense forces; Major-General Božo Novak; and commander of the CVŠ (Central Military School) Major-General Grujo Borić. All signed a letter to the Republika Srpska assembly rejecting Karadžić's announcement and declaring Mladić commander of the VRS. *De facto* Mladić emerged from this civil-military clash victorious – symbolically, morally and, most of all, in practice, given that he retained his position. He had confirmed his power and control over the situation, the latter being one of his great strengths. Indeed, only once, at the beginning of May 1995, had his effective control over events and, even more important, his belief in his ability to control and to have everything done on his terms, been disturbed. At that point the British officer commanding the UN force in Bosnia and Hercegovina, General Rupert Smith, had temporarily outmaneuvered the Bosnian Serb general, including using air strikes (only to be undermined by his superiors, who refused to allow further action of this kind, at the time). Within a month of the letter, however, Mladić's control over events was effectively removed, as NATO, amplifying the approach taken by Smith earlier in the year, used force decisively.

Throughout the summer, the prospect of NATO air action had been building, catalyzed by the events at Srebrenica and Žepa. Mladić had already crossed the threshold, the only question remaining was what exactly would precipitate action, and when. General Smith and General Mike Ryan, the US commander of air forces at NATO's southern command in Naples, had spent the summer working out operational plans for extensive air strikes, galvanized by strong encouragement from their governments and relevant organizational hierarchies to be ready to use the force available – indeed, there was a clear consensus that they should not wait for approval the next time there was a Serbian affront looming. After years of international hand-wringing over the use of force, finally they would be allowed to strike and to strike seriously.

The prompt for air attacks was a VRS mortar attack on Markale Market in Sarajevo that killed 37 people and wounded 90. General Smith took time formally to confirm that the missile had been fired by the VRS, as well as delaying the attack until he was sure that the British contingent in Goražde,[17] the only UN troops remaining exposed by that stage, had secured an exit – which they did, against ABiH resistance and with VRS and VJ help, via Serbia. Once Smith got word that the Welch Fusiliers were safe, he called in air strikes.[18]

Forty-eight hours after the market place massacre, NATO aircraft, with artillery support from the Franco-British–Dutch Rapid Reaction Force on the ground around Sarajevo, opened what the Serbs regarded as 'massive attacks' (in fact, although extensive, they remained limited) on the VRS.[19] The basis for this action was a new and more expansive interpretation of the mandate for protecting the UN–Security Council declared 'safe areas', foremost of which was Sarajevo, than had previously been used. Although the artillery was only used in the first two days (after which the UN mission leaders ordered that it should no longer be used), it inflicted substantial damage to VRS positions around Sarajevo – in line with the principle that the best way to deal with artillery (the Serbian guns on the hills around the town) is precisely targeted artillery return fire. The air campaign, however, was to continue.

Although some in NATO wished to see a pause, had there been a break in operations this would have fatally undermined the success that was to come – indeed, whatever happened, they might not have recommenced. Mladić understood this and hoped to be able to finesse a deal from discussions with the French General in overall

[17] Although the source of a similar incident against the same target in February 1994 had been unclear at the time, later evidence appeared clearly to confirm VRS sponsorship. By contrast, there was no doubt over the August 1995 mortar – but, ironically, even if there had been, by that stage, it might well have made no difference, given that the UN Force and NATO were poised to act, ready if another atrocity were to occur.

[18] Unfortunately, space does not permit a detailed account of the air campaign. Aside from official studies, two have been provided, both strong in detail. Colonel Mark Bucknam of the USAF produced an excellent Ph.D. thesis on the role of theater level commanders in the air campaign. (Mark A. Bucknam, 'The Influence of UN and NATO Theater-Level Commanders on the Use of Airpower Over Bosnia During Deny Flight: 1993–1995', Ph.D. dissertation, King's College London). Tim Ripley, *Operation Deliberate Force: The UN and NATO Campaign in Bosnia, 1995*, Bailrigg Studies no. 3, Lancaster: CDISS, 1999, although ostensibly on the NATO air action, also offers extensive, generally reliable detail on military operations in Bosnia and Hercegovina.

[19] Janjić, *Srpski General*, p. 196.

command of the UN forces in former Yugoslavia, Bernard Janvier, at a meeting, on the night of 1–2 September, at Mali Zvornik, just on the Serbian side of the border formed by the River Drina. Over the next few days, in an exchange of letters by fax, Mladić proposed terms for an agreement between NATO and the Rapid Reaction Force, on one side, and the VRS, on the other. Janvier rejected Mladić's proposals outright, the key provisions of which were that NATO and the Rapid Reaction Force should cease hostile action immediately, that there would be an agreement on the 'safe areas' in line with the Geneva Conventions of 1949 (which for Mladić meant a change from the provisions of UN Security Council Resolutions 824 and 836, which permitted Bosnian government forces inside the areas and the international use of force to protect them, whereas Mladić sought a 'demilitarized' zone, that he could, one day, occupy when the crisis had passed), in return for all of which, the VRS would desist from attacks on the remaining 'safe areas' of Sarajevo, Bihać, Tuzla and Goražde. This was not much of an offer – though it was surely intended less as an offer to be accepted than as a tactical gambit with which to begin a dialogue that would require the air operations to be suspended. It did not work – but it was a clear indication that Mladić had lost control of the situation, unlike any stage before – even the beginning of May 1995, when General Smith had seen through, and so rattled, him.

The NATO and Rapid Reaction Force action began at 0155 on 30 August, with bombs and missiles knocking out the Post and Telecommunication Office (PTT) facility at Kmur kod Srbinja, which was again struck at 0225 by another seven missiles. Shortly afterwards, at 0212, the one major SA-6 Surface-to-Air Missile defense site in eastern Bosnia, at Sokolac, was hit. At 0230, another four rockets destroyed the PTT facility at Stražica kod Čajniča, killing one person and wounding another. Meanwhile ten strike aircraft attacked the relays and communications facilities at Stolica on the Majevica Hill. Damaging and, if possible, destroying Bosnian Serb communications facilities was vital. So too was suppressing any chance of air defense activity, hence an array of air defense targets was also part of the early targeting. The Rapid Reaction Force launched artillery barrages against Serbian gun and mortar emplacements, which were often located in residential areas. The focus was on targets in Ilidža and Hadžice, which contained military repair and support facilities and a major anti-aircraft artillery capability. The bout of artillery fire between 0405 and 0715[20] also landed on Mirkovici and Bariće kod Sarajevo. The Bosnian Serbs had not faced action of this scale and quality before and they were immediately put in an impossible position – unable to respond and weak in the face of their local adversaries' ground advances.

The air campaign – named *Deliberate Force* – continued for thirteen days. NATO strikes targeted key Bosnian Serb economic and energy resources, VRS positions and, especially, communications facilities. Knocking out the latter, as well as eradicating their air defense, rendered Mladić and his forces ever more helpless (nonetheless, while fixed air defense assets were eliminated, the VRS demonstrated great adeptness in playing on-off cat-and-mouse games with NATO aircraft, meaning that the latter could never be absolutely safe, or absolutely eliminate the Serbian capability).[21] Some of the most severe damage was inflicted on communications facilities around the VRS-VJ military command center at Han Pijesak. The TV and radio transmitters there were key successes on Day 3 of the NATO action. Microwave transmitters had been attacked early in *Deliberate Force*, while other operations against PTT facilities throughout VRS-held territory meant that the underground landlines, which were a great strength of the Serbian military capability, were largely unusable. Communications – whether microwave, radio, or landline – between Han Pijesak and the field were severely disrupted.

The Bosnian Serbs had been placed under an information and communications blockade, with Generals Smith and Ryan dissecting the VRS, separating one Corps from another, making it impossible for them to talk to each other, or to the command at Han Pijesak, and rendering mobility – and therefore support from one part of the VRS to another – all but impossible. Mladić was defenseless, and had completely lost control of the situation. This was General Smith's precise purpose, a psychological advantage he reinforced by ordering raids to destroy ammunition dumps near the Bosnian Serb general's home, designed to make sure that his family and others there understood that, in classical military terms, Mladić's

---

[20] These are Bosnian Serb timings – NATO timings suggest the assault commenced at 0432.

[21] Significant elements in the following paragraphs draw on Janjić, *Srpski General*, pp. 208–18.

position was untenable. The typically arrogant and self-confident general was silenced and retreated from the scene to Belgrade where he was admitted to the Military Medical Institute hospital – ostensibly unwell, with gallstones, but in a position also to take Belgrade's political and military advice. His hospital treatment and hence absence from the battlefield were, so Serbian disinformation claimed, the reason for the poor performance of the VRS. The real explanation, however, was military impotence in the face of NATO air power. Indeed, once he accepted an agreement that ended the NATO air operations, Mladić emerged from his 'sick-bed' and returned immediately to the frontline. 'Mad at the losses' suffered at the hands of the Croatian-Bosnian joint advance, albeit under cover of the NATO operations which had rendered him defenseless,[22] but freed from the helplessness created by those NATO attacks, Mladić took control again, though in a much weaker position. First, he stabilized the frontline – a task accomplished relatively easily against the Bosnian army when NATO power was not overwhelming his ability to communicate and maneuver. He then mounted a significant counter-offensive that pushed back the Croatian-Bosnian advance, especially when his only opponent became the ABiH, which at the end acted alone, after Croatian forces ceased operations – see Chapter 9. His success in regaining land taken by the ABiH in north-western Bosnia brought the war to and end, as the Bosnian government realized that it would be better off agreeing to a ceasefire at this stage rather than risk losing further territory, as Mladić regained his touch and again 'notched up successes'. Croatian and Bosnian forces, moreover, clearly could not 'accomplish what they had planned.'[23] Ključ fell easily to Mladić, as did Krupa-na-Uni and Petrovac, although he suffered further reverses. The ceasefire was signed on 9 October, to come into effect 24 hours later – a final day of fighting that went against the VRS as 10,000 rounds (in renewed Croatian engagement) were fired on Mrkonjić Grad, which fell, as did Sanski Most, finally, in its wake – one of the key psychological objectives that the ABiH had previously failed to capture.[24] That success, once the NATO operations

[22] *Telegraf*, 27 September 1995.
[23] Janjić, *Srpski General*, pp. 216–17.
[24] Sanski Most, along with other targets the ABiH sought in vain to capture, were important because of their experience of ethnic cleansing in 1992 which prompted the desire to restore honor by enabling forcibly expelled Muslims to

had finished, also confirmed that it was Alliance air power, not Croatian and Bosnian ground forces, that defeated the VRS – and would have done so without the contingency of ground forces being there to compound the anguish of the impotent.

NATO's use of air power was, without any doubt and contrary to the predominant opinion of Western commentators (especially in the US), the decisive element in ending the war in Bosnia and Hercegovina. As Milošević, no less, was to confirm to a senior US general in December, Mladić was defenseless against NATO air strikes: it was Alliance air power that was decisive in removing Mladić's grip on the situation – communications between the field and Han Pijesak fell from minutes to forty-eight hours, or more. While Croatian and, to a far lesser extent, Bosnian forces on the ground could exploit this position, they could never have put the Bosnian Serb general in such a predicament. Indeed, once the air action had ceased, the manner in which Mladić was able to recover and launch successful counter-offensives suggests that arguments emphasizing the role of Croatian and Bosnian forces on the ground – of which there were many – are spurious. Air power was decisive.

---

return, as well as, no doubt, taking revenge on Serbs, no matter how far they had participated in, or supported, the cleansing.

8

THE ENDS: THE QUEST FOR OLD
BORDERS IN THE SOUTH – KOSOVO

Almost four years after Serbian strategy in Bosnia and Hercegovina
had been decisively reversed by NATO air power, Serbian forces
had again to defend themselves against Alliance aerial attack. By
1999, the focus of Serbian operations had moved south to the province of Kosovo, formally part of Serbia, but with an ethnic-Albanian majority population. Allied action was a response to Belgrade's
campaign against the Albanian inhabitants and the insurgent force
that emerged from them, the Kosova Liberation Army (*Ushtria
Çilimtare e Kosovës* – UÇK). Alliance air power significantly determined the outcome in both Bosnia and Hercegovina and in
Kosovo. Whereas success in the former resulted solely from action
that removed the Serbian commander's control of the situation and
rendered the VRS helpless, in Kosovo the outcome was less straightforward. While Alliance planes and missiles were credited with playing a similar role in overwhelming Serbian forces and breaking the
military-political leadership's control of events, the effect was less
conclusive. Against the background of major air power achievements, it required a complementary contingent factor – indictment
of the Belgrade leadership for war crimes – finally to turn the tide.

That tide was turned and the Serbian project initiated a decade
earlier by Slobodan Milošević was terminated in June 1999 despite
the Serbs' considerable success, both in defying NATO's might
(even if that might was always certain to prevail), overrunning the
insurgent force and evicting at least half the ethnic-Albanian population of the province. For Belgrade – and, in the course of events,
for many outside observers, and even for NATO – the war was
fought on two levels. One was the original campaign on the ground
against the UÇK and the ethnic Albanians. The other was air defense
against Alliance air operations. Strategically, the two were intertwined, although at the tactical and operational levels they were
mostly discrete.

As had been the case in the earlier campaigns in the west, statehood was the issue and the point of the campaign was to establish control of territory by removing the possibility of any political, or military, resistance. In both theaters, the aim was to secure territory by removing not only armed opposition but also the entire potentially antagonistic local populations. Whereas the quest in Croatia and in Bosnia and Hercegovina had been to establish new borders, in Kosovo the mission was to reinforce existing ones.

The southern front: from ground operations to a two-level battle of Kosovo

The restoration of Serbian control over Kosovo, which had been granted substantial autonomy as a province within Serbia, had been the starting point of Milošević's Serbian political agenda in the late 1980s. From that point until the campaign that Belgrade launched in 1997 and which began in earnest early in 1998, the prospect of anti-Albanian action always cast an ominous shadow.

There had been expectations of assistance and certainly of significant regeneration of the Serbian economy after the signing of the Bosnian peace accords in 1995. But two years after the ending of hostilities in the Bosnian and Croatian theaters, the expected rewards had not materialised. Formal UN sanctions were only suspended, not lifted, hence sufficient uncertainty remained to deter most potential international investors. And even when formal sanctions had been removed, other politically defined measures remained. These included the EU ban on travel by an elite group of individuals to any of its member states and the US commitment to an 'outer wall' of sanctions – barring Serbian membership of international organizations and agreements with international financial institutions – all of which destroyed business confidence. Early in 1997, Milošević seems to have given up on the international community and any expectation of movement on these impediments to Serbia's development. At that point, other options were considered and attention turned to Kosovo, where major operations were to begin in spring 1998.

The Serbian action after March 1998 was, in part, a reaction to the emergence of an ethnic Albanian armed force under the label of the Kosova Liberation Army. Serbian security services were indeed fighting the UÇK to restore Serbian control but there was considerably more to the Serbian campaign than this. Ostensibly a reaction to the UÇK uprising, Belgrade used the pretext of the insurgency to begin a new campaign of ethnic cleansing.

This Serbian campaign to cleanse at least part of Kosovo reflected the clear understanding of FRY President Slobodan Milošević that, in the long term, Serbian control of the province could only be secured by the elimination of the ethnic Albanian population. Otherwise, an already bankrupt country would be ever more burdened with the need to maintain some provision for state authority in Kosovo. Milošević, used action in Kosovo to ease himself out of a tight political corner in early 1998 (given the international presence in Bosnia and the opposition of Montenegrin leader Milo Djukanović), and he exploited divisions in the UN Security Council (between the US and the UK, on one side, and France and Russia, on the other, over Iraq, as well as the decision by the US and the UK to commit forces to the Gulf for at least six months) to move on Kosovo.

In this situation the only realistic solutions for the province were as follows. First, there could be Kosovo with an ethnic Albanian population, but self-governing outside Serbia and, possibly, outside the Federal Republic of Yugoslavia. Second there could be Kosovo without ethnic Albanians and inside Serbia. Third there could be Kosovo divided, with one part held by Serbia and without ethnic Albanians and the other outside Serbia, probably outside the Federal Republic of Yugoslavia, but with an ethnic Albanian population. (The separation of Kosovo, or part of it, from the Federal Republic of Yugoslavia could imply full independence and an international personality for that territory, or it might signify association with another state.)

The Serbian campaign had been on the agenda politically since the early 1990s and in operational terms for at least a year prior to the beginning of action in March. MUP and Serbian Security Service Special Forces, and the Yugoslav Army had been deploying and reinforcing in preparation for this action. By October 1997, the MUP was deployed in full-combat mode in Kosovo, with MUP and VJ units in reserve, deployed in the field, ostensibly on maneuvers, around the edges of Kosovo, inside Serbia proper.[1] To have reached this level of readiness by October, preparations

---

[1] Confirmed to the author by an officer in Belgrade, October 1997.

must have begun the previous March, which implies that a decision must have been taken at the political level perhaps in February. While it is highly unlikely that a formal record of this political decision was made, it is a surer bet that it was taken at a small meeting possibly involving no more than three people – probably Milošević, Radovan Stojičić (known as 'Badža'), at that time Serbian Police Minister, and a third person, perhaps most likely to have been the head of the Security Service, Jovica Stanišić.[2] This was the manner in which Milošević conducted such business. The timing also appears to be consistent with the first intelligence reports to Western governments that ethnic cleansing in Kosovo was on Belgrade's agenda – the only question, it appeared, was when it would happen with Stojičić representing a hard-line lobby. Implementation was subject to variation, depending on circumstances. While care was taken to keep action below thresholds that would prompt external intervention in the early stages (as there had been during the campaign in Bosnia), this was overturned in early 1999, when the prospect of NATO action was strong and Milošević apparently calculated that this could be used to apparent advantage – as is argued below.

When operations began in 1998, initially only Serbian forces participated. Later, the VJ was involved in border areas and then in providing artillery and helicopter gunship support to the Serbian security forces. At all times in this period the VJ was kept in a secondary role, a fact that appears to have created discontent among its most senior officers. Some of these including General Dragoljub Ojdanić, who became Chief of Staff in October 1998, replacing the sacked General Perišić (whose failings, inter alia, included objecting to the Kosovo campaign), seemed keen to take action in Kosovo, concerned that their institutional position could be further weakened by the emphasis on the Serbian Special Forces. The Serbian MUP Special Force units were already considerably better paid than their army counterparts, were better trained and had better equipment (although the Serbian Special Forces did not have artillery, heavy armor, or air support).

Aside from one period in July 1998, Serbian forces did not focus only on UÇK operational targets. Rather, they targeted civilian

[2] Given that Stojičić was killed on 10 April 1997, the only certain confirmation of this meeting could come from Milošević, or a third person.

population centers, ensuring that something in excess of 300,000 Kosovan Albanians fled as refugees and displaced persons. In many cases there were mass murders as in Drenica in March. When Serbian action appeared only to be directed against operational targets in July, this was probably a step taken to diminish external pressure for international intervention. In this case, Serbian forces could be said to be doing that which any government might reasonably claim the right to do: suppress an armed insurgent force acting against the state. However, after July, the measures against civilians, which were clearly designed to kill them or drive them out, continued. These were supplemented by the planting of anti-personnel landmines to ensure that there was no prospect of return.

Over the next few months, the Serbian campaign continued, although it was careful to remain below any threshold that would push the hesitant and divided ranks of the West into action (see Chapter 10). Eventually NATO issued an ultimatum: the Serbian campaign had to stop, MUP and VJ force numbers in Kosovo had to be reduced to normal levels – 6,500 of the former (mainly local and reserve forces) and 10,600 of the latter – and returned to barracks, and there had to be an agreement to allow an international presence in Kosovo. If these conditions were not met, NATO would use its air power against Belgrade's forces. The deadline was 27 October. Milošević understood that this threat, unlike earlier noises emanating from Washington, London and Brussels, would be backed by action and thus decided to reach an accommodation with the US Envoy Richard Holbrooke. The latter had prepared an immediate fallback position regarding an international presence – an OSCE observer mission, rather than an armed peacekeeping force underpinned by NATO.

By the 27 October deadline set by the NATO air-strike ultimatum for withdrawal of Belgrade's forces from Kosovo and from the field, the VJ was down to the level that NATO had judged to be its standing force in Kosovo – 1,000 personnel on the borders with Albania and Macedonia, as well as 10,600 personnel in barracks at Kosovska Mitrovica, Peć, Djakovica, Prizren, Uroševac, Gnjlane and, the provincial capital, Priština. The last of these was also headquarters to 52nd Corps and the joint command for all VJ and MUP operations in Kosovo. The same October withdrawal agreement allowed for 6,500 MUP personnel to remain in Kosovo in 28 locations, meaning that all others had to be withdrawn by the NATO deadline if air strikes were to be averted. In the end, around three companies – 360 men – failed to meet the deadline but there was no question of NATO's using air strikes because of this oversight, given that in the last twelve hours before the mid-night deadline, Belgrade had withdrawn 4,126 MUP personnel from Kosovo, thereby signaling effective compliance.

The withdrawal of forces did not constitute a complete re-turn to the status quo ante as some key units, such as the VJ 215th Armored Brigade, did not return to their barracks (in this case, at Niš), suggesting that they were deployed elsewhere in southern Serbia, ready to return to Kosovo should the order be given. In addition, other units within Kosovo continued to be deployed in the field although the Belgrade authorities complied with a 29 October deadline to supply full information on all MUP and VJ forces stationed in Kosovo and their locations to international observers (see Chapter 10).

In Kosovo itself, the ceasefire met challenges, including several killings. Nonetheless, for over a month it could be judged gener-ally to have held and to have been successful although an increasing number of incidents indicated that the security situation remained unstable. The main element in this appeared to be the role of units of the UÇK, although the UÇK cited Serbian provocation for its actions. While the UÇK had been badly beaten by Serbian and Yugoslav forces, superior in quality and numbers, the ceasefire enabled elements of the UÇK to re-emerge and take up positions where Belgrade's forces had been withdrawn. In consequence there was international indulgence for the continuing presence in the field of limited VJ and MUP units from within the standing force for Kosovo.

The VJ and MUP presence in the field never ceased on the east side of the road from Djakovica to Klina and along the road from Suva Reka to Stimlje, while MUP units established new positions in the Mališevo area. In all cases these deployments were judged at this stage by international observers to be defensive positions, in response to UÇK progress and provocation. More ominously, MUP and VJ units withdrawn from Kosovo to meet the October deadline hovered just outside the borders of the province.

As the momentum established at the end of October fell away, the expectation that Belgrade was using the agreement to gain a breathing space in which to reconfigure its operational plans for

Kosovo began to be confirmed by events on the ground. A small increase in the MUP and VJ presence had been tolerated because of UÇK provocation. However, this was the tip of a wedge that was being driven gradually but firmly into the province. Using the distraction of the Christmas and New Year holiday season, Belgrade tested the international response with small-scale operations inside Kosovo. Using the pretext of conducting a winter 'exercise', the VJ attacked Podujevo on 25 December. The test proved successful. There was no real international response – a ticking-off from the OSCE KVM mission meant little to those preparing the way for a new version of the Serbian campaign. Indeed, for Belgrade, criticism was welcome: so long as it was not accompanied by actual, or threatened, use of NATO air power.

With growing confidence, Serbian forces moved ahead with their preparations. The next point at which they would test the international tolerance threshold would prove to be a turning point, however. NATO had indications that Belgrade would act next at Račak and the KVM, increasingly obstructed and abused by Serbian forces, had been alerted. However, there was nothing that could be done to prevent forty-six ethnic Albanians apparently being massacred there by forces led by General Sreten Lukić. When the KVM Chief Ambassador, William Walker, reached the village, he recognized the hallmarks of cold-blooded execution from his earlier experience in Latin America – bodies with hands bound and gunshots through the back of the neck. Serbian sources claimed that the dead had been killed in combat, which was risible. Račak was, confirmation, if confirmation were needed, of the impending Serbian campaign and it spurred international action (discussed in Chapter 10), with indications that this would begin in earnest in the spring.

The spring cleansing

In the hiatus following the October agreement, Belgrade had refresh its long-standing plans for a solution to the Kosovo problem. The ethnic Albanian insurgency had to be stopped. Amid the otherwise insurmountable conditions of an antagonistic and overwhelmingly hostile majority population in the province, reverse-Maoism was the only strategic response. Popular support for the insurgency could only be brought to an end by removing the population. Initial probes had been successful enough to suggest that a campaign in the spring might meet with only a feeble and divided international response – something familiar from previous years. However, the orders permitting NATO to use air power, which had been important in finally making credible the saber-rattling of various Alliance members and the Secretary General, remained. Because these orders had not been 'turned off', there remained the significant chance that a NATO response might meet the planned campaign.

In contemplating the open order authorising the use of air power, Belgrade had three options. The first was to refrain from crossing a threshold that might lead to air action in practice. The second was to prepare to defend against it, should an air response begin. And the third, which Milošević appears to have taken, was to exploit the situation. Thus, he decided to call NATO's bluff and to reject the first option. The second thus became inevitable, but it would not be the only approach. As international attempts to pre-empt the coming campaign faltered, it seems that Milošević concluded that there could be advantage in what was expected to be a short-lived NATO air campaign. Rather than trying to avoid an aerial assault, and partly reassured by the probability that any bombing would last no more than three weeks (and might last only three days), the Belgrade leader seems to have set out to provoke such an attack. While this eventually proved to be a miscalculation, it was not an unreasonable judgment to make in light of information available to him about Alliance operational planning.

Serbian logistical preparations became geared for two simultaneous operations. One was to defend against NATO attacks, the other was to prepare the mass eviction of ethnic Albanians, at least from the northern parts of Kosovo. The starting point for this would be operations in the south and west, which would provide the open end of a horseshoe-shaped area of territory marked approximately by the towns of Djakovica and Prizren, with Serbian forces pressing along the two prongs and the arc of that shape the cleared path through which hundreds of thousands of ethnic Albanians could be forced to leave Kosovo. The enormous logistical provision necessary for the forcible emptying of major towns was put in place, with buses (as at Srebrenica – see Chapter 7) and trains made ready for large scale evacuation. Milošević had moved from ducking beneath thresholds to actively counting on NATO bombing. His approximate calculations seen to have been as follows: withstand several days of NATO bombardment in exchange for the opportunity to use those attacks as cover for large-scale and

high-speed cleansing of Kosovo – operations at a pace and on a
scale never previously feasible because of the imperative of avoiding international armed action – and blame NATO for the situation, assured that there would be more than enough gullible people to accept his version of events and so generate international
public opinion hostile to NATO.[3] Thus, as outsiders hurried to
forge a diplomatic agreement to prevent the approaching Serbian
campaign, they were chasing a lost cause. Indeed, because most of
those engaged in international diplomatic and military efforts to
deter the imminent Serbian campaign had no idea of Belgrade's
real intentions, they raced headlong into a trap.

The Serbian campaign would have happened, with or without
the various international initiatives, but it was just these initiatives,
backed by threats of the use of force, that allowed Milošević to
draw NATO and the international community into a position where
they would have no option but to use force or else risk losing face
and strategic credibility. All this was to Belgrade's advantage. Assuming, as the planners there did, with some reason, that air action
would last considerably less than one month, it seemed like a win-
win situation. Either NATO would crumble and not use force,
which would be a significant strategic victory for Serbia, or, as expected, air attacks would be ordered giving the Serbian campaign
the perfect cover for going into overdrive. The latter is what happened.

After a series of failed international negotiations aimed at stav-
ing off the Serbian offensive, Belgrade's plan swung into action in
the second half of March. The plan was reportedly codenamed
'Horseshoe'[4] though that designation – if not the plan itself – was

---

[3] In a sense, this decision was similar to that of General Rupert Smith over
using force in Bosnia and Hercegovina in 1995 (see Chapters 7 and 10). In both
cases, all that had changed was the mindset of the actor involved: Smith decided
no longer to allow the prospect of hostage-taking to intimidate the international
force and effectively limit its room for maneuver; Milošević decided not to be
intimidated by the threat of air action, the avoidance of which had previously
been a restraint on his scope for action. A key lesson from this is the need to
check information and assumptions about an adversary's mindset and likely
behavior when contemplating the use of force – especially where the force to
be used and the objectives at stake are limited and a coercive approach is predicated on the assumed understanding of the opponent's threshold of pain and
likely actions.

[4] The original publication and fullest treatment of details pertaining to this
operation, including the name 'Horseshoe', was in the *Washington Post* on
11 April 1999. The picture painted there is generally correct, although there are

probably a product of confusion and interpretation. One of the
key points of confusion arose over the original word. The first
announcement that a plan existed was made by the German Foreign Minister Joschka Fischer, on 6 April. In Germany the original word was said to have been 'Potkova', but as a German general
on retiring was later to note, that word would more likely be used
by Croats, whereas the more conventional Serbian word would be
'Potkovica'[5] (the latter is a diminutive of the former – a 'little horseshoe').

While there was both a specific plan for the operations in Kosovo
and, it would seem, some other plan apparently named (in the
original) Potkovica (not Potkova), the two were not the same. One
element in the confusion stems from the origin of the report in
which the term 'Potkova' is used. This was variously said to have
come from Bulgarian, Austrian or Slovenian sources before it reached Germany – although there was specific information available to
NATO capitals on the actual plans, 'Potkova' may well have referred to something else. The most likely interpretation is that in
the *ex post facto* attempt by surprised Western politicians and officials to see why they had not understood how fast and widespread the Serbian campaign would be, somewhere in the German
(or some other) system different elements had been conflated.[6] These
included trawls through background intelligence reporting, where

---

some nuances and details that are inaccurate, or not as clear as they could be.
For example, the assertion that 'Milošević and his generals had prepared over
many weeks' is not wrong, in the short-term and with reference to the specific
version that was Operation Horseshoe, however, it is equally wrong in that the
name does not appear to have been correct and the specific plan was merely the
latest iteration of one that had evolved over months and years, with the disposition of units in summer and fall 1997 suggesting that the first decisions and
plans had probably appeared in February or March that year. A second useful
journalistic account was published in *The Observer* (18 July 1999) in the wake
of the 1999 hostilities, although the focus is on the surprise caused by the scale
of the operation, despite prior knowledge of it, there is generally less detail and,
of course, the name 'Horseshoe' is mistakenly repeated.

[5] After retiring, Brigadier-General Heinz Loquai, who had gone to work for
the OSCE, questioned the use of 'Potkova' rather than 'Potkovica' and suggested
that, because his former boss, the German Defense Minister Rudolf Scharping,
had sought to disguise the origins of the information, the evidence to support
the allegations was 'at best terribly meager.' See *Sunday Times*, 2 April 2000.

[6] It seems likely that only some decades hence, if ever, will the exact details
of this confusion emerge.

evidence of a 'Horseshoe' plan was found. This may well have been added to a descriptive analysis of Serbian operations, which almost certainly was of Bulgarian origin,[7] in which the 'Horseshoe' image left by the shape of the operations was noted. All of this was combined with awareness of information circulating in NATO capitals about the Serbian plan to eradicate the Kosovo Albanian insurgency by removing the water in which its guerrilla fish swam – the province's ethnic majority. Despite later public confusion over its name, this was the operational plan for which Serbian forces were mobilized and waiting only for the signal to start.[8]

With an integrated force of over 50,000 VJ and MUP troops poised as the last members of the KVM left Kosovo on 20 March, the Milošević machine rolled into action. Its forces darted into Kosovo, if they were not already deployed there, and spread across the province with some 300 tanks and half as many pieces of heavy artillery, destroying 600 towns and villages as they both harrassed and dissipated the UÇK, as well as murdering thousands of people, mainly ethnic Albanian men, and forcing close to one million of their ethnic kin to flee for their lives.

In this operation, VJ and MUP units, which had previously co-ordinated operations in the province, began to operate as one integrated force, for the first time, with a single integrated command

[7] According to German reporting in *Die Woche*, cited in the *Sunday Times*, 2 August 2000.

[8] The generally excellent writer Tim Judah was skeptical of 'Horseshoe' though not because of the lexical issue. He seems broadly to have doubted the idea of a planned operation, citing officials, including those in the UK, who suggest that there had been no warning – although, in reality, the various reports probably ran into three figures. The significance of these reports was simply not registered or properly assessed for the most part – although some in the British Foreign and Commonwealth Office were already struggling with the enormously complex issue of how to respond to a cleansing campaign in mid-1997. This skepticism acknowledges that for some time, if not forever, 'the real picture will remain unclear.' This is a positive modification of a position he expressed in Edinburgh on 20 October 1998, where he and I addressed a meeting of Scottish humanitarian NGOs, led by Edinburgh Direct Aid. At that stage, he had dismissed my suggestion that mass ethnic cleansing was in the pipeline and that the emptying of Kosovo should be anticipated, unable to believe that Belgrade would contemplate such a move ('what? One or two million people'? Never!). Events, unfortunately, confirmed that suggestion, even if the admirable qualities of skepticism continued to make the idea of plans to cleanse on such a scale hard to embrace. See Tim Judah, *Kosovo: War and Revenge*, London and New Haven: Yale University Press, 2000, pp. 240–1.

in Kosovo, under General Nebojša Pavković, commander of the 3rd Army (previously commander of the 52nd Priština Corps, based in Kosovo, and later to be Chief of Staff of the VJ). This integration was the culmination of years of preparations in which joint MUP-VJ 'counter-terrorist' operations had been the focus of training and education, and had been prominent in Belgrade military publications.[9] Joint action had been an issue of dispute within the military, with some, such as the former Chief of Staff, Perišić, arguing that the VJ should preserve its identity and not become enmeshed in the work of the MUP, while others, including his successor, Ojdanić, believed that the only way for the regular army to compete in terms of status and resources – including salaries – was to embrace the relationship with the Serbian MUP and to claim a primary role in any operations in Kosovo.[10]

Special and paramilitary units complemented the VJ and MUP forces. These were intended for some of the close-quarter killing missions and, as had been the case in Bosnia, some of the groups involved were not averse to looting. Among the latter, the best known were Arkan's Tigers, based in one of its old training camps, outside Mitrovica, as well as in the southern part of the province at Velika Hoča, south-east of Orahovac, on the road to Suva Reka. These units and others (irregulars and Special Forces of the JSO) were organized by Frenki Simatović, head of operations in the Security Service. Their bloody presence was not only a sign of what was to come, but was also intended to be read as a sign, sending fear into the hearts and minds of local Albanians.

Symbolism was certainly not the limit of their presence. Within hours of Ambassador William Walker's departure they were in action. Operating in their conventional squads of around twenty, 'Frenki's forces' spread out across the province, striking at mostly militarily inactive towns and villages, as well as at UÇK strongholds. In the

[9] The army bookstore in Belgrade from the mid-1990s began to carry a range of titles dealing with the joint army-interior ministry and police counter-terrorist and counter-insurgency operations.

[10] Since 1997, the MUP had been predominantly responsible for operations in Kosovo, with the VJ relegated to no more that a background supporting role – and consequently, to a smaller share of the security sector pie. Milošević's, at best, uneasy relationship with the regular army from the outset of the Serbian project led him to use what were, from his perspective, more 'reliable' Serbian forces (see Chapter 3).

latter category, there were blows to the heart of the ethnic Albanian insurgency around Drenica and Podujevo. Serbian forces had begun to move on the UÇK, attacking its positions, even before the KVM had completed its exit from Kosovo. These attacks had quickly dispersed the Albanian forces, tending to confirm VJ-MUP assumptions (based on experience the previous summer) that it would take little more than a week for them to complete the rout of their opponents. The only problem would be to prevent their reemergence at some stage. This left the focus of the Serbian action on civilians. In Srbica and Suva Reka, among other places, men were rounded up, taken away and shot by JSO units wearing distinctive red berets and ski-masks, or balaclavas. Such was the swift and ruthless conduct that characterized the conflict.

From the first moments of the Serbian campaign on 20 March, villages were shelled or simply razed while the strike units of persecution murdered, raped and tortured. The campaign was a fluent combination of forces. The shock troops of the JSO and the paramilitaries moving rapidly from one location to another in armored vehicles were at the sharp end of a joint operation supported by MUP and VJ infantry, including VJ Special Forces in places (such as Srbica and Suva Reka, as well as Djakovica, Priština and Peć) and crucially by VJ artillery and tanks, with the latter, in particular, demonstrating the fruits of reflection over the preceding years, with emphasis on the capacity of armor and mechanized units to provide surprise and dynamism through fire and movement in local operations.[11] This integration was a product of careful preparation – which also involved significant non-military matters.[12]

The VJ had quickly gained control of communications routes. One of the first moves of the campaign had been to deploy tanks to block the main routes and supply lines from Macedonia into the province, while dispatching armored units into the hills to seize the area and eradicate any UÇK presence. Elements of the 15th Mechanized and 211th Brigades moved along the north-south road and rail links between the capital, Priština, and one of the key

---

[11] Col. Milinko Stišovic, 'Iskustva iz Lokalnih Ratova o Pripremi i Angažovanju Oklopnih Mehanizovanih Jedninica', *Vojno Delo*, vol. XLIX, no. 1, 1997.

[12] Among the ways in which the campaign had already been well rehearsed was the collection and removal of public records from many towns. The same was true of valuable cultural artifacts, including important pieces of religious heritage, presumably taken away for safekeeping.

strategic towns, Podujevo, establishing firm control. While the former moved out from the capital, the latter entered the province from Serbia proper, with the two forces meeting at Podujevo. Other 15th Brigade elements, along with the 37th and 125th Brigades, struck west from Priština towards the heartland of support for the UÇK around Drenica. By 26 March, the VJ had established a grip on the key axes of communication.

With a framework of control established, on 29 March, with the VJ operating jointly with MUP units, the Serbian attack was in full spate. By this stage, the ethnic Albanian insurgency was largely dispersed and had been driven into deep retreat, its communications broken, while population centers were emptied of their remaining residents – both through murder and forcible expulsion – and the buildings destroyed by artillery fire, by flamethrowers (in the hands of white uniformed VJ special forces), or simply by tanks and bulldozers knocking dwellings to the ground. The 15th, with a command hub in Priština, played a vital role, at the core of joint operations. With elements already deployed north to Podujevo and west to Drenica, it extended its reach into the south, both west and east, accompanying units from the 125th in a drive on the key areas that would form the open gate for cleansing expulsions. For these operations in the south, the 243rd Brigade joined the fray, devastating towns such as Mališevo and later, under the command of Colonel Krman Jelić, directing artillery fire onto tens of thousands of displaced ethnic Albanians exposed in fields. Enormous numbers of ethnic Albanian civilians fled across Kosovo and into neighboring Macedonia and Albania, having been herded from their homes into holding areas, robbed and stripped of their identity documents – thus effectively removing any claim that they might make to return at a later date.

A special unit spearheaded the most ferocious attacks on ethnic Albanian villages, comprising troops from the 15th and 125th VJ Brigades and MUP SAJ units, with JSO and paramilitary squads attached, commanded by Colonel Seba Zdravković, of the 125th. This composite force was responsible for the primary mission in the first days of the campaign – to clear the pathway between the ends of the horseshoe at Djakovica and Prizren. All villages and the entire population along and beside the E-27 road were therefore emptied, creating a corridor between the two towns. Once this stage was completed, by early April, additional forces were moved into the area, with the 252nd Airborne – veterans of earlier campaigns in Croatia and Bosnia and Hercegovina in the 243rd Motorized Infantry, the 549th Motorized Brigades and elements of the 52nd Artillery Brigade. The joint operation moved systematically clockwise from Dečani to Peč to Klina to Orlate,[13] creating an iron rim that drove the population and any remaining insurgents southwards, where they would meet alternative flows of ethnic Albanians coming from other directions, all of whom would be forced towards the borders with Macedonia and Albania.

In some cases rural ethnic Albanian departees were driven into larger towns, such as Djakovica, but in most cases this was merely a temporary refuge. On the night of 27–28 March, in an operation that resonated with images of Nazi Germany more unambiguously than any other Serbian action in ten years of war and terror, there began the mass deportation of ethnic Albanians from the towns. Overnight, hundreds of thousands of people were herded onto trains and buses and taken directly to Kosovo's borders, where they were forced at gunpoint, without money, personal belongings and identity papers, to head into Albania or Macedonia. In the big towns of Prizren, Peč and the capital, Priština, MUP units established checkpoints, stopping all vehicles and directing the occupants to collection points on foot, where other ethnic Albanians had been ordered to go after MUP personnel had conducted door-to-door searches. These massive corralling operations began on the outskirts and worked their way inwards towards the center, with over 200,000 people in the capital ushered at gunpoint to the railway station, before being crammed into railway cars for the short 64 km journey to the Macedonian border that some did not survive, particularly the elderly.

From the perspective of Serbia's image in the struggle against NATO air operations, the deportations were a negative move that quickly required modification. The images of so many people crammed into railway carriages focused international opinion and support, where before there had been division and criticism of the NATO campaign. In the midst of the operation, Belgrade's resolve cracked, trainloads and buses of ethnic Albanians, some of which

[13] This corresponds with the movement General Sreten Lukić was reported to have described to Western officials in September 2000, when he suggested that a massive operation on this arc would wipe out the UÇK, completely. Cited in *The Observer*, 18 July 1999.

had already reached the border, were turned back, but it was not clear where they could, or would go.[14]

When the inhabitants of Kosovo's towns and those who had been forced from the countryside by the Serbian campaign returned to the crossing points out of the province, Srebrenica cast its shadow. Men between the ages of twenty and fifty were disappearing. As the columns from Djakovica reached the border, there were no males present among the 60,000 ethnic Albanians from that town alone. While some men had fled, or were in hiding, there were also reports emerging of forcible separation of men. In Ostrozub 1,000 men were separated from the rest of the population and taken away. In Velika Kruša, the number of men separated and taken away was 3,000. The same pattern occurred elsewhere, often in smaller numbers, at any one time. Tens of thousands of ethnic Albanian males ended up concentrated in makeshift prisons – the munitions factory at Srbica, the metalworks at Glogovac in the north.

By the end of the war, 10–11,000 ethnic Albanians, mainly men, had been killed. Two years after the end of hostilities, more than 3,000 of them had not yet been found or accounted for. In part, this was because of the massive cover-up operation undertaken by Serbian forces from March 1999 onwards, to remove any evidence of the mass murders. In some cases this meant unearthing bodies from mass graves; in others, it may have involved their incineration at the Trepča lead mine furnaces, near Mitrovica. Credible reports during the conflict suggested that thousands of bodies were destroyed there. Even though preliminary forensic investigations at the mine revealed little, this did not necessarily rule out the fact that remains had been destroyed – as was the case with the missing men of Srebrenica. This was later confirmed by evidence emerging after the fall of Milošević which indicated that Serbian Special Forces had burned bodies as part of the cover-up. Based on testimony of some of those involved in the cover-up operation, it was

[14] This led to curious twists and turns at NATO, where initial condemnation of the forcible expulsions into neighboring countries was transformed into demands that those who had been pulled back from the brink of expulsion should be returned from wherever they had been taken in order to be forced out. These NATO convulsions were the result of fears that the humanitarian disaster of dealing with nearly a million refugees was a better option than tens of thousands of refugees disappearing – a notion that might have seemed incredible had there not been experience of mass disappearances from Srebrenica.

estimated that about half the 3,000 missing Albanians had been ground in an ore processor before being fed into the blast furnace conveyor belt.[15] This appallingly inhumane disposal of corpses was testimony both to the cruelty of the Serbian campaign and to the awareness of those involved that war crimes lay at the heart of their strategy.

Facing NATO: decoys and deception, communication and control

There could have been little surprise that the situation in Kosovo gained worldwide attention. There was already a major international stake in the future of the region covered by the former Yugoslav federation. That in itself would have brought attention to the conflict in Kosovo, notwithstanding its savage nature. Even without knowledge of the necro-nihilism of robbing graves to destroy potential evidence, or of the Nazi-style railway deportations, the Serbian campaign in Kosovo was such that it was bound to generate an international response. The audacity of Serbia's criminal strategy, however, ensured that, despite some doubts over motivation, means and ends in the international public sphere there was broad agreement that action was warranted, a response that found its echo in the generally high level of support in NATO countries for a response. NATO was ready to act, while Milošević appeared to have lured it into his plans to cleanse Kosovo – using Alliance attacks as the catalyst. Even so, confronting NATO and its massive air capability was a major challenge for Belgrade – one not easily mitigated by the eroneous assumption that air action would last no more than three weeks.

An important part of the equation both for Brussels and Belgrade was what NATO air power could achieve. It could destroy and denude Serbian capabilities, limiting their use against Albanian civilians and the UÇK, but Milošević's blitzkrieg cleansing operations reduced the usefulness of this option. Beyond this, the strategy could only work if raids were targeted against the pressure points of Milošević and his regime. While the logic of the situation pointed to eventual Serbian capitulation, there was always the chance

---

[15] *The Times*, 26 January 2001. This report referred to an earlier broadcast in the US by NPR, produced by American Radio Works, a unit of Minnesota Public Radio.

that the logic might not apply. Belgrade clung to the hope that, even when its assumptions about NATO's operational planning and stamina proved so misplaced, there was a possibility of outstaying the Alliance. In a peculiar form of asymmetric conflict, the leadership in Belgrade knew that, as with guerrilla campaigns, if it held on and avoided admitting defeat, it could, in the end, actually win – in such a conflict, for the weaker party not to lose is to win. With some experience of NATO airpower over Bosnia and Herce-govina – and also having discussed NATO capabilities and how to respond to them with officials from other countries with an interest in the question, such as Iraq – the Belgrade planners could imagine a scenario in which wily tactics in face of a vastly superior opponent might just enable the VJ to withstand NATO action.[16] What could NATO do to make Milošević change his mind, and how long might all this take to achieve?

The deployment of ground forces was a prospect that clearly worried Milošević, but it was also one which he ought to have had plenty of time to anticipate. He might gamble on surviving the bombing while his country and its armed forces were destroyed, in the hope that NATO would grow war-weary, or split, or that 'something might just turn up.' However, practical considerations meant that NATO ground forces were always perhaps three months away from mobilization as an option, until the decision to begin a build-up had been taken. And before practical issues were addressed, the Western allies would have to make a political decision that the use of air power would not work quickly enough – one that went to the core of the NATO military-political approach (see Chapter 10).

One of Milošević's most vulnerable points was control of communications and information. His power in Serbia had been secure in large part because of the adroitness of his information policy.

[16] Cunning, deceit and similar characteristics are judged to be important aspects of Serbian military tradition and culture. See Colonel Novica Stevanović 'Ratna Lukavstva Srpska Vojska', *Vojno Delo*, vol. XLVII, no. 2, 1997. Other significant factors in Serbian military culture are the ideas of being motivated only by defense and fighting ferociously in that spirit. See Božidar Jovović 'Tragovima Srpske Vojničke Etike', *Vojno Delo*, vol. XLVI, nos 1–2, 1994. Both ideas have some foundation in experience. It is intriguing that Milošević and his agents couched so much of what was a campaign of territorial expansion in terms of defending Serbia and Serbs, paving the way for explanations of war crimes in terms of the ferocity of Serbian defensive actions.

This permitted the existence of small, alternative sources of information, which appealed to those opposed to the regime, but any one of which could always be stifled using some legal technicality if it were judged to be too threatening. The major means of information dissemination was the Milošević controlled-RTS television, whose news broadcasts were the major (if not only) source of news for over 80 per cent of Serbia's population. Thus Milošević controlled the message, and even if he couldn't wholly control the way they received it, the scale of official public opinion polling in Serbia always gave his information managers an excellent sense of the public mood and how messages had been received. The targeting of Serbian TV broadcasting was thus a priority for both NATO and Milošević. It would show Milošević that he could not control events entirely – much as the use of NATO air power over Bosnia and Hercegovina in 1995 had entirely removed General Mladić's control of the situation. While this undoubtedly increased the pressure on Milošević, it could not absolutely force him to back down, if he simply chose to be defiant, sit out the bombing and absorb the pain inflicted. The same was true of operations that targeted his home, which was used as a command and control facility, and his party's offices in Belgrade. These brought NATO's destructive message close to the man himself. Again while Milošević was apparently panicked by being targeted personally, it was also clear that it would not necessarily force him to change course.

If the use of air power in any particular manner could not guarantee that Milošević would alter his policy, then his priority was to avoid the cumulative impact of various Alliance air operations before NATO's campaign succeeded. To be sure, over time, NATO would prevail. That success might come suddenly, overnight; equally, it might come suddenly after three months, or even eighteen months. While a shorter time frame was always more to be expected, as NATO's action hampered the effectiveness of the Yugoslav army and the Serbian Security forces, whether because of fuel shortages, lack of spare parts, or low morale, there was always a reasonable chance that it might just drag on a lot longer. For Milošević, the stakes were as high as they could be. Undoing his instruments of rule and oppression was unacceptable and he envisaged no circumstances in which he would capitulate. For him – as it turned out, in the end – there was nowhere to go but The Hague, or his grave.

If NATO could not be certain of making Milošević change his

mind, then he had to be removed from the equation. Both the army and the security forces knew that their strategic assets were being wasted as NATO wrought more damage, even if they had often been quite successful in terms of tactical force protection in the field in Kosovo. Overall, few personnel had been killed, leaving the military commanders some scope for satisfaction, as well as reassuring them that they were in control of the situation. But, this was not to remain the case as NATO's campaign intensified. Increasingly, personnel were being caught in groups and the number of casualties rose rapidly throughout May, especially in the second part of the month.

Many in the military must have questioned Milošević's leadership, and some appear to have been ready to get rid of their President to save themselves and their institutions. With the military being hit hard by NATO, their best option would be to replace Milošević with another politician, whether from within Milošević's party, such as Serbian President Milutin Milutinović, or from the Serbian opposition, or, even, perhaps with Montenegrin President Milo Djukanović, who had stayed neutral in the conflict (a possibility that saw Milošević, inevitably, repeatedly trying to get rid of his Montenegrin foe, as a sub-text of the war). The military malcontents were, however, discovered by Milošević's Security Service and several generals who had formed a group around the sidelined General Momčilo Perišić were placed under house arrest in Belgrade at the beginning of May, at the height of the conflict – although they were later released, once the threat had passed.

Breaking Milošević's strategic control of communications and information had opened the way for word-of-mouth transmission by reservists returning to their homes, whose numbers and reports were so great that the broken instrument of RTS could not project a complete enough message to counter the truth. Milošević's eventual capitulation was a disappointment to most of the military actively engaged in operations. Even though fatality levels were rising rapidly, the generals saw no reason to give in, certainly not at such an early stage. For them, not only had the ground campaign against the ethnic Albanians been a success, but the defense against NATO was also a source of great satisfaction and pride. From the outset, the VJ had drawn on its own experience and whatever it could glean from others to ensure that NATO air operations would face greater difficulties than had been the case against the VRS in Bosnia and Hercegovina almost four years earlier. Among their greatest sources of pride was the tactical success of the VJ's elaborate engineering works, in part derived from experience gained within the Belgrade military in Croatia and in Bosnia and Hercegovina.[17] VJ engineers had created a false army, in addition to the one that was actually deployed. Using mock-ups and models, as well as camouflage, they created enough false targets at the tactical level in Kosovo that NATO planes spent much of the time destroying decoys.

Thus, while the Pentagon and NATO initially claimed to have destroyed 450 artillery pieces, including mortars, 220 armored combat vehicles and 120 tanks,[18] these figures were later revised downwards, in part due the realisation of the extent of Belgrade's use of decoys, despite the VJ's major clear-up before it withdrew from Kosovo. The final figures of 389 artillery pieces, 153 armored vehicles and 93 tanks were around one fifth down on the initial end of operations estimates. However, the relative success of Serbian operations and tactics has to be measured against NATO's strategic objectives, which did not focus primarily on destroying the tactical level forces in Kosovo (even though many commentators in the West believed that this was what NATO was trying to accomplish and what it ought to be doing). Despite the qualification, the Serbian success in strategic deception was rightly a source of pride – and despite having many fatalities, running to perhaps even 5,000,[19] especially after mid-May, there was no objective military operational reason to suppose that this success could not have been sustained longer, had not this and other factors generated a change at the political level which brought the conflict to an end.[20]

Another significant boost to Serbian morale was the shooting down of a US F117A Stealth bomber. The first – and in the end almost the only Serbian air defense kill came on the night of 27–28 March. Not only had the air defense downed a NATO plane,

[17] See for example Colonel Dušan Stanižan and Major Branko Bošković, 'Iskustva iz Inžinjeriskog Obezdjenja Borbenih Dejstava u Graždanskom Ratu u Hrvatskoj', *Vojno Delo*, vol. XLVII, no. 1, 1995.

[18] For reasonable analysis of NATO's destructive record at the tactical level, see Ivo Daalder and Michael O'Hanlon, *Winning Ugly: NATO's War to Save Kosovo*, Washington, DC: Brookings Institution Press, 2000, pp. 153–5.

[19] In one A-10 attack alone at the end of the conflict, it was estimated by NATO that some 800 VJ personnel, flushed out by skirmishes with the UÇK, had been killed on Mount Paštrik at the end of May.

[20] For discussion of these factors, see Chapter 10.

it had destroyed one of America's elite aircraft, designed to be extremely difficult to detect on radar. While Daalder and O'Hanlon have discussed Western media speculation on how the plane was brought down,[21] their explanations are inadequate. One of these was that Serbian radar caught the supposedly invisible aircraft while its bomb doors were opened, thus momentarily removing part of its stealth covering, enabling air defense forces to target it. Another was that an SA-3 missile had locked on to the aircraft. It seems more probable that there was a mixture of luck and good judgment in the downing of the aircraft. While stealth attributes significantly reduce detection by radars, they cannot guarantee absolute prevention. One factor could be the type and generation of equipment used – while Belgrade was flush with both Western and Russian radar and air defense detection and response equipment,[22] it also used what would be deemed museum pieces in more advanced armed forces. While the modern Western and Russian systems were precisely the kind that stealth had been designed to fool, the VJ was also operating radar equipment of a vintage and limited potential that the plane's 'stealthiness' might not have been designed to meet.[23] In any case, when wet, the planes may become partly visible to radar, although not necessarily as a stealthy military aircraft. In those circumstances, however (and the night in question was one of many in which poor weather bedeviled NATO air operations early in the campaign), it may well be that the best – and in this case, the successful – approach is to launch rapid and random anti-aircraft artillery fire at the target and into the space along its trajectory.

The stealth success was one of the few positive gains for the Serbian air defense campaign,[24] even though there was a creditable defiance put up throughout the NATO attack. Other attempts,

---

[21] Daalder and O'Hanlon, *Wining Ugly*, p. 118.

[22] Among the Western equipment were systems made by Westinghouse and Marconi.

[23] This is reasoned speculation, which seemed plausible when suggested to British air force officers. The scenario has some parallel with the end of one of the *Star Wars* films, produced and directed by George Lucas, in which the evil Empire is defeated by aircraft so small and primitive that their defenses are unable to cope.

[24] On 1 May NATO lost two more aircraft, one accidentally, the other through Serbian air defense action – demonstrating the capacity to cause damage, even using relatively old missile defense systems.

some of which went beyond simple air defense, floundered. For example, at an early stage, the VJ air force sought to widen the conflict by taking hostilities into Bosnia and Hercegovina, where they sought to intercept NATO aircraft and, especially, to target NATO SFOR targets with attacks by its elite force of MiG-29s, among the most advanced combat aircraft in the world (although not necessarily the most appropriate machine for Serbian needs, given its primary role as an air superiority aircraft). However, the first two aircraft were so quickly dispatched by NATO aircrews that the others following in the flight turned back and made for base. This effectively put an end to any attempt to widen the war into Bosnia and Hercegovina.[25] The fate of the MiG-29s had been foreshadowed by the downing of three planes of this type, flying against NATO attacks over Kosovo on the first night of the air operations. They had been downed relatively easily by pilots from different NATO countries, with the first being a Dutch kill. The relative ease with which NATO aircraft were able to limit the use of MiG-29s, the most potent anti-aircraft air capability in Belgrade's arsenal, could never lead to complacency over air superiority and control. Despite NATO's holding the initiative, the VJ was able to maintain enough of a credible threat to keep NATO continually on guard in its attacks.

The attempts to use MiG-29s in the first line of defense probably contribute to explaining one of the most interesting Serbian approaches to combat with NATO: the failure significantly to turn

---

[25] It can reasonably be supposed that Milošević intended to create some kind of a second, complicating front, by applying pressure on Macedonia to the south. One specific way of doing this had been to organize rent-a-mob protesters from the strong ethnic-Serb community in the northern Macedonian town of Kumanovo, who, at the instigation of the Serbian Security Service, had burned and attacked the US and other NATO embassies in the capital Skopje, the previous day. Another, more general way, was by forcing unprecedented numbers of ethnic Albanian refugees into the country, where there was a delicate balance in intercommunal relations between the ethnic minority of Albanians and the ethnic majority of Slav Macedonians. There was also evidence of preparations by the VJ to conduct operations just outside the borders of Kosovo against ethnic Albanian communities in the Preševo Valley. Although conceived, in part, as a means of widening the war into Macedonia, which would almost inevitably have become involved, this action remained no more than a potential option. However, this operational concern was to emerge as a more significant issue after the end of hostilities. There was also strong concern about Belgrade's intention to attack Montenegro, at this stage.

on and use air defense radars and systems, especially in the first days of the NATO attack, and certainly for any extended period. At first, the non-use of radars could have been a complement to the first-line use of the MiG-29s – not using Serbian air defense capabilities minimized the risks of an own goal, in which Belgrade's planes would be downed by friendly fire. But this is by no means the only explanation of this seemingly unusual tactic, one that baffled NATO commanders.

The likely thinking from Belgrade's point of view has two axes. On one axis was the question of force protection and preservation. The VJ command knew perfectly well that, if the radars were turned on, NATO aircraft could detect and destroy them relatively easily. Put simply, restricted use, or no use, ensured that valuable assets were not wasted unnecessarily at the outset of the campaign – indeed were not significantly used in a campaign where their deployment might render them inoperable on another occasion. The other axis was the benefit of denying the Alliance easy early successes and, for more than good measure, confusing NATO's commanders: in essence, Belgrade was not playing ball – at least, it was not playing the onset-of-modern-military-operations game the way that US doctrine expected.[26] This was one of Belgrade's biggest assets in an unusual conflict: the capacity not to allow the conflict to be conducted exactly the way that the US, at the air power core of NATO, wanted. Apart from frustrating the Alliance and creating scope for disagreement in the West, it was also a source of great satisfaction and moral strength for the VJ, in particular, and Serbia, as a whole. They could not win, but they had shown pride, wit and some skill in attempting to counter NATO – all qualities notable by their absence in ground operations against ethnic Albanians.

Belgrade's campaign to eradicate the UÇK was eventually undone, despite general success, by the need to fight a second front against NATO. A sense of being cheated by the international

[26] Belgrade's military researchers had studied US strategy and operational doctrine, since the end of the conflict in the Bosnian theater – although it is not clear whether these studies contributed significantly to the conduct of the campaign against NATO in 1999. See, for example, Todor Mirković, 'Strategija Elastičnost i Selektivnog Vojnog Angažovanja Sjedinjenih Američkih Država', *Vojno Delo*, vol. L, no. 1, 1998 and 'Vojska u Spoljnoj Politici Sjedinjenih Američkih Država', *Vojno Delo*, vol. XLVIII, nos 4–5, 1996.

community in its failure fully to reward Belgrade for signing the Dayton Peace agreement in 1995 may well have been a factor in turning the Serbian strategic focus onto Kosovo. Undesirably, for Belgrade, it was international action that ended that campaign (see Chapter 10). As in Croatia and in Bosnia and Hercegovina, perhaps considerably more so, Serbian forces had the measure of their local adversaries but could not withstand the flexible strategic application of air force by NATO. In the southern campaigns, as in the west, it was the strategy of war crimes that prompted international military action, which in all cases had the *de facto* effect of feeding into the Serbian project's local adversaries' strategies and relative success along the way. The strategic approaches of those ranged against the Serbian project – first, local, then international – are considered in the following two chapters.

9

THE NEIGHBORHOOD ADVERSARIES:
AIMS, STRATEGIES AND OPERATIONS

While the Serbian project for new borders in the context of the SFRY's break-up was the core of the Yugoslav war, no armed conflict involves only one party. Moreover, while the Serbian strategy of war crimes dominated the war, there were other parties whose conduct included and even embraced acts that constituted crimes against humanity and war crimes. Indeed, the difference between a strategy founded on the commission of war crimes and one in keeping with the conventions, customs and laws of war was starkly apparent in the contrast between the conduct of most actors from within the region and that of those engaging with international purpose – most notably, NATO's operations over Kosovo in 1999 defined the difference. Contrary to some fairly wild assertions,[1] even by otherwise responsible groups, the NATO operations – sometimes to the frustration of US generals – were predicated on propriety and legality, with every mission legally vetted and enormous care taken to minimize deaths, even of combatants, most of the time. Those who lodged allegations against the Alliance betrayed ignorance, for the most part, of the relationship between war crimes and war – as discussed in the first chapter – and of the realities of military operations and war. (Of course, the overall character of the operations did not exclude the possibility that in some way, despite one's best efforts, transgressions would occur – as discussed in the final chapter.) Both the careful approaches of

[1] See for example, Michael MccGwire, 'Why Did We Bomb Belgrade?', *International Affairs*, vol. 76, no. 1, 2000, or Amnesty International 'Violations of the Laws of War by NATO During Operation Allied Force', 7 June 2000. Among the wildest of all is Robert Hayden, who asserts that the Alliance committed 'text book' war crimes (R. Hayden, *Blueprints for a House Divided: the Constitutional Logic of the Yugoslav Conflicts*, Ann Arbor: University of Michigan Press, 1999, p. 175).

those from outside the region who opposed the Serbian project and the frequently malign approaches of those inside the region opposing it require some attention. Even though this book's focus is on the Serbian project, it would be wrong not to consider the desires and situations of the other parties to the war.

Although Serbian aims, strategies and operations easily did most to define the war, they were to some extent shaped by the approaches adopted by each of the other parties, as well as creating the conditions for them. And – just as Nazi German and Imperial Japanese ambitions set the agenda during the Second World War, although there were other countries whose purposes were also embedded in the conflict – however much the Serbian project defined the war, there were many, collectively and individually, not working in the direct interest of that scheme who sought political and personal benefit from it. The aspirations and actions of those opposed to the Serbian new state project should be considered.[2] While these approaches, with the part exception of Slovenia, were contingent on the Serbian strategic approach, each had salient characteristics. The common strand running through each was that the strategies adopted were those of the weak, largely because the relative strength of the Serbian military through most of the war defined the terms on which others would have to engage – including Slovenia and, with some qualification, the UN and NATO (for the latter, weakness was often self-inflicted by political reluctance and division).[3]

For the most part, there was a general and ostensible war aim shared by the non-Serbian parties. Whereas the Serbian campaign was to create new borders, the position of all the other parties was, in the first instance, to secure the existing borders of the various SFRY republics as they gained independence. Thus, for Slovenia, for Croatia and for Bosnia and Hercegovina, the primary objective was to secure independence within agreed borders, while international actions, however confusing, limited and lacking in will they were at times, were generally geared to upholding key principles

---

[2] The opponents of the Serbian project are understood here to be the authorities in Slovenia, Croatia, Bosnia and Hercegovina and the political leadership of the Kosovo Albanians, as well as those engaged with the extra-Yugoslav international response to the Yugoslav war.

[3] See James Gow, *Triumph of the Lack of Will*, and Ivo Daalder, *Getting to Dayton*, Washington, DC: Brookings Institution Press, 2000.

of international society and both Western and international values. Croatia and Bosnia and Hercegovina had other war aims, some of which involved campaigns against each other. The Muslim-Croat conflict in Bosnia and Hercegovina demonstrated clearly that, however much the Serbian project dominated the war, there was considerably more to understanding the conflict than simply label-ing it Serbian 'aggression' – a term often used by non-Serbian protagonists from the region and by their sympathizers elsewhere. Despite helping to reflect primary responsibility for the onset of armed conflict, such terminology could also be unhelpful and misleading: it disguised the roles played by others and deflected attention from the genuine political questions on the Serbian side that were obscured by the decision to use force and its manner of application. The next two chapters seek despite the appropriate emphasis on analyzing the Serbian project in the remainder of this book, to contribute to this debate and counter an overly simplistic reading, via a review of Slovenian, Croatian, Bosnian Kosovan ap-proaches to the war, in the present chapter, and international res-ponses in the one that follows.[4]

Slovenia: armed forces, aims and approach

Slovenian strategy relied heavily on the doctrine of General People's Defense adopted in the SFRY,[5] the essence of which was to use guerrilla tactics to prevent an opponent fighting on its own terms while demonstrating to the world a capacity and a commitment to defense of the country. For Slovenia, this meant mobilizing its territorial defense forces (TOs) in order to engage the JNA in a series of armed clashes, rather than frontal combat. The purpose of this was twofold. First, it was intended to harass the enemy, and second, it was intended to convey the message to the outside world

---

[4] It should be noted that each of these reviews covers topics each of which deserves further book-length and Ph.D. research as topics in their own right, as well as having the potential for even more specific research on their sub-aspects – just as each of the chapters on the Serbian project contains the potential for book-length research and writing. For analysis of the international strategic res-ponse within the overall context of international engagement in the Yugoslav war until 1995 (thus excluding the Kosovo campaign) see the author's *Triumph of the Lack of Will*.

[5] More detailed treatment of the war in Slovenia can be found in James Gow and Cathie Carmichael, *Slovenia and the Slovenes: a Small State in the New Europe*, London: Hurst, 2000, Ch. 6.

of a country bravely defending itself. To this end, Slovenia established an international media management center in advance of the conflict and used the former Deputy Minister of Defense as Information Minster to brief the international press, who then carried Slovenia's message to the world, based on its armed action. This integrated strategy of military encounters and media management worked effectively for Slovenia.

Slovenian officials studied the Gulf War as part of a comprehensive review of the international community as they formed their strategy for independence. However, they were not distracted by events in the Gulf, nor did they assume that they would be more likely to secure outside armed intervention than they would have been had there been no Gulf War. In fact, they relied on the well-established Yugoslav doctrine of General People's Defense in calculating the possibility of mobilizing outside support.

Although the Gulf War featured in the Slovenian analysis of the world they were seeking to join, their key assessment involved the commitment of Western governments to supporting the Federal government of Ante Marković and opposition to any suggestion of independence. Their somewhat realistic assessment was that, apart perhaps from sympathetic neighborly support from Austria, they could not expect help from any Western country. There would only be hope of mobilizing external support if they were prepared to help themselves and this implied reliance on an effective defense should there be a use of force against their attempt to become independent.

Two features of the Gulf War were factored into these preparations. One was the importance of a short campaign with a big impact. Slovenian defense planners formed the belief that, if it came to a fight, they would need to be efficient in combat in order to secure a quick and favorable outcome. Indeed, it was judged that their aims could only be realized through a short, sharp campaign in which the 'occupier' was beaten as soon as possible. The second was that use of the media would be vital. To this end, the Ministry of Information organized what was in reality a massive propaganda campaign. The Ministry hired a conference center in the Slovenian capital Ljubljana, the Cankarjev Dom, and established it as a slick, modern media hub on the eve of the declaration of independence, from where they presented their case to the world, mobilizing support in Western countries in particular. The Press Center understood that one of the best ways of controlling the media was by

'making their lives easy' and giving them efficient, regular brief-
ings on the state of events. To this end they also proved adept at
manipulating information.[6]

Media management was the vital component in an integrated
strategy adapted from the old Yugoslav General People's Defense
doctrine. This doctrine required avoidance of frontal war. Instead
guerrilla operations to initiate armed clashes on Slovene terms were
inaugurated, giving the Slovenian military the advantage. But this
asymmetric strategy required publicity to work – without magni-
fication through the media, these limited efforts would prove futile.

The emphasis at the operational level was on action against tanks
and armored vehicles. Combinations of wholly local troops and
mobile units were used to trap vehicles, perhaps by using felled
trees along a mountain road, and then to attack them with short-
medium range anti-armor weapons, using Singaporean copies of
German Armbrust rockets at ranges often considerably less than
the 2,500 meter capability of that weapons system. Utilities were
cut to JNA facilities. With regard to JNA air power, Soviet-made
Strela-7 anti-air rockets were used against both helicopters and fixed
wing aircraft.[7] The primary purpose of TO operations was to harry
the JNA, but not with any illusion of being able to beat it purely
through this action. The operations were conducted only with a
view to projecting a message to the world: that the Slovene people
were bravely defending themselves.

Croatia: armed forces, aims and approaches

Croatian aims were ambiguous throughout. Zagreb wanted to preserve Croatia's territorial integrity from Serbian incision while Croatia and its Bosnian Croat proxies sought to create an ethnically
Croat statelet in Western Hercegovina and Central Bosnia that would

[6] For example, the Minister for Information, Jelko Kacin, briefed journalists
about the location of a burned-out JNA armored personnel carrier; the journalists raced off to get pictures of it, assuming that it had been destroyed by anti-
armor fire; it later emerged that the vehicle had been abandoned by its crew and
later set ablaze by local youths. Kacin had not lied, but had given the journalists
enough information to allow them to jump to conclusions which supported
Slovenia's case.

[7] In addition, Slovenia made limited use of the Gazelle, Augusta and Hirondelle
helicopters available to it from the Slovene Police force, although essentially for
medical and reconnaissance purposes only, with a few instances of ground attack.

be annexed to Croatia itself. Herceg-Bosna was the key to this aggressive strategy. On 3 July 1992, just as Croatian forces were successfully removing Serbian forces from around Mostar and taking control of the western part of the town, Croat leaders in Bosnia and Hercegovina declared the formation of the 'Croatian Community of Herceg-Bosna' at Grude in western Hercegovina. At what was described as a meeting of this entity's Presidency, a set of measures on civil and military authority in the area were proclaimed for the undefined entity thought to include the estimated 30% of Bosnia and Hercegovina under the military control of the local Croatian armed forces. It was announced that the capital would be in Mostar, and it was clear that the broader motive was the creation of a 'Greater Croatia.' The move put Croatia and President Franjo Tudjman in an embarrassing and awkward position given Croatia's arguments regarding its sovereignty and integrity, although it chimed harmoniously with his personal ambitions for a 'Greater Croatia.'[8]

Croatia's position, was marked by elements of ambiguity. On one level, although Croatia's first concern was to secure independence within borders for Croatia itself, there was also an interest in securing control of territory in Bosnia and Hercegovina to be annexed to Croatia, just as the Serbian republics were to be federated

---

[8] In the mid-nineteenth century, Croatian nationalists in the Croatian Party of Rights (HSP – Hrvatska Stranka Prava), founded by Ante Starčević and Eugen Kvartnik, promoted the idea of re-creating the maximal borders of the medieval realm of King Tomislav. It is this notion of a historic territory from which discussion of Greater Croatia derives. The basic 'right' sought by the HSP was the right to form that historic nation-state. While Starčević appears to have developed his idea in line with French revolutionary nationalism – all inhabitants within the territory are French and have citizen's rights, but are not allowed, for example, to be Catalan – Kvartnik was of a more openly anti-Serb and anti-Semitic complexion, regarding the former as an obstacle to the achievement of Croatian nationhood. After Starčević died in 1896, the HSP took on an overtly anti-Serbian line. The Nazi-puppet Independent State of Croatia, formed after the Axis invasion of April 1941, went some way towards the creation of the boundaries of greater Croatia, incorporating Bosnia and Hercegovina and parts of Vojvodina. That state resorted to a policy of genocide, in part, as a solution to the problem for a nationalist, anti-Serbian government that half the population within these borders was non-Croat. As the communist regime in Croatia came to an end, the proponents of a Greater Croatia, which would incorporate the whole of Bosnia and Hercegovina, plus parts of Vojvodina, Montenegro and Sandžak re-founded the HSP under the leadership of Dobroslav Paraga and argued for the establishment of Greater Croatia.

with Serbia. The Croatian approach echoed that of Serbia, with the evolutionary development of an 'Association of Municipalities in Herceg-Bosna' in November 1991 and the aforementioned 'Croatian Community of Herceg-Bosna'. Eventually, this self-proclaimed status would be formally subordinated to the creation of the Federation of Bosnia-Hercegovina, under the US-brokered Washington Agreement of January 1994, which brought the Bosnian-Croatian war to a close.

The Croatian approach to Herceg-Bosna could be seen in two lights – either as compensation for loss of territory in Croatia itself, or, in an ideal situation, as an addition to a Croatia whole within its designated borders. The essential ambiguity of this position meant that, to some degree, Croatia could not lose out completely in any eventual settlement: if border changes were to be accepted, then any territory lost to Serbian forces would be compensated for by the acquisition of territory from Bosnia and Hercegovina, formed around the large Croatian minority areas; and if the maintenance of existing borders were to be confirmed, then Croatia would not gain land from Bosnia and Hercegovina but would secure the borders of Croatia itself. In an ideal world Croatia might have its cake and eat half of it too – as could be argued to be the case with the outcome of the war: Croatia's independence within borders was confirmed, but it also gained great influence in Bosnia and Hercegovina, even if territory was not formally acquired. Moreover the evidence of campaigns in central Bosnia and Hercegovina, as well as in Croatia, indicates that 'ethnic cleansing' could be identified as a Croatian war aim.

Suspicion surrounding Zagreb's ambitions was fanned by Croatian decisions to abandon their allies in certain areas (Bosanski Brod, for example), the refusal to fight in others at crucial moments (Sarajevo) and the decision to stifle arms supplies through Western Hercegovina (the principal route for imports) to army units in central and northern Bosnia. In October 1992, local Croat forces in Prozor and Gorni Vakuf began to 'cleanse' the areas of Muslims, but these remained isolated cases until the spring of 1993, when friction between the two was exacerbated by the Vance-Owen Plan.[9] The HVO command gave the Bosnian Army an ultimatum to withdraw by 15 April from areas they claimed were 'given' to the Croats

[9] See Gow, *Triumph of the Lack of Will*, pp. 249–50, n.55.

under Vance-Owen's creation of ten provinces within Bosnia. There followed a spate of horrific clashes between Croatian forces and the Bosnian Army in the central part of the country, including 'cleansing' operations on Muslim villages, in which the inhabitants were shot and burned.

The Croatians used four forces in the course of the war: the official Croatian Army; its Bosnian Croat proxy-cum-paramilitary force in Bosnia and Hercegovina, the Croatian Defense Council; Ministry of the Interior Special Forces; and, lastly, private paramilitary groups. Not all of these forces were operational throughout the whole of the period.

The Croatian Army (Hrvatska Vojska – HV) was formally established in September 1991. It absorbed units of the Croatian National Guard (Zbor Narodne Garde – ZNG), formed on 12 April 1991, initially from interior ministry special police reservists organized by the Croatian Ministry of Defense as the core of a standing army. At that time, Croatia also had around 20,000 troops in Special Units of the Interior Ministry (MUP); these were also placed under the operational control of the Ministry of Defense. Originally over 20,000 strong, there were plans for a force of 75,000, but by late 1991 the level had swollen to perhaps 200,000.

Even this reflected no more than partial mobilization – Zagreb appeared hesitant, even when it ordered full mobilization, and faced challenges in ensuring that its developing army had sufficient manpower available. Although armed hostilities erupted in the Republic of Croatia at the end of June 1991, it was not until 6 October 1991, three months later, that the Croatian Parliament mandated an immediate general mobilization. However, there had been specific regional mobilizations previously – for example, around Zadar, in September 1991 – and, given the immediacy of armed hostilities in this period, it is likely that local mobilization also occurred in the Split region.

The peak point of potential mobilization throughout the war occurred in October 1991. The highest mobilization levels applied only to this month, and possibly to the months either side of it.[10]

---

[10] For example, in one Dalmatian enterprise, the number of employees performing some kind of military duty was 1,528 in October 1991, a peak reached between September's 1,073 and November's 1,310, with the December figure falling away to a little more than that for September at 1,082. These were the highest levels of manpower lost to defense needs during the war.

Despite this, the October general mobilization was neither comprehensive, nor complete. By 12 November 1991, it was necessary to issue a specific mobilization call for the Dubrovnik area – which at the time was under a major attack. The fact that Defense Minster Gojko Šušak made this call indicated the degree to which the official full call-up of October had not begun to be fulfilled. And on 21 November 1991 the Defense Ministry restricted the movement of all men of call-up age, a measure that would not have been necessary had the general mobilization been successfully completed.

Several important issues qualify the discussion of mobilization. In particular, there was concern that military mobilization might affect manpower at industrial facilities in Croatia.[11] The impact depended on the type, duration, or location of those involved, but it is quite likely that a number performed Civil Protection duties rather than service in the armed forces.[12] In general, to limit the impact of the draft on industry, Zagreb had made specific provision to ensure that certain categories of worker would be excluded from the call-up. 'Strategic' labor was legally exempt from mobilization.

Mobilization did not last far beyond the ceasefire of 2 January 1992. After this truce in Croatia, although some units of the 30,000-strong MUP forces continued to be associated with the HV, most, especially reserve units, were demobilized. The first wave of formal demobilization for the HV – 20,000 personnel – was announced on 26 February 1992 and implemented on 12 March 1992, although de facto this process may well have begun before, regarding

[11] For instance, records for one shipyard in Dalmatia indicate that 1,418 workers played a role in the war between 1990–93.

[12] The term Civil Protection refers to one specific component of the General People's Defense doctrine of the SFRY which was based on a two-tier armed force. The first of these was the JNA, the regular army. Its function in the event of an armed attack was to protect the borders of the SFRY and to delay the aggressors while the second tier of the armed forces was mobilized. This was the Territorial Defense (TO – Teritorijalna Odbrana). Unlike the JNA, which was run and commanded by the SFRY Ministry of Defense, the TO was organized by a ministry of defense in each of the constituent states. The TO was to provide resistance in depth, through low-intensity guerrilla operations which would drain the capacities of the invader. The TO system was complemented by Civil Protection (CZ – Civilna Zaštita), the purpose of which was civilian support of the armed forces, especially the TO, through the exercise of tasks such as first aid and ambulance work, as well as, crucially, maintaining morale in the community. CZ was a civilian function, which would not necessarily require anyone serving in this capacity to be away from their homes.

local mobilization. A second wave of demobilization occurred the following May, aimed at reducing Croatia's armed forces to around 70,000. There would be further brief periods in which reservists would be called up, such as prior to military operations in January and September 1993 and in 1995, but these were not general mobilizations.

The army consisted of two elements, the ZNG (Croatian National Guard) and the Home Guard. The ZNG comprised elite mobile brigades for use in any part of the country, while the Home Guard formed local territorial defense units based on a reserve cadre. In the spring of 1993, the ZNG officially had seven brigades, each up to 2,500 strong, while the Home Guard totaled between 80,000 and 90,000 troops. The official total for the HV was 105,000 troops, although a more accurate figure was, perhaps, 150,000. It was equipped with 200 tanks, mostly T-54/T-55, but with some older M-34s and some more up-to-date M-84As, as well as 150–200 artillery pieces of 76 mm., 105 mm., and 155 mm. caliber. A small air capability had been acquired, involving 250 personnel and around ten aircraft, including two MiG-21s. A slightly more significant coastal naval capability was built up, a consequence of Croatia's having four out of five of the naval bases in the former Yugoslavia (Split, Šibenik, Ploče and Pula, with Boka Kotorska (the Bay of Kotor) in Montenegro, the fifth). The Croatian Navy had 800–1,000 personnel in 1993 and thirty craft, including five missile boats. Croatia also committed around 15,000 troops, with 50 M-34 and T-54/55 tanks, plus 60–80 artillery pieces of varying caliber, to the support of the Croatian Defense Council in Bosnia and Hercegovina (see below). In addition, Croatia used Mi-8 helicopters and light aircraft of the Croatian Air Force to carry troops and supplies into Bosnia and Hercegovina.

During the war in Croatia several paramilitary groups emerged which were either partially or wholly outside the control of the government in Zagreb. The 'Wolves of Vukovar' was a renegade unit of the ZNG, led initially by Branimir Glavaš, head of defense forces in the Osijek area. Glavaš, an extreme right-wing member of Tudjman's Croatian Democratic Community (HDZ) was said to have created his own cell within the Osijek police force, as well as a parallel military force some months before the war. This force was around 1,500 strong. The Zebras was a small group of 180 men organized by an émigré Croat from Austria, who was responsible for arming them. The group, which included some non-Yugoslavs, was said to be responsible for capturing the army barracks at Petrinja – although the town was later lost again by the ZNG. The Zebra group's political program was not clearly expressed, although it was clearly closer to neo-fascist elements than to Zagreb's official forces, of which the Zebras were critical. Indicative of its views was its appearances alongside the Ustaški Prepored (Ustasha Revival), which, although it did not appear to be large or have significant weaponry at its disposal, clearly invoked the heritage of Ante Pavelić's 'Ustasha' regime. The two groups operated side by side in Sisak. Also present there was the Crna Legija (Black Legion), which was also active in Vukovar alongside the ZNG and other groups. This was a relatively small outfit, perhaps no more than 300 strong, which operated alongside and within units of the Interior Ministry Troops (MUP) as an 'anti-terrorist brigade.' It consciously adopted the wartime Ustasha's uniform and symbols. The Legion was not exclusively Croat in composition: its commander, Alija Šiljak, described himself as a 'Croat of Muslim faith' – and there were clearly other non-Croats in its ranks. The Legion was identified by Croatian information minister Branko Salaj as neo-fascist. He warned that it would be 'eliminated' unless it accepted full integration in the republic's regular forces, even though it had already been cooperating with MUP units.

The Legion was said to have formal links to the extremist Croatian Party of Rights (HSP), although in this respect it was overshadowed by the overt link between the HSP and the largest of Croatia's party-armies, the Croatian Defense Union (Hrvatski Obranbeni Savez – HOS). HOS was estimated to have 10–15,000 men and took the initiative in Croatian counter-offensives, setting a lead which Tudjman's ZNG had to follow. Tension between Paraga's people and the government grew as the impression quickly spread that where HOS was involved, Croatian forces appeared more successful than where they were not. This helped HOS to win support in the same way that Tito's party-army, the Partisans, had done during the Second World War: people were attracted simply because the movement was offering resistance. The pressure this put on the Tudjman government, in addition to the failure to gain recognition, led to serious tensions between HOS and government forces, including shooting incidents. In one of these, the HOS leader (and Paraga's deputy in the HSP), Ante Paradžić, was killed by ZNG members. Paraga was arrested in November 1991 and during his detention the Croatian authorities were able to assert their authority over HOS within the republic. This was a process facilitated not only by Paraga's incarceration, but also by the prospect of imminent international recognition. By the end of the year, the Chief of Staff, General Anton Tus, claimed that all elements of HOS, the other party-armies and a brigade of emigrés and international volunteers had been brought within the ranks of the ZNG and no longer carried their own insignia.[13] At this stage, HOS established itself in Bosnia and Hercegovina, with around 5,000 troops, which based themselves there at the end of the war in Croatia – although contemporary estimates suggested that they numbered up to 16,000 in Western Hercegovina.[14] This seems to have been partly a move to avoid coming under Croatian command and control and partly a reflection of the degree to which Croats from Hercegovina were represented in its ranks. In August 1992, HOS units in Bosnia and Hercegovina were formally absorbed by the Croatian Defense Council.

Commonly referred to by the abbreviation of its Serbo-Croat name, HVO (Hrvtska Vijeća Odbrana), this force was organized by local representatives of Tudjman's Croatian Democratic Community (HDZ) party and by the Croatian security service, in a manner not dissimilar to that taken by the Serbian side in forming proxy forces. The force was established locally; but it was supplemented by up to 15,000 personnel from the Army of the Republic of Croatia who initially brought with them over 50 tanks (the figure grew by almost four times by 1995) and many artillery pieces. These forces were engaged both in western Hercegovina and in the north. The HVO was formally organized by the Croatian Democratic Community, the political entity to which it was attached, from the summer of 1991 onwards, although it was not until early 1992 that

[13] *Danas* 31 December 1991.

[14] *Oslobodjenje*, 13 January 1992; *Politika*, 14 January 1992; 'Weekly Review', *RFE/RL Research Report*, 6 March 1992. These HOS figures are those cited in James Gow, 'Military and Political Affiliations in the Yugoslav Conflict', *RFE/RL Research Report*, vol.1, no. 20, 15 May 1992. In a curious footnote, presumably based on confusion, Steve Burg and Paul Shoup report that the HOS figure in this article is put at 45,000, 'which is probably an overestimate.' They appear to be confused between HOS and the HVO, taking the upper figure for Croatian forces as a whole, rather than the estimates purely for HOS. Burg and Shoup, *The War in Bosnia-Herzegovina: Ethnic Conflict and International Intervention*, Armonk, NY: M.E. Sharpe, 1999, p. 427, n. 53.

arms began to be distributed. The HVO also gradually incorporated HOS forces in Bosnia – a process that was formally completed in August 1992. HVO force strength was 30–35,000, reaching up to 45,000 with Croatian Army supplements. Although nominally allied with the Army of Bosnia and Hercegovina for most of the war, especially at the beginning and end of the phase in Bosnia and Hercegovina, the role of the HVO was always ambiguous and there was suspicion and tension between the two, both before and after they clashed in 1993. The generally stronger Croats were rightly suspected by Sarajevo of seeking their own fiefdom, with a view to creating a 'Greater Croatia.'

Croatia had three discrete approaches to the war. In the early stages in Croatia itself, defense was the objective. In the middle phase of the war, the purpose was to seize territory in Bosnia and Hercegovina, primarily at the expense of the Bosnian Muslims and the Bosnian government – hence an ambiguous and putative alliance with the Army of Bosnia and Hercegovina (ABiH) dissolved into open conflict. In the final phase of Croatia's war, a modernized offensive approach was taken against Serbian forces, both in Croatia itself and, once more in uneasy alliance with the ABiH, in western Bosnia and Hercegovina.

Croatia's approach to defense and the achievement of international recognition differed from that of Slovenia, despite significant co-operation in advance of and soon after the declarations of independence, although the Slovenes felt betrayed by Zagreb's lukewarm support once the war had begun. The Slovenian authorities had determined that their ambition would only be fulfilled by thorough planning and efficient execution of that plan, based on General People's Defense. Croatia, on the other hand, did not make such thorough preparations and, once fighting broke out, rather than taking the initiative, sought to maximize its status as the victim of aggression. Among other things, this was to result in a conflict between Croatia's President Franjo Tudjman and his then defense minister, Gen. Martin Špejglj, who argued for both better preparations and a more active defense. The latter resigned over the issue in August.[15]

Franjo Tudjman's strategy was for his forces often to do as little as possible – although hidden, easily achieved successes in ethnic

[15] *Nedeljna Dalmacija*, 11 August 1991.

cleansing were not excluded (whether or not officially determined by Zagreb, they were certainly condoned). Doing little did not mean doing absolutely nothing. They had to do some defending in order to show the world that Croatia was a victim needing assistance, namely by granting recognition. In 1992 Croatia's official representative in London argued that there were parallels between his country's plight and that of Kuwait, the emphasis on Croatia as a 'victim of aggression' drawing clear allusions to the situation in the Gulf. This was a message that was echoed by those outside Croatia opposing Serbian acts of aggression. The Serbian President, Slobodan Miloševic was characterized as the 'Saddam Hussein of the Balkans', and as the UN Security Council met in September and aired the possibility of recognition, this was interpreted with reference to the Gulf War. Recognition, it was thought, would place Croatia in the same position as Kuwait had been. The official Croatian news agency, HINA, issued a statement indicating that it had 'already been confronted with the difficulties in northern Iraq of the Kurdish uprising' and seemed to see a precedent for Croatia's situation in the Security Council resolution, which had required Baghdad immediately to stop its aggression.[16]

Croatian commentators realized that the significance of taking the Yugoslav issue to the UN Security Council was that the United States would be necessarily more involved in the situation in Croatia. The US role was summed up in one article which commented that, 'What God wants, without Bush, will not be!' The author supplemented this with the judgment, expressing a common view, that, 'if nothing else, America cannot lose the initiative from the Gulf War.'[17] A review of the principal newspapers in Croatia from June to October suggests that such associations were not necessarily a primary issue internally. In fact these comparisons may have been made by Western journalists first and later taken on board by the Croats.

Notwithstanding the efforts of external representatives to link the cases of Croatia and Kuwait, the peculiar attempt by the Tudjman government to depict Croatia as a victim, and the timing of the change of strategy, suggest that Zagreb was making calculations of

[16] *HINA*, 21 September 1991.
[17] Jože Vlahovič, 'Kaj god bu, bez Busha to ne bu!', *Vjesnik*, 22 September 1992.

this kind. Zagreb announced a full mobilization and took the military initiative in a variety of ways after 7–8 October 1991. This date marked the end of the moratorium on implementation of the declarations of independence by Slovenia and Croatia agreed with EC mediators on the island of Brioni in July. It also followed the meeting of the WEU a week before, on 30 September, which removed any vague hint of a European military intervention, even as a peace-keeping force, from the agenda. In the absence of hard evidence, caution is necessary, and one can only speculate whether the proximity of the WEU meeting and the Croatian change of strategy were linked. Given the efforts of the external representatives and the timing of the decision, it is possible that Croatia could have based its 'victim strategy' on the Kuwaiti example. It was certainly inconsistent with the traditional Yugoslav strategy put to good use by Slovenia in which external support was mobilized by active resistance and respect, rather than passivity and hopes of a sympathetic intervention from countries with no immediate interest in doing so.

Croatia's depiction of itself as a victim was masked by in coherence in its media management and in use of armed forces. Early in the conflict journalists complained about poor media facilities and the dearth of information emerging from Zagreb, with the result that many international journalists took the trouble to go to the field, or to other sources, to gather information – often producing reports that ran counter to Zagreb's interests (although there was much sympathetic reporting in Germany and Austria).

In its use of armed forces, Croatia took two operational and tactical approaches during the first phase. The weaker was to take up fixed positions in areas under attack – around police stations, for example – thereby playing into their opponents' hands, given the Croats' lack of weaponry, especially of heavier types, and the relative paucity of manpower. The other, which had mixed results, was to encircle JNA bases and to cut off utilities, thereby putting a stranglehold on these military facilities. While pressure was exerted to good effect in some cases – JNA troops withdrew, handing over weapons – in many others, it proved an irritant which prompted a much more forceful approach than would have been the case otherwise (this was the case at Split, for example). The JNA response was sometimes more punishing than the benefit gained from placing facilities under effective siege.

The key to Croatia's victim strategy was to force international recognition of its independence: the more Croatian towns were attacked, the more likely it became that international support for Croatia would grow. The 'victim strategy' was apparent in Zagreb's dealings with those in Croatia who were taking the initiative in a more active defense, such as the defenders of the besieged town of Vukovar. By offering strong resistance, Vukovar both epitomized and went against the grain of Croatia's 'victim strategy'. Zagreb refused to send material support, claiming that it was impossible to reach the town – even though others offered contradictory evidence.[18] Whereas the 'Wolves of Vukovar' criticized the Zagreb regime and its strategy, Zagreb did not offer unequivocal support, but was also unable to denounce the town's defenders because they symbolized a growing desire to resist and were putting pressure on the Tudjman regime.

The tension between Vukovar and Zagreb was evident when the town eventually fell after a three-month siege. Mile Dedaković, a Serb known by the *nom de guerre* 'Jastreb', a military leader in Vukovar, was arrested by the Zagreb authorities initially for 'desertion', although he claimed that he had been ordered to leave his position by the General Staff. The charges were dropped and Dedaković was, instead, ordered to take ten days' leave. In the meantime, he was further accused of misappropriation of funds and of being an agent of the federal military counter-intelligence, KOS, but this occurred only *after* he had demanded at a press conference that the government explain what had happened to the $17 million that the finance ministry had dedicated to the defense of Vukovar. Whatever the details, the tension between Zagreb and Vukovar's defenders was obvious and explains the government's actions against Dedaković. Vukovar's resistance not only embarrassed the Tudjman regime, but also undermined the government's strategy. Vukovar was finally surrendered in the run-up to the Maastricht Summit of the European Council – the supreme intergovernmental body of the then-European Community – where Germany and other countries promoted recognition of Croatia's independent international personality – exactly as Zagreb intended. Vukovar could

[18] *Danas*, 28 January 1992, carried an interview with Liljanja Toth, wife of one of the town's defense chiefs, in which she derided official claims that supplies could not get through, claiming that it took them a maximum of three quarters of an hour to get from where the official convoys stopped into Vukovar.

probably have held out indefinitely, had there been a commitment to its defense, but the political will was absent.

During the middle phase of the war, Croatia's strategy in Bosnia was more direct. Initially elements of the Croatian army (HV) were used in conjunction with the Croatian Defense Council (HVO) forces and paramilitary groups, but the latter soon became an integrated component of the HV. Units of the HVO carried out ethnic cleansing of Muslims in central Bosnia during 1993, fuelling tensions between the former putative allies. After initial successes in 1993, Croatian forces in Bosnia were defeated by the Bosnian Army in the second half of the year. Following this reverse (although a shotgun-wedding between Croatia and Bosnia and Hercegovina organised by the Americans in early 1994 permitted the Croats to gain a political victory from imminent defeat) Croatia changed tack in the final phase of its war. Under emerging US influence, it began to build up its forces, in all services. While the degree of American influence cannot be precisely gauged (and is surely exaggerated in most quarters),[19] it is undeniable that in 1995 Croatian forces began to show improved capability in terms of plans and operations, as well as the competence to implement them with a degree of maneuver reminiscent of NATO forces, especially the US (although the Croatian capability remained limited, its real impact was amplified by Serbian weaknesses – as discussed in Chapter 6).

However, one significant difference from any NATO force was that the Croatian armed forces practised ethnic cleansing during their operations – albeit after most Serbs had left the Krajina region in Croatia, in advance of the HV assault. The 150,000 ethnic Serbs had been told to leave by the withdrawing Serbian military commanders. Some, mostly elderly, remained, only to meet an advancing Croatian Army, units of which, under the ex-heating engineer (and later boss of Crodux, a tanker company) General Ivan Čermak[20] and General Ante Gotovina, conducted themselves in a

---

[19] This was the view put to me by one US official who had been attached to Croatian forces in 1995.

[20] Žunec 'Operacije', p. 95 notes the importance within the HV/HVO of the 'party line', that is those individuals throughout the forces who were mostly, if not all, members of the ruling HDZ party and who were appointed because of their political role in order to carry the 'inner', or 'secret', orders, which began in all cases with the Minister of Defense, Gojko Šušak and, in some cases, with President Tudjman, who, only after his death, was named as an accomplice to alleged crimes by the Prosecutor at the ICTY. According to Žunec, General

manner to attract the interest of the International Criminal Tribunal for the former Yugoslavia and the new Croatian authorities, elected in 2000, who began war crimes investigations into events in Krajina in 1995, resulting in indictments and arrests.

The HV had swept to victory, but its success was marred by the conduct of some of those on the ground. It was also diminished by Serbian withdrawal although it was hastened by the strategic dominance that the HV had gained. The key to this was the earlier capture of Kupres in Bosnia and Hercegovina – probably the single most important operation in the land war in the west.

Bosnia and Hercegovina: armed forces, aims and approaches

As in Croatia, the Gulf conflict precedent was invoked and the attempt to mobilize international intervention became part of the Bosnian government's strategy. Unlike Croatia, which exaggerated its weakness and criticized those who, by resisting, undermined this image and who craved the status of victims, the Bosnians were bona fide victims who in spite of their relative military impotence often fought bravely with the few means available to them.

For the authorities in Bosnia and Hercegovina, the primary war aim of maintaining the territorial integrity and survival of the newly independent country was supplemented by a further, unstated objective, namely to protect the Muslim community. This was because the political leaders were themselves primarily Muslims (although there was always an effort to ensure representation from other communities in order to preserve an image of multi-culturalism) and because the Muslims had, undoubtedly, been the primary victims in a conflict which had strategically targeted the civilian Muslim population on both the Serbian and Croatian sides.

The definition of forces loyal to the Bosnian government (and the government itself) as victims is based on two factors. First, the Bosnian leadership, having first tried to engineer compromise deals which would keep Yugoslavia together, then went out of its way to co-operate with both European Community and UN mediators, as well as the leadership of the JNA in the Bosnian capital,

---

Čermak was the next most senior in this chain, which was also believed to include the prominent Bosnian Croats Dario Kordić and Ivica Rajić.

Sarajevo, to work for peace as the republic teetered on the edge of, first, violence and, later, independence with violence. The second factor was an extension of this. The Bosnian President Alija Izetbegović and his interior ministry forces co-operated with Col. Gen. Milutin Kukanjac, the Sarajevo Corps commander, in efforts to disarm all paramilitary groups and to place the weapons of the Bosnnian Territorial Defense under army control. A corollary of this was that the Bosnian government, both despite and because of the storm clouds gathering, undertook no formal preparations for defense of the republic, lest these be mistaken as preparations for belligerence. Bosnian officialdom left itself and its republic defenseless in its efforts to avoid war. In doing so Izetbegović was perhaps placing his trust in the local leadership of the JNA (which was hostile to him) and the representatives of the international community with whom he was working closely.

The co-operative relationship with EC and UN representatives gave Bosnia's leadership the impression that good behavior would see his newly independent republic being rewarded with more international protection than had been offered to Croatia.[21] In a rather helpless position, Bosnia's only real chance of containing Serbian forces depended on the actions of the international community, whether this was a matter of lifting the arms embargo on Bosnia and Hercegovina, exerting economic and diplomatic pressure, or the engaging of military forces at one level or another.

The Bosnian foreign minister Haris Silajdžić sought support for a *Desert Storm*-type intervention at the UN: 'The United Nations can provide the umbrella for such an operation just like the one we had in the Gulf.'[22] Ejup Ganić, Izetbegović's deputy demanded that, 'Either the UN should pass a resolution to send in intervention troops or they should allow us to get weapons'. Comparing Bosnia with Kuwait, he somewhat bitterly expressed a generally perceived distinction between the two: 'If you are a small country without oil, without strategic resources, the world only sends you messages like "stay brave".'[23]

When the UN Security Council voted to allow the use of 'all necessary means' to ensure the delivery of humanitarian aid in Bosnia

[21] This is based on interviews with Haris Silajdžić, Foreign Minister of Bosnia and Hercegovina.

[22] Quoted in *The Guardian*, 16 May 1992.

[23] Ibid., 1 August 1992.

and Hercegovina, the Bosnian leadership gave it a mixed recep-
tion. Although Izetbegović was glad of international moves to relieve
the suffering in his country, he pointed out that his people 'dreamed
of a Western intervention,' not just humanitarian aid.[24] However,
as Col. Gen. Lewis MacKenzie, UN Commanding Officer in Sarajevo (a seemingly persistent opponent of intervention in support
of the Bosnian authorities) indicated, for the Bosnians, even humanitarian intervention would serve their purposes. He said that
one of the government's advisors had told him: 'Let Bush come
with humanitarian aid, take control of the roads, get his troops or
his helicopters shot at . . . and pretty soon he'll find he's fighting
the same war as us.'[25] It would appear therefore that the enfeebled
Bosnian government at no stage gave up hope of a greater international commitment. Until the moment in 1995 when limited
NATO and UN action spurred an end to the war in Bosnia and
Hercegovina, the primary strategic aim of the Bosnian Government was to precipitate such action.

Military weakness explains the Bosnian Government's reliance
on existing international involvement and its attempt to increase
the likelihood of the international presence using force. Sarajevo
had always been on the back foot in terms of the armed forces
at its command. The Army of Bosnia and Hercegovina had three
tributaries: very limited elements of Bosnia's Territorial Defense
(most had come under Serb control, or been denuded), the Bosnian
MUP and several small paramilitary groups – most significantly, the
Patriotic League, the private army of Izetbegović's SDA (Party of
Democratic Action), the chief Muslim party in Bosnia and Hercegovina.

Of the various paramilitary groups the Patriotic League played
a key role on the side of the Bosnian government. It is fair to
characterize the activities of these paramilitary groups, and indeed
possibly of Territorial Defense and HVO units, as being private
armies in the chaotic confused circumstances in which units were
being formed without an overall, well-established, hierarchy. The
label 'Green Berets' came to be used to refer to these groups –
although in an ill-documented period, and characterized by im-
provisation, separating which units were which was never easy

---

[24] *The Guardian*, 12 August 1992.
[25] *The Independent*, 13 August 1992.

confused the press generally labelled all such groups as 'Green Berets'. This perception was reflected in the relevant UN Expert Commission report, which tends to group all the different Muslim paramilitary groups as one.[26] The proper connotation for the Green Beret label,[27] however, is the Patriotic League, which was formed by the SDA leadership early in 1991 and was operating by June of that year. In organizing the defense forces of Bosnia and Hercegovina, the Patriotic League and the Green Berets played a key role as a loyalist strand within the security forces, around which a framework for other elements of defense, including Territorial Defense, could be built. Moreover, it was the Patriotic League that most worried Belgrade's generals at the time.[28]

The role of the Patriotic League paramilitary units was to be the guiding influence in defense structures – almost a party-army in fact. They comprised those elements of the military most closely linked to the SDA Muslim leadership, a band of loyalists who would organize defense and other activities. The framework for the ABiH came not from the Territorial Defense structures but from the Patriotic League.[29] Thus the Patriotic League provided the elite, or political, guidance that the JNA or the Communist Party would have offered under the old Yugoslav system.

The ABiH was officially the national army of the Bosnian State. Although usually referred to as a Muslim army in press reporting, the Bosnian Army was a multi-ethnic force in which, although it was predominantly Muslim, Serbs made up over ten per cent of the troops, with Croats and Jews also present. By the spring of 1993 it had 120,000 troops (with reserve components, 200,000),

[26] UN War Crimes Expert Commission 'Final Report'. Annex III, UN doc. S/1994/674/Add. 2 (vol. I), 28 December 1994.

[27] For a good indication of the significance and cultural resonance of the 'Green Berets', see Xabier Agirre Aranburu's fine study on the various armies and societal civil-military relations *Yugoslavia y los Ejércitos. La Legitimad Militar en Tiempos de Genocido*, Madrid: Los Libros de la Catarata, 1997, pp. 207–10. On the evolution of armed forces in Bosnia and Hercegovina, see also Chapter IV in Xavier Bougarel's excellent *Bosnie: Anatomie d'un Conflit* (Paris: La Découverte, 1996).

[28] *Narodna Armija*, 12 March 1998.

[29] One former Chief of Staff of the ABiH, Sefir Halilović, who was also an original member of the Patriotic League, provides some material on this process, while promising at a later stage to reveal full details, from the creation of the League onwards. Sefir Halilović, *Lukava Strategija* (Sarajevo: Maršal, 1997), pp. 5 and 165–8.

of which 40–50,000 were fully equipped and 80,000 in combat units. Throughout the war in Bosnia and Hercegovina the Bosnian Army was outgunned by its opponents, first on the Serbian side, later on the Croatian, a reflection of the arms embargo imposed by the UN Security Council on the Socialist Federative Republic of Yugoslavia and the disarmament of Bosnian Territorial Defense Forces by the JNA in 1991 and 1992.

The ABiH was formally established on 15 April 1992, although it was not until later in 1992 that a formal structure began to take shape. In the spring and summer of 1992 the Bosnian army, as such, was not fully in existence. So TO units continued operating, as did units of the HVO and several paramilitary groups. In some areas, notably in eastern Bosnia, there were largely autonomous groups of Muslim guerrillas operating against Serbian forces – although they were later incorporated within the ABiH and most likely had some connection to it at the time (the group was reportedly led by the enigmatic Naser Orić, who later commanded ABiH units at Srebrenica). Despite the lack of formal structures and integration, all these units fought against the Serbs at the time.

The TO became the Army of Bosnia and Hercegovina. After initial confusion, the Patriotic League, elements of the Interior Ministry and also Territorial Defense units all merged to form the ABiH. The presidency was supreme commander and appointed a general staff and a chief of staff. The latter nominated commanders for regional military authorities and below that lower levels would be appointed by the chief of staff on the recommendation of reports from further down. The ABiH's evolution continued with the designation of seven administrative districts, which are sometimes inaccurately referred to as corps.

Following from the creation of military districts and, later, tactical groups, in November 1992 the ABiH began finally to take shape with five corps being organized answering to the General Staff and command in Sarajevo. The 1st Corps was based at Sarajevo, the 2nd Corps at Zenica covered central Bosnia, the 3rd Corps at Tuzla covered eastern Bosnia, and the 4th Corps, notionally based at Mostar – though in practice, never able to be based there – covered Hercegovina and central Bosnia, while the often largely autonomous 5th Corps was based at, and operated out of, the Bihać pocket. The 6th and 7th Corps were largely notional – the 6th Corps should have been based in Konjic and the 7th Corps was supposed to be based at Travnik in central Bosnia. Although the 6th Corps did not emerge during the war, the 7th Corps, at well below anything like genuine corps level, emerged to operate in the Muslim-Croat conflict during 1993 but only really took shape as the instrument of co-operation between the ABiH and the HVO in capturing the strategically vital point at Kupres.[30] Not till the latter stages of the war did this corps structure begin to furnish an operational level capability, because the Bosnian military was severely impeded by its fractured geography, resulting from initial Serbian successes and its strategically weak position – especially its difficulty in obtaining arms.

In April 1992, the Bosnian authorities mobilized the Territorial Defense units in Bosnia and Hercegovina, but, this was, quite evidently, not universally obeyed – on the whole, Croats and Serbs did not respond to this call – or if they did, they did so by joining the armed forces of their own ethnic community. For example, in Konjic, the local Territorial Defense force, where mobilized, should have had a complement of around 2,000 personnel, but Serbs and Croats in the area, as was broadly the case across the country, did not heed the call. However, typical of the somewhat anarchic circumstances of the Bosnian defense forces, paramilitary groups also operated in this area, supplementing the TO. Most were small, little known groups but there were others that would come under the umbrella of the Green Berets or Patriotic League. Moreover, as happened in other parts of Bosnia and Hercegovina, the JNA had previously moved weapons from TO facilities and concentrated them under its own control. The weapons of the Konjic TO were transported to the JNA's Ljuta barracks, along with TO weaponry for the neighboring municipalities of Prozor and Jablanica.

The regional headquarters for Konjic Territorial Defense should have been at Mostar, but was located in Sarajevo to which Konjic was reporting. The formal TO headquarters, in relation to Konjic, at Mostar, was not functioning. Relations with the HVO mostly explain this situation.

A joint regional command was formally established between the TO, or the Bosnian army, and the HVO. It appears not to have succeeded, in so far as it ever functioned. After the HVO capture

---

[30] Suad Arnautović, *Kako se Branila Bosna Vojno-Politički Eseji i Komentari*, Sarajevo: Promocult, 1997, p. 129.

of west Mostar in early July 1992, relationships broke down and there was no question of joint command, or common procedures, after that time, until the very last phases of the war.

The ABiH chain of command was not clear early in the war, nor was it well established. Formal relationships did exist, but the degree to which all elements were integrated into one whole gives some reason to suppose that the situation was not at all clear. In the Konjic area, again, from May to July 1992, unconventional steps were taken in relation to the military structure there. In addition to the evolution and development of certain units, it was decided to designate a coordinator, a role that was given to Zejnil Delalić, who later gained the rank of general in the ABiH.

The coordinator's role involved carrying out tasks which an officer commanding might perform, but not as part of the formal hierarchy in a situation where there was no officer commanding at that stage. 'Coordinator' is not a usual military term, but it is one sometimes used.[31] It was not a term used by the JNA, although, in evidence in The Hague, General Jovan Divjak stated it was a term used in the JNA in some circumstances. The Konjic context, again, can assist in clarifying the coordinator's role. There, a number of in-

---

[31] 'Coordinator' is not a normal term in military structures, nor does it fit into a generally understood framework, although it does have its uses. One way of explaining the role of a coordinator is by reference to British special forces in the Second World War, in which several small units, sometimes designated 'private armies' – indeed one of them was known as 'Popski's Private Army' – were formed for special missions. They are devised either for very special purposes or at the initiative of a particular commander, and in a situation where there are uncertain lines of command or where units do not fit into the traditional formal hierarchy of command and control. The private nature of these armies offers a particular role for a coordinator. In the context of British Special Forces where these units were beginning to emerge, one man, John Hackett, was appointed with the job of coordinator. His role was to know what was going on, to deal with all the different units and to be sure they did not carry out private initiatives, undertake the same mission or end up fighting each other. (See Julian Thompson, *War Behind Enemy Lines*, London: Pan, 1999, esp. pp. 101–2.) If a coordinator's role is to be successful, it depends on two qualities. The first is full knowledge, that is, the ability to know exactly what each of the relevant units is doing, and also capable of doing, otherwise there could be serious problems in operations; and the second is a degree of authority, perhaps personal authority, to facilitate dealing with the sometimes highly charged egos of commanders of such units; that is they would have to respect the coordinator, otherwise information, for example, would not be given. This would impede the coordinator's chances of doing the job successfully.

dependently organized armed forces – i.e., lacking a formal, organized, hierarchical command structure, normally associated with
an armed force – were operating. In that context, there was a degree
of fluidity and uncertainty. But, the overall intention was to carry
out operations against the hostile Serbs. In designating the role of
coordinator, the purpose was to exploit an individual's knowledge
and the authority with which he approached various units and,
without the benefit of formal order, could give guidance, make
requests, indicate what might or might not be appropriate and
helpful, see to the requirements of a particular unit and find ways
in which to satisfy these. This would involve some of the qualities
that an officer commanding might have in a more organized military structure, but in fluid and changing circumstances it could not
be a formal command position.

In the Konjic municipality, the coordinator in question may have
been given that role because of his personal wealth and an ability
to carry out certain tasks, including the purchase of provisions, as
well as his being a member of the Green Berets. Perhaps on the
basis of personality, Delalić appears to have been trusted by all sides.

There were three entities operating in Konjic at that time, the
War Presidency, the HVO and the TO, so there was a need to co-
ordinate activities of the HVO and the territorial army and also
to make sure the War Presidency's orders were carried out by the
other two entities. The coordinator was the link between these
different elements, especially between the War Presidency and the
two main military elements, the HVO and the TO, which remained
discrete entities, as well as with the smaller paramilitary groups.
Coordination was particularly important because the HVO did not
recognize the command authority formally given to the War Presidency at the local level. The requirement for the coordinator, therefore, was to have the trust of both sides and to deal with both sides
on the basis of a degree of personal authority – to be able to say,
'these are the things that would be useful, or these are the things
which such and such a unit might need; let us put it all together
and make it more coherent.'

As indicated, there was an intermediary period between the appointment of coordinators and the establishment of the corps, during
which tactical groups were set up in some areas. A tactical group
was a set of units brought together for specific tactical purposes for
a temporary period – and unlike the designation of a coordinator,
it was an acknowledged option in JNA literature. A tactical group

was created in a context where the regular structures and the regular organization of units were not judged to be appropriate to the circumstances. It could be one of two types: either designed specifically for one objective, in which case designated units would be brought together to achieve that objective; or, in other circumstances, it would be brought together as a group in order to act to some extent independently, within the broad scope of objectives to be achieved, to accomplish whatever was possible. In Bosnia and Hercegovina the latter type was more relevant.

Tactical Group 1, however, fell somewhere between the two. Its broad objective was to carry out actions which would facilitate lifting the siege of Sarajevo. This was a somewhat desperate approach adopted by forces in a position of grave weakness who were still working out what operations could be carried out. A tactical group would normally have five units attached to it for particular operations. On 27 July 1992, however, all units to the west and south of Sarajevo were put under the Tactical Group 1 commander, so there was an evolution not only in the role played and the formal position, but also in the area over which formal command authority was relevant.

Delalić, who had previously been appointed as coordinator in Konjic, was appointed as Tactical Group commander on 11 July 1992,[32] following a short period in which Colonel Mustafa Polutak had held the post. Considering the special circumstances, it is likely that the Tactical Group commander was appointed because of personal authority. In some ways, as in the case of Delalić, the move from coordinator to Tactical Group commander was a logical progression. Although there is a clear difference in the formal authority between coordinator and Tactical Group commander, there would be de facto similarities. Whereas a coordinator might carry

---

[32] He was subsequently re-appointed on 27 July, but with a clarification or possibly an extension of the scope of his authority. There may have been a degree of personal rivalry between Delalić and Captain Esad Ramić. There were times while Delalić was coordinator where Ramić did not respect his role fully, and there appear to have been differences. This also seems to have been the case after Delalić had been appointed Tactical Group commander. The clarification of Delalić's earlier appointment was an attempt to reinforce his formal position as officer commanding. There were some instances where Ramić disputed Delalić's authority over his particular command – including the assertion recorded in one communication that 'tactical group commander is not commander over me and my units because we are not assigned specifically to the tactical group.' The 27 July appointment very clearly changed that position.

out many of the functions of an officer commanding, a coordinator would not have any formal authority within the military hierarchy. A Tactical Group commander, in contrast, would have formal authority within the military hierarchy, would issue orders rather than, for example, make requests or give advice, and would be backed in doing so by the regular structures of the military and its disciplinary system.

Throughout 1992 the Bosnian military was fighting Serbian forces and clashes with HVO units were beginning. By the spring of 1993 the ABiH was engaged in armed hostilities with Croatian forces to the west, as well as with the Serbian forces to the north, east and south. The conflict with the Croatians lasted for about nine months, to the end of 1993; the armed conflict with the Serbian forces continued until 1995, by which time the ABiH had been boosted by the contribution of Croatian forces, with which an uneasy alliance was formed again in 1994, and by international military engagement.

Against the backdrop of the development of the Bosnian armed forces, the Bosnian government's strategic approach sought to maximise its victim status to influence international opinion through the news media. To this end it deployed several American educated politicians who could articulate the Bosnian position for international consumption. Because of Bosnia's predicament and the degree to which the Muslims, in particular, were victims of the Serbian project in 1992, the international media became generally receptive to this strategy.

The second level involved using its armed forces to attack either its own positions, or those of the UN, which, from the outset, had a base in Sarajevo. Thus, unlike Slovenia where there was an integrated media management strategy based on creating a story of successful defense, the Bosnian army had a complementary, if not integrated, approach which relied on maintaining international attention because of certain types of attack – attacks which were attributed to the Serbs, even though they were fired from Bosnian positions. This strategy was ultimately counterproductive as it eroded much of the sympathy of representatives of the international community, which it was intended to stoke. In particular, it built up a reservoir of mistrust with the troops deployed by the international community in Bosnia. Nonetheless, it was effective in that it conveyed a message to international diplomatic circles, even if the outcome always fell short of the desired outcome for the Bosnian authorities – full intervention of a major international expeditionary operation.

On many occasions the Bosnian Government's story of victim status was underlined by the weakness and incompetence of its armed forces. The ABiH was clearly weak – and whenever it attempted operations, for example, to lift the siege of Sarajevo in late 1992 and again in early 1995, it failed miserably. For much of the war, morale-boosting success stories were few and far between – occasional celebrity for the 5th Corps at Bihać, or the victory against Croatian forces during the Muslim-Croat conflict of 1993. One of the success stories, from the Bosnian perspective, came from Muslim guerrillas, carrying out ruthless asymmetric operations against the better equipped VRS – albeit at the cost of undermining the purity of Sarajevo's victim image for those watching closely, as the group had no compunction about murdering Serb civilians. Operating in eastern Bosnia, most notably, around Bratunac, these Muslim guerrillas carried out the kind of hit and run raid which Tito's Partisans used to build their force during the Second World War. Their chief aim was to capture weaponry from Serbian forces and to inflict reprisals on Serb communities – up to 1,000 Serb civilians were massacred near Bratunac. This force of 2,500 was responsible in early 1993 for several significant feats, in and around Bratunac, in which, with an element of surprise, Serbian forces were pushed across the River Drina. This took hostilities to Serbia itself for only the first time since war began in Bosnia and Hercegovina and only the second time in the war of dissolution. In response, the VJ became openly engaged in Bosnia for the first time since it withdrew in May 1992.

Bosnian strategy changed from 1994 onward. There were two components to this change. The first, negatively driven, imperative was the use of artillery detection radar by UN forces in Bosnia to prove indisputably that the Bosnian army had been shelling both its own UN positions. The second, more positive, element was that having had limited successes against Croatian forces during the latter part of 1993, the Bosnian army began to improve its tactical level competence, which had emerged in some areas, as well as developing its operational level capability and, even, the strategic. To some extent, the influence of US thinking on Croatia also had resonance in Bosnia, although its impact was more limited.

In spite of the limitations, the focus shifted in the military sphere more from victim status to demonstrating the capability to fight back – whereas in the political and diplomatic spheres a victim stance continued to be presented. Nonetheless, even this became less pronounced as the Bosnian President Alija Izetbegović effectively made it clear that, whatever the reservations of his government, the priority for Bosnia was to keep British and French troops there to hold the situation. In the course of 1995 the Bosnian army demonstrated its capabilities and limitations. In the spring, an operation to lift the siege of Sarajevo failed, but the operation revealed, for the first time, the ability of the Bosnian army to co-ordinate operations on a scale which could incorporate simultaneous action all around Sarajevo. That capability was again demonstrated at the operational level, in conjunction with Croatian forces, as Serbian control of territory was released in the summer and autumn. In this context, the strategic capability was provided by Croatian forces, as was demonstrated by the way Bosnian army troops struggled to achieve objectives such as Prijedor once Croatia had decided not to complete the joint strategic plan for a three-pronged assault on Banja Luka, the major urban center in Serb-controlled Bosnia. Whatever the limitations of the forces themselves at this stage, the overall approach, including the diplomatic and media rhetoric, shifted from being one of eternal victim to one of self-help, with the victim demonstrating the will and training to do enough to maintain the support of those who would help. Crucially, however, it still relied on help from elsewhere.

The final push involving joint Croatian-Bosnian operations had begun in November 1994 with the capture of Kupres. The Kupres Heights dominate the eastern Adriatic landmass – both towards the Dalmatian coast in Croatia and into central Bosnia – and had remained an Axis stronghold against Tito's Partisans during the Second World War, only being relinquished after surrender. Hence Kupres was one of the most vital objectives for all parties in the war in the west.[33] Although the operation was jointly planned and conducted, the politics of the situation meant that the Croats would be allowed to complete the capture of Kupres – the ABiH needed

---

[33] See Jovan Janjić, *Srpski General Ratko Mladić*, Novi Sad: Matica Srpska, 1996, p. 164, and Ozren Žunec, 'Operacije Bljesak I Oluja' in Magaš and Žanić (eds), *Rat*, p. 103.

Croatian support far more than the HV/HVO required Bosnian assistance at this stage. In a short operation, lasting around two days, Croatian forces moved from the south and west, while the ABiH moved in from central Bosnia. The attack left VRS forces exposed and overstretched, with surprise a key element – while it was a vital target, the attempt to seize such an important and, theoretically, defensible position was audacious. With daring rewarded, the keystone had been laid for Croatian and joint Croatian-Bosnian land operations that would transform the strategic position during 1995.

In July 1995, following the HV's successful Operation *Flash* and shortly before its sweep of Krajina with Operation *Storm*, significant joint operations were renewed in western Bosnia. The first stages of these operations, pushing northwards from Kupres, along the Dinaric Mountain Range, were preliminaries both to planned operations in Bosnia and to Operation *Storm*. With control established along the high ground inside Bosnia's borders with Croatia, the HV was in a position not only to sweep across Krajina from within Croatia, but also the OS RSK's rear. Although Serbian forces withdrew in advance of the attack, there can be little doubt that the HV had established a position that promised certain success, as its forces moved across the Kupres Heights and descended through the Dinaric Mountains to Knin, the RSK 'capital.' Joint preparatory operations in July and planned moves on the VRS throughout western Bosnia saw rapid successes initially. The successful push through Glamoč began to define the limits of Croatia's support, however. Further joint operations were planned to culminate in the capture of the Bosnian Serb political and military stronghold of Banja Luka in a three-pronged attack.

The Croatian General Staff provided the strategic level perspective and planned the operations to be implemented in alliance with the ABiH. The HV and HVO 4th Corps, along with the ABiH 4th Corps and elements of the 2nd Corps, were to continue their push from Kupres, along the heights, reaching beyond Glamoč to Bosanski Petrovac and eventually becoming the southern prong of the final assault on Banja Luka. There, it would have met a second prong, created by the ABiH 5th Corps' breaking out from the Bihać pocket, once Operation *Storm* had ensured that its rear would be secured by the collapse of the OS RSK, across the River Una from it in Krajina. The 5th Corps thrust would provide a sharp, rapid jab to puncture VRS defenses to the west and to close on forces retreating in advance of the Croatian-led joint advance from the south. The final prong of the attack was to be provided by the HV alone, entering Bosnia from the north through Bosanski Brod and driving south, directly towards Banja Luka, severing VRS lines to the north of Banja Luka – meaning that the only direction in which the Serbian forces could retreat was to the east. With Banja Luka captured, the original aim was to press the VRS all the way to the Posavina Corridor – there was no intention to do more than this, for fear that action in eastern Bosnia in the approaches to the River Drina and the border with Serbia might prompt Belgrade to launch a heavy counterattack, something which could otherwise be ruled out, in the circumstances.

None of the above transpired. Despite the decisive, but contingent, contribution effectively provided by NATO airpower, the Croatians pulled out of the final phase of operations. Although Croatia's change of heart has been attributed to US pressure – a standard line argues that American urging, including Special Envoy Richard Holbrooke's very firm instructions to Zagreb to stop the operations was decisive – others, including the author, believe the Croats were not going to see the joint-venture through to the end. Already, before the NATO air operations gave implicit impetus to the scheme – and perhaps encouraged Croatia to continue a little longer than it would have otherwise, the push on Banja Luka was effectively dropped – even before the Serbian mortar attack on the Markale Market in Sarajevo on Monday 30 August had occurred.[34] Aside from any role US pressure might have played, there were two reasons for Croatia's decision to ease up. One was politically cynical: ceasing support for the ABiH would remind it of its weakness and dependence on the HV/HVO and leave Zagreb in a position of strength *vis à vis* Sarajevo. Perhaps more importantly, there had begun to be discontent in the ranks and fears of desertions, if not mutiny. Once Croatian forces had pushed past Glamoč, they began to question the point of continuing. The Croatian interest as far as Glamoč was clear enough. But, in their eyes,

---

[34] In discussions with the author in Zagreb the week before the mortar landed and NATO air power had mobilized, military and civilian officials said that the Banja Luka operation would not happen. The description of the plan here is based on an interview, in August 1995 with an ABiH officer familiar with it.

there seemed little point in fighting on to achieve what were essentially Muslim-Bosnian government objectives. With morale otherwise high in the Croatian military, there was a strong desire to avoid dissipation and disillusion.

Without Croatian support from mid-September (although help was renewed in the final stages of the war), the ABiH pressed on until October. However, as noted in Chapter 7, without the all-important cover of tangential NATO air action and the full effect of Croatia's military clout and strategic level capability, the Bosnian military floundered. In difficult and slow operations, it struggled to take the symbolically important towns of Sanski Most, Prijedor and Bosanski Novi. Even where there were successes, the ABiH could not hold the territory. Sanski Most, captured finally on the last day of the war, had to be given up in the ensuing peace negotiations. Nonetheless, having struggled to capture the towns and barely able to hold them if it came to a fight, the ABiH withdrew from them, under the terms of the Dayton Accords. The Bosnian government and the ABiH had, in the end, achieved far more than many could have dreamt of in 1992, but their relative success in protecting the position of the Muslims was overshadowed by several key events.

One of the darkest shadows concerned the eastern enclaves of Srebrenica and Žepa. The effective decision to concede them, in July and August, was, on the one hand, wise – the position was untenable. The less-than-honest manner in which these enclaves were cast adrift, however, left a bitter twist of doubts and questions. Rather than facing up to losing the towns at the negotiating table, the Bosnian government effectively withdrew the command from Srebrenica and abandoned its defenders – only the much (and mostly unfairly) maligned Dutch UN battalion offered any real resistance in a lost situation. The Sarajevo government, which would normally be on the phone to the UN Headquarters in Sarajevo the moment anything happened, was notable by its silence during the first two days of the Serbian capture of Srebrenica. It was only when it began to emerge that thousands of people were missing, along with reports that they had been murdered, that Sarajevo reacted in the usual fashion. This suggests that the Bosnian government had not anticipated mass murder on this scale, but, until that point, everything was as it was expected to be. It is undeniable that after years of using the unhappy people of the eastern Bosnian enclaves to manipulate international opinion and seek the political and moral high-ground, their government callously left them to their fate. Whatever the precise truth of the Bosnian government's knowledge and actions, and recognizing the continuing weakness of Sarajevo's armed forces, it is at least reasonable to question the government's partial responsibility for what transpired, which on a superficial reading was of a far higher order than that of the Dutch military.

In the end, the absence of a strategic capability and severe weaknesses at the operational level also cast a shadow over the relative success of 1995. This had, in reality, only served to underline the chronic weakness of the ABiH. The difficulty with which it finally scraped to take Prijedor and the fact that this key objective then had to be conceded, as well as the inability to resist Mladić's counter-attack once the NATO air operations were over, are testimony to the hollowness of those, including soldiers of the ABiH, who later claimed that they had been denied the fruits that they were about to reap. The truth is that without assistance from elsewhere, there would have been only further desperate struggle, further failure. Yet, notwithstanding their reliance on external help, the Bosnian defiance of the odds and formation of an army while already largely overrun, was heroic and, on many levels, partly successful.

Kosovo: armed forces, aims and approaches

Opposition to the Serbian project in Kosovo was always in the weakest position among all the adversaries, yet it emerged with one of the more obvious successes. This relative success, even though nowhere near absolute, did not, however result from either of the two main strategic approaches taken by the Kosovo Albanians. These radical alternatives – pacifism or armed engagement designed to provoke atrocities – were promoted by different factions among the Kosovo Albanians, factionalism being a prominent characteristic of the Kosovo military-political order at all stages. Given this and other major weaknesses, it is unlikely that once the Serbian project was clearly focused on Kosovo, the Albanians would have stood much of a chance.

The leadership of the majority ethnic-Albanian population in Kosovo had for several years conducted a campaign of peaceful resistance to Serbia's forced re-integration of the province and re-pression of the local people. This was based both on the desire to show that the ethnic Albanians deserved the respect of the West because they had not resorted to violence and on the reality of the community's weakness. After ten years of living in conditions akin to a police-state the Kosovo Albanians had little opportunity to arm themselves and, especially, to organize and build an army of liberation. Notwithstanding their small caches of weaponry, these were nothing compared to the arsenal available to the Serbian side. The Albanians were acutely aware of this and, hence, over several years, largely accepted the strategy of civil protest and disobedience advocated by their leader Ibrahim Rugova. This approach also involved, during 1992, the setting up of parallel state structures of governance in the province, including provision of education and other public services.

As Yugoslavia disintegrated, Rugova and his colleagues came under great pressure to abandon their pacifist approach and foment an uprising. However, apart from references made by some Alban-ian representatives to the mineral resources of Kosovo, which may have implied there were physical (and hence strategically valuable) resources worth securing there, the Albanians drew a stark conclu-sion from events in Bosnia and Hercegovina: had there ever been belief that initiation of an otherwise suicidal uprising might pro-voke the international community to defend the Albanians, this was now a lost cause. Watching events in Bosnia and Hercegovina, including the progress of Serbian 'ethnic cleansers', with the inter-national community unprepared to stop what was happening, led to the obvious conclusion that there would be no greater keenness in the West to protect Albanians than there had been to protect Bosnian Muslims. The Kosovar leadership seemed completely to rule out the remote possibility of a futile uprising to present them-selves as victims, but there were some Kosovo Albanians at home and overseas who read events differently.

Despite growing unease, there was always strong support for Rugova and his policy inspired by Gandhi. This was tested by continuing Serbian repression, with support waning in some areas as voices began to call for violence. This was accompanied by grow-ing dismay among Kosovan Albanians that their position had been effectively ignored by the international community during the break-up of the Socialist Federative Republic of Yugoslavia. The

conclusion was drawn that Slovenia, Croatia and Bosnia and Hercegovina had been internationally recognised because they had waged
war while the Serbian project had not been entirely unsuccessful
in Bosnia and Hercegovina because the Republika Srpska had been
established as an entity within an existing country.

This was a clear misunderstanding. Among the factors involved
in a complicated set of processes and decisions, it is important to
note the international view of Kosovo's position in the break-up
of the old Yugoslavia. The question of Kosovo was treated differently from Slovenia, Croatia and Bosnia and Hercegovina because
of the different status accorded to these territories under the old
federal Yugoslav constitution, which was used as the basis for discussion by all concerned. That constitution defined each of the six
states which comprised the federation as sovereign, giving them
the notional right to independence in the event of the federation's
ceasing to function. This is how the break-up was interpreted.
Kosovo, as well as the other province in Serbia, Vojvodina, did not
qualify formally by the attribute of sovereignty. So they were not
included in negotiations on dissolution, or considered as being
eligible for recognition as independent entities on the same basis
as the federating republics.

This distinction was important when considering the conflict
in Kosovo and the prospect of intervention. Kosovo was formally
regarded as part of Serbia and part of the common federal state between Serbia and Montenegro. Thus all international discussion
was officially about the maintenance of international order and
predicated on preserving the borders of the Federal Republic of
Yugoslavia. A change was hard to envisage on this question without agreement from the Serbian and Yugoslav authorities in Belgrade.
This however gave the Belgrade authorities a considerable degree
of protection in carrying out action against Kosovan Albanians because of the conventional understanding that sovereignty offers protection against external interference in internal affairs. It is on this
basis that Yugoslav President Slobodan Milošević repeatedly rejected
international appeals regarding the conflict in Kosovo from March
1998 onwards, having specifically said that the situation in Kosovo
was an internal matter.

The incremental disenchantment with the pacifist approach
of Rugova led to two developments. One was that clans in certain parts of Kosovo began to harass and attack Serbian police and

security forces. The other, beginning around 1995, was the formation in exile of an armed organisation – the Kosova Liberation Army (*Ushtrie Çilimtare e Kosovës* – UÇK).[35] This body was established secretly in Switzerland with funds raised by Jashar Salihu under the Homeland Calling network and with leadership provided by Bardhyl Mahmuti. The UÇK was tightly organized at its center according to Leninist principles, and until 1998 numbered no more than 300 members all told, inside and outside Kosovo itself. In 1996 and, in particular, 1997, it launched terrorist attacks against Serbs and Serbian targets in Kosovo. These only ensured that Serbian repression was maintained and strengthened. The Serb response precipitated a change of mood among the people in Kosovo, who remained strongly loyal to Rugova, yet many of whom wondered if taking matters into their own hands and using force might not be the only route, in the end, by which to end Serbian repression. In response to this, there was an attempt by the would-be political leadership of Kosovo led by Rugova's prime minister in exile Bujar Bukoshi to form an alternative, 'official', force, loyal to Rugova. Despite recruiting some former JNA officers, this alternative force never really took form and many of its members quickly transferred to the UÇK as events unfolded during 1997 and 1998.[36]

[35] The precise date of formation for the Kosova Liberation Army is obscure, in large part because of its rather nebulous form, having several constituent elements both from movements based outside Kosovo, primarily in Switzerland, and from clans and groups within the province. An important precursor, feeding into its emergence, was the Popular Movement for Kosovo. This was one of two small groups to emerge from a split in the Popular Movement for the Republic of Kosova (the other was the National Movement for the Liberation of Kosova). The spawning organization was a radical group formed by anti-Rugova, primarily Marxist, ethnic Albanians from Kosovo and Macedonia whose agenda was for the establishment of Kosovo as a republic and for union of the various Albanian communities. The creation of an armed force and the nature of its use had been one factor in breaking up the original movement and one of the first decisions of the leadership of the Popular Movement for Kosovo concerned the name – Kosova Liberation Army – of the terrorist-guerrilla armed wing that was being formed. However, although there were activists, it was not until 1995 that the armed wing really began to take shape and not till 1996 that regular operations were launched. For a fuller treatment of the UÇK's origins in and development from the Popular Movement for the Republic of Kosova, see Judah, *Kosovo: War and Revenge*, pp. 103–20 *passim*.

[36] I am grateful to Tim Judah for alerting me to the distinction between the armed movement for which Bukoshi was attempting to raise funds and the UÇK.

The UÇK also benefited from a Croatian link – earlier in the 1990s, two battalions within the HV had been formed by ethnic Albanians, a step seen at that stage as a move towards a possible alliance. They participated in operations during 1995 that brought the war in the west to a close and one of the most significant military figures in the UÇK, General Agim Çeku, served with those units.

By March 1998, when the conflict erupted, two broad, very different elements had begun to coalesce into the force that became the UÇK. The twin strands of armed Albanian action in Kosovo that came together were the core group of disciplined activists organized from Switzerland and Germany, and local groups, such as that of the clan leader Adem Jashari. Contacts had been made and Jashari and others were associated with the UÇK, if not completely formally part of it (although this was changing as events unfolded and 'UÇK' became recognized as a brand with which others wished to be associated and, therefore, an organization of which they wanted to be a part). This created an armed force with a core organisation from the UÇK of a few hundred people supplemented by local groups acting as auxiliaries. The numbers involved swelled to several thousand, although certainly not to the levels of tens of thousands sometimes suggested in press reports, or the 17,000 formally claimed by the UÇK in discussions with Western representatives. There was a core command to the movement, which had a loose-leaf structure. This meant units could act autonomously, but, for the most part, the suggestion of autonomous action was likely also to be a deception similar to that used by all sides in the war in Croatia and in Bosnia and Hercegovina – that is, the creation of apparently autonomous and uncontrolled units so that responsibility for action could be denied by military and political leaders. Weapons were obtained primarily from Serbian, or Yugoslav, sources, not from Albania, as often reported, although some weaponry came from chaotic northern Albania during 1997. The UÇK lacked heavy weaponry and armor. In terms of armament and organisation, in the course of the conflict the Serbian forces were easily superior.

In the first part of 1998, Jashari's and other forces had established a degree of control over considerable parts of western Kosovo, creating no-go zones for the Serbian security forces in some cases. This control was only established in the absence of Serbian opposition – as noted in Chapter 8, when Belgrade's forces moved to roll up the UÇK in July and August 1998, they faced little problem in doing so. The Serbian action after March was undoubtedly, in part, a reaction to the UÇK's filling a vacuum in areas where there was no real Serbian presence, and Serbian security forces were fighting the UÇK to restore Serbian control. There was more to the Serbian campaign than this, however. Ostensibly, it was a re-action to the UÇK uprising, but it was really used as the pretext to begin ethnic cleansing. Ironically, but predictably (in line with guerrilla war theory), while the Serbian action demonstrated the incoherence and weakness of the UÇK, it also helped to boost popular support for it.

Following the withdrawal of Belgrade forces under the October Agreement (see Chapter 8), the UÇK's position improved and it once again began to control territory. The UÇK had been reduced from around 7,000-strong to no more than 2,000 and was deeply divided over its immediate political goals. But its constituent el-ements could relatively easily take over where Serbian forces had withdrawn and quickly began to do so, reestablishing positions in some areas.

On 9 November 1998, UÇK units attacked the MUP headquart-ers at Mališevo, while MUP Special Forces engaged Kosovan Albanian targets at Stimlje. In each of these areas there was tension and incidents occurred. Where MUP units had withdrawn, the UÇK moved in to operate, for example, in Drenica, Podujevo and the parts of Mališevo not defensively held by the MUP. In some places, there was UÇK action against Serb positions. There was also growing evidence of UÇK action against ethnic Albanians, for example, at Bukoš, where a 25-year-old was shot in the back of the head. This was an apparent act of intimidation, or disciplining, by the UÇK and was not isolated. UÇK elements also fired on and interfered with the freedom of movement of the Kosovo Diplo-matic Observer Mission (KDOM) and the OSCE's Kosovo Verifica-tion Mission (KVM) preparatory personnel in their clearly marked orange vehicles.

In many ways, the UÇK was fortunate. Its unnecessary action against the international monitors was overshadowed by the men-acing character of Serbian activity. In the months between Octo-ber and the renewal of the Serbian campaign, the following March, representatives from Western countries, notably the US, established links with the UÇK, attempting to identify and find its leadership and to bring it into discussions – which happened at Rambouillet and subsequently in Paris, where it emerged that its leading figure was Hashim Thaçi, one of the younger generation of radical activists involved in the UÇK in Switzerland. The links formed were to be important for the UÇK after the renewal of hostilities and the onset of the NATO air campaign. From being in a hopeless military position *vis à vis* Serbian forces, these links permitted a curious, implicit, alliance to be formed by NATO and the ethnic Albanian force. As the conflict developed, the US (perhaps sometimes too naïvely and clumsily) began to rely on cooperation with the UÇK, primarily for transmission of information, but also for some degree of coordination between the ethnic Albanian force's actions on the ground and tactical air operations by the Alliance.

In practical terms, this coordination made sense. It was carried out primarily, it would seem, through CIA channels, as well as by liaison between US forces stationed in Albania supporting the Apache attack helicopters (based there for possible use in the NATO operations, but in fact never sent into action) and the Albanian army, which was in contact with the UÇK. The US then fed information into NATO's tactical operations' planning, enabling the Alliance to take advantage of UÇK operations that forced clusters of VJ, in particular, and MUP units into the open, where they could be struck and, in some cases, receive high casualty levels. Moreover, with a strong degree of coordination, as emerged, the UÇK could generate tactical targets for NATO action – even if this creative and flexible approach was not as well understood by the Pentagon as it was by NATO's top military figures in Europe (Supreme Allied Commander Europe General Wesley Clark, an American, and his Deputy, Lieutenant General Sir Rupert Smith, a Briton). The practical tactical logic of this was undeniable – as was the corollary, which was that if VJ units dispersed to avoid devastating air assault, in smaller, more isolated groups, they became vulnerable to UÇK operations, as NATO's top military man, General Clark explained.[37]

There were good reasons for the Alliance to have avoided this

[37] Wesley K. Clark 'When Force is Necessary: NATO's Military Response to the Kosovo Crisis', *NATO Review*, vol.47, summer 1999. See also Clark *Waging Modern Warfare: Bosnia, Kosovo and the Future of Combat*, New York: Public Affairs, 2001, pp. 328–9.

coordination, or at least to have ensured that it was minimal. These ranged from the more practical to the political and philosophical. Regarding the former, the UÇK was self-serving, had a different set of values and objectives from NATO and hence could not be relied upon either to provide reliable information, or to respond to requests. At the other end of this scale, while NATO clearly desired success, its headline purpose in carrying out the operations – responding to an impending, then actual, humanitarian catastrophe and the gross abuse of human rights (even though this was by no means the only motivation, for, in reality, Alliance credibility was also at stake in major ways) – could only be tarnished by association with an insurgent group whose intent was to secure the independence of Kosovo and which was prepared to use all means, including those anathema to Alliance members, to achieve its ends.

For the most part, the UÇK, despite some crowing after Serbian forces had eventually been driven from Kosovo, demonstrated no greater cohesion, coherence or capacity for independent success when faced with significant Serbian forces than it had during 1998. Its function on the ground in relation to NATO air operations was undesirably important for the Alliance, which in turn meant that when the UÇK got into trouble against the VJ, NATO close air support became imperative. For example, General Clark regarded it as an absolute priority that key UÇK positions on Mount Paštrik, close to the border with Albania, were not lost and that all possible air force should be applied to ensuring that control was maintained.[38] In the end, it was the UÇK's practical relevance as a limited ground complement to NATO's tactical air operations over Kosovo that bought it a place at the political table after the conflict. It was an ironic success for what remained a small, relatively ineffectual force – an historical curiosity and anomaly. It was probably the weakest insurgent force ever to achieve the key items on its political agenda and had done so only because of the peculiar circumstances of NATO involvement, especially air operations, in probably the shortest time it had taken any similar force to achieve its goals.

Among the neighborhood adversaries, Slovenia, Croatia and Bosnia and Hercegovina all had a primary focus on preserving their statehood and the integrity of their borders. Each was acting from

[38] Clark, *Waging Modern Warfare*, p. 335.

a position of weakness and adopted a general strategic approach which reflected this. Slovenia's strategy was the most coherent and successful. Relying on armed clashes where its opponent was engaged on Slovenian terms, action was reinforced and magnified by its integration with media management. Slovenia also benefited from being a relative complement to the Serbian project – a contingent conflict on the way to others, of greater immanence.

The other two countries both adopted victim strategies for much of the conflict. In neither case was it a particularly coherent approach, and nor did it produce all the results desired – notably the presence of an armed international expeditionary force that would engage, in effect, on its behalf, against Serbian forces – although, for various reasons, international engagement was greater in the case of Bosnia and Hercegovina than in that of Croatia. Ultimately advantage could only be taken of that international engagement, however, and better results could only be achieved by Croatia and by Bosnia and Hercegovina, when they took matters more into their own hands and, critically, after they stopped fighting each other, as in 1993, and formed a common strategic approach predicated on success on the battlefield, rather than failure on all levels.

The approach of the Kosovo Albanians was different, but, by the time they were involved in major armed hostilities it represented something of a blend of the victim and self-help approaches, both geared towards taking advantage of international engagement to counter the Serbian project. With only a very limited military capability, but with such an overwhelmingly clear-cut designation as victim in terms of human rights abuses, and with the earlier campaigns shaping thinking, the UÇK benefited from more straightforward, more prompt and more comprehensive international military engagement. Ironically, the cause of the Kosovo Albanians was the one point at which the key question of statehood, in the international purview, ran against Serbia's local adversaries. Despite this complication, the clear inference to be confirmed by the Kosovo experience was that the only serious opposition to the Serbian project would come from outside the Yugoslav lands. The theme of the next chapter – international military engagement, principally Western air power – was the vital counterweight to Serbian strategy.

10

THE INTERNATIONAL ADVERSARIES: AIMS, STRATEGY AND OPERATIONS

The international approach to the Serbian campaign of the 1990s was rarely straightforward.[1] Caught between the complexity of events and the difficulties of achieving coherence in international affairs, the international strategic approach was always defined by the 'least bad' option available, given the various conditions that applied in a particular phase of involvement. There were different approaches, at different times, but the chief aim, at each stage, was to uphold the key principle of international order – that state borders should not be altered by the use of force – and to resist gross, policy-driven, abuses of human rights, and, in doing so, effectively to oppose the Serbian project. However this opposition could never be straight forward, given the comparable ambitions (though on a lesser scale) of the other protagonists, the geographical and ethnic intricacies of the conflict, and, lastly, the diffuse and sometimes contradictory perspectives and ambitions of the international actors involved. This is a range of problems that I have discussed elsewhere regarding early phases of the war in the western theaters.[2] Hence only a summary of early international approaches is required to characterize the evolution in the international strategic approach, this chapter's emphasis being on the latter phases of the war, in Kosovo.

---

[1] The term 'international' is not, itself, straightforward, as indicated in Gow, *Triumph of the Lack of Will*. In the present context, given the drift in international handling over the years, the inner 'Western core' of that term has become even more important, and, certainly more obvious. However, despite the exposure of a clearly (and largely, solely) Western approach in one phase of handling the war in Kosovo, there remained notable ways in which the approach, while dominated by the West, for the most part, had broader dimensions. Thus, 'international' is retained, rather than using the term 'Western'.

[2] Gow, *Triumph*.

Croatia, Bosnia and Hercegovina and the testing of international strategic ingenuity

War in the Croatian and Bosnian theaters provoked international engagements both diplomatic and military; it was also one of the most testing challenges that could have been faced by anyone at any time. The number of interlinked factors meant that any strategic calculation needed to be calibrated against not only the immediate needs of a particular situation, but also against others in the overall picture. There was never going to be a simple strategic approach to the questions posed by the Serbian project and its adjunct problems in Croatia and in Bosnia and Hercegovina. However, as the war continued, the issues of using force coherently and with political will became ever more focused. Unfortunately, earlier, often understandable, strategic decisions had made it harder than it would have been to work out the correlation of means and ends required.

The international military intervention provoked a major academic and practitioner debate on the character and capacities of peacekeeping, peace support operations and other operations short of clear-cut war – that is, the range of operations in which the ends fall short of clearly defined political objectives that oblige the 'enemy' to do one's will. This philosophical and practical debate was, at its core, one about the conditions for using force and the utility of doing so.[3] It was a debate begun by the decision of the UN Security Council in February 1992 to authorize deployment of one of the largest ever UN peacekeeping operations, UNPROFOR (United Nations Protection Force), in Croatia. Unlike traditional UN missions, UNPROFOR's mission was not to monitor a single ceasefire line, but to patrol zones, described as UN Protected Areas. This wider patrolling mission necessitated a force of 14,000, compared with an average level for UN peacekeeping operations closer to 2,000. However, the terms of engagement were still clearly in the domain of traditional UN peacekeeping: the force was to be neutral, it was deployed on the basis of consent, and, even though it was considerably better armed than conventional UN missions, its only scope for using those armaments was in response to direct

---

[3] This debate and the deployment and use of international forces in the Croatian and Bosnian theaters is discussed more extensively in *Triumph*, chapters 5 and 6.

attacks on units in cases where those firing could immediately be identified and targeted.

When a force came to be deployed to Bosnia and Hercegovina in the fall of 1992, the existence of UNPROFOR, including the optimistic decision to base its headquarters in Sarajevo,[4] and the strategic linkage forced on that country and its western neighbor by the Serbian state project, meant that any operation in the former could not be divorced from the latter. The existing mission would, in part, define the new one – and, as a consequence, the latter was treated as an extension of the former for its first two years.[5] This constraint on the new force in the Bosnian theater was not the only one.

In terms of the means–ends equation of strategy, international engagement in Bosnia and Hercegovina was never favorably placed. Aside from the need to take into account the existing UN force in Croatia, the strategic challenge involved several complicating factors. There were two principal international aims – to reject the attempt to disrupt the territorial integrity of Bosnia and Hercegovina by use of force and to respond to, oppose and, if possible, prevent, ethnic purification, two political objectives that required different approaches. The former could involve no more than a diplomatic refusal to recognize the accomplishments of Serbian force, but it might also involve a resort to armed force. In contrast to the case of Iraq and Kuwait in 1990, the Serbian attempt to dismember Bosnia and Hercegovina was not a militarily clear-cut question of one army's invading and occupying another country and needing to be ejected.

[4] This decision was optimistic in that it made no military sense to locate the mission's headquarters hundreds of kilometers away in a neighboring country, but there was some vain hope that the demonstration of interest in Bosnia and Hercegovina might serve as a deterrent.

[5] By 1994, UNPROFOR had three commands, Croatia, Bosnia and Hercegovina and – a radical departure – a preventive force deployed in Macedonia symbolically to deter any Serbian moves there and as a tripwire should any occur. In 1994, recognizing the practical and political complexities of treating all three cases as one, especially regarding pressures on the force in Bosnia and the need to divorce these from the other situations as far as possible, three separate forces were created. The force in Bosnia inherited the title UNPROFOR, while the force in Croatia was reconstituted as UNCRO (United Nations Conflict Resolution Operation) and the preventive mission in Macedonia was renamed UNPREDEP (United Nations Preventive Deployment).

As noted in earlier chapters, a key part of the Serbian strategy involved ambiguity and attempted deception: by dividing the JNA into the VRS and the VJ, issues were clouded. The VRS mostly comprised Bosnian Serbs, making any action against it not only resistance to the Belgrade project, but also a measure taken against one of Bosnia's communities, albeit a movement bent on rejecting Bosnia and Hercegovina as a country. Because that movement appeared credibly to represent a substantial part of the Bosnian Serb population, there was no easy way to conduct international military engagement purely against Serbian forces as if they were analogous to those of Iraq in Kuwait.

The imperative to resist ethnic cleansing was a factor in considering the use of force against the Serbian project in Bosnia and Hercegovina. Because it had support from many Bosnian Serbs, any action against it would be action against Bosnian Serbs and, in the circumstances (and without any intention on the part of international actors) might result in the displacement and flight of Bosnian Serbs and hence of accusations of ethnic cleansing against the international actors.

Because of the risk of a mass Serbian exodus following a hypothetical international use of force, the options for such a direct use of force were constrained – although they were by no means non-existent. The personnel deployed were authorized, in effect, to use force to prosecute a mission of humanitarian relief, one that sought to resist ethnic purification, implicitly (at least), by bringing humanitarian relief to communities under threat from Serbian troops, thus enabling surrounded and besieged populations, as far as possible, to remain in situ without being forced out. In part, this was a mission to save lives – one that was accomplished.[6] It was also, in effect, an attempt to impede ethnic cleansing by sustaining otherwise cut-off and beleaguered communities and assisting people to remain in their homes.

The humanitarian mission also kept in mind the perspective of resisting the dismemberment of the country. A spider's web of long communication lines was established throughout the country, ensuring that the humanitarian mission also had a role in rejecting

---

[6] Of the estimated 200–250,000 people, predominantly civilians, killed during the war in Bosnia and Hercegovina, approximately 150–200,000 died in the first six months of the Serbian campaign.

the attempt to change borders by force. An alternative, militarily easier, operation might have involved providing assistance, but only behind safe lines that, in practice, if not principle, conceded the territorial question to the ethnic cleansers.[7] This is infact what happened in 1995 when, as a result of several events, including the use of NATO air power and European artillery on the ground (see Chapter 7), as well as the fall of Žepa and Srebrenica, international troops on the ground were effectively brought behind one line that could then permit the use of air power.

There were three other important factors which fed into the international approach First, because the US was reluctant to be involved whereas European countries, after the London Conference of August 1992, were committed to acting, the options for deploying ground forces with credible command, control and communications capabilities to meet the needs of the Bosnian context were very limited. While it seemed that many European soldiers were available, in practice there were few combat-ready troops available – with the largest capability for the most forceful of missions involving 30,000 British and French troops for six months. Anything larger and more sustainable was not feasible – a problem that, despite some measures to improve the situation in the mid-1990s, was largely still the case when action over Kosovo became an issue in 1998–9 – discussed below. In the end, the force initially deployed throughout Bosnia and Hercegovina was 8,400, predominantly from European countries.

The lack of credible troops was both a product of and a compound to another limitation on international means: a political reluctance to use force, even where there was recognition that this might well be the only way, in the end, to confront and halt the Serbian project (although few, if any, of these considerations were significantly aired in public). The absence of US forces was significant. As happened later in the case of Kosovo, the main European Allies lined up behind a US lead on using force – something that only became practicable because of US commitment. However,

[7] When French troops led Operation *Turquoise*, the humanitarian operation belatedly launched in Rwanda, following the 1994 genocide there, they did so only in the south-western part of the country, neighboring the border with Burundi, which made the construction and management of military operations easier – even if it did not address questions of political purpose and ethnic advantage.

even among those who were prepared to contribute forces in the absence of US engagement, such as France and the UK, there was no great appetite at the political level for advice that recommended a more forceful strategic approach, even within the limitations of the ground force already deployed.

The questions over use of force, political will and the disposition of the force on the ground were made more acute following the creation by the UN Security Council of the six 'safe areas' noted in Chapter 7. On the ground, there were two major changes resulting from declaration of the 'safe areas': greater troop numbers were deployed and the formal authority to use air power became more pronounced. First, the force level for UNPROFOR in Bosnia and Hercegovina was significantly increased, eventually rising to some 24,000 troops. An international force was deployed to each of the areas and based within it. At the tactical level, these forces played a sometimes important role in blocking the Serbian project (as well as its Croatian counterpart, much of the time, during 1993). While the forces in most cases were too weak to frustrate major Serbian attacks (as was the case, in the final analysis, at Srebrenica – see Chapter 7), in some cases, notably Goražde, the contribution was critical. At one key moment, it was engagement by the Royal Welch Fusiliers that saved the town from being overrun.

When General Mladić began what was intended to be his final sweep of the safe areas in eastern Bosnia by attacking the largest of them, his forces were presented with stiff opposition. With troops in Observation Posts (OPs) at key points and Checkpoints (CPs), the outnumbered Welch Fusiliers engaged in sustained battle with a considerably larger VRS contingent over several hours on 28 May 1995.[8] Despite an adverse ratio of at least 1:10, the Welch Fusiliers held out to protect the most vital of the three positions, the high point of Mala Biserna (Small Pearl) marked by OP3 on the eastern bank of the River Drina. The Serbian attack reached the OPs around

[8] For more on the performance of the Royal Welch Fusiliers see Gillian Sandford's excellent reporting in the the *Yorkshire Post*. Several of those involved received honors for their role in the protection of Goražde, although the picture she paints, inevitably in the context of a newspaper, lacks further detail, of which she must undoubtedly have been aware, noted in official classified material. See also the Welch Fusiliers' own account of tours in Bosnia and Hercegovina, which, of necessity at the time it was published, keeps much of the detail implied 'between the lines'. 1st Battalion Royal Welch Fusiliers, *White Dragon: the Royal Welch Fusiliers in Bosnia*, Wrexham: Royal Welch Fusiliers, 1995, pp. 49–50.

the middle of the day. Some of the OPs were easily surrounded and obliged to surrender, with the VRS taking 25 men prisoner, and at least one was vacant. At other points the much larger and more heavily armed Serbian force was kept at bay. After a ferocious engagement, at 1545, OP2 was overwhelmed and the eight soldiers defending it were captured and held hostage (although their leader, Corporal David Parry, still managed to maintain secret communications with force commander Lieutenant-Colonel Jonathan Riley) and, at around 1600, forces were ordered to withdraw from OP1 and CP1. This left OP3, the key military position that dominated the strategic terrain down towards Goražde. The British troops engaged in constant firefights on OP3, reinforced by three Saxon armored cars dispatched from units on the eastern bank of the River Drina below. After almost four hours of uninterrupted exchanges, several hundred ABiH soldiers from Goražde, whom the British commander had expected would be there sooner, arrived to defend Mala Biserna. With the Bosnians in place and having withstood hours of intense fire, the British troops withdrew, having ensured that Mladić would not overrun Goražde – indeed, that he would not come as close to doing so as he had in April 1994 (see Chapter 7) – and that he would turn elsewhere to mop up Bosnian government-controlled-cum-UN 'safe area' blotches on his Bosnian Serb landscape.

The second factor involved a clear shift in formal terms towards the prospect of using air power to protect the areas, albeit one that was limited by consideration of the troop configuration on the ground. Long lines of communications and small numbers of troops deployed in cut-off positions meant a decidedly vulnerable ground force. In the event of air strikes, these troops would be highly vulnerable, whether to hostage taking, or to direct hostile attack. With a perfectly understandable first priority of force protection, the use of air power was thus deeply constrained – a reality that caused some heated discussion and friction, not only in public discourse, but in relations with the United States – which, with the arrival in office of the Clinton administration, for a long while took a somewhat simplistic approach to the use of air power, whereas the Europeans, with troops on the ground, were acutely aware of the complexities involved.

In the end, these issues were reconciled on three fronts: the realization on both sides of the Atlantic that this issue needed to be resolved and that air action would be needed for NATO's strategic credibility, if the very nature and existence of the Alliance were to be preserved; the fall-out from the collapse of the safe areas at Žepa and Srebrenica (see Chapter 7); and the orchestration of a reconfigured ground force by the British Commander of UNPROFOR in Bosnia and Hercegovina, Lieutenant General Rupert Smith, complemented by the deployment of a Rapid Reaction Force, comprising artillery and light armor from three European countries (see also Chapter 7). As a result, a new approach, involving the decisive use of force, emerged, primarily using air assets – again as shown in Chapter 7. This was to have a keen impact on operations in Kosovo a few years later.

The road to Rambouillet: the failure to deter the Kosovo campaign

As the Serbian campaign in Kosovo developed during 1998 (see Chapter 8), and as the outside world was drawn ever more sharply into the conflict, international diplomatic approaches sought an end to the conflict. Throughout the summer, as Serbian offensives displaced over 300,000 refugees, there was increasing discussion of the use of force, although for most of that period the voices of deterrence had a very hollow ring. Gaining information from sources inside NATO, Belgrade knew full well that there was no agreement inside the Alliance on the legal grounds for an intervention. Only when this came, in October, was Milošević finally persuaded to suspend operations. Even then, the prospects were never great for the peace to hold. Leaving aside the ambitions of the UÇK, there was no provision for a military force to secure implementation of the agreement. Moreover, although there was no dispute over allowing an OSCE monitor force to be deployed, the tardy international progress in actually getting it on the ground meant that the agreement and the political agenda slipped, making a return to hostilities and a new Serbian campaign certain.

Several weeks after NATO went to the brink of using air power over Kosovo, the province's security situation remained fragile. Both the military and the political dimensions of the arrangement agreed by the authorities in Belgrade to avert NATO air strikes in October were less expeditiously implemented than was foreseen. The relatively slow pace of deploying unarmed international verifiers by the OSCE and NATO armed reaction force to protect them meant that the sense of inevitability that had cemented the Dayton Peace Accords for Bosnia and Hercegovina in 1995 was missing. Without this sense of inevitability, the situation in Kosovo continued to be strategically dynamic, with Serbs and, especially, Albanian extremists, believing that the use of violence could still produce benefits for them. Thus if the pace of international verification of the ceasefire and force agreement could not be increased, the political progress needed in negotiations between the Serbs and Albanians, conducted indirectly through American offices, would not be achievable. Yet, political progress was essential to avert any breakdown in the delicate ceasefire which had largely stayed in place, but which remained insecure and was under constant threat.

Under the terms of the agreement between Yugoslav President Slobodan Milošević and US Envoy Richard Holbrooke, signed in Belgrade on 14 October, provision for elections to be held in Kosovo within nine months was due to be agreed by 9 November but disagreements on procedural matters for holding elections led to further delays. This was because implementation of the agreement signed between Milošević and Holbrooke had slipped behind schedule. Agreement on elections was part of a tightly worked out timetable imposed by Holbrooke, with elements entered into in an ostensibly voluntary way by Belgrade. This US approach reflected the substantial and painstaking preparatory work that had been carried out with the Kosovan Albanian leadership by the US Ambassador to Skopje, Christopher Hill. Unfortunately other dates in the timetable had already been allowed to slide backwards, notably the date for agreement on procedures to reach a political solution – 2 November.

There were two principal reasons for this slippage. The first was difficulties presented by both the Belgrade authorities and, particularly, the Kosovan Albanian leaders. The second was the greater period of time required than planned to put international verification and protection forces in place. While discussions between Hill and the Kosovan Albanian leadership had settled on the notion of an interim agreement for three years, political divisions meant there was reluctance to accept this interim period without commitment to steps towards independence being taken later. The arrangement was intended to persuade the Kosovan Albanian leadership that any agreement need not necessarily be forever, while ensuring that whatever agreement there was would recognize the perspective shared by Belgrade and the international community that Kosovo could not become independent without Belgrade's consent.

Because discussion surrounding the Holbrooke arrangement and its implementation emphasized that there would be no direct move towards independence after three years, the Kosovar Albanian leadership was subject to divisions regarding acceptance of arrangements for self-governance within the Federal Republic of Yugoslavia (Serbia and Montenegro). Under pressure from those such as Adem Demaçi, political spokesman for the UÇK, either not to agree to anything at all, or only to agree to an arrangement which ultimately carried the promise of a referendum on the status of the province in southern Serbia, the negotiating team was unable to follow easily the line expected of it by US diplomats. In an effort to narrow the respective positions, the US State Department deputed a lawyer to assist the Kosovan Albanians in negotiating an agreement in which they could be confident of that which had gone into the agreement and of a US commitment to ensuring that it was upheld. In this context, US officials let it be known that they were not unduly worried by the delay, as Hill's role in mediation and negotiation between the parties was continuing in a positive manner, even if it was behind schedule.

This position might have appeared weak, given that less than two weeks earlier the US and others in the international community had been reinforcing their position that the threat of NATO air strikes would remain in place if the terms of the agreement, as well as the eleven points to be incorporated in any political arrangements for Kosovo, were not kept. However, given the difficulty on the Kosovan Albanian side politically, there was no reason to rush to a use of NATO air power against the Serbian and Yugoslav side, even though the Activation Order for use of air strikes regarding Kosovo was maintained indefinitely by the North Atlantic Council (NAC) on 27 October. Even though ultimately all aspects of the agreement, most notably the military ones, required agreed political structures to be in place, the international community was relaxed about the pace of implementation falling behind because it was unable swiftly enough to deliver its part of the bargain – a verification force to oversee implementation.

While the existing Kosovo Diplomatic Observer Mission (KDOM) continued to operate and experienced a 'surge' in numbers, including the recruitment of 'local staff' (including some regarded by observers as 'private soldiers') to take on some of the roles assigned to the OSCE Kosovo Verification Mission (KVM), the KVM itself was not likely to begin operating until late November or early December. Advanced parties had been in Kosovo preparing to establish a 300-strong headquarters for the operation, which would total around 2,000 personnel – primarily unarmed soldiers in civilian dress. But progress on the ground, as well as in composing the full force, was taking longer than had been hoped initially.

In addition to the delay in gathering and deploying the KVM, there was also a further dimension to delay. This concerned provision by NATO to protect the force. An armed protection and extraction force, supplied under NATO auspices, was to be deployed to the former Yugoslav Republic of Macedonia, the existence of which would significantly safeguard the KVM, once both were in place. This could be expected to stabilize the situation sufficiently to facilitate implementation of any political agreement and subsequent elections.

Almost as significantly, this potentially resolved the critical and long drawn out problem faced by NATO countries regarding appropriate legal authority for the use of armed force. When the NAC finally issued its Activation Order to the military commanders in October, the issue of legal authority for use of force had been fudged. While the US and the UK argued that a compound of legal bases, including UN Security Council Resolution 1199, provided appropriate authority, a number of their allies, including The Netherlands, Italy and Germany, strongly believed that an explicit UN Security Council Resolution was required. With the deployment of the KVM, complemented by a new UN Security Council Resolution, 1203, using full authority of enforcement powers under Chapter VII of the UN Charter, a previously vague situation was transformed with the appearance of two clear legal bases for the possible use of force.

The first of these was the right to self-defense, meaning the right to protect nationals involved in the KVM. The other was the recognition in Resolution 1203 that the OSCE mission would need to 'consider arrangements to be implemented in co-operation with other organizations' to provide for action to ensure their safety and freedom of movement'. The problem had ceased to be so much the legal authority to use force. But this was not the end of all problems, as the composition of the force itself had to be decided. This immediately presented NATO with an old Transatlantic dilemma: the US contribution to such a force would not be ground troops, despite the presence of US ground personnel in Macedonia, leaving Europeans to carry what they might interpret as the burden of a US-inspired policy. While planning for various options was accelerated on the assumption that US ground personnel would not be directly involved, the exact nature of the likely force in the absence of Americans remained open.

The difficulties in establishing the international mechanisms to support implementation of the various agreements made in mid-October, including that between the Supreme Allied Commander Europe, General Wesley Clark, and the Chief of Staff of the Yugoslav Army (VJ), General Momčilo Perišić, meant that international actors were not forcing the pace to achieve agreements that they were not yet ready fully to oversee. This was despite the deadlines, which had been established earlier. The absence of these mechanisms permitted the pace of political negotiations to falter. That in turn meant that the pressures on the fragile security situation grew. The October ceasefire and withdrawal of Serbian and Yugoslav forces, either from Kosovo, or into barracks, came under pressure.

The first main challenge to the ceasefire was that, in the absence both of political agreements according to schedule and of effective mechanisms to be offered by the KVM and its back-up, there was no confidence in the likely success of the political negotiations. (By contrast, in Bosnia and Hercegovina at the end of 1995, what proved vital was the existence of a political agreement and international commitment, including a role for US troops, to see it implemented, that created a mood of inevitability which greatly facilitated the embedding of the ceasefire.) Unless the political timetable could be recovered soon after implementation provisions were finally in place, then it was likely that any confidence in the agreement succeeding would be eroded. The other big challenge, again encouraged by the fact that the prospect of a political agreement had fallen behind timetable and that the verification presence had not arrived, was that backsliding by the Serbs on the military provisions of the October agreements was being implicitly condoned by the international community, while, in the absence of a stronger international presence, elements of the badly beaten and divided UÇK had begun to exert an influence on the ground, both against Serbs and against ethnic Albanians.

The October agreements insisted that Belgrade should remove the additional forces it had deployed to Kosovo for its crackdown, which began at the end of February. Belgrade had two types of force deployed. The larger and better armed was the VJ. Over 20,000 additional troops had been sent to Kosovo in the year preceding the crackdown, meaning that over a third of the VJ's total strength was deployed there. The other element involved interior ministry units. These were of three kinds – regular police (albeit relatively heavily armed), special anti-terrorist units and special combat forces. The first of these constituted the 6,500 MUP personnel considered normally to be based in Kosovo, while the last two, especially the third, constituted the additional units deployed to Kosovo, said to have numbered at their peak around 13,000. It was the MUP Special Forces that carried the attacks against the UÇK and, above all, against villages and towns, in the course of the seven-month campaign earlier in the year.

UÇK elements directed fire at and impeded the freedom of movement of KDOM and KVM preparatory personnel in their clearly marked orange vehicles. VJ forces also later opened fire over the roofs of OSCE vehicles, giving rise to official protests and to a warning by NATO Secretary-General Javier Solana in Rome on 17 November that 'serious consequences' would follow continued attempts to intimidate international observers, or to impede their freedom of movement. UÇK activity, as well as killing ethnic Albanians, also included renewed attempts to recruit. In these circumstances, the international community did not rush to condemn the Serbian and Yugoslav presence, although protests were lodged. Rather it temporarily (at least) quietly acquiesced in what had probably involved a small increase in the MUP and VJ presence in the field, in order to provide greater security than would otherwise have been the case – NATO air strikes, for example, could not seriously have been employed against UÇK forces too small and too disparate to be susceptible to this kind of treatment. The Serbian presence only served, however, to increase tension with the UÇK.

Faster progress on deployment of the KVM and its back-up NATO reaction force in Kosovo was needed in order to ensure that the delicate security situation in Kosovo would not completely break down, crucial to which was the need for political agreement on the interim arrangements for governing Kosovo, which could pave the way for elections. Political agreement required the underpinning to be provided inter alia by the KVM. Both were essential if the momentum for peace was to be maintained in what was not yet a strategically static situation, as both sides, but especially the UÇK, believed that more could be gained through the further use of violence. Momentum was partly lost, with slippage in the original timetable, regarding agreement on interim political arrangements by 2 November and for elections under those arrangements by 9 November. This slippage was not yet fatal – challenges to the ceasefire could still just about be maintained. However, gradual erosion meant that time was running out and eventual collapse was becoming inevitable. As information and understanding on Serbian preparations for a new and decisive campaign of ethnic cleansing began to be digested in Western capitals, the quest to avert that Serbian campaign gained urgency. The massacre identified at Račak by the KVM was the final warning of what was to come.[9]

To avoid further atrocities of this sort significant political progress from the talks under the aegis of Ambassador Hill was required. Hill's initiative bolstered a Franco-British initiative to seize the diplomatic agenda in order to press for a political agreement, based on the Hill talks, that would permit agreed deployment of an international implementation force. This led to negotiations in France, initially at the Château of Rambouillet. Contrary to the wholly false (and, it is tempting to think, sometimes consciously false) analysis offered by some, concerning the aims, purposes and conduct of this process,[10] the aim was to get agreement and deployment before the Serbian campaign due to be launched in late March. Time was of the essence and a strict timetable was put in place. International diplomatic agreement would provide the political

[9] On Račak, see Chapter 8.

[10] For accurate and essential discussion of the Rambouillet process and some of its prominent and less shrewd critics, see the fine article by Alex Bellamy 'Reconsidering Rambouillet' in *Contemporary Security Policy*,Vol. 22, No. 1, 2001. Aside from describing Serbian President Milutin Milutinović as Prime Minister, Bellamy provides a comprehensive, commonsense, and sound attack on some of the arguments put forward. The curious assortment of authors he discusses includes: Michael Mandelbaum, Henry Kissinger, Colin Gray, Ken Booth, John Pilger, Noam Chomsky, Christopher Layne, Peter Gowan, Eric Herring and Michael MccGwire. Of these, MccGwire's 'Why Did We Bomb Serbia?', *International Affairs*, vol. 76, no. 1, 2000, is a particular personal disappointment, not least because I made him aware of evidence which he appears to have ignored in this piece.

mission for military implementation – and a NATO-led international military force on the ground would halt the Serbian campaign of ethnic cleansing.

At Rambouillet the Western intention was to secure an agreement that would provide broad-ranging and effective self-government for the province of Kosovo – short of its gaining full independence – and *inter alia*, secure the withdrawal of most Serbian and FRY forces. It would also facilitate the deployment of an international armed force under NATO leadership, command and control (the euphemism that came to be adopted later was 'effective', as only NATO could provide something that would be effective). This would remove any possibility of Belgrade being able to initiate ethnic cleansing operations against the Albanian population. It was desirable that such an agreement should be broadly international and have the backing of the UN Security Council, and with this is mind, and given the role of the International Contact Group in dealing with the break-up of the old Yugoslavia, there was a great desire to ensure Russia's involvement.

There was a fine line to be walked between the desire for a truly international character to the agreement and the imperative of blocking the imminent Serbian campaign. For those focused on Western interests – including the viability of the NATO-led operation in Bosnia and Hercegovina and the credibility of the Alliance itself – an effective response to the problem posed by Belgrade was more important than securing broader international support, if that decision had to be made. This was especially the case because Western leaders, after years of dealing with Milošević in a variety of ways, had concluded that he would only accept an agreement if there were a credible threat of force – as had been most recently demonstrated by his accepting the October Agreement with Holbrooke.

The negotiations at Rambouillet were led by the French and British, on behalf of the EU. The talks were also reinforced by the continuing NATO threat to use force against Belgrade, if it did not cooperate. While these were technically separate tracks of international involvement, the fact that London and Paris were prominent in both cases and that the US was very close to each process, in a strong sense, meant that the two tracks were part of the same Western approach. Its aim was to avert Belgrade's spring campaign against the UÇK and the wider Albanian population in Kosovo. While there was no doubt that success in this would depend on the use of Western armed forces, the issue of how best to use the military was not straightforward.

The issue of using NATO's unique capability began to be discussed seriously as the conflict in Kosovo developed during summer 1998. At that stage, NATO capitals were threatening the use of air power, though the threat remained a hollow one at that stage. Different governments had different views on the legal grounds for such action. In Britain, when the lawyers offered an unhelpful opinion, the Prime Minister Tony Blair told them to work on it and return with an interpretation of international law that would be relevant. In The Hague and in Bonn, there was a strong and simple conviction that there could be no legal use of force without clear authorization to do so from the UN Security Council. Some at NATO Headquarters cited duty to act under the Genocide Convention – although this presented significant difficulties, among which was the definitional concern that the events in Kosovo, at that stage, while unacceptable, perhaps did not meet the definition of genocide in the Convention. Thus, a variety of legal interpretations emerged, but no agreement between the Allies on a single common interpretation (and problems with some Allies agreeing that action was needed, irrespective of its legality).

In the end, there would be no single interpretation on the legality of using force. After several months of political and planning activity, during which time the 'legal basis' box on the agenda remained unchecked, once everything else was in place and the key decision occurred in October, the NATO Secretary General Javier Solana displayed his diplomatic ingenuity. He sidestepped the discussion over competing versions of the legal authority for action and instead simply asked if it was agreed that action would be legal – with no one against, the final box came to be checked. Each of the Allies could operate according to its own interpretation of international law. As a consequence, however, when air attacks eventually began in March 1999, Alliance spokesmen were never able to give an explicit legal rationale for the action – there was no single line that could be advanced and no possibility of a composite explanation.

The differences within NATO over the legal grounds for action vied with concerns over how force might be applied. One key issue was consideration of using ground forces. During the summer of 1998, while Washington and London, in particular, were uttering empty threats on using air power, General Michael Jackson and a team from NATO Allied Rapid Reaction Corps (ARRC) Headquarters investigated mounting a ground operation. In August they went to Albania and Macedonia to assess conditions as part of the operational planning process. The ARRC team reported that any major ground operation required the infrastructure in both countries to be built first. The problems in Albania were particularly significant because the Greek government had made clear that the use of Thessaloniki, the major strategic port facility in the whole sub-region, would not be made available owing to domestic political pressures. Nor were Albania's port facilities at Vllöre and Dürres equipped to cope with either the scale, or the scope, of NATO's capability. And had the port facilities been suitable for handling NATO's military might, the internal road and rail infrastructure was close to non-existent, given the size and quantity of NATO's 'kit.' A single, narrow, winding mountain road up to the border between Albania and Kosovo-cum-Serbia-cum-the FRY was not the type of strategic thoroughfare required to accommodate the enormous US Abrams M-1 main battle tank, or even the slightly smaller German-made Leopards, used by a number of NATO members, and the British Challenger – all of which dwarfed the standard Soviet-derived T-55 tank predominantly used by the VJ. With the road leading into Macedonia from Albania also through the mountains, there was no alternative route. Leaving aside the almost non-existent infrastructure offered by Albania, routes in Macedonia were also inadequate for NATO's needs – and air base facilities there were too small and too limited, especially for the serious heavy lift capability that insertion of a major armored force would require. The only option for using a major ground force, therefore, would require construction both in Albania and Macedonia.

In practice, this meant that a ground operation was not a serious option. There were three reasons for this, the first of which was the equation of cost and equipment: not even the governments most strongly in favor of forceful action over Kosovo would find it easy to countenance such a massive construction project. The cost would have been simply too great in terms of finance and manpower to contemplate for something that both might not be required, if other approaches proved to be successful and, above all, would not be easily explained to, or received by, domestic and international political audiences.

The second reason was that apart from justifying the cost in those arenas, it is highly likely that any such engagement by Alliance countries would have been interpreted negatively, both domestically and internationally. It is hard to imagine even the most sophisticated phrasing by Whitehall mandarins, or the smartest professional marketing campaign, that could counter the same suspicions and allegations that would be made 'in face of any direct explanation'.

A direct explanation – that it was preparation for the eventuality of action to prevent ethnic cleansing by Belgrade, would almost certainly have met with a negative response. Rather than being lauded as an act of prudent preventive action in a good cause, there would have been strident voices declaring that the build-up was evidence of NATO's anti-Serbian prejudice, its being no more than a demonstration of the Alliance's determination to bully Belgrade, for the sake of nothing more than its own power projection. It is hardly likely, for example, that Moscow, or Beijing, could have been reassured of necessity and benign intent in such a situation. The evidence from the period of armed hostilities during 1999 only confirms this. The reaction of some governments and of large sections of the media and public opinion, even in NATO countries, had no (or occasionally next-to-no) connection with that which was actually happening, or at stake. Instead, assorted critics invented and imagined spurious scenarios, and fairy-tales, couched in NATO's malign intent and Belgrade's innocence, rather than in consideration of the politically and operationally awkward attempts of the former to come to terms with and confront Milošević's brutal intent.

It was the Serbian leader's brutal agenda that provides the third and decisive reason for there being no serious choice about mounting a ground option: time was of the essence. Already in October, as Milošević was agreeing to the terms negotiated with Holbrooke, his Chief of Staff, General Perišić, had somewhat obliquely indicated concern to his NATO counterparts in negotiations – Supreme Allied Commander Europe (SACEUR) US General Wesley Clark and Chairman of the NATO Military Committee, the German General Klaus Naumann. Over the subsequent months,

it became ever more clear and likely that Milošević would go beyond testing the limits of international tolerance and move against
the Kosovo Albanians. Moreover, as this scenario developed, with
MUP and VJ units evidently preparing for action (protesting, as
had the JNA at the beginning of the decade, that they were merely
conducting normal exercises), Western governments understood
clearly that there was a deadline for any action to counter Belgrade's
campaign – on or around 24 March.

Given the infrastructure required to mount a major ground operation in a non-permissive environment, by the time the Serbian
timetable was known early in 1999 and the necessity of action had
become clear, there was simply no time to make Macedonia and
Albania NATO-compatible. In truth, even if there had been the
same certainty over Milošević's exact intentions in October, or even
in July and August – and even if political leaders who were not recognized for making major commitments that were costly, hard to
explain and hard to justify in many arenas had ignored the inevitable flak and built the two countries' infrastructure and deployed
forces to them – there would probably not have been enough time.
As it was, the impossibility of mounting a ground operation tal-
lied with the political preferences of leaders, especially those in
Washington, who had little taste for putting ground forces in harm's
way, lest this have an impact on domestic political opinion. On
the other hand, those same leaders were relatively comfortable in
authorizing what was seen as a largely risk-free use of air power –
especially if it involved the use of standoff weapons.

Given these constraints, two broad options remained. One was
to use air power and the other was to seek a permissive environment in which a NATO-led international peace support force could
be deployed. The former became the fallback plan, as the latter was
pursued. NATO-led implementation of any agreement was vital,
both to ensuring that the agreement held and to establish a serious,
physical-military impediment to the use of the Serbian military.
Milošević would not be able to move on Kosovo with a major
international force in place. But, the permissive arrangements for
deployment would make all the difference: there would be less
need for major logistical back-up and reinforcement to insert the
force into a hostile environment, meaning that a smaller force and
lower level of protection would be needed. The problems of deployment would remain, but they would be manageable – all the

more so if the far better option of force transit through Serbia were a part of that package.

Deploying troops through Serbia was automatically included in the plans for deployment of an implementation force that were added to the political agreement being negotiated in France. Appendix B of the draft agreement became notorious and the centerpiece of criticism and conspiracy theories (discussed above) depicting NATO as a provocative bully, delivering ultimatums that contained terms that were alleged to have been designed to be unacceptable and, therefore, to do no more than serve as the pretext for an air campaign that the Alliance was determined to initiate. Appendix B was the basis of this utterly ridiculous notion.

Some European NATO countries, with the UK notably in the lead, had deployed troops to Macedonia in February in anticipation of an agreement that would require immediate readiness to implement – these forces would join with those already deployed there under NATO auspices. What the draft planning and the Appendix envisaged, first of all, was an agreement that would (according to Chapter 7 of the Interim Agreement – the Rambouillet document) result in the parties' inviting NATO 'to constitute and lead a military force to help ensure compliance' with the provisions of the agreement and which affirmed the 'sovereignty and territorial integrity' of the FRY.[11] The version of KFOR proposed at that stage, in Chapter 7 of the agreement was, primarily, much narrower than that eventually deployed after armed hostilities ended in June 1999. Whereas the latter gave KFOR a wide-ranging security remit in the province, under the Rambouillet terms, the mission would have been limited to supervising demilitarization and ensuring there was no retreat on that position and no armed hostilities. Nor would it have had the role it took, in the end, regarding Kosovo's borders with Albania and Macedonia, as Rambouillet would have permitted a continuing VJ presence of 1,100 troops for border monitoring, as well as 6,500 ordinary MUP for public security purposes, whereas the eventual deployment of KFOR saw the complete removal of all Serbian forces. Belgrade would clearly have been better off, in terms of its connection to Kosovo, under Rambouillet than it proved to be afterwards.

[11] For considerably fuller discussion of these issues and the fallacies of the critics, see Alex Bellamy's excellent 'Reconsidering'.

In terms of the Appendix itself, this was a more-or-less off-the-shelf Status of Forces Agreement, similar to that for SFOR in Bosnia and Hercegovina. Whereas the authority to move freely throughout the latter was not seriously contested, a similar provision regarding the FRY was seen by critics, and willfully by Belgrade, as contentious and unacceptable. Paragraph 8 stipulated freedom of movement throughout the FRY for the force – something simply transferred from the Bosnian model without particular thought, in the first place, but once thought about, carrying significant logistical and transit advantages, given the physical difficulties of relying on Albania and Macedonia. Interpreted as a mandate for an occupation force, this was, in truth, a mixture of lazy borrowing from an existing template and the realization of greater practicality in using access from Bosnia and Hercegovina and, particularly, from Hungary, to transit the rest of Serbia into Kosovo. Rather than being a device designed to be unacceptable, as critics suggested, it was something normal and sensible in military planners' terms. But, equally, it was something about which there could have been discussion, had Belgrade shown even a smithereen of interest in negotiation.

The paramount fallacy in what Alex Bellamy has called the 'orthodoxy' over the military appendix is the charge that is was non-negotiable.[12] In fact, as noted in Chapter 8, it was Milošević who refused to contemplate discussion over the annex. With perhaps seven points still to be agreed on the political part of the plan, Milošević told Ambassador Hill that the military implementation arrangements were wholly unacceptable – that not a country in the world could accept such terms (ignoring, as discussed above, that these were the same terms that Bosnia and Hercegovina had agreed, in large part because of him). Hill said that the Serbian leader should suggest what would be acceptable and that he would see what he could do. He offered Milošević a pen to mark the text. The latter sat with his arms firmly folded and what can only be imagined as a childish stubborn sulk on his face and did not speak again. Hill's efforts were not the only ones. Secretary of State Madeleine Allbright, in what must have been an uncomfortable act of personal concession, also secretly called Milošević, by arrangement, to make it clear that the US (and, therefore, it could be presumed, its allies and partners) was prepared to negotiate the terms of the

[12] Bellamy, 'Reconsidering'.

military annex. However, despite these offers, the Serbian strongman would not even begin to discuss the possibility. By now, he had clearly made up his mind and had set course for conflict, expecting NATO air action and waiting to exploit it, apparently.

It was Milošević who actively thwarted the possibility of peace. The international approach to preventing conflict in Kosovo – that is to stop the imminent Serbian campaign – was not easily achieved. The strategic equation was by no means straightforward – attempting to stop something that there was eminently good reason to believe was about to happen, but unable openly to show that this was the case, or needing to prepare a military capability, but one limited politically and practically by the circumstances for preparing such a capability, especially one for ground operations. Once the various efforts being made and the range of impediments to action are understood, namely the combination of needs and pressures in the strategic equation faced by the West, then an appreciation of the real conditions of international efforts can be gained – and a very clear understanding of just why the legion of critics and refuse-to-believers were always wrong. When the NATO Kosovo campaign began, it was by no means because NATO had sought to provoke it – as its conduct confirmed.

Struggling strategically with limited war: NATO's Kosovo air campaign

NATO operations over Kosovo were not straightforward. The move from Phase I of the plans for Operation *Allied Force* to Phases II and III raised different political questions within the Alliance, as action shifted from obvious initial air defense targets to others in the strategic infrastructure that were military-political and which, because of the political aspect, sometimes political leaders found it hard to comprehend the targets' value to the mission. The fact was that the air campaign was always working on two levels – the strategic, attacking Belgrade's assets and political-military-economic infrastructure and points of vulnerability that could break Milošević's will to resist, and the tactical-cum-strategic, seeking to prevent Serbian ground operations in Kosovo itself, always the more difficult of the two and, to some extent, dependent on the former, to be successful. The difficulties presented by poor weather – hard for some to understand – were not insignificant. There were questions raised by the occasional accidents and mistakes made by Alliance air attacks – some, bizarrely, could not recognize the difference between deliberate war crimes and regrettable contingent killing of innocent civilians in mistakes (for example, when a train was hit as it crossed a bridge at Leskovac that had already been targeted and fired on by a NATO plane, or when a column of refugees at Djakovica was mistaken for a Serbian troop column reported by a Forward Air Controller). There can be no doubting that in operations involving some 38,004 sorties, of which 10,484 were strike missions, over 78 days it was remarkable how few serious errors there were. This should be seen as a tribute to the care taken and the technological and skilful precision of Operation *Allied Force*, in complete contrast to the targeting of civilians by Serbian forces.[13] Similarly, those inclined to see another striking mistake, an attack on the Chinese Embassy in Belgrade, in spurious conspiracy theory terms fail to grasp the extent to which such a diplomatically disastrous action could not have been planned and that the Federal Procurement Executive building had been the intended, and far more obvious, target.[14] One of the big issues associated with mistakes, as well as with criticism of NATO's

[13] The one area in which any question of war crimes might be raised concerns the use of cluster munitions. Although personally the use of these munitions should not be regarded as contravening the laws and customs of war, there might be more of an issue concerning their use, albeit not a particularly strong one, than implied by the dismissal of this issue by the Prosecutor at the ICTY, along with a range of other allegations raised against Alliance operations (among others by the US-based Human Rights Watch), on the grounds that this weapons system was not specifically proscribed by any legal instrument.

[14] The immediate impact was not small: aside from denting belief in NATO's competence – particularly that of the US, which had been responsible for the action, and its CIA, which had supplied the erroneous target information – this *faux pas* seriously complicated the diplomatic environment for Alliance operations. In the not-too longer term, the US was obliged to pay China compensation significantly higher than the rebuilding costs of its Embassy and, far more damagingly, to ease various pressures on Beijing regarding human rights issues – a policy applied for ten years, since the massacre of protesters in Tiannmen Square in 1989 – and to withdraw opposition to China's entering world trade forums, all of which were degrading for Washington and involved major diplomatic climb-downs. A longer-term consequence of the obligation on the US to soften its position was to allow Beijing to emerge from a decade of seeking international rehabilitation following Tiannamen, which came to be exploited with

limited ability to put a break on Serbian operations at the tactical level in Kosovo, concerned the 15,000-feet ceiling on air operations – leading some to suppose that this generally sensible, primarily force protection, measure in some way constituted cowardice and, worse, criminal negligence (all of which discussion failed to register important aspects of detail – a 15,000-feet ceiling was not a basement and meant that, in practice, planes were flying at heights of 10–14,000 feet, that pilots mostly found this the optimal height for using the types of munitions with which their aircraft were equipped; and that there were arrangements for many types of operations where the optimal level was to fly at lower altitudes of 5–6,000 feet). In brief, for the most part considerable confusion and misunderstanding surrounded the air campaign. Given all of these considerations and the inevitable temptation to draw conclusions from the Kosovo campaign about the conduct of limited warfare, it is important to grasp exactly what happened and why it proved to be successful.

The intention in the present section and the one that follows is both to investigate and explain the conduct of the Kosovo campaign itself and to address the implications for the conduct of such action in the future (although, writing at a time still fairly close to the events, all provisional conclusions must be open to later revision, as information becomes available). Contrary to the view of Ivo Daalder and Michael O'Hanlon, the 'overall verdict' on Kosovo is not 'less likely to offer new lessons than to affirm old truths.'[15] There are new things to be learned and there is an old orthodoxy that hampers thought on limited warfare that needs to be explored and revised, although space and focus does not permit that exploration here. Military and political analysts and practitioners have struggled to come to terms with the end of the Kosovo conflict because they have generally been looking for answers in the wrong place and in the wrong way.

There were three broadly touted explanations for the end of the conflict. The first was that NATO air power alone was successful. The second focused on the prospect of NATO's moving to use

---

painful vengeance when a US spy plane was forced to land on Chinese territory after an air incident in April 2001.

[15] Ivo Daalder and Michael O'Hanlon, 'Unlearning the Lessons of Kosovo', *Foreign Policy*, no. 116, fall 1999; see also Daalder and O'Hanlon, *Winning Ugly*.

of ground forces. The other emphasized the role of Russia. The second and third explanations are not mutually exclusive, but they are exclusive of the first. Moreover, they are both counters to the first. As with most things in life, a number of factors contributed to such an explanation, but the key one appears to have been the announcement of an indictment against Milošević by the International Criminal Tribunal for the former Yugoslavia, as I shall argue below. Thus, the most decisive element was action away from the battlefield and beyond the control of NATO's military and political leaders. This does not mean that lessons cannot be learned from the campaign regarding the use of armed force, but they do have to be understood in the proper context and strategic light. I shall treat the case for success by air power alone in the remainder of this present section while the ground force, Russian and indictment options will be considered below. The most important question to answer is why did Milošević give up? More precisely, as we shall see, the key question is, in fact, a refined version of this one. It is not simply a matter of finding out why the Serbian leader capitulated, but why he caved when he did.

The case for an air power victory is simple. NATO used only its air capability in the campaign to secure Serbian withdrawal from Kosovo, and Serbian forces were withdrawn. At face value, this is to be taken as the first example of a successful air-only campaign, giving the lie to the countless armchair critics, sensible professionals and sound academics, such as Robert Pape,[16] who argued that air power alone had never, and could never secure victory. That there can be no guarantee of victory without ground forces is a truism: physical commitment of forces on the ground is the only guarantee of success. However, being the only guarantee does not mean that a successful outcome despite it is impossible. Success without ground forces is possible – it just cannot be guaranteed. (It might well be that some other form of guarantee might be available, albeit with great difficulty, as we suggest below.)

NATO conducted a 78-day campaign over Kosovo. It destroyed, damaged and degraded Belgrade's strategic capability. The chief element in traditional terms was the damage done to Serbian oil facilities and supplies. The destruction of all refining facilities and

[16] Robert Pape, *Bombing to Win: Air Power and Coercion in War*, Ithaca, NY: Cornell University Press, 1996.

the majority of oil supplies meant that the VJ and the MUP were on a diminishing life support system. Logistical support and reinforcements were badly impeded. But these were not stopped and, until the end of the conflict, there was enough fuel to enable forces in the field to operate at some level of salience. Similarly, destruction of communications routes, such as bridges, major roads and railway lines, impaired the ability of the VJ and the MUP to sustain their operations. But, this was still not enough to render such operations impossible by the end of the conflict. Despite the impact of strategic level damage regarding oil and communications, Belgrade had not been reduced to a position where it was impossible to continue, had there been a political decision to do so.

But things were getting worse as the NATO campaign continued and intensified: according to the official NATO count, of the ninty-three tanks hit by NATO planes, only twenty-six were classified as destroyed. The majority of the others were deemed to be 'mobility kills.' This meant that they were disabled, but not beyond repair and future redeployment. The thing that made mobility kills as effective as destruction was the strategic level success that gravely diminished VJ and MUP ability to reinforce and re-supply. These tanks might have been capable of resurrection, but not in the circumstances of NATO's continuing campaign over Kosovo.

A major problem in assessing the success of NATO's air campaign is that Brussels and Belgrade were largely operating on different levels. Brussels was carrying out a strategic level air campaign, while Belgrade's strategy was focused on tactical level action. The VJ and MUP had the cleansing of Kosovo in their sights. Aside from armor and artillery bombardment, the most immediate aspects of Belgrade's campaign of horrors were carried out by squads of around twenty specially trained troops. Whether it was these groups of twenty, relying on close quarters shooting, torture and mutilation, or the relatively dispersed and covered tanks and guns in the field, these were not easy targets for NATO, in the best of circumstances. As it was, most of the NATO campaign concentrated on the big picture, not on the smaller frame. This is a point clearly missed by most observers and critics of the NATO campaign, who appear to have expected NATO to attempt the somewhat impossible task (given different strategic, geographic and temporal starting points) of engaging VJ and MUP units directly at the tactical level, blocking their actions as they attempted to perform them. This is a wholly naïve perspective that demonstrates no real understanding of military operations and certainly no sense of the political and strategic terms on which the NATO campaign had to be conducted. Over time, NATO's approach would take the life out of the Serbian campaign. But day-to-day, as critics opined, it did little to save or directly help the Kosovan Albanian civilians.

To some extent, this changed in the latter stages of the conflict. As NATO's campaign continued, there was a greater concentration on the forces in the field in Kosovo. First, the weather improved significantly. Poor flying weather, compounded by political concern not to take operational risks such as flying in less than ideal conditions, meant that NATO's scope for attacking Belgrade's forces in the field was severely circumscribed through much of the early part of the conflict. Secondly, the VJ was more and more forced to reveal itself. It had proved itself adept in deploying an asymmetrical strategy that avoided using its air defense systems, disguising units and equipment on the ground. However, by the second half of May, it may be presumed to have been suffering heavy losses, both of personnel and equipment. The overwhelming majority of the hardware lost was judged by the Pentagon to have been destroyed in the last two weeks of the campaign. In this period, forces on the ground were being driven from cover by UÇK harassment, presumably coordinated with the US. A-10s were then able to concentrate fire on 'kill-boxes' of VJ units in the open. This also reflected a shift in policy: while NATO had done all that it could throughout the first two months of the campaign to avoid not only civilian, but even military, deaths there was now clearly preparedness to be lethal by necessity, not only contingency.

The UÇK role in this context has led some to suggest that the UÇK was a proxy ground force for the Alliance's airmen. This would be significantly to exaggerate both the group's role and its capability. While there was a good deal of harassment, especially close to the borders with Albania, this did not amount to operations that could threaten Belgrade's forces. In the absence of NATO air power, the UÇK stood no chance operationally against the VJ, as had been demonstrated many times during the previous year. On every occasion, VJ and MUP operations had rolled back the UÇK insurgency. Aside from the convenience to the NATO air campaign, there is no suggestion that the 'revitalized' UÇK operations in May were in any way substantial. They were not directly threatening to Serbian forces. Reports at the time suggested that, despite the losses incurred by NATO bombing of troops drawn into the open, the VJ was finding no problem in rebuffing UÇK action. Thus, while some recognition has to be given to the fact that the UÇK was present and that its raids played a limited role in making Belgrade forces more vulnerable to air attack, it is hard to infer that the UÇK was NATO's proxy ground force. Not all NATO's successes were in the UÇK area of operations close to the border with Albania and the only thing that could be said regarding the UÇK action in those areas is that it provided a small scale catalyst to that which would have happened anyway, once NATO had taken the decision politically to accept deliberate killing of Belgrade troops, if necessary in pursuit of the military objective.

Thus, a fairly strong, though not conclusive, argument in favor of the success of NATO's air campaign could be made. While the UÇK's role was too feeble to support claims of its being a proxy NATO land force that made all the difference to the use of air power, there is no evidence or reasoning that points to the connection between aerial bombardment and the point at which Belgrade sought an end to hostilities. Air power was the sole military instrument that made the difference. Paradoxically, however, there was nothing obvious in the scale of the damage and destruction wrought on Serbian asserts to suggest that Belgrade could not have prolonged the conflict, had it chosen to do so.

Despite the perception that air power had secured its first ever 'victory' without assistance from other services, air power enthusiasts have avoided triumphalism. Indeed, where credit has been claimed it has been sublimated in discussion of how the air campaign might have been better managed, crucial to which is the tenet of strategic air power theory that hitting hard and massively at the beginning gives air power its greatest advantage. The combined destructive and psychological impact of the initial phase of attack compels an adversary to do one's will. For adherents of this school, the NATO campaign was flawed because it began in a graduated way – for reasons which I shall not discuss here – and its success became apparent only after escalation confirmed this to most proponents of air power theory.

However, if we consider the question raised earlier regarding the point at which Milošević conceded, this argument has to be in question. The scale and scope of attacks was increased. But there was nothing in these broader and more painful attacks that would obviously make the Belgrade leader change course abruptly and decide to sue for peace. Thus, any theory that air power's success rests on the decisive use of massive hammer blows cannot be sustained on the evidence available and it seems improbable that it can be sustained in the case of Kosovo. As will be seen below, however, this does not mean that air power was not significant in creating the conditions for capitulation. But, the way in which it plays a role has to be understood in a more refined way. General Henry Shelton, Chairman of the Joint Chiefs of Staff, had a point when he told the US Senate Armed Forces Committee: 'We are a hammer, but not every problem we face is a nail.' His point showed that there was a need for some flexibility in thinking. The implication that the hammer could not be used for other purposes, or in a more subtle way, was misguided, however.

Why Milošević caved in when he did

Surprise is a key component in warfare and its importance was amply confirmed by the outcome of NATO's campaign over Kosovo between March and June 1999.[17] There was astonishment at the precipitate ending of the conflict by Slobodan Milošević. The onset of hostilities had also surprised many observers. Milošević had not behaved as expected by key figures in Washington and other Western capitals. Equally, it is reasonable to infer that Milošević and his confidants were taken by surprise when NATO, in a mirror of its own misjudgments of Belgrade, did not behave as expected by the Serbian leadership. There was surprise, then, both at the conduct of military action and in it. Belgrade did not deploy its air defenses early in the NATO attack, baffling the standard thinkers at SHAPE. Despite the initial decision to switch off air defenses, the Yugoslav air and air defense service (RV-PVO) managed to bring down a stealth bomber. While surprise is not an unknown feature in warfare – the element of surprise is after all a key principle of all military thinking – so much surprise in such a short space of time seems of a diferent order. For the most part, the surprise involved was

---

[17] The following section is based on a presentation made with my colleague Jan Willem Honig at the Center of International Studies, Princeton University. Our discussions on limited war in this context and others have been particularly helpful.

not that of one side's outwitting the other with an unexpected move, rather it seems more to be the product of accident.

If there is a strong, but inconclusive case for air power, it is conceivable that the alternatives of a looming NATO ground force or the role of Russian diplomacy might offer better guidance. In terms of the former, the case is thin. NATO ground forces had always been part of the plan, on one level. The original intention had been to introduce them as a result of presumed diplomatic agreement at Rambouillet, and when this did not materialize the terminal point of any NATO action was the deployment of a ground force. As with a post-Rambouillet deployment, the assumption was that there would be a permissive environment.

The only shift in this position during the air campaign was that open reference to the possibility of deploying ground forces in a less than permissive environment was introduced, as active planning for such a possibility was stepped up. A land operation was not about to begin at the end of May, that much is clear. Milošević may have believed that it would come in July, and there has been some suggestion that the Russians had told him that it would come in August.[18] The reality is that 13 September was the probable starting point for what was designated Operation *Bravo Minus* in the UK. Whichever of these dates is considered, none of them presented the Serbian leader with such an imminent threat that he would make a complete about face. Indeed, over the years, it became clear that he was someone who would never do something unless he believed that he had to. Moreover on past evidence he did only one thing at a time, at the last moment – if not several moments beyond it. It defies credibility that he would abruptly alter course overnight because he believed that there was an impending NATO ground operation between six weeks and four months hence. While the prospect of NATO ground forces' being introduced even in a non-permissive environment must have affected Milošević's thinking, there is no reason to suppose that this proved decisive in making him suddenly end the conflict when he did so.

The Russian dimension also fails to explain the Milošević *volte-face*, if timing is deemed to be crucial. Russia's clear-cut message that it would not support the Serbs was delivered by Viktor Chernomyrdin on 4 June, a week after the Serbian leader had quite

---

[18] Robert Pape, presentation at the Institute of War and Peace Studies, Columbia University, October 1999. Stephen T. Hasmer, *The Conflict over Kosovo*, RAND, 2001, emphasises this point while ignoring Milošević's character and record.

abruptly begun his change of heart. Indeed, on 27 May, quite the opposite picture of Russian engagement and delivery of an ultimatum had been suggested. On that day Chernomyrdin was visiting Belgrade. His public statements were directed against NATO and he said that this would be his last visit there unless NATO, which had intensified its air attacks, ceased operations. There was no point, he believed, in pursuing diplomacy while NATO bombing continued. NATO, far more than Belgrade, was clearly the guilty party. That he was making one set of comments in public and another in private to Milošević cannot be excluded entirely, yet it is hard to conceive of anything that would have made the Serbian leader switch positions so immediately, even though he was capable of making instant, intuitive responses.

The Russians might have offered a military deployment so as to facilitate Belgrade's ambitions to salvage partition from Kosovo. This would imply a change in the Russian position that, in reality, only came about one week later, in response to Belgrade's new line, not prompting it. The change in the Russian position was said to date from 3 June, according to well-placed figures, including the NATO ground force commander General Jackson, and Chernomyrdin delivered his message on 4 June.[19] Moreover, even if the offer had been made on 27 May, there was no reason for Milošević to have reacted by immediately reversing his position. Even had there been a Russian ultimatum attached to such a message, there is nothing in the Serbian leader's record to suggest the behavior change on 27 May. As it is, 4 June remains the key date for Russia's intervention – and so, quite clearly, cannot explain Milošević's sudden change a week earlier, very helpful though Moscow's intervention undoubtedly was in facilitating Belgrade's climb-down.

27 May is crucial in determining why Milošević changed his position. On that day, the International Criminal Tribunal for the former Yugoslavia publicized an indictment against Milošević and four others suspected of committing crimes in Kosovo. This was clearly unexpected, perhaps as much by the Allies as the indictees themselves.[20] It was a personal issue which delivered precisely the kind of psychological blow that proponents of air power argue

---

[19] Duško Doder and Louise Branson, *Milošević: Portrait of a Tyrant*, New York: The Free Press, 1999, pp. 273–4.

[20] Indeed, both Washington and London, having got wind of the imminent indictment, apparently made efforts to persuade Chief Prosecutor Louise Arbour

results from initial massive attack. Against the background of other events, including the prospect of a NATO ground operation and mounting losses in the field which, it may be presumed, his generals must have told him could no longer be hushed up, Milošević's command of the situation and sense of control were overturned. Inadvertently, the Tribunal's indictment had helped NATO's strategic purpose.

Timing is crucial to a reasoned explanation of the Milošević transformation. On 27 May Chernomyrdin published a piece in the *Washington Post* threatening to end his mission, not because of the Serbian leader but because of NATO's intensified air bombardment. He was at that point embarking on what he said might be his last mission in search of peace. However, he emerged from discussions with Milošević the next day to announce that Belgrade would accept all the G8 principles (that is, the terms for a cessation of hostilities agreed between the G8 – the Group of seven advanced industrial countries, plus Russia). That day also saw the Yugoslav government issue a statement declaring not only that it accepted the G8 principles, but also that it would begin a unilateral withdrawal, irrespective of NATO's action. While this was probably disingenuous, it was in marked contrast to any previous statement from Belgrade. It represented what one source close to the Yugoslav government termed a 'psychological shift' on the part of the President, who suddenly was seeking any way in which to co-operate with the West. In the space of one day, Milošević had made a 180-degree change.[21] The only explanation consistent with this about-turn is the publication of the indictment by the Tribunal in The Hague.

The crucial thing about the indictment was the psychological impact. Milošević had lost control. By changing tack so abruptly and diametrically, it might well be that he was hoping to regain control by a return to the kind of business-like co-operation he had established with Western figures in the past. Given that the indictment was (wrongly) seen as a NATO instrument by Belgrade, it must be supposed that the Serbian leader believed that a different approach might lead to withdrawal of the indictment, or immu-

---

not to issue the indictment at this time – or at least to keep it under seal – for fear that it could jeopardise negotiations to end the air campaign.

[21] BBC News, 30 May 1999.

nity. He had probably always believed that it was possible to cut a deal – and his interaction with some in the international diplomatic circus that had performed around him no doubt deeply reinforced his native outlook. Indeed, the deep shock the indictment brought indicates that he believed that some arrangement for immunity was already in the air – possibly, even, that one of his interlocutors had mooted this possibility at some stage.[22] Unfortunately for Milošević the Tribunal's action was independent of any Western government's policies, even where there was co-operation and common interest.

If Milošević was seeking to regain control of the situation, this was not only because the indictment had completely thrown him, even though it appears clearly to have been decisive. The prospect of no further support from Moscow – which emerged in the following week – weakened his ability to feel that he could control events. The increasing losses in the field in Kosovo also generated the context for sharp panic in face of the indictment, not so much because the Serbian leader was concerned at the losses themselves, but because he also appeared to be losing control over the dispersal of information. Having ridden to power on media manipulation of the major messages circulating in Serbian society, his defenses had suddenly been breached.

This breach was caused by two factors, both resulting from NATO's use of air power. The first was NATO's shift to attacks that would be likely to inflict large troop fatalities on the VJ (which had been avoided hitherto), and the second was NATO's action against Milošević's control of communications and information dissemination. Regarding the former, NATO had, from early- or mid-May, finally accepted that previous attempts to avoid killing Serbian troops, if possible, would have to give way to attacks on concentrations of troops, in which high fatality levels would be registered. This approach was applied at the tactical level in Kosovo. Coordinated action with the UÇK and NATO Special Forces Units liaising with it, saw VJ units, especially, being flushed out of their highly

[22] The most obvious Western candidate to have broached this topic, or to have acted in this way (possibly without full official backing) was Richard Holbrooke. However, when presented with this reasoning by the author – which reasoning was accepted as a plausible extrapolation – two senior US figures, neither close allies of Holbrooke, could not countenance this interpretation in reality – as one of them put it, 'not even Dick would do that.'

successful concealment. UÇK harassment forced the VJ into the open to conduct direct land engagements as they harried the ethnic Albanian armed force. However, the action had been designed to draw them into kill-boxes, where US A-10 aircraft, in particular, were able to inflict heavy losses. It is likely that VJ losses ran into thousands – perhaps up to 5,000, although Belgrade concealed the true figures, even when making statements on losses.[23] While it is certain that the VJ command and reports from General Dušan Lazarević, the officer commanding in the field, in Kosovo, were recommending continuing with the campaign and were unhappy with capitulation when it came, it is also highly likely that they were telling Milošević that they could no longer suppress information on fatalities, given the scale. For them, this was not a problem. For Milošević, it began to be one.

In response to the growing losses, numerous protests had begun to emerge in Serbian towns, charging that the regime was not publishing the full details of those killed and wounded in Kosovo. These protests were spontaneous and were focused on reservists returning to their homes and finding that the real story was not being told. However, what distinguished these protests from others in Serbia over the years was the sense in which information was spreading by word of mouth and through other means. The Serbian people appeared briefly to be empowered.

Empowerment, protest and the spread of information contrary to the interests of the regime regarding the conflict were made possible by the second thing altering Milošević's control. This was the use of lethal, but interestingly also, non-lethal weaponry by NATO, against the Serbian leader's grip on communications and information dissemination. A decisive blow was the well-known strike on the Belgrade Radio Television Serbia (RTS) tower. This generated negative publicty in the West – not least because of the personal friendships of some of the Western journalists and their Serbian colleagues.[24] While no one could have wished for those deaths, the number was higher than it might have been. Belgrade had advance warning of the attack but rather than choosing to reduce the number of people in the building actually increased it – presumably in the hope of either deterring it, or, more likely,

[23] Belgrade's official losses were stated to be 576.

[24] The BBC's John Simpson, who knew some of those who died, was so emotionally and vociferously critical of the attack on the TV studios that the British Prime Minister Tony Blair dubbed him a mouthpiece of Belgrade.

maximizing the negative impact of the bombing. Although the survivors and the families of the victims condemned the attack, they also bitterly turned on the government itself.

In the end, however many people were working inside the building, an attack was inevitable. There had been considerable agonizing at the political level in NATO countries over authorizing such a strike, in the circumstances of limited operations under a primarily humanitarian rationale – both the possibility of incidental innocent civilian casualties and the symbolism involved in targeting media facilities were not easy for Western leaders to contemplate. Against this, however, was the overriding strategic importance of the RTS tower in communications, and the vital role it played. Crucially, for the government, it was the means by which they mediated information to most Serbian citizens.[25] So long as a grip on information could be maintained, the possibilities of opposition to the government and of undermining the Kosovo operations remained limited. But this was not the only role. While RTS might have limped on with a limited return to broadcasting within 24 hours (the Alliance had not destroyed the whole building), in what would have been a gesture of defiance by the regime, its strategic position had been significantly degraded by the loss of key communications infrastructure.

Given the negative impact of using lethal munitions to attack Serbian communications, NATO operations began to emphasize a non-lethal capability. Graphite bombs were used to take RTS off the air intermittently, thus striking a decisive blow at the heart of the Milošević message. In the gaps created while Belgrade's main instrument of manipulation was off the air for perhaps 12 hours at a time, there was opportunity for the messages of protest to be spread by word of mouth, rather than ignored or denounced by RTS. The intermittent disruption of broadcasts ruptured official control and allowed the public space briefly and haltingly to form alternative views. As with the NATO campaign in Bosnia in 1995, where air power was responsible for removing General Ratko Mladić's control over events and effectively delivering him into Milošević's hands to enable peace,[26] so it played a role in removing the latter's control in 1999.

[25] See Mark Thompson, *Forging War: the Media in Serbia, Croatia and Bosnia-Hercegovina*, London: Article 19, 1994, and James Gow *et al.* (eds), *Bosnia by Television* London: BFI, 1996.

[26] See Chapter 8.

International military involvement in the Yugoslav War had many dimensions, but all were facets of a practical and philosophical enquiry into waging modern war, the key aspects of which were problems of state conflict, the limited character of the military operations involved, the ways in which armed forces might purposefully be used and the constraints on their deployment, such as political commitment and the availability of appropriate means and approaches. The theological struggles confronted through years of engagement in Bosnia and Hercegovina shaped thinking on the approach to handling Kosovo. Kosovo became the critical case – but the situation was not exactly the same and the lessons learned over the years were only partly relevant.

Of all the surprises that emerged during the Kosovo campaign, the most striking was the ending of the conflict; a clear understanding of it has been difficult. Strategists and others have struggled to come to terms with the management of limited war. The NATO campaign against Serbia was limited both in objective and in conduct – indeed, in the care given to avoiding collateral damage, it was perhaps the most limited in terms of conduct ever. By accident, probably more than design, the 1999 NATO campaign against Serbia showed that the crucial factor in limited war is not turning it into unlimited war, but finding the points at which the adversary is forced to change position. This may well not be the result of destruction *per se*.

In the case of Serbia and Milošević, it seems that non-military factors were important. Both the accidental strategic accomplishment of the indictment by the International Tribunal and the more deliberate, though possibly inadequately understood, use of graphite bombs and more destructive munitions to interrupt information control, suggest that the key to success lay in careful targeting. This meant knowing the adversary well. Understanding that which counted for Milošević was crucial to gauging how to prosecute the NATO campaign successfully. That this was achieved, in part, not by design does not undermine might the potential lessons to be drawn. To some extent, these might involve looking beyond the obvious. In part, they might mean consider the way in which a hammer might be used not to smash window or to hit nail hard on the faced, but to extract a nail,. It certainly means a need for flexibility of approach, tailored to a particular conflict or situation, rather than standard operating procedures. Most of all, it should involve knowing the case well, *sui generis*, which in turn requires good information and the means to understand it.

Correct analysis of the Kosovo campaign contradicts the conclusion that the only way to conduct a limited war is to use massive force, by air, land and sea, from the outset – an approach often falsely attributed to the Powell doctrine (which was more about clarity of purpose and the decisive use of force than simply about its massive use).[27] The use of armed force does not have to be all or nothing, rather, its use needs to be adjusted to the task at hand. The way forward for a better strategic approach to limited warfare rests on flexibility, and on good information about and good understanding of the adversary. Defeating Slobodan Milošević proved to be a struggle because the means used reflected conventional thinking. The surprising outcome was a product of hitting the right target by accident. Less conventional thinking might have shaped a different campaign that hit the right target intentionally at an earlier stage.

[27] See Daalder and O'Hanlon, *Winning Ugly*, pp. 212–15.

11

CONCLUSION

MEANS, ENDS AND JUSTICE

In the beginning and in the end, war crimes were central to the Yugoslav War of the 1990s. At the core of the war was the Serbian state project and the strategy of war crimes adopted to achieve it. In a layer around that core, the record of Serbia's local adversaries was often also characterized by war crimes and crimes against humanity. In this cruel environment, international engagement and humanitarian concern were challenged to find ways to oppose the aims and the means of the Serbian project and, to a lesser extent, the worst of the local adversaries' demeanor. Militarily, this meant care and attention to the shaping and conduct of operations that were as far apart in character from those of the Serbian project as could be.

Over nearly ten years the war provided not only empirical evidence of war crimes and crimes against humanity on an exceptional scale, their being the very purpose of the war, but also offered material for a more philosophical examination and exploration of strategy and war crimes. If the Serbian strategy of war crimes and the Yugoslav War brought some small benefit, it was to raise the issue of that which is outside the bounds of acceptability in war and to prompt radical developments in the international sphere to address it. The emergence of the Yugoslav *ad hoc* Tribunal and its Rwandan counterpart, along with the rapid and radical moves towards establishment of the permanent International Criminal Court, were unimaginable before the Serbian project changed the tone of the post-Cold War world. While the impact of the ICC was likely to be felt more in the political realm and its relations to standards of military conduct in hostile operations, this in itself increased the focus on war crimes and the way in which these aberrations gave definition to the excellence of professional soldiers, grounded not only in military skills but also in a broader understanding of their business, including the ethical and practical importance of restraint. Above all, in a world where war had to be taken as a matter of fact that could only be constrained, but not erased, Serbian strategy, in provoking extraordinary and unprecedented international judicial intervention, made it clear that war with criminal breaches of international humanitarian law and standards as its very essence, in its exceptional nature, could not be tolerated.

The relationship between war crimes and war is not a straightforward one – even in circumstances such as those of the Yugoslav War. Each era and culture might provide a pattern of rules and restraints that would not be appropriate in another place at another time. However, in all circumstances, there are limits on war. Any discussion of breaches of the laws and customs of war must be contextual. This is true not only of time and place, but also of situation. The laws of war are dependent, to a considerable extent, on interpretation, discretion and judgment. The very same act might well be a war crime, at one moment, but not at another – for example, military necessity in a peculiarly adverse situation where force protection might override the taking and good treatment of prisoners, might justify this action, in terms of the law – but the same approach in relatively benign conditions, i.e. not taking prisoners, would surely constitute a breach of the Geneva Conventions. Because of the difficulties in gauging the responsibilities placed on officers and their troops in difficult circumstances and under great pressure, in practice, prosecutions have tended to be raised only for acts committed against non-combatants and outside the immediate course of battle.

To a large extent, this was true of the approach to war crimes in the Yugoslav context. It was the design of a strategy in which various types of persecution – from murder *en masse* to rape, torture and forcible expulsion – were central to achieving political ends that provoked a response. However, in considering some aspects of that strategy, questions might be raised, such as, given the relative lack of manpower available to the Serbian project, was the strategy adopted justifiable, in its own terms? The strategy was precisely a way of reconciling the available means and the desired ends. Thus the aim of winning new borders for the Serbs was to be achieved with the available means – limited manpower and considerable stocks of weaponry. If there was insufficient manpower available to achieve control of territory and to secure it against any potential resistance (and leaving aside the acceptability of the aims in the first place), there might at least be a self-contained and self-defined logical extreme where removing the population could be seen to make strategic sense. In such a case, a force commander, or political superior, might argue that there was military necessity in the policy, or the way in which policy was implemented.

Against this, there is an ethical – and, indeed, more common sense – approach that questions the acceptability of such an action, under any conditions. There could be no conditions under which the considerations of military necessity and proportionality could justify such inhumanity. While this must be the assumption of any approach to war crimes and crimes against humanity, because of the contextual character they have, it is hard absolutely to exclude the hypothetical possibility of arguments of military necessity and proportionality being applicable – even for gross acts committed against civilians, where most people would find it impossible to conceive of conditions in which these acts might be justifiable.

Conventionally, where war crimes and crimes against humanity have been identified and measures taken to address their commission, this has been for action against civilians. However, one of the issues to emerge from the Yugoslav War, notably from Serbian strategy, has been the appearance of indictments not for actions outside the normal scope of war, such as mass murder of civilians, but for soldiers ostensibly doing the things they are supposed to do. The key example of this concerned the use of siege and artillery bombardment. This gave rise to questions about the commission of war crimes, even though General Stanislav Galić and other soldiers indicted could be said to have been accused of doing something akin to that which might be expected of them in war. They were not face to face with victims, deliberately murdering innocent civilians, raping them, or mistreating prisoners, all acts outside the boundary of that which is acceptable in combat. They were engaged in armed operations with resolute opponents.

The Sarajevo indictment inter alia raised the charge of disproportionate artillery bombardment. However, in seeking to understand the strategic equation to be settled by Serbian commanders – as discussed in Chapters 3, 6 and 7 – one can see how in protecting their own soldiers, of which there were too few to mount an attack of a different kind to capture major cities, the bombardment might make military sense. There are ways – perhaps difficult to embrace – in which the constraints on the creation of force available to General Galić and his fellow commanders might be compared with those operating on international, especially NATO, commanders, as they approached the task of countering the Serbian project. The strategic approach of encirclement and shelling, where there were hostile forces in the town, was not an entirely novel approach to war and it was certainly not one that was clearly outside the limits of acceptability in war purely by definition. While the twisted intention to torture the military and civilian inhabitants of Sarajevo and other towns, captured in General Mladić's cruel orders, quoted in Chapter 7, was a telling factor that could not be ignored in considering allegations of disproportionate artillery bombardment, this, in itself, did not necessarily do anything to alter appreciation of the strategic logic involved. Given Serbian means and ends, and notwithstanding the difficult aspect of proportionality (deciding whether, say, ten shells are enough, but eleven would be too many), such use of artillery need not be absolutely regarded as unacceptable – any commander might consider the same approach, given the same calculation, to achieve his military objective.

For the most part, allegations of war crimes and crimes against humanity represent a basic sense of wrong and right, one that might not be reflected in law – either in part, or at all. And where it is reflected, small technicalities, or broad ones, such as jurisdiction, might result in those who commit acts escaping justice, not for want of evidence but because it is not recognized as a crime in the eyes of the court, as certain conditions for considering it have not been met. Recognizing this reality defies the common sense idea of justice that many people have when confronted with challenges of the kind thrown up by the Serbian project. A similar kind of common sense also makes it hard for lay observers to accept that the standards of criminal justice demand evidence beyond reasonable doubt, not a general understanding that, for example, 'everyone knows' that Slobodan Milošević lay behind a strategy colored with crime. Even the standards of evidence employed in scholarly and related literature fall short of the courtroom test to be met in a criminal case. It is certainly not enough to have read about Milošević's role in a newspaper – even if the newspaper article is entirely accurate, this cannot, in itself, be persuasive of criminal liability in a courtroom.

A broad and important aspect of meeting the conditions required for Trial Chambers even to consider the evidence in a case concerns jurisdiction. In a conflict characterized by transition, ambiguity and complexity, at different times and in different ways, the issues of jurisdiction were not necessarily straightforward. The international character of conflict was clouded by three factors. First, the old Yugoslav federation was breaking up. Thus what at the beginning of 1991 was regarded as internal, in terms of international law, by some time in 1992 had become international (although, at the time of writing – and presumably for some considerable time to come – issues of when certain questions became international is open to discussion). Secondly, the independence of both Croatia and Bosnia and Hercegovina was rejected by a significant part of their Serb populations (and, following independence, the statehood of Bosnia and Hercegovina was rejected by significant Croatian political forces). And, lastly, although Belgrade fuelled Croatian and Bosnian Serb disquiet and generated war with the material provided by those communities, it disguised its initiating and guiding hand through security forces in those countries composed of individuals primarily from those countries and the conscious attempt to deceive the outside world by designating them as separate armies. However, in the end, Belgrade's directing role and general responsibility for the generation and application of force, using Croatian and Bosnian Serb agents for its project, could not be disguised. While there was clearly an internal dimension to the war in Croatia and in Bosnia and Hercegovina, Belgrade's initial, continuing and ultimate responsibility and involvement meant that internationality provisions were applicable. And, in the case of Kosovo, which more clearly seemed to have an internal character, it too gained a clearly international character with the opening of major NATO hostile operations after 24 March 1999.

In terms of the widespread-or-systematic criteria required for jurisdiction in other cases, including internal ones, and the apparent complexity of the Yugoslav conflict and fallacies of culturally and sociologically based collective violence (often introduced with the purpose of obscuring issues), there was a need to disclose the character of the Serbian project (and of some counter-projects) as a planned, organized and instrumental campaign of crimes. Ethnic cleansing was not a contingent phenomenon of a primitive, or bestial, culture, but a strategy involving rational calculations and decisions on the creation and use of means to achieve the ends.

Even where it is recognized that there have been gross abuses of human rights, abuses that might constitute war crimes, or crimes against humanity, there are often major differences between the perspectives of civilians and soldiers regarding attribution of criminality. Where human rights activists might well make allegations and seek to elevate atrocities, on certain matters, such as the use of artillery, the more sober soldier with a professional appreciation of military necessity and proportionality, as well as elements feeding into strategic, operational and tactical calculations, might have more understanding of the forces at work on a commanding officer seeking to reconcile means and ends. In the end, it may well be that there are some aspects of the war crimes canon, despite the outrage of civilians, where only professional soldiers are qualified to make assessments over the type and degree of use of force in a particular case. There can be no doubt that military judgment, not that of human rights lawyers, has to be paramount in such cases – just as the professional assessment of lawyers tends to take precedence over that of non-professionals on legal matters. About truly atrocious crimes, however, there can be no doubt – and civilians and soldiers will always concur: mass murder by men (or women) in uniform besmirches the honor and humanity of the military profession.

Understanding how and why an action came to be taken does not necessarily exonerate it. In this context, the undiplomatic lack of sympathy shown by US officials for ethnic Serbs being harassed by Kosovo Albanians as Belgrade's troops withdrew and NATO moved in at the end of the Kosovo conflict reflected understanding of the desire for revenge against those held responsible for such widespread use of inhumane means. When Pentagon spokesman Ken Bacon suggested he would not remain in Kosovo if he were an ethnic Serb, although defensible as an honest and accurate observation, it was the kind of statement that, had it been uttered by Belgrade spokesman Goran Matić would have been taken as a threat of ethnic cleansing – better go now before it is too late. The apparent condoning of reverse criminal actions was not fitting, even if they might in some way be mitigated by being generally (but certainly not entirely) lesser in quality and scale, just as those actions themselves might reflect understanding of the desire for revenge, or justice, on the part of victims. That enormous crimes had been committed in prosecuting the Serbian project did not justify retributive persecution. The measure provided by criminal justice, not the immoderation of revenge, had to be sought, if the damage created by ethnic cleansing were to become sensitive scars, rather than open wounds.

The imperfections and technicalities of due legal process might, on occasion, leave unsatisfied the emotional desire for justice – especially where victims and those close to them see those accused of crimes go free. Moreover, it is noteworthy for those who doubted the value of prosecuting war crimes, on any level, that the seeking of justice, in which voices are heard and stories told, is cathartic and, it might reasonably be presumed, contributes to the healing process after a war of war crimes.[1] Reconciliation between victims and perpetrators might be too great an aspiration, but the role of international criminal justice in helping victims to be reconciled within themselves was not beyond imagination and in reality had some impact. Peace and justice were intertwined, contrary to conventional academic approaches to these issues: without the peace constituted by the end of armed hostilities, there could be no scope for justice; but without a process to render justice once that version of peace had been established, there could be no guarantee that revenge would not motivate renewed hostilities in the future and therefore that peace, in the deeper sense of removing the conditions for war and war crimes, had been created.

Ensuring that the ending of hostilities would be translated into a lasting peace was a cardinal imperative for the international actors engaged in the region. Addressing the legacy of war crimes was paramount, but it was not purely a matter for the International Tribunal. It was also something that required the cooperation of governments all around the world, as well as in the region. Most of all, given the investment made by Western countries and the role played by NATO, it was incumbent on those countries to assist the Tribunal, whether through providing resources, supplying crucial evidence or assisting in the apprehension of those suspected of having committed war crimes.[2] This was one of many tasks facing the Alliance, which had acted justly throughout but in doing so had set itself vital challenges. NATO had to be even more successful in peace than it had been in halting Milošević and the strategic campaign of war crimes.

[1] See the excellent Aurélien Colson, 'The Logic of Peace and the Logic of Justice', *International Relations*, vol. XV, no. 1, April 2000.

[2] See David Gowan, 'Kosovo: the British Government and ICTY', *Leiden Journal of International Law*, vol. 13, 2000.

Although the Yugoslav War proved not to be completely at an end with the effective demise of the Serbian project after the fall of Slobodan Milošević, it was very largely so. The main challenge thrown up by the war had been tempered – and, although the accomplishment of ethnic cleansing and strategic war crimes could not be overturned, they were virtually at an end. Serbia had emerged from the war in a far poorer position, in every sense, than it had been at the start. Neighboring countries were in ruins. Millions of people's lives had been ruined, while hundreds of thousands of lives had been lost. The only way in which those who had actually suffered this misery could possibly find peace was by rendering justice – in whatever sense this could be achieved – and finding some degree of reconciliation, if only in the abstract. Only justice, in the end, would truly begin to temper the effects, mostly direct but also indirect, of the Serbian project and its strategy of ethnic cleansing.

The Serbian project ultimately came to nothing. It took significant international action as well as the discrete efforts of various neighborhood actors to achieve this – and not least among the latter, in the end, were those in Serbia itself who worked to oust the Milošević regime. When his fall came in late 2000, troubles for the region were not at an end – as the incipient conflict in Macedonia demonstrated. But, the skies were clearing slowly. A strategy defined by war crimes had eventually been undone by those very crimes. Milošević and many of his agents, rather than being proud beneficiaries of opportunism and ruthless war-making, were trapped figures, hostage to their dark record and the toll of the Tribunal's bell, waiting to face trial and justice one day or another, in one way or another, if they did not die first.

INDEX